D1256546

ROBERT GROSSETESTE

*The Growth of an English Mind
in Medieval Europe*

R. W. SOUTHERN

CLARENDON PRESS · OXFORD
1986

Oxford University Press, Walton Street, Oxford OX2 6DP

Oxford New York Toronto
Delhi Bombay Calcutta Madras Karachi
Petaling Jaya Singapore Hong Kong Tokyo
Nairobi Dar es Salaam Cape Town
Melbourne Auckland

and associated companies in
Beirut Berlin Ibadan Nicosia

Oxford is a trade mark of Oxford University Press

British Library Cataloguing in Publication Data

Southern, R. W.
Robert Grosseteste: the growth of an English mind in medieval Europe
1. Grosseteste, Robert
I. Title
189   B765.G74
ISBN 0–19–826450–X

Printed in Great Britain by
The Alden Press, Oxford

CONIUGI
PER XLII ANNOS
CARISSIMAE

Preface

First of all in this book I have attempted to place Robert Grosseteste in the provincial setting of England from about 1170 to 1253, and to view the international currents of thought and action during this period from an English point of view. It is likely that this way of looking on the international scene will produce some distortion of vision, but I wanted to see things as Grosseteste saw them—to capture his personal view, and to understand how he arrived at it. It is only in this way, I believe, by groping and questioning, that we will come to a better understanding of Grosseteste and his relationship to the cross-currents of thought and action in his own day and in the minds of later generations.

The distant origins of the thoughts which I express here go back to about 1937 when I examined Grosseteste's *Dicta* in order to compare them with those ascribed to St Anselm. The comparison was not flattering to Grosseteste. Of course, it was the wrong comparison to make: it was like comparing an English shire horse with a race-horse, both noble animals but built on different lines for different purposes.

The contrast left me with some awkward unsolved puzzles, which promised to be cleared up many years later in 1955, when the scholars whom I admired most in Oxford produced a volume which gave a first over-all view of Grosseteste in the light of modern scholarship. It was (as I explain below) a notable work, but it left me with a sense of unease. This gradually took the form of a conviction that, if there was a Grosseteste who lectured on Arts and Theology in Oxford and Paris in the years between 1200 and 1214, and was elected chancellor of the University of Oxford in or around 1214, there must have been another Grosseteste who taught and wrote on Arts and Theology in Oxford between 1220 and 1235, and became bishop of Lincoln in 1235. For, besides the difficulty of imagining the same routine being repeated after an interval of twenty years or more, there was the evidence that the 'second' Grosseteste was only a deacon in 1225 and received his earliest

recorded benefice in this year: a situation scarcely to be reconciled with academic eminence as a doctor of theology ten
years earlier.

I must have given more publicity to this view than I realised
for I see that Professor McEvoy ascribes it to me in his recent
book on Grosseteste's philosophy. I had, however, abandoned
it in about 1975. The immediate cause of my change of mind
was an article by Mr Graham Pollard which set out to prove
conclusively that Grosseteste must have been elected Chancellor of Oxford in 1214. The evidence which he adduced had
precisely the opposite effect on me: it made it seem in the
highest degree unlikely that his election could have taken place
in that year, and pointed to a later date.[1] The point is of small
importance in the history of the University, where the creation
of the office in 1214 is much more important than the obscure
question of the person appointed. But in Grosseteste's career
the question of his election is pivotal. It provided the only
evidence we have of Grosseteste's connection with the schools
of Oxford and Paris before 1214, for it was argued, and surely
correctly, that the masters who returned to Oxford in this year
would only have elected him as their corporate leader in the
face of episcopal opposition, if he had been well-known among
them both before their exile and during their intervening years
in Paris. But, if he was *not* elected chancellor in 1214, but
perhaps ten or fifteen years later, then his career began to
assume a quite different shape. The change of view, which
gradually imposed itself on my mind, required many further
changes which I have tried to work out in the course of this
volume.

Naturally, I think that the revised chronology of career and
intellectual development set out in this book is more consistent
both with the external evidence and with Grosseteste's internal
growth than the earlier alternative. On all these matters the
reader must judge. I have tried only to plot the stages of Grosseteste's intellectual journey, and its consequences for the future.
There still remains much to be done. To quote one of his characteristic and most attractive phrases, 'I can only hope that others

[1] For Pollard's article, see *Oxoniensia*, 39, 1975 (for 1974), 62–72. For my criticisms
and revised chronology in the context of the history of the University, see *HUO*, i,
1984, 26–36.

may be stimulated to enquire more deeply, and to do better, and to discover more than I have been able to find out.'

Despite the length of this approach to the Grosseteste problem, I do not think I should have ventured to come so late into so complicated a field of study, in which Fr. Gieben, Professor Dales, Professor McEvoy and others were already producing editions and studies of the greatest interest and importance, if I had not in the summer of 1979 received an invitation from the electors to give the Trevelyan Lectures in the University of Cambridge, and if in the course of conversation Dr G. R. Evans had not encouraged me to work out more fully my ideas on Grosseteste's career and intellectual habits as a possible subject for these lectures. Whether or not the result fulfils their expectations, I must thank them for giving me the opportunity and incentive to undertake this work, and the Master and Fellows of Sidney Sussex College for their kindness and hospitality during the term when I gave the lectures.

All the main points were outlined in the lectures which I delivered in the spring of 1981, but most of them have been considerably enlarged and some of them modified since then. In the course of this work I have incurred many debts, in the first place to the work of the scholars I have already mentioned. To these I must add the names of Richard Hunt and Beryl Smalley whose influence will be found in several parts of what follows; also the name of S. Harrison Thomson, whose work on the *Writings of Robert Grosseteste* (1940) still remains the essential tool for anyone working on the subject and has long deserved a revised edition. I have also greatly benefited from correspondence with Professor Richard Dales on many textual problems, and I have to thank him and Professor E. King for their permission to quote some passages from their shortly to be published editions of Grosseteste's *De Cessatione Legalium* and *De Decem Mandatis*. Professor W. C. Kneale has been kind enough to read and send me valuable comments on some of the more philosophical, and consequently more shaky, parts of these pages. Dr Diana Greenway has helped me over the intricacies of the diocese of Lincoln, and Mrs Cheney has given me judicious advice on the subject of the Chancellorship of Oxford University. I thank them all, and declare them to be innocent of my errors. I owe a special debt to the librarians of

Durham Cathedral and Eton College for depositing volumes in the Bodleian for my use, and to Dr A. C. de la Mare and other members of the staff of the MSS department in the Bodleian for their invariable patience in many demands made upon them.

I do not think I should ever have brought the work to an end without the unflagging energy, skill and endurance of Elaine Hyams and Ita Hollinshead in putting the whole work into a form fit for publication by processes beyond my comprehension; and I am grateful to the Oxford University Press for making these processes possible. Above all, without the help and patient understanding of my wife, who endured the long process of writing and corrected many infelicities, I should have given up long ago.

Contents

PART II
GROSSETESTE'S THOUGHTS ON NATURE, MAN, AND GOD

Abbreviations

The following list contains only common abbreviations. For abbreviations used for individual books and articles, see below, pp. 323 ff.

AHDLMA	*Archives d'histoire doctrinale et littéraire du Moyen Âge*
BGPM	*Beiträge zur Geschichte der Philosophie des Mittelalters*, 1891–
BL	British Library, London
BLR	*Bodleian Library Record*
BRUO	*Biographical Register of the University of Oxford*
MGH	Monumenta Germaniae historica
Coll. Franc.	*Collectanea Franciscana*
CPR	*Calendar of Entries in the Papal Registers relating to Great Britain and Ireland*, ed. W. H. Bliss, vol. i, 1893, London
EHR	*English Historical Review*
Ep.	Roberti Grosseteste *Epistolae* (referred to by number)
Franc. Stud.	*Franciscan Studies*
JTS	*Journal of Theological Studies*
MARS	*Mediaeval and Renaissance Studies*, London
Med. Hum.	*Medievalia et Humanistica*
PG	Migne, *Patrologia Graeca*
PL	Migne, *Patrologia Latina*
RTAM	*Recherches de théologie ancienne et médiévale*
RS	Chronicles and Memorials of Great Britain and Ireland published under the direction of the Master of the Rolls, London, 1858–96
SB	*Sitzungsberichte*
TRHS	*Transactions of the Royal Historical Society*, London

I

GROSSETESTE AND THE
EUROPEAN SCENE

The Grosseteste Problem

I. DIVERGENT VIEWS

THE thoughts and actions of all notable historical characters offer grounds for wide differences of interpretation. But Robert Grosseteste offers more grounds, and has been the subject of more widely contrasting interpretations, than most. Observers in his own day, and interpreters ever since, have tended to portray him either as an extremist, in varying ways original, eccentric, discordant; or as an essentially moderate and representative figure in the central stream of European scholastic and scientific thought, and of papally directed ecclesiastical reform and pastoral care. The second of these views has won an increasing measure of support in recent scholarship, but his contemporaries and their medieval successors were more evenly divided. Two of the main reporters of the thirteenth century, Matthew Paris and Roger Bacon, emphasize (for blame or praise) his eccentricity and his violent—or at least prolonged and determined—opposition to some of the main tendencies of his day. This view was later taken up and developed by Wycliffe and the Lollards, who saw him as their main medieval precursor. On the other hand, we have good contemporary evidence of his urbanity and large hospitality, and several later writers—conspicuous among them the Oxford theologian Thomas Gascoigne—insisted, against the Lollard enthusiasts, on the learned centrality of his thought.

Which of these views is right?

As a preliminary to the enquiry, we must briefly put him in his setting. He was born of humble parentage in the county of Suffolk, probably in the village of Stow Langtoft not far from Bury St Edmunds, at a date which cannot be later or much earlier than 1170.[1] The evidence for the first fifty-five years of

[1] The evidence for these details is discussed below in chapter 4.

his life is meagre in the extreme. Then, quite suddenly, a change
sets in. From 1225 we can be quite sure that he was lecturing
on theology in Oxford, at first in the secular schools of the
university, and from about 1230 in the recently established
community of Franciscans just outside the city walls. Then in
1235, quite unexpectedly, he was elected bishop of Lincoln.
The next eighteen years are as notable for the abundance of
documentation as the earlier years are notable for its absence.
When he died on 9 October 1253, he was one of the best known
and least understood men in England.

His life, therefore, covered the central period in the consolidation of institutions, habits of thought and religious practices of medieval Europe: the development of papal government
from Alexander III to Innocent IV, and of scholastic thought
from the first users of Peter Lombard's *Sentences* to the maturity
of Albert the Great and Thomas Aquinas; the growth of Canon
Law from the first commentators on Gratian's *Decretum* to the
first users of Gregory IX's *Decretals*; the translation and penetration into the schools of the whole body of Aristotle's scientific works with their Arabic commentators; the great series of
General Councils of 1179, 1215 and 1245; the short-lived Latin
Empire of Constantinople from 1204 to 1260. This whole body
of events expressed and defined the expansion and unification
of the Western world in Grosseteste's life-time. It is against this
background that the question of where Grosseteste stood in
relation to his contemporaries must be answered.

But no one lives only in the context of great events. Grosseteste must long have struggled with the brutal problem of
mere survival. In order to understand him it is necessary above
all to explore the almost impenetrable silence of the first fifty-
five years of his life. The first requirement for this task is an
open mind. This is not easy, perhaps not possible, to achieve.
It is inevitable that—at least as a first approximation—he
should be fitted into one or other of the recognizable patterns
of his day. This has generally meant the pattern which the historian finds most abundantly documented. Grosseteste has
shown himself in this respect remarkably adaptable. To recent
scholars, the most plausible pattern of his early life and training
has been that of other successful scholar-bishops of his time,
and there is an inherent probability in this pattern. Nearly all

the great scholar-bishops of the period had come up the same ladder of training in the great schools of Paris or Bologna and had acquired a normality of outlook which fitted them for the highest positions in the Church. The position at which Grosseteste belatedly arrived in 1235 seems to require the normality which we find in other men in similar positions. He became a bishop at a time when the procedure for making a bishop was very complicated and required a wide variety of assents. No one could become bishop of the largest diocese in England unless he was acceptable to the pope and king, as well as to the canons of the cathedral. As a body, the bishops of his time were the most important group of administrators and upholders of order and orthodoxy in the country. There were not many among them who had risen from poverty, unless they belonged to a great religious Order or had the support of a great patron. Grosseteste was a friend of the Franciscans, but he belonged to no Order; so far as we know he had no patron; his origins were extremely humble. He had a unique combination of disadvantages. To rise despite these drawbacks would seem to argue not only great abilities, but also an easily recognizable normality of beliefs, social attitudes, and intellectual background. The great schools of Europe provided the best training grounds for these qualities; proficiency in their methods of thought was the best guarantee of doctrinal consistency. The more we know of government in the thirteenth century, the more important a background of international scholastic training appears to be. It seems self-evident that, in order to rise as he did, Grosseteste must have shared this background with the other learned bishops of his day. Yet the contemporary observers who described him most fully say nothing about it. Their emphasis is on his oddity rather than his conformity to contemporary standards of thought and action. This is the first problem with which we are faced.

II. CONTEMPORARY WITNESSES

We may take as our starting-point the accounts of him given by two contemporary, or near contemporary, writers who saw him from very different points of view. The first observed him at fairly close quarters, and wrote down his impressions from year to year during the last eighteen years of Grosseteste's life. The second may never have seen him, but he knew well some of his closest collaborators and he had access to his literary remains. What he learnt from these sources made him feel that he was the heir to Grosseteste's thought, and perhaps the only man who could carry it forward. The first of these writers was Matthew Paris; the second Roger Bacon. Neither of them has a very good reputation among modern scholars for judgement, accuracy or veracity. But with this warning we may turn to what they say. And first to Matthew Paris.

Matthew Paris

Matthew Paris, whatever his demerits may prove to be, had one great advantage over all other observers: at St Albans he was a monk of the greatest monastery in Grosseteste's diocese of Lincoln. Moreover, at the moment when Grosseteste became bishop, Matthew Paris was in the process of taking over from his predecessor, Roger Wendover, the duty of historiographer in the monastery.[2] The historian and the bishop who was to play a central role in his history for the next eighteen years both emerged from obscurity in the same year, and both made their mark at once. The historian announced the new management of the Chronicle by sharpening its tone. Having at first written that the new bishop was 'a worthy and religious man, competently learned in ecclesiastical law', he scratched this out and substituted a phrase of similar length but very different emphasis. The new bishop, he wrote, was 'a man of too much learning, having been brought up in the schools from his early years'.[3] So here, right at the beginning of his independent history, we have an indication of what to expect: a sharp reporter, who does not hesitate to strike out a complacent meaningless phrase and substitute a pointed and abrasive one. It may not be right, and it is certainly not based on deep knowledge or long consideration, but it records a vivid first

[2] For details of the change of authorship, see Richard Vaughan, *Matthew Paris*, Cambridge, 1958, 28–30, and Richard Kay, 'Wendover's last annal', *EHR* lxxxiv, 1969, 779–85, where it is shown that Roger of Wendover wrote his last annal in spring 1234. From this point Matthew Paris was the sole author, at first retaining the general style and attitude of his predecessor, but rapidly developing his own personal style and point of view.

[3] He omitted both descriptions when he enlarged the passage in his final revision (see below, p. 11).

impression. It is not likely that Matthew Paris knew much about Grosseteste's early years, but he knew that he came straight from the schools of Oxford, and immediately from the school of the Franciscans—a body of men whose influence he distrusted. All this inclined him to think that Grosseteste had too much book-learning and knew too little of the world.

This first impression was not contradicted by the experience of the next few years. Almost at once he saw the bishop engaged in an endless, expensive, acrimonious and—so far as he could judge—stupidly pointless disagreement with the canons of Lincoln over his right to examine and correct their behaviour and the conduct of their affairs. And he saw this as only one example of Grosseteste's insistence on his personal responsibility for the spiritual welfare of every single soul in his diocese, except those formally excluded from his responsibility by an earlier papal privilege. Civilized behaviour, custom, established usages, the common way of life, seemed to mean nothing to this strange bishop. He acted with brutal truculence, and all, so Matthew Paris was inclined to think, for nothing: his actions were a vast waste of energy and resources, a breach of all charity, an implacable effort to insist on changes which could do little good at best, and at worst caused pointless ill-feeling.[4]

From Matthew Paris's point of view, this unfeeling violence was especially odious in the bishop's treatment of the monasteries in his diocese. His own monastery had almost nothing to fear from the bishop's pastoral care. A hundred, no less, papal privileges of recent date and unparalleled particularity protected St Albans and all its dependent churches from any interest that the bishop might take in their welfare. But St Albans had been lucky in having a pope, Hadrian IV, who was almost a son of their church. He had showered privileges on them with a liberal hand, and his successors had followed his example.[5] Other monasteries were less securely guarded. They had to rely on the goodwill of bishops who respected established rights and found in them an essential support for the peace and serenity of the whole fabric of the Church. But

[4] For Paris's opinion of this quarrel, see *Chron. Maj.* iii. 528–9, 638–9; iv. 497.

[5] For Hadrian's privileges granted to St Albans, see Holtzmann, *Papsturkunden in England*, Abh. der Akademie der Wissenschaften in Göttingen, 1952, iii. 100–13, 117–19; those of his successors, *passim*.

Grosseteste came from the great mass of the underdogs of the world. Unlike most bishops he had not learnt from childhood to respect ancient rights and possessions, because he had never enjoyed them. What others saw as rights, he saw as attempts to evade the rigours of religious observance and the pastoral care of the bishop of their souls.

Matthew Paris saw things differently. The civilized life and religious amenity of a great abbey provided the inspiration for all his work. Inevitably, his first suspicions about Grosseteste were hardened into hostility when he found him an unrelenting, persistent, unreasonable and violent enemy, not only to the rights of the canons of Lincoln, but also to the rights of the religious communities in his diocese. Strangely enough, Matthew Paris did not mention, as the Dunstable annalist did, that in his very first episcopal visitation, within a year of his election, Grosseteste deposed no less than eleven heads of religious houses for irregularities of one kind or another.[6] But he saw plenty of other examples of similar wholesale and, as he thought, disproportionate severity towards members of religious communities: 'If all the tyrannies which he practised in his visitations were recorded, he would be reckoned not just a severe man, but a heartless and inhuman one.'[7] Such was Matthew Paris's considered verdict on this side of Grosseteste's activity. The two men were incompatible in their outlook. Matthew Paris, by his upbringing, tastes, and the traditions of his Order, was a humane man. Grosseteste was not. He drove everything to extremes; and, in his pursuit of even good ends, he behaved with a violence which was at least as objectionable as the disorders he sought to eradicate. This was Matthew Paris's view, and he provided abundant detail to support it in his chronicle.

But, in addition to the vivacity and immediacy of his impressions, Matthew Paris had another quality which made him a first-rate journalist: his eyes were open to events of many different kinds, and he gradually became aware of other sides of Grosseteste's character. His first distinctly favourable impression was recorded in 1242, when he reported that the bishop had been responsible for getting hold of, and translating

---

[6] *Annales de Dunstaplia*, 1235 (*Ann. Mon.* iii. 143–4).
[7] *Chron. Maj.* v. 226.

from Greek, a hitherto unknown Old Testament text, which the Jews were alleged to have suppressed because of its testimony to the coming of Christ.[8] This was the work known as the *Testaments of the Twelve Patriarchs*, and Grosseteste's enterprise in making it available to Latin Christendom aroused the chronicler's enthusiasm: it was 'a glorious treatise for strengthening the Christian faith and confounding the hatred of the Jews'. And it appealed to the chronicler's local patriotism, for Grosseteste translated it with the help of Nicholas the Greek, who was connected with the Abbey of St Albans. For the first time, he could express a warmth of admiration for the bishop.

After this date, Matthew Paris found other points to admire. He began to see that the rough violence which was so intolerable when directed against monks, nuns, clergy and common people, could be exhilarating when directed at other targets. He observed that, whenever there were discussions among bishops or at meetings of bishops and lay magnates, it was always Grosseteste who sharpened their resistance to royal encroachments, rallied their wavering pusillanimity and pressed for the excommunication of the enemies of Magna Carta. Also, and increasingly, he saw and applauded his implacable resistance to papal financial demands. On this point, Grosseteste stood out as a friend of local liberties, and Matthew Paris was careful to preserve the proofs in a remarkable collection of documents.[9]

As these varied symptoms of a large and ruggedly independent personality and spiritual presence gradually displayed themselves to his observation, Matthew Paris warmed in his appreciation. In his final summing up he paid him a magnificent tribute in which he tried to do justice to a very

[8] Ibid. iv. 232-3.

[9] The first occasion on which Paris reported with approval a speech of Grosseteste was in October 1244 when he stiffened the resistance of the bishops against a papal demand for their consent to a subsidy to the king (*Chron. Maj.* iv. 366: for the date and circumstances, see F. M. Powicke, *Henry III and the Lord Edward*, Oxford, 1947, i. 298-30). See also *Chron. Maj.* v. 325-6, for Grosseteste's intervention in October 1252 to prevent the payment of a papally supported subsidy to the king for the Crusade; v. 377-8, 395-400, for his excommunication of breakers of Magna Charta; and v. 355 for his calculation that the 'present Pope Innocent IV' had impoverished the church more than all his predecessors put together. All these incidents were recorded with favourable or neutral intention. For the main documents relating to Grosseteste preserved by Paris among his *Additamenta*, see *Chron. Maj.* vi. 134-44, 148-50, 152, 186-7, 200-1, 213-17, 229-31.

complex character. Grosseteste, he wrote, was 'an open re-
prover of pope and king, a critic of prelates, a corrector of
monks, a director of priests, a preacher to the people, a sustainer
of scholars, a diligent student of Scripture, a hammer and
despiser of the Romans; hospitable, liberal, urbane, cheerful,
affable in his hall; devout, tearful, contrite in church; diligent,
grave, untiring in his episcopal duties'.[10]

These words must have been written immediately after
Grosseteste's death.[11] Then came reports of miracles at his
tomb, and Matthew Paris entertained the thought that, besides
being a riveting personality, Grosseteste might even be a saint.
He contemplated this possibility with sympathy, but with some
scruples. What was he then to make of all the excesses he had
reported in the course of his Chronicle? This is how he dealt
with them:

Let no one be disturbed by the violent acts which he did in his
life-time, as recorded in this book—his treatment of his canons whom
he excommunicated and harassed, his savage attacks on monks, and
even more savage against nuns . . . They arose from zeal, though
perhaps 'not according to knowledge'. And I confidently assert that
his virtues pleased God, though his excesses displeased him. It was
like this too with David and St Peter. In David, I admire his mildness
while reprehending his betrayal of Uriah; in Peter, I admire his
constancy while reprehending his thrice-repeated denial.[12]

Then more miracles followed, and Matthew Paris, who was
making an abbreviated version of his Chronicle, edged a little
further towards complete conviction by altering the assessment
of the above paragraph to a 'confident assertion that his virtues

[10] *Chron. Maj.* v. 407.

[11] Matthew Paris originally intended to bring his Chronicle to a close in 1250 and
he wrote an elaborate ending at this point (*Chron. Maj.* v. 198). But after an interval
of a year or two he resumed it and brought it down to the end of 1253 (v. 420). The
final entries of this year give the impression of being written at the same time as the
events they describe: for instance, the first summing up of Grosseteste's character
quoted above appears immediately after his death. But then came reports of daily
miracles at his tomb, and Paris wrote a new summing up, repeating some examples of
Grosseteste's violence, but expressing confidence in his sanctity (v. 419, as quoted
below). Then, a little later, *c.*1255, Paris made his abbreviation of the annals for these
years, and he curtailed the examples of Grosseteste's violence (probably erasing one of
them in *Chron. Maj.* as noted by the editor) and strengthened the confident note of the
final sentence.

[12] *Chron. Maj.* v. 419.

pleased God *more* than his excesses displeased Him'.[13] In the same revision, he took the opportunity to revise his initial impression of Grosseteste's election. He recalled facts which he had not thought worth reporting in 1235: the acute divisions and long altercations among the canons of Lincoln during the election, and the totally unexpected unanimous decision in the end to elect Grosseteste, whom no one had supported except the Franciscans. Matthew Paris did not know, or did not report, from whom the initiative which brought this decision had come, but he took the chance to strike out his earlier estimate of the man and to give a new account based on his later experiences: Grosseteste, he wrote, was 'born from the very humblest stock, a man of refined learning in both trivium and quadrivium, unconventional in his manner of life, following his own will and relying on his own judgement, as the narrative which follows will make plain'.[14] These words, written in his own hand, survive to give Matthew Paris's final judgement on the man he had observed over a period of eighteen years.

These small touches have a greater significance than might at first appear, for two reasons. First, because in this revision of his work Matthew Paris was engaged in a drastic reduction in length to about one-eighth of the original narrative. So any *additions* which he makes had some special importance for him. Generally, they indicate his growing interest in the intellectual and scientific movements of his time; and his growing appreciation of Grosseteste is to be seen in this context. Then, they show that Matthew Paris was a more reflective and conscientious observer than is often realized. Too often he is portrayed as a slap-dash writer who used his Chronicle as a medium for his own prejudices without much regard for truth.

[13] *Hist. Angl.* iii. 148-9.

[14] Ibid. ii. 376. The printed text is unintelligible at this point, so I give a corrected version of the essential sentence from BL MS Royal 14 C vii f. 123^r: 'Ipse autem Robertus ex humillima stirpe procreatus, eleganter tam in trivio quam quadrivio eruditus, sui ipsius consilio non alieno regi volens, singularis erat conversationis et propriae sectator voluntatis, suae innitens prudentiae, quod perspicue postea manifestavit, sicut sequens narratio manifestavit.' The erasures and alterations in the manuscript bear witness to the care with which the whole passage was composed. A slightly later corrector was responsible for a misunderstanding of the phrase 'sui ipsius consilio non alieno regi volens', which has got into the printed edition: he read 'volens' as 'nolens', wrongly understood 'regi' as meaning 'to the king', and added 'praesentari' in the margin in a desperate attempt to make sense. It is in this corrupt form that it is generally quoted.

But a closer attention to his changes shows that he was a laborious reviser of first impressions, a conscientious collector of evidence, and one with wide views and some refined scruples. This does not mean that he can be accepted without question; but it does mean that he should not be dismissed lightly.

This remark is especially relevant when we come to the longest and most dramatic scene in his whole account of Grosseteste—his death-bed. Matthew Paris was fully aware of the importance of death-bed scenes in winding up accounts of both saints and sinners. This was the moment when eternity impinged on this world in prophecies, visions, premonitions, unusual natural phenomena and miraculous events. It was the time for special revelations about the future course of events; the time too when the dying person might be expected to sum up the experience of a life-time in pregnant phrases, to leave a last message for his disciples, to pass a final judgement on hostile powers, and to give an example of the art of dying. Matthew Paris worked most of those themes into his account of the last days of Grosseteste. The dying man is represented as speaking with force and indignation about all the griefs of his later years—the general neglect of pastoral care, the universal presence of heresy and unbelief in the Western Church, the cause of these evils in the worldliness of the papal curia, which amounted to nothing less than apostasy and foreshadowed the coming of Antichrist. His words blaze with hostility to Innocent IV and the Roman curia as the source of the manifold evils of Christendom. In the light of these evils, the dying man believed that a general disaster was imminent.[15]

Matthew Paris's account of those conversations has not been well received by modern scholars, and we shall have later to examine the grounds for this distrust. All that needs to be said at present is that, if the account turns out to be unreliable, the cause cannot be found in Matthew Paris's blindly one-sided picture of Grosseteste, for we have seen some evidence of his thoughtful and even delicate assessment of the varied strands in Grosseteste. Nor can it be due to indifference to the current ideal of a holy death, for he had recently written a full account of a model death in his biography of Archbishop Edmund of

---

[15] *Chron. Maj.* v. 400-7; abbreviated in *Hist. Angl.* iii. 145-6. See below, pp. 291-5.

Canterbury.[16] Matthew Paris certainly knew how the elements of contrition, confession, supreme unction and Holy Communion should contribute to such a scene. He gave them a large place at the death-bed of Archbishop Edmund; but he ignored them all in his account of Grosseteste's last days. Despite this, he was willing to believe that Grosseteste too was a saint. Certainly not a conventional one: a seer rather; a man whose heartless persecution of sinners was governed by a deep concern for souls, and whose violence of speech hid a man who in daily life was affable, courteous, hospitable and open-handed. He had long wrestled with the complexities of Grosseteste's character and outlook; and, if he left him mysterious and perplexing in the end, this may be a tribute to the honesty of his reporting. We shall see.

Roger Bacon

We turn now to our other important contemporary witness, Roger Bacon. In every way, both in what he says about Grosseteste and what he himself was, he forms a striking contrast to Matthew Paris. The chronicler had seen Grosseteste in action over a period of nearly twenty years: as a monk in his diocese he had observed and experienced his activity; he had disapproved of much, been puzzled by more, and had felt the appeal of an intense earnestness and power in all that Grosseteste did, without understanding the connecting links which held it all together. Roger Bacon had seen nothing of all this. Indeed, it is not even quite certain that he had ever set eyes on Grosseteste in person: he may have known him only from the reports of his friends and associates, and more especially from Grosseteste's chief friend and disciple, Adam Marsh.[17] But also, after he became a Franciscan in about 1257, he had access to

---

[16] Printed in C. H. Lawrence, *St Edmund of Abingdon: A Study in Hagiography and History*, 1960, pp. 264–71.

[17] Roger Bacon seems to have been born in about 1219. His career is at all points extremely elusive, but his early writings on the liberal arts appear to be connected with Paris. In 1267 (in his *Opus Tertium*, p. 59) he says that he has been buying scientific books and instruments for twenty years, but there is no firm evidence for his presence in Oxford or knowledge of Grosseteste before he entered the Franciscan Order, perhaps in 1257 and probably in Oxford. For Bacon's early career, see S. C. Easton, *Roger Bacon and his Search for a Universal Science*, Oxford, 1952. Also A. C. Crombie and J. N. North in the *Dictionary of Scientific Biography*, ed. C. C. Gillespie, i, 1970, 377–83.

the literary remains which Grosseteste left to the community at Oxford. It was from these sources that Bacon got a picture of Grosseteste which was clear, consistent and inspiring, entirely lacking in the dark corners and contradictory features of Matthew Paris's portrait. The contrast points to an essential difference between the two observers. Matthew Paris saw Grosseteste as a contemporary in his everyday world. Bacon saw him as a man of an earlier age, a forerunner.

So far as we can judge, Grosseteste left no mark on Bacon's early studies nor on any of his writings before he joined the Franciscans. But from 1267 onwards, he wrote a series of works inspired by a new vision of scientific, linguistic, and biblical study designed to save Christendom from its internal and external enemies. The key document in this second phase of his life is a letter, now lost, written to Pope Clement IV in 1265/6 giving a brief account of his ideas and the obstacles under which he laboured. The pope replied on 22 June 1266 asking him to send a full account of his ideas as soon as possible, in secret and without regard to the orders of his superiors. Bacon replied in 1267 by sending his *Opus Minus* as an introduction to his new programme, and his *Opus Maius* which gave a full account of his whole plan. He also set about preparing an intermediate work, his *Opus Tertium*. This was going ahead in 1267.

Clement IV died in 1268 and it is doubtful whether the *Opus Tertium* was ever finished, but Bacon went on expounding his programme in several forms until 1292.[18] His plan became an obsession, and the works in which he developed it are extraordinarily detailed, complicated, and repetitive. They are frequently bizarre and always idiosyncratic. They have the

---

[18] The best survey of Bacon's works is still A. G. Little's account in *Roger Bacon Commemoration Essays*, Oxford, 1914, pp. 373-419. For our present purpose it will suffice to mention the *Opus Tertium* and the *Opus Minus* printed in *Rogeri Bacon Opera hactenus inedita*, ed. J. S. Brewer, RS, 1859; a supplementary fragment of *Opus Minus* printed by Cardinal Gasquet, *EHR* xii, 1897, 494-517; and a supplementary part of the *Opus Tertium*, ed. A. G. Little, *Brit. Soc. of Franciscan Studies, iv, 1912; the Opus Maius*, ed. J. H. Bridges, 3 vols. 1897-1900, with supplements ed. by E. Massa, *Rogeri Baconis Moralis Philosophia*, Padua, 1953, and by K. M. Fredborg, Lauge Nielsen, and Jan Pinborg, 'An Unedited Part of Roger Bacon's *Opus Maius: De Signis*', in *Traditio*, xxiv, 1978, 75-136. Later works of Bacon on related themes are his *Compendium studii philosophiae* (1271) in Brewer, op. cit., pp. 393-519; and *Compendium studii theologiae* (1292) ed. H. Rashdall, *Brit. Soc. of Franciscan Studies*, iii, 1911.

grandeur and impracticability of passionate conviction and unremitting zeal. In all of them he mentions Grosseteste with extravagant praise as his precursor in every main branch of his proposals: it is this that gives his programme a special interest to us here.

What Bacon urged was that Western Christendom should change the direction of its studies: first, that it should master the philosophical and scientific resources of its enemies with a view to meeting them on their own ground; and, secondly, that it should clarify its own position by discarding harmful accretions and concentrating on the central documents of its tradition. For the first of these aims, it was necessary that the Latins should learn the languages—especially Greek—in which scientific knowledge, hitherto available only in debased translations, was to be found most fully expounded. Having done this, it would then be possible to master the sciences to which these writings were no more than the introduction. For the second aim, a deeper understanding of the Bible was the primary requirement. To achieve this, a knowledge of Greek and Hebrew, and a much greater familiarity with the writings of Greek theologians and commentators than the West had hitherto possessed, were essential. Add to these studies the use of science to clarify the symbolism of the Bible; cut out the distractions of Peter Lombard's *Sentences* and the obsessive interest of the West in Roman Law; and the West would be on the road to recovery and able to meet the Muslims both in the field of action and in debate.

In support of this programme in all its branches Bacon invoked the name of Robert Grosseteste. In his view, Grosseteste had pioneered every one of the developments which he advocated. Bacon had gone further—much further—but it was Grosseteste who had shown the way. That is how Bacon saw the situation, and his point of view explains several oddities in his account of his predecessor. In the first place, it accounts for his very extravagant praise of Grosseteste and his associates. Then also, despite the praise, it accounts for his constant tendency to criticize Grosseteste and to follow him very rarely in detail. And it explains why he always and only saw Grosseteste as a proto-Bacon. We can see all these tendencies at work as we go through his references to Grosseteste one by one.

The most extravagantly laudatory passage is one in which he described the heroic Grosseteste brushing aside the wholly inadequate translations of Aristotle and going straight to the sciences. Bacon was very eloquent on the subject of the uselessness of the earlier translations: they were so useless, he said, that the more they were read, the less they brought understanding of the subject. Grosseteste alone had had the courage to ignore them :

Robert, formerly bishop of Lincoln of blessed memory, neglected the books of Aristotle and their arguments and, by using his own experience and other authors and other means of learning, he worked his way into the wisdom of Aristotle and came to know and write about the subjects of Aristotle's works a hundred thousand times better than those who used only the perverted translations of these works. You can see this in his treatises on Rainbows, on Comets, and other works which he wrote.[19]

This passage has often been quoted, and as a factual statement it is absurd. Grosseteste did not neglect Aristotle; and he was not unduly bothered by the short-comings of the existing translations. And yet, if we can imagine Bacon as a Franciscan in Oxford reading Grosseteste's little scientific treatises for the first time, noticing their freshness of approach, their arguments from the phenomena themselves, their interest in the geometry of celestial movements, and their independence with regard to Aristotle; and if we further imagine Bacon meeting the men whom Grosseteste had inspired to undertake the greatest co-operative work of translating Greek sources ever attempted in the West; and if we make allowances for the highly charged, superlative-laden, style of writing to which the Franciscans (not least Adam Marsh, and even Grosseteste himself) were addicted, then Bacon's reconstruction of Grosseteste's achievement is understandable. So also are his criticisms. If the lack of adequate translations had forced Grosseteste to plunge into the sciences without a reliable guide, this explained why his methods were sometimes clumsy and his conclusions wrong. He had the great merit of seeing the fundamental role of mathematics in science, but his mathematical methods were crude

---

[19] *Compendium studii philosophiae*, ed. Brewer, p. 469.

and old-fashioned.[20] A similar critical note is struck when Bacon refers to Grosseteste's work on the calendar—the only subject on which Bacon wrote a rival work, perhaps intended to replace Grosseteste's. He criticized Grosseteste for retaining the common distinctions of spring, summer, autumn, winter, instead of following the philosopher Abu Ma'shar in dividing the seasons, in a manner consistent both with nature and reason, into three periods of growth, equilibrium, decline.[21] Yet, despite this weakness, which we may be inclined to see as a preference for common sense over highfalutin theory, he saw Grosseteste as the only modern man who had understood the sciences: 'Only Boethius, the first of all the translators, understood the power of languages; only Robert Grosseteste knew the sciences. The other translators were defective both in languages and in sciences.'[22]

Bacon revered Grosseteste also as a pioneer in the study of languages, but he had started too late, for—so Bacon tells us—it was only towards the end of his life that he was sufficiently competent to translate Greek without help.[23] Modern scholars have thought that Bacon was here, as elsewhere, too severe; but he was not far from the mark, and if he unduly depreciated Grosseteste's linguistic ability, he did full justice to his energy and foresight in collecting Greek books and gathering together a group of translators. Bacon mentions their names: Adam Marsh, Robert Marsh, Thomas Wallensis, William Lupus, and William of Sherwood. Strangely enough, he does not mention the earliest and most notable of them, John of Basingstoke, who had died the year before Grosseteste in 1252, and this is another indication that Bacon knew about Grosseteste's life only from those who survived him.

His mention of Grosseteste's work as a translator brought Bacon to another of his favourite themes: the need to enlist the

---

[20] For Grosseteste's understanding of the fundamental importance of mathematics, see *Opus Maius*, i. 108; and for his technical shortcomings, *Communia mathematica*, ed. R. Steele, *Opera hactenus inedita Rogeri Baconi*, fasc. 16, 1940, pp. 117–18.

[21] Roger Bacon, *Compotus*, ed. R. Steele, 1926, p. 40.

[22] *Opus Maius*, i. 67; cf. *Opus Tertium*, p. 33, and *Compendium studii philosophiae*, p. 472. Also *Opus Minus*, p. 317, for a probable reference to Grosseteste on rainbows and similar phenomena: 'Certus sum quod nullus apud Latinos praeter unum qui est sapientissimus Latinorum poterit satisfacere in hac parte.'

[23] For Bacon's assessment of Grosseteste as a Greek scholar with the names of other translators (chiefly Grosseteste's helpers), see *Opus Maius*, i. 73.

help of the old Greek theologians in understanding the Bible. His list of neglected authors in need of study and further translation runs thus: Origen, Basil, Gregory of Nyssa, John of Damascus, Denys, Chrysostom. Grosseteste had been responsible for bringing all of them except Origen to wider notice in the West. So here too Bacon could claim Grosseteste as the originator of the programme which he advocated.[24]

Then, last and most important of all, he claimed Grosseteste and his friend Adam Marsh as the chief men of his own day in maintaining the primacy of the Bible over all other texts for the study of theology.[25]

Brief though these notices are, they form a magnificent eulogy of Grosseteste as the initiator in all parts of Bacon's ambitious programme—in the study of science and Greek, in organizing translations, in the primacy of the Bible, against the main scholastic tendencies of the period before about 1220. No doubt Bacon pressed Grosseteste too firmly into his own mould. They were men of very different temper. Bacon was a grandiose and systematic planner of an ideal scheme of studies designed to lead to effective action against the enemies of Christendom. Everything that he wrote in his later years, for which he claimed Grosseteste as his exemplar, was directed to this end. But there is not the slightest reason to think that Grosseteste was interested in grand plans of scholastic reform. We shall find him going from one activity to another as circumstances and the inspiration of the moment led him. Bacon was altogether more

[24] Roger Bacon's words on this subject deserve to be quoted because they put Grosseteste's translations in their correct theological context and emphasize their scale. Bacon has been speaking of the need for new translations of Greek scientific works, and he continues: 'Innumerabiles etiam libri expositorum Hebraeorum et Graecorum desunt Latinis, ut Origenis, Basilii, Gregorii, Nazianzeni, Damasceni, Dionysii, Chrysostomi, et aliorum doctorum nobilissimorum tam in Hebraico quam in Greco. Dormit igitur ecclesia quae nihil facit in hac parte, nec aliquid a septuaginta annis fecit, nisi quod dominus Robertus, episcopus Lincolniensis sanctae memoriae, tradidit Latinis de libris beati Dionysii, et Damasceni, et aliquibus aliis doctoribus consecratis. Mirum est de negligentia ecclesiae, quia a tempore Damasi papae non fuit aliquis summus pontifex nec aliquis alius inferior, qui solicitus fuit de promotione ecclesiae per translationes, nisi dominus praefatus episcopus gloriosus.' (*Compendium studii philosophiae*, ed. Brewer, p. 474; cf. also *Opus Maius*, i. 70, on the same theme). For the justice of Bacon's estimate of Grosseteste's importance in this field, see below, chapter 8.

[25] *Opus Minus*, ed. Brewer, p. 329. Bacon marks the generation gap between himself and these *maximi viri* by referring to them as *sapientes antiqui*, some of whom he had nevertheless seen with his own eyes.

aggressive, systematic, polemical, and scholastic in outlook. Grosseteste could indeed on occasion be both polemical and aggressive, but only under the impact of immediate events. In his scientific and theological writings, in his Greek studies and his translations, he took up subjects as they presented themselves to his notice, and it is very unlikely that he would have approved the framework in which Bacon placed him. Yet Bacon correctly identified the four areas of his essential originality. This perception entitles him to a high place among the interpreters of Grosseteste's achievement: he was the first to pick out the things which are most worthy of attention.

A member of Grosseteste's household: fr. Hubert

A different aspect of Grosseteste's complexity is revealed in the lavish hospitality and urbanity which (as Matthew Paris saw) presented a vivid contrast to his harshness in action. This sunny side of Grosseteste's character was beautifully portrayed in a brief biography, or rather lament, written shortly after his death by an unknown friar Hubert.[26] Biographically, this effusion tells us no single fact about him which was not already known. The writer seems to have known nothing about Grosseteste's early life, except that he was born in Suffolk. His words would have been no more than a general eulogy if they had not provided a serene and convincing picture of Grosseteste in the circle of his *familia*, to which the writer evidently belonged. The portrait is both moving and life-like. We should not have guessed that such a man lay behind the details which occupy so many pages of Matthew Paris or formed the subject of Roger Bacon's observations. Here we see him as a courteous and lavish host, a great spender of his revenues, intensely interested in the education of the noble children in his household, amenable, encouraging, talkative to all around him, sombre yet light-hearted, perpetually active, deeply contemplative, dedicated to prayer and worship; the protector of the poor, the critic of kings and popes, the patron of both orders of friars. This was the man as his intimates knew him, as contrasted with the

[26] This lament was discovered and printed by R. W. Hunt, 'Verses on the Life of Grosseteste', *Medievalia et Humanistica*, NS i, 1970, 241–51. There is a full and sympathetic account of it in McEvoy, 1982, 40–2. McEvoy's 'Portrait of Grosseteste', ibid., pp. 3–48, deserves to be studied as a whole, and I have not thought it necessary to go over again the ground which he covers.

man whom others knew either as a disturber of worldly peace
or as an intellectual innovator.

III. LATER HISTORICAL RECONSTRUCTIONS

Grosseteste presented several different views of his aims and
activities to his contemporaries. All of them responded to him
in ways which reflected their own circumstances and interests;
and later scholars and chroniclers down to the present day
have continued to make similarly weighted responses. The first
important new alignment of the Grosseteste material is to be
found in the various recensions of Ranulf Higden's Chronicle
during the fifty years after 1327.[27] It was Higden who first drew
the outlines of a national hero suffering for his resistance to the
papacy. And it is interesting that he did not draw the material
for this portrait, as he might have done, from Matthew Paris:
rather, it would seem, he drew from the experiences of the
canons of Lincoln, whose long-continued efforts to obtain
Grosseteste's canonization had been finally repelled by the papal curia shortly before 1330.[28]

On an objective view, the curia had good reasons for their
refusal. But this was not how it seemed to his local advocates,
and Higden adopted their point of view. Brief though his account is, it contains several elements which were to endear
Grosseteste to the Lollards fifty years later: Grosseteste's opposition to papal exactions, his excommunication, his posthumous judgement on Innocent IV, followed by the refusal of the
curia to canonize him despite the miracles at his tomb. Later, in
the 1340s, Higden added more details, including an imperfectly
understood reference to Grosseteste's speech to the pope and
cardinals in 1250, which does not seem to have been noticed by
any earlier chronicler. So here we see that in the mid-fourteenth

---

[27] See *Polychronicon Ranulphi Higden*, ed. J. R. Lumby, RS, 9 vols., 1865–86, viii. 240–
3. The growth of the text at this point can be made out with the help of the analysis of
the recensions of Higden's Chronicle in John Taylor, *The Universal Chronicle of Ranulph
Higden*, Oxford, 1966. It was Higden who gave currency to the story, beloved by the
Lollards, that Grosseteste had been excommunicated by Innocent IV. In Matthew
Paris's account the cardinals persuaded the pope not to proceed to extreme measures,
and it is likely that he was simply suspended from some or all of his episcopal duties.
Nevertheless, the generally well-informed Lanercost Chronicle (p. 43) preserved an
earlier Franciscan tradition that he died excommunicate.

[28] For the attempts at canonization, see E. W. Kemp in Callus, 1955, 241–6.

century the picture of the uncanonized saint and heroic anti-papal figure, in whom Wycliffe and the Lollards were later to see their great exemplar, was already being built up.

Wycliffe and the Lollards perfected this picture of the persecuted saint and religious teacher who suffered for his denunciation of the worldly papacy and its curialist minions.[29] Two centuries later, the 'Protestant Grosseteste' received his final consummation in Foxe's *Book of Martyrs*. Foxe took some care in constructing his portrait of Grosseteste. He made full use of Matthew Paris, and he examined Grosseteste's literary remains 'in the Queen's Majesty's Library at Westminster'.[30] His book continued for another two hundred years to keep the Wycliffite Grosseteste alive in many remote parish churches. But Foxe's account was the last gasp of Grosseteste the religious agitator. A few years after the publication of the *Book of Martyrs*, an equally eccentric but less significant figure was given a wide circulation in Holinshed's Chronicle. Holinshed ignored the anti-papal bishop, but extracted from Matthew Paris a portrait of a sour martinet. He chose details which portrayed a busy-body bishop, who excommunicated sinners and negligent officials with a hasty hand; a prurient investigator of monastic sins, who in his visitations of monasteries 'entered into the chambers of the monks and searched their beds, and, coming to the houses of the nuns, went so near as to cause their breasts to be tried that he might understand their chaste livings', and so on.[31] All these details are indeed to be found in Matthew Paris, and it is by no means clear that Grosseteste was incapable of these actions. But they had lost their interest, and Grosseteste was effectively dismissed from the pages of national, still more international, history for three hundred years.

What brought him once more to a central position in the history of his time was the constitutional theme as developed

---

[29] This subject is sufficiently important to require fuller treatment below, pp. 299–310.

[30] John Foxe, *Actes and Monuments of thynges passed in every kynges tym in this realm* (generally known as the *Book of Martyrs*), edition of 1570, pp. 404–10. Among other works of Grosseteste, Foxe saw 'one sermon writen and exhibited in four sondry skroles, to the pope and other four Cardinals beginning "Dominus noster Jesus Christus" '. This was the speech distributed to the pope and four cardinals and read to the curia in 1250 (see below, p. 276), almost certainly the copy in BL MS Royal 7 F ii.

[31] R. Holinshed, *Chronicles of England, Scotland and Ireland*, edition of 1585, pp. 242, 244, 246, 249, quoting Matthew Paris, *Chron. Maj.* v. 226–7, 256.

by William Stubbs. The few pages which Stubbs devoted to
him marked a decisive new beginning in Grosseteste studies.
For the first time, serious historical scholarship was brought to
the interpretation of Grosseteste, not as an eccentric extremist
or lonely figure in a hostile age, but as an essentially moderate
and central influence in the greatest of the medieval centuries.
To Stubbs he was as great a hero as he had been to Wycliffe
and Foxe, but in a different mould: 'the most learned, the most
acute, the most holy man of his time, the most devoted to his
spiritual work, the most trusted leader and confidant of princes,
at the same time a most faithful servant of the Roman Church.'
'The great mauler of the Romans' of Foxe has become a far-
sighted statesman whose 'attitude to the papacy was not one of
unintelligent submission'. In Stubbs's pages Grosseteste emerged at last as a central figure in a great age of construction:
'the prophet and harbinger of better times coming', 'the friend
and adviser of the constitutional opposition', 'more than once
the spokesman of the constitutional party in parliament; the
patron of the friars who represented learning and piety as well
as the doctrines of civil independence in the universities and
country at large'.[32] Stubbs wrote about Grosseteste with a quite
unaccustomed warmth. He was the first scholar to see Grosseteste as a representative of all that was best in the thirteenth
century, a great man in a great age displaying all the normality
of a superior mind.

A hundred years have now passed since Stubbs wrote, and
an ever growing number of studies have been published which
have concentrated attention on scientific and theological works
which Stubbs scarcely knew. These studies have largely undermined Stubbs's picture of Grosseteste as a great figure in the
constitutional development of England, and they have increasingly placed him in the setting of European scholastic
thought. But they have all preserved one essential feature of
Stubbs's portrait: Grosseteste's centrality. As the constitutional
theme has withered, Grosseteste has emerged as a central exponent of the scientific and theological developments of the
early thirteenth century.

The first, and still in its general outlines the best, expression
of this new normality is to be found in the collection of studies

---

[32] W. Stubbs, *Constitutional History of England*, ii, 3rd edn. 1887, pp. 74, 313-15.

edited by Fr. Daniel Callus to commemorate the seventh centenary of Grosseteste's death in 1953.[33] I linger over it, for it is one of the most distinctive products of the school of history associated with Sir Maurice Powicke, to which I have had the honour to belong.

To understand its emphasis it is necessary to recall the circumstances of its publication and the aims of what may broadly be called the Powicke school of history. It had always been the special aim of this school to assert the normative role of the twelfth and thirteenth centuries in the development of European civilization, and to emphasize the importance of European influences in English history. Grosseteste seemed to offer an ideal illustration of these two principles: he could be seen as an Englishman fully immersed in the European tradition, reflecting all that was latest and best in the scholastic tradition of Paris and Oxford, exemplifying this tradition in his own writings, and giving effect to the recent legislation of the Fourth Lateran Council of 1215 in his work as a bishop.

This was the general picture; and the moment was peculiarly propitious for giving it a new expression. Its guiding principles had been fashioned in the inter-war years, under the growing threat of a war which seemed likely to destroy everything of most importance in European history. The threat had risen to its climax, and had (as it seemed) finally receded. A subject which revived the hopes of earlier years was, therefore, approached with a certain sense of euphoria. At last it was possible to take a long and peaceful look at Grosseteste in the light of the great advances which had been made in the study of European scholastic thought during the previous generation. He could be portrayed as Oxford's, and perhaps as England's, greatest exponent of the all-embracing European normality created by the joint influences of the great schools, the papacy, and the new religious orders—as a link connecting these European themes with the university of Oxford and with the legislation of the English church.

All these aspects of the subject were brought together in Powicke's introduction to the volume. Then the tale was taken up by Father Callus, certainly the most profound and sympathetic Grosseteste scholar of the time. He saw Grosseteste as

---

[33] *Robert Grosseteste, Scholar and Bishop*, ed. D. A. Callus Oxford, 1955.

a joint product of the schools of Paris and Oxford, exhibiting
the fine polish of a highly developed scholastic training, following (or even leading) the fashion of writing a *Summa Theologiae* on the model of Peter Lombard's *Sentences*, contributing
to the growth of ideas in almost every branch of contemporary
study:

one of the greatest glories of the university of Oxford, her first chancellor in the crucial years of her formation . . . he gave a powerful
impetus in every department of intellectual activity in which he himself excelled, and left behind him a tradition of learning which was
destined to grow, increase, and deepen throughout the centuries.[34]

These two contributions set the tone for the whole volume.
Even when it came to a consideration of Grosseteste's diatribes
against the papal curia, the note of moderation which separated
him—despite all superficial resemblances—from Wycliffe was
strongly maintained: 'Grosseteste, I think (wrote Dr Pantin),
envisaged an unlawful command as a temporary aberration,
which deprives the superior's command of validity *pro hac vice*,
but does not permanently destroy the superior's authority or
the office that he holds . . . Wycliffe on the other hand, at least
in his final stage, seems to regard reprobate popes and prelates
as permanently lacking authority. Even the epithet 'Antichrist', which Grosseteste used more than once of the pope and
papal curia, despite its 'ominous sound to modern ears', was
given an interpretation which brought it well within the bounds
of normality: 'what he (Grosseteste) has in mind is a moral,
not a doctrinal failure, and he does not envisage the possibility
of the papacy or the Church erring in doctrine.'[35]

Fr. Callus's volume of is so full of wise and balanced words,
so impregnated with civilized sentiments, and has so strong a
hold on the minds of those who have lived with it, that it is
hard to call in question the attitude it expresses. Yet one must
ask whether it does not drain the life out of a tempestuous
character and flatten the contours of a strongly independent
and unconventional thinker. Have not the jagged edges, the
violence of feeling, the extremist tendencies in thought and
expression, been smoothed away? Have not the actual cir-

[34] Ibid., p. 69.
[35] Ibid., pp. 191-2.

cumstances of his life, and the influences which they brought to bear on him, been forgotten? These are questions to which we shall often return in the pages which follow.

2

Grosseteste and the Pattern of Scholastic Thought

THE first step in clarifying the extent of Grosseteste's eccentricity is to ask how far his manner of tackling problems
conforms to the models developed in the European schools
where the mainstream of scholastic thought is to be found.
There is ample evidence that the great impetus to scholastic
development in the early twelfth century came from the urgent
need for clear and authoritative solutions to questions about
marriage, baptism, and the eucharist; about authority in secular society and in the Church; about God, Creation, Purgatory,
Heaven and Hell. The most important schools of the twelfth
century—and pre- eminently those of Paris and Bologna—
owed their huge success to their methods of answering such
questions, and in the course of the twelfth century they developed techniques for accumulating, arranging, dissecting and
reorganizing the materials in such a way that convincing answers could be given to almost all the important questions that
were asked. This body of material and techniques formed the
scholastic tradition which was available in the greater schools
of Europe by the time of Grosseteste's youth. So our first question is the extent of his immersion in this tradition, his mastery
of its methods, and his capacity to extend its results.

If, as we have good reason to think, Grosseteste was born
about 1170, we must look to a time about twenty years later
when he would be exposed to the full force of scholastic thought.
By this time the schools, and especially those of Paris, had
produced a huge and varied body of literature which took
many forms: organized collections of authorities; commentaries
on the Bible and on authoritative texts in all subjects; collections of questions, discussions, and conclusions: outlines of
knowledge covering large or small parts of the recognized disci-

plines. The total body of scholastic literature had become very large, but all of it bore the marks of its origin in its methods of argument and in the common effort to reach clear and definitive conclusions. Despite its general unity of aim and method, this literature displays many personal and regional differences which often make it possible to suggest the school or 'circle' to which an anonymous work belongs. The products of a long co-operative effort could scarcely fail to bear some marks of their origin, some recognition of contemporary or near contemporary influences. Indeed it was often the glory of a writer to be able to show himself the pupil of great masters. If Grosseteste is to be given a place in this scholastic scene, it is important to ask whether his works fit into the general scholastic pattern, and how they are related to the works of his contemporaries and predecessors in the schools.

I. THE PROBLEM OF SPURIOUS TEXTS

Before answering this question, it is necessary to take a general view of the works which can safely be used to explore the main outlines of his personality and habits of thought. We are faced with a small core of essential works surrounded by a large penumbra of the spurious and doubtful. Grosseteste was not a careful or self-conscious writer. Relatively few of his works circulated in his lifetime in a definitive form: his *De Sphera*, his commentary on the *Posterior Analytics*, his *De Decem Mandatis* and *De Cessatione Legalium*, and his so-called *Château d'Amour*, are in their different spheres the outstanding works which he left in a finished form. Even a relatively carefully composed work like his *Hexaëmeron* shows a marked deterioration in argument in its final sections, and it was never brought to a definite conclusion; and his comments on the Psalms and on the Pauline Epistles, his Sermons, his *Dicta*, his comments on the *Physics* and *Ethics*, his short treatises on Rainbows, Comets, Light, the origin of sounds—all these and several others seem to have been left in confusion, several of them unfinished, among his books which he left to the Oxford Franciscans at his death. It was this bequest which ensured their survival; but it also ensured that, in the absence of any firm editorial control, they came out into the world by the choice of readers who had only indifferent standards of authenticity.

It has too often been forgotten by writers on Grosseteste how little evidence sufficed for scribes and bibliographers to ascribe works to great names: an *horreur d'anonymité* is as pervasive a feature of the human mind as an *horreur du vide*. Fifty or a hundred years after the death of a notable man false ascriptions were easily made, and even more easily accepted, by bibliographers anxious to give completeness to their lists of writings. These attributions are like entry tickets in a lottery: they contain some winners but many losers. Yet, surprisingly often, scholars add up late ascriptions and quote their number as a substantial argument in their favour. They should rather be quoted as a warning of a common disease. Grosseteste has long suffered from the effects of this disease. Through the work of many scholars, he is now emerging from this world of shadows, but the clouds still hang around him. Even when attributions have been shown to be false or unlikely, the character of a systematic scholastic writer, which they have helped to stamp upon him, still lingers. I think especially in this connection of two large surveys of natural science, the fragments of a *Summa Theologiae*, and a complete set of lectures on the Gospels. All of them are well supported by attributions, by association with genuine works, by a wide consensus of bibliographers; and all are either certainly or probably spurious.

Perhaps the most strongly supported by manuscript attributions and bibliographical consensus was an outline of natural science, a *Summa Philosophiae*, a work of great length and widely ranging learning. It forms by far the largest item in Ludwig Baur's epoch-making edition of Grosseteste's scientific works. He devoted more than half his volume to it, and he called it 'one of the most significant and interesting works of the Oxford school in the thirteenth century'. It was ideally suited for a leading place among Grosseteste's scholastic works. But a single chance reference to the death of Simon de Montfort, which happened twelve years after Grosseteste's death, destroyed it. No one now believes that it is Grosseteste's. But, if it is not, it leaves an even greater puzzle unresolved. It is certainly an important work in Grosseteste's own special field of study, written in England and probably in Oxford not long after Grosseteste's death. The author mentions many names among his authorities, some of them the names of Grosseteste's contemporaries—notably Albert the Great and (among Englishmen) Alfred of Shareshill and Alexander of Hales. How then does it come about that he does not mention Grosseteste or show any traces of his influence?[1] Were his scientific works not read in the Oxford schools?

Baur, who discovered his error while editing Grosseteste, had earlier discovered another false ascription. This was a *Compendium Philosophiae*, similarly supported by a long line of scholarly and bibliographical opinion, and described not unreasonably before Baur's time as 'the most important of Grosseteste's works from the point of view of the history of knowledge'.[2] It was a systematic survey of the sciences that anyone might have been proud to own, and it was Baur who discovered that its true author was a scholar of the twelfth century, Dominicus Gundissalinus, and that all the references of bibliographers were consequently worthless.

These errors are now ancient history. But the image of the systematic scholastic writer which they helped to foster still lingers. Not least it lingers in the volume edited by Fr. Callus which I have already mentioned. One of the works which justified the continuing vitality of this image was a *Summa Theologiae*, of which Fr. Callus believed he had discovered fragments in an early fourteenth-century manuscript in Exeter College, Oxford.[3] It was not ascribed to Grosseteste in the manuscript, but it was in the company of other works which were, and Grosseteste's authorship had some support from later bibliographers. Fr. Callus edited it and pointed out some similarities between the doctrine in these fragments and in other works of Grosseteste. The fragments were clearly the remains of a large general survey of theology in four books based on

[1] For the text, see Baur 1912, pp. 275-643. For Baur's account of the work, see pp. 126*-141*. The fatal reference to Simon de Montfort is on p. 587. Thomson 1940, p. 265, lists the testimonies of MSS and bibliographers in Grosseteste's favour.

[2] This description occurs in F. S. Stevenson, *Robert Grosseteste*, London, 1899, p. 49, but it represented the view of more notable scholars. Baur, op. cit. pp. 124*-126*, gives an account of the false attribution.

[3] Several *Summae Theologiae* were attributed to Grosseteste by medieval cataloguers and bibliographers. Fr. Callus listed and disposed of all of them except the fragments of theological *quaestiones* in Exeter College, Oxford, MS 28, ff. 306ʳ-307ᵛ, which he believed were the sole surviving remains of a genuine *Summa* by Grosseteste. He published the fragments in *Studies in Medieval History presented to F. M. Powicke*, ed. R. W. Hunt, R. W. Southern, and W. A. Pantin, Oxford, 1948, pp. 180-208.

the *Sentences* of Peter Lombard. The plan and the manner of
treatment placed the work in the central tradition of Parisian
theology, and Fr. Callus concluded that the fragments 'belong
undoubtedly to Grosseteste's early years', and that they 'cor-
roborated the tradition of his pursuing his theological studies
in Paris'.[4]

I believe this is quite mistaken. If Grosseteste wrote these
fragments they cannot be an early work, for they contain a
quotation from Ps.-Denys's *De Divinis Nominibus*, and there are
good reasons for thinking that Grosseteste was not familiar with
this work till 1230 at the earliest.[5] But, if it is a late one, then
we have a quite large body of work with which it can be
compared, and in method and content it is quite unlike his
works of this time. Moreover, the similarities of doctrine and
expression noted by Fr. Callus are very general and are can-
celled by at least one notable difference.[6] No doubt, ingenuity
might discover an explanation which could reconcile all these
oddities with Grosseteste's authorship. But the need for ingenuity in so doubtful a case is itself a sign that the argument

---

[4] Callus 1955, p. 29. McEvoy 1982, p. 489, thinks that the association of the
Quaestiones with Grosseteste's authentic works in the only surviving manuscript is more
persuasive than the doctrinal similarities adduced by Fr. Callus. I have already given
reasons for thinking that the way in which Grosseteste's works were preserved made their
association with unauthentic works unusually easy. And it is peculiarly fragile in
this case. The *Quaestiones* form part of a series of additions made to a large collection of
school texts in a fourteenth-century manuscript. The first addition consists of two
works, *De Veritate* and *De libero arbitrio* (Baur, pp. 130–43, 130–226), with full ascriptions
to Grosseteste. Then, after a gap and on a new page, without any ascription, are the
Quaestiones, which end with some unrelated passages from St Anselm and a few lines,
also without ascription, of a work *De Statu Causarum* (Baur, p. 120), which is ascribed
(possibly, but not certainly, correctly) to Grosseteste in some later manuscripts.

[5] Grosseteste does not quote any work of Ps.-Denys in his lectures on the Psalms,
not even in the second part of those lectures in which quotations from Greek theologians
are frequent. These lectures are the main record of his theological teaching in Oxford
during the years from about 1225 till 1230, and the earliest of his theological works
known to us. His first known quotations from Ps.-Denys are in the *Hexaëmeron* and *De
Cessatione Legalium*, which both belong to the years 1230–5. In the first of these works
his quotations come from Ps.-Denys via the commentary of Hugh of St Victor. In the
second he uses a different translation from that used in the Exeter College fragments.

[6] The *Summa Theologiae* (p. 196) uses the phrase *causa antecedens* to express the constitution of nature which ensures that similar events (like conjunctions of sun and moon
in relation to the earth) will be followed by similar effects (e.g. an eclipse), and *causa
coniuncta* to describe the act of God which causes things to be what they are. Grosseteste
in his *De Scientia Dei* (Baur, op. cit., p. 145) reverses this terminology, calling that
which makes things to be what they are *necessitas antecedens*, and the course of nature,
which ensures that the same causes have the same consequences, *necessitas consequens*.

is on the wrong track, and I do not think that Fr. Callus would have persisted in following this track if he had not been previously convinced that Grosseteste was a scholastic writer drawing his inspiration from the schools of Paris.

This leaves us with two other important scholastic works. The first is the set of lectures on the Gospels knowns as the *Moralitates super Evangelia*. The manuscript attributions of this work to Grosseteste are much better, and the character of the work is much closer to that of his authentic works than the *Summa Theologiae*. Consequently, these lectures have been widely accepted as a record of his Oxford lectures, and in 1955 Dr. Smalley saw in them 'a measure of his influence in Oxford'.[7] But once more a posthumous attribution, however attractive, turns out to be a fragile support. It now appears almost certain that it was no more than an intelligent but mistaken guess made about fifty years after Grosseteste's death, when his name was more than usually in the public eye owing to the campaign for his canonization.[8]

Another work which I shall exclude from consideration is a set of lectures on Aristotle's *Sophistici Elenchi*, which is attributed to Grosseteste in a single manuscript of about 1300. These lectures are the most conventionally scholastic of all the works for which his authorship has been confidently claimed. They are difficult to read, but what can be read is uncharacteristically lifeless and I have found no trace in them of his familiar mannerisms. It is perhaps just possible to imagine that Grosseteste wrote them in Oxford between about 1220 and 1225 as an academic chore. No teacher can ever be quite immune from such a corvée; but they tell us nothing about him, and it is more likely that the ascription is another error.[9]

The removal of these dubious or spurious works still leaves us with a number of works which in one way or another are associated with his teaching in the schools: his treatise *De Sphera*,

---

[7] See Callus, 1955, pp. 71-4.

[8] E. J. Dobson, *Moralitates on the Gospels: A New Source of Ancrene Wisse*, Oxford, 1975, first pointed out in detail the extreme shakiness of the attribution to Grosseteste, which if not absolutely fatal to his authorship, leaves it without any solid support.

[9] Sten Ebbesen, *Commentators and Commentaries on Aristotle's 'Sophistici Elenchi'* (Corpus Latinum Commentariorum in Aristotelem, 7), 3 vols. , 1981, i. 202, iii. 120, accepts the attribution to Grosseteste, but only (as he kindly tells me) because he has never found strong evidence against it: 'I find the *Elenchi* commentary dull, but I lack a knock-down argument for its inauthenticity,' he writes.

his commentaries on Aristotle's *Posterior Analytics* and *Physics*, and on the Psalms and *Epistles*, and his treatises *Hexaëmeron* and *De Cessatione Legalium*. In a later chapter, I shall develop some lines of enquiry designed to penetrate to the personality and course of intellectual development which lie behind these works. As an introduction to this task, a small example of Grosseteste's manner of answering a typical scholastic question may help to put us on the right track.

II. SYMPTOMS OF AN INDEPENDENT MIND

1. An unscholastic answer to a scholastic question

Of all scholastic forms of writing, the *Quaestio*—that is to say the posing of a problem for which authoritative statements existed pointing in two different directions—is the most common. And for good reason. A large part of the procedure of the schools was designed to bring such problems to light and to solve them: the large collections of organized material performed the first of these tasks; the elaboration of rules of analysis and debate, and the final *sententiae* or judgements of the master performed the second. All scholastic masters had to be skilled in these procedures; and Grosseteste was sometimes asked questions which demanded their use.

The earliest of his surviving letters contains his answers to two theological questions from a young master, probably in the period 1225-9.[10] The first of the two questions was, 'Is God the first Form and Form of all things?' Anyone with a sound scholastic training would know that this was a particularly awkward question: a negative answer had to explain away some strong statements of St Augustine; but an affirmative answer would come close to the pantheistic heresy for which David of Dinant and his followers had been condemned with great publicity and ignominy at Paris in 1210.[11] So we have a

[10] Grosseteste, *Ep.* no. 1, pp. 1-17, addressed to Master Adam Rufus, for whom see below, p. 123. Professor McEvoy has made an exhaustive examination of the date in *Franc. Stud.* lxiii, 1981, 221-6, without finding conclusive evidence for a narrower dating than 1220-30; but the theological reading which the letter presupposes suggests a date after 1225, and a date before 1229 when Master Adam had joined the Franciscans seems almost certain.

[11] See G. Théry, *Autour du Décret de 1210: David de Dinant. Étude sur son panthéisme matérialiste*, Bibliothèque Thomiste, 6, 1925, pp. 7-8, 13-15.

situation of the kind that the skills of scholastic debate had been particularly devised to deal with. What was needed was a careful laying out of the authorities on both sides, an acute distinguishing of the meanings of technical terms with a view to discovering any loopholes in the opposing positions, and a final solution which would do justice to Augustine while keeping well clear of David of Dinant. If we want to see an expert handling the question, we have only to turn to Albert the Great's discussion of it in his *Summa Theologiae* of about 1250.[12] Here we have the careful laying out of texts, a breaking down of the question into its component parts, a reference to the Parisian condemnation of forty years earlier, and a final solution in a negative sense in line with this condemnation.

Not so Grosseteste. With him there was no careful laying out of texts, no discrimination of technical terms, no reference to the condemnation of 1210. He rushed in at once, in his first sentence, to give his answer in the affirmative: 'I reply straightaway that in my view God *is* form and the form of all things. . . And if you ask me what moves me to this opinion, I reply: the great authority of the great Augustine.[13] He then proceeds to quote Augustine for the next six pages: Augustine and no one else.

These are very significant pages. They flout every principle of scholastic method. There is no organization of material; no setting out of authorities or arguments *pro* and *contra*; no mention of a previous condemnation, nor of any contemporary or near-contemporary debate or opinion; just Augustine—and Augustine quoted in such large gobbets that the relevance of the quotations to the *precise* issue is often unclear. In addition, it is remarkable that the decision comes first, the evidence and discussion later. Indeed there is, strictly speaking, no discussion at all; Augustine is cited, not as a basis for discussion, but as an

[12] Albertus Magnus, *Summa Theologiae* (Opera Omnia, vol. xxxiv, part 1, ed. D. Siedler, 1978), tractatus 4, Q. 20, c. 2, pp. 102–4: 'quaeritur utrum deus sit forma omnium vel sit materia omnium . . . Solutio: Dicendum quod deus nec forma essentialis, nec materia alicuius nec est nec esse potest . . . Ex hoc ulterius patet, quod non procedit ratio, qua probare videtur quod deus et noys et materia prima idem sint.'

[13] 'De re itaque grandi, petitione tua compellente, pauca non granditer locuturus, in primis tuae dilectioni respondeo me sentire hoc verum esse, scilicet quod Deus est forma et forma omnium . . . Si autem quaeras quid me moveat ad sentiendum Deum esse formam et formam omnium, respondeo: magna magni Augustini auctoritas' (*Ep.*, pp. 1–2).

appendix of supporting evidence for a decision already taken. Moreover, the phrases used by Grosseteste in delivering his decision—'respondeo *me sentire* hoc verum esse'; and 'si quaeras quid me moveat *ad sentiendum* Deum esse formam'—are words of personal feeling, insight, opinion, rather than the grave words of a definitive judgement which was the hallmark of the scholastic exercise.

Various reasons may be given for this indifference to scholastic forms and formulae. It may be argued that in this letter Grosseteste was writing in a relaxed mood to a young man whom he knew well, and that it should not be used as a measure of his thought as a whole. Clearly caution is needed here. But the objection cannot be pressed very far. For one thing, although it is a letter, it is not in our sense a private letter. Grosseteste wrote it as an old master to a young master; and what he wrote was a letter of instruction, very long and very emphatic; and it soon became a document in public circulation.[14] Besides, its personal style, its way of using authorities to support a privately reached conclusion, and its extremely emphatic manner of expression, are all features of a great mass of Grosseteste's work.

Another possible explanation of his method, which has sometimes been given as a description of Grosseteste's theology as a whole, is that he was 'old fashioned'. There is certainly some truth in this, but it is misleading. It implies that he lagged behind his most advanced contemporaries. But Grosseteste was not just lagging behind the scholastic leaders of the day: he was in a different world, in which the dissection of authorities, the refinement of doctrines and the hair-line distinctions of scholastic discussion played no part. His pre- or anti-scholastic state of mind was like that of Rupert of Deutz a hundred years earlier—a world in which those who had read their Augustine and Gregory felt so confident of possessing the spirit of their spiritual fathers that they could speak on their behalf and shape their words as if they were their own. Nothing is more common in Grosseteste's writings than this mixture of the personal 'I say' or 'I believe', juxtaposed without any connecting argument

[14] The letter was split into two parts and circulated as two treatises, 'De unica forma omnium' (or 'Quod Deus sit forma omnium') and 'De Intelligentiis'; see Baur, op. cit., pp. 95*-99*, 106-119; and, for a list of MSS, Thomson, 1940, p. 99.

to a succession of passages from the basic texts, far longer than was required by the precise question under discussion, and often of scarcely visible relevance. There is a whole world of difference between the carefully selected scholastic quotation, coolly examined in measured words, and the torrential out-pouring of one who is immersed in the stream from which he draws.

2. The tentative approach

Another symptom of Grosseteste's unscholastic method which is displayed in this letter and in many other parts of his writings is his habit of dealing with well-worn questions as if they were new. He had certainly no dislike of tradition. Quite the contrary, he revelled in it; but he felt himself to be so much a partaker in the tradition that he could speak for it in his own words. He goes back to the sources, ignoring all the careful work of the schools in solving problems or drawing boundaries. He brushes aside the collections of authorities which twelfth-century scholars had laboriously compiled. He grubs up the roots once more, makes his own individual selection of au-thorities, and, as often as not, reaches only tentative conclusions. In this he might be thought to represent a throw-back to a more primitive stage of scholastic discussion a hun-dred years earlier, when scholars collected conflicting authorities without proceeding to the further stages of analysis and decision. But Grosseteste's indeterminism is quite different from this: the early scholastic compilers had laid authoritative foundations on which others could build, and were often con-tent when they had done this. Grosseteste did not lay foun-dations of this kind. If he did not see the solution, he threw out some suggestions, and then confessed his inability to see any further.

At one point in his *Hexaëmeron* he writes: 'I wish the reader to know that I say this not by way of asserting its truth, but to stimulate him to enquire more deeply and better, and to ex-plain more clearly what he has discovered.'[15] A critical master of the schools might have felt very impatient at this remark.

---

[15] *Hex.* IX. ii. 6, p. 268: 'Volo autem lectorem scire me istud dicere non tam asserendo quam lectoris ingenium exsuscitando ut investiget aliquid secretius et melius et in-ventum explanet dilucidius.'

What reason had a master to speak, if not to assert truth or uncover error? What was the nature of the more searching enquiries in which he incited his hearers or readers to engage? There is here a spirit of individual enquiry very different from the corporate activity of the schools. His remark reflects two of his least scholastic traits: first, the value he attached to tentative suggestions; and second, his expectation that new knowledge was to be found, not so much by refining the definitions of the past, as by reaching out beyond the present limits of knowledge.

Of course, reaching out to new truths was characteristic also of twelfth-century scholastic thought, typically expressed in the well-known saying of Bernard of Chartres (borrowed, like much else in the twelfth century, from an ancient source, and given a new context) that the scholars of the present age, pygmies though they were, could see further than the giants of the past, because they stood on their shoulders.[16] This has long been recognized as a splendid image of the forward looking aspirations of the schools of the twelfth century. But it represents a way of looking forward quite different from Grosseteste's. For Bernard of Chartres, those who stood on the shoulders of the giants saw the same view, only more clearly and a little further. Grosseteste's remark, like his practice, suggests that sharp eyes count for more than giants' shoulders; that new views can be obtained by personal effort, and that there is an element of uncertainty, as well as the possibility of indefinite advance, in all knowledge.

This tentative quality in Grosseteste's thought, combined with the hope that others will see further than he could, points to another contrast. Scholastic thought aimed at objectivity— at clarity and certainty which would be the same everywhere, for everyone, for ever. This was the core of the whole scholastic enterprise: to reach definitive conclusions on important problems. At a time of vigorous doctrinal definition, when developments of immense importance in the organization of corporate life were based on these definitions, much more depended on the success of the schools than is customary in academic exercises. Never before, and never again until the late nineteenth century, had Europe depended so much on the

[16] For the source and context of the remark, see R. Klibansky, 'Standing on the Shoulders of the Giants', *Isis*, xxvi, 1936, 147–9.

successful outcome of an academic programme. Of course, Grosseteste did not stand wholly outside this programme, and he was not opposed to certainty where it could be found: in matters of dogma, ecclesiastical discipline, and in scientific conclusions based on observation and sound doctrine, he stood as firm as anyone could wish. But he also pushed out into many speculations in which he felt himself to be going beyond all previous enquirers. He rejected (as we shall see) the legal compromises which had emerged from the scholastic debates of the twelfth century. Theologically, he did not seek to advance by refining the verbal or logical distinctions of earlier scholars: this line of consolidated advance could best be followed in the great schools where there was a tradition of persistent clarification and reshaping of achieved results. He stood outside this tradition, and contributed towards diversity, not towards consolidation. Hence there arises the paradox which runs through his whole career: with all his zeal as a promoter of order, he was also a prophet of dissolution—not a revolutionary prophet, but a quiet and persistent dissolving influence, at first in his inclination towards the tentative and individual, and later in his distrust of the practical results of the organization that he saw around him.

3. The importance of insight

One of the symptoms of Grosseteste's tendency to break away from the structure of scholastic thought can be found in the importance he attached to his *obiter dicta*. These scattered thoughts posed a problem for at least one of the lecturers to the Oxford Franciscans who succeeded him, Fr. William of Alnwick.[17] About half a century after Grosseteste's death, he was engaged in a dispute about eternity, and his opponent had quoted a statement of Grosseteste in support of his argument. William of Alnwick objected:

Grosseteste did not say this as an assertion but as an opinion. Hence he uses such words as 'I believe' or 'I think', or something similar.

[17] See *BRUO* i. 27, for his career: he entered the Order *c.*1290, and was successively theological student, lecturer in theology, colleague and literary executor of Duns Scotus, lector to the Oxford Franciscans *c.*1316-17; then regent master in Paris; he died at Avignon, 1333.

These words are written in his own hand in the margins of his copy of Aristotle's *Physics*. He did not expound this work formally (*studiose*) or completely, as he did the *Posterior Analytics*; but when any notable *imaginatio* came to his mind he wrote it down so that he would not forget it. So he wrote many scraps which are not all authoritative (*authentice*), and these fragments which he wrote in the margins of the *Physics* have no greater authority than the other scraps which he wrote. They are all preserved in the Franciscan library at Oxford, and I have seen them with my own eyes. They must be distinguished from his authoritative sayings in his comments on Denys, or in his *Hexaëmeron*, or on the *Posterior Analytics*.[18]

This is one of the earliest, and also one of the most interesting comments about Grosseteste's habits of thought, and we have abundant evidence to illustrate the truth of William of Alnwick's observation—and the wrong-headedness of his explanation.

To take first his explanation. William of Alnwick had a special reason for wishing to distinguish between Grosseteste's *authoritative* judgements and his *obiter dicta*. He had to answer an opponent, who had quoted Grosseteste as an authority against him, and there were various kinds of answer he could make. He could say that, properly understood, Grosseteste was really on his side; or he could quote a superior authority, or give some other ground for thinking that Grosseteste was wrong. But what he chose to do was to distinguish between different levels of authority within Grosseteste's own writings, and to allege that, unlike the statements in the formal works, this particular statement was not intended to be magisterial. Scholastically this distinction was unimpeachable.[19] But it breaks down when Grosseteste's works are considered as a whole. It is true, as William of Alnwick says, that a large part of Grosseteste's surviving writing consists of notes, of which some had originally

[18] This important passage in the *Determinationes* of William of Alnwick was printed by A. Pelzer, 'Les Versions Latines d'ouvrages de morale conservés sous le nom d'Aristote en usage au XIIIe siècle', *Rev. néo-scolastique de philosophie*, xxiii, 1921, p. 398 (reprinted in *Études d'histoire littéraire sur la scholastique médiévale*, ed. A. Pattin and E. van der Vyver, 1964, p. 170).

[19] Pelzer, op. cit., p. 171, quotes a passage from Walter Burley, a slightly younger contemporary of William of Alnwick at Oxford and Paris, making a similar distinction between statements in Aristotle which were *autentica* and those which were spoken *in parte declarativa aut narrativa* and not to be received *tamquam autenticum*. The need for this distinction implies a growing sophistication in the interpretation of authoritative texts, but it is about eighty years later than the main writings of Grosseteste.

been written in the margins of his books. But he often included
them, and remarks similar to them, in his more formal works:
they were an essential part of a single process of thought, beginning with perceptions and ending in tentative conclusions
and suggestions as in the passage I have just quoted from his
Hexaëmeron. William of Alnwick's distinction between authoritative comments and casual remarks is sound scholastically,
but it does not represent Grosseteste's practice.

What makes Fr. William's evidence precious is his realization
that the problem existed. He had seen and handled Grosseteste's books with their notes and marginalia. For scholars, they
were one of the curiosities of Oxford. They were still, and
more than ever, objects of interest in the fifteenth century. The
voluble Dr. Thomas Gascoigne never wearied of repeating that
he had seen the comments of *Lincolniensis* written with his own
hand in the margins of the Pauline Epistles and on the Psalter—
not, he was careful to emphasize, on the whole text, but on
certain passages.[20] This was always Grosseteste's manner. When
a passage struck him, he 'considered' it in elaborate detail and
in all the freedom of his own special knowledge. When he had
nothing to say, he passed on. This was the foundation of all his
best writing.

4. Consideration

'Consider' was one of his favourite words, and it became a kind
of code-word among his close associates. 'Consider', they would
write in the margins of books, 'Consider most diligently the
explanation of the time of the coming kingdom of Christ in the
prophecy of David'; 'Consider that no one sees God who is not
altogether dead to this world'; 'Consider the necessity for a
knowledge of Greek for understanding Holy Scripture'; 'Consider what is said about the literal and spiritual understanding
of the Law and how the Law is the dawn of the Gospels';
'Consider how the "one" in which *we* are one with the Father,
Son and Holy Spirit also holds together the substance of Father,
Son and Holy Spirit.'[21] These were memoranda for thought. He

[20] For further details, see below, pp. 314–15.
[21] The examples quoted above come from Grosseteste's works and from manuscripts
associated with Grosseteste and his circle: Lincoln College, Oxford, MS lat. 33, ff. 48,

liked to identify the important points which needed unhurried thought, and then to settle down to consider them from every angle. The results of these 'considerations' became essays and several of them were incorporated in his later sermons and treatises. He explained his method when he made his collection of *Dicta*:

These are words which I wrote down briefly and cursorily when I was in the schools lest I should forget them. They are not on a single theme and they are not connected. I have given them titles to help the reader to find what he wants, but the titles often promise more than he will find.[22]

This is the relaxed mood in which he gave wider publicity to some of his thoughts. Everywhere the note is one of informality, freedom and abundance.

5. Imagination

There is one phrase used by William of Alnwick about these jottings which deserves special attention: 'when any notable *imaginatio* occurred to him'.

The faculty of imagination was closely linked with Grosseteste's practice of consideration. To understand this we must begin by distinguishing between the modern and medieval meaning of the word. The faculty of imagination in its medieval context was not primarily or properly concerned with invention: indeed, invention was generally a symptom of diseased imagination. Properly, imagination was the power of fixing the fluctuating impressions of the senses in a lasting and definitive form as a preparation for the processes of reason. In performing this function, imagination had a double task of discrimination and retention: it had to establish the permanent features of

108; Bodleian MS Laud misc. 746, ff. 14^v, 22, 29, 48; St John's Coll., Cambridge MS 47, f. 6^v; BL Harleian MS 3111, f. 154^v; and Grosseteste's *Hexaëmeron* I. i. 2, p. 50. See also *Hex.* VIII. v. 5, p. 226; *De Cessatione Legalium*, I. ix. 7, p. 226. In *Hex.* I. i. 2 we can observe a transition from the *considera* formula in an early recension to a final statement in another. An interesting example of Grosseteste's usage is also quoted in *Fasciculi Zizaniorum*, p. 137. Dr R. W. Hunt was the first to notice this symptom of Grosseteste's mind and influence, and to point out several examples in manuscripts belonging to or associated with him: see 'Manuscripts Containing the Indexing Symbols of Robert Grosseteste', *Bodleian Library Record*, iv, 1953, pp. 243-4.

[22] For the context of this remark, see Thomson 1940, p. 214.

recurrent sense impressions of the same object; and it had then to retain those features in a lasting image.

The full complexity and importance of the contribution made by the faculty of imagination to the processes of reasoning was evolved in a series of stages throughout the twelfth century. The early stages, which occupied the first half of the century, were chiefly concerned with mapping the areas of the brain where the various functions of mind were thought to be performed. They were distributed between different areas of the brain: the collecting of sense impressions in the frontal cell, the memory at the back. Between them, there were two intermediate cells, of which the most important was that in which the processes of reasoning were performed. A more ambiguous and subordinate role was assigned to the other intermediate cell, the *imaginativa* or *phantastica cellula*, which linked the area of sense impressions with that of reason. This was the area of imagination, the holding area of images, where sense impressions were stamped on the mind and retained for the use of reason when required: a kind of memory-bank of images waiting to be activated by the higher faculty of reason.

The progress in mapping can be followed in some detail in a series of authors from about 1120 to 1170.[23] By this time the

[23] The earliest medieval accounts of the parts and functions of the brain come from the first half of the twelfth century. In particular William of Conches in his *Philosophia Mundi* (c.1115- 20), iv. 24 (*PL* 172, col. 95) divides the brain into three *cellulae*: the frontal cell combines the function of sense impression and imagination (*visualis et imaginativa*), the middle cell the rational function, and the rear cell memory. He distinguished sense impression from imagination in assigning to the first the perception of objects which are present, and to the second the perception (or, strictly, the revival of images) of things which are not present. Thierry of Chartres (c.1130-40) in his Commentary on Boethius's *De Trinitate*, ii. 3-87 (ed. N. M. Haring, *Commentaries on Boethius by Thierry of Chartres and his School*, 1971, p. 269-70), gave imagination a somewhat larger role as the 'vis animae comprehensiva formarum atque figurarum necnon imaginum tactu materie corruptarum absenti materia'. This tendency to give imagination a larger function than the mere retention of sense impressions was continued by Clarembald of Arras, a pupil of Thierry, writing some twenty years later: 'Cum per imaginationem anima ipsa rem quamlibet secum retractat, tanto subtilius eam considerat quanto in eius retractione subtiliori utitur instrumento' (N. M. Haring, *Life and Works of Clarembald of Arras*, 1965, p. 108). Thierry had already indicated that imagination was a more refined instrument of cognition than sense impression, and Clarembald elaborated this point also: 'In parte quippe capitis anteriori quae phantastica dicitur, multus aer cum exiguo humore includitur cui eorum quae per sensus cognoscuntur figurae imprimuntur atque eo aere cum pauca humidate in imaginando anima utitur pro instrumento. Quanto igitur aeris substantia compositione manus vel oculi vel nervi subtilior est, tanto imaginationis cognitio subtilior est sensuali' (ibid.).

main locations and functions had been determined in a form which would last for the next four hundred years. But the processes at each stage between sense impression and conceptual thought, and more particularly the processes of the imaginative cell, had not been fully examined. So far as the imaginative faculty was concerned, progress during the next fifty years took place along a number of routes. First there were the physicians and naturalists who, by about 1200, were announcing that the imaginative faculty was peculiarly active and discriminating in certain states of bodily activity—for instance in the act of coition when imagination could impress physical features on the foetus and excite the brain to subtle speculations.[24] Then there were visionaries like Hildegard who received the messages of God 'in the eyes and ears of her inner being, *in pura mente*'.[25] And, most important of all, there were students of one of the most influential translations of Arabic science which became available in the second half of the century.[26] This was the translation of Avicenna *On the Soul*, a work of immense learning, which first (even before Aristotle's work on the same subject) made clear to Western readers the refinement and range of the operations of the imagination faculty in its powers of discrimination. According to John Blund, the first English scholar who is known to have studied the work— probably in Oxford a few years before 1200, the students of Avicenna believed that, through the faculty of imagination, the soul could apprehend the *summum bonum* and be moved by a vehement desire to enjoy it.[27]

By 1200, therefore, imagination had come a long way from its primitive portrayal a century earlier. It was a faculty, not only installed at a central point of the *piano nobile* of the human organism, but equipped with powers scarcely less important than those of reason itself. From being a somnolent ante-room,

[24] See especially *The Prose Salernitan Questions*, Auctores Britannici Medii Aevi, 5, ed. Brian Lawn, 1979, pp. 19 (paragraph 35), 21 (paragraph 42).

[25] For Hildegard's account of her experiences, see her letters in J. B. Pitra, *Analecta Sacra*, viii. 1882, 332-3, and in her *Scivias*, PL 197. 383-1038 *passim*.

[26] Avicenna, *Liber de Anima*, ed. S. van Riet, i-iii, 1972, iv-v, 1968, Leiden. The translation was made in Toledo between 1152 and 1166, and the earliest known manuscript (which is of English origin) is early thirteenth century. For its influence on Grosseteste's doctrine of the internal senses, see McEvoy 1982, 297-9.

[27] Johannes Blund, *Tractatus de Anima*, Auctores Britannici Medii Aevi, 2, ed. D. A. Callus and R. W. Hunt, 1970, p. 5, paragraph 13.

it had become the junction of many roads bringing new images to the aid of reason.

Grosseteste was one of the first to appreciate its new importance. Even if we had no other evidence for this than the marginal symbols with which he annotated his books, we would have some insight into the scope of imagination in his thought. In annotating his copy of Augustine's *City of God* he put his symbol for Imagination against passages which illustrated the capacity of this faculty to create images: of corporeal substances and of their beauty; of the Trinity; of God's revelations to the soul; and of the fantasies of the diseased mind. In a word, a wide range of creative operations, designated appropriately by one of his most striking symbols, was performed by the imagination.[28]

The power of imagination was peculiarly important for him in his close examination of natural phenomena, whether for scientific purposes or for their symbolic and theological meaning. For all these purposes he needed the discrimination and constructive power of the imaginative faculty. He saw the image of the Creator in every detail of the universe. Everything therefore had to be looked on, not just analytically, but with a response of the whole soul. In providing the grounds for this response, the imaginative faculty had a primary role. In one of his boldest images he saw the relationship between the observed object, the impressions of this object on the senses, and the stabilizing of these impressions by the imagination, as an image of the three Persons of the Trinity—the object 'begetting', the sense impressions 'begotten', the imagination uniting both object and impressions in a lasting and stable harmony.[29] It was entirely appropriate, therefore, that when he spoke of the Trinity he sought to inflame dry arguments with memorable images drawn from his imagination:

[28] Grosseteste's copy of the *De Civitate Dei* is in Bodleian MS Bodl. 198. His marginal symbol for Imagination ( ) is found on ff. 29ᵛ, 45ᵛ, 48ᵛ, 79ᵛ, 104ᵛ against passages which mention these varied forms of image: viii. 5; viii. 6; xi. 2 (with Grosseteste's comment: 'Qualiter loquitur Deus animae'); xi. 26; xviii. 18; xxii. 22. For these symbols and their significance for Grosseteste's thought, see below, pp. 188–93. It is of some interest that the nearest analogue to the symbol for Imagination is that for Eternity:

[29] *Hex.* VIII. iv. 8, p. 223.

Let us be content for the present with these arguments proving the Trinity in unity, and let us bring forward some examples whereby that which has been proved may be impressed in some way on the imagination. For it is in the highest degree necessary for us to understand the Trinity: love of the Trinity is the salvation of our souls, and without this love there is no salvation. But the Trinity is loved in proportion as it is grasped by faith and understanding; and it is beauty which inflames the love of the believer and the understanding of the thinker.[30]

This theological programme, directed towards the stimulation of love rather than the piling up of proofs and the answering of objections, was something that Grosseteste had learnt from St Anselm and St Bernard, not from the schools. But for the moment we are concerned less with the content of his theology than with the importance he attached to the consideration of images. It was through these images that he tried to impress the idea of the Trinity on the minds of his hearers.

He treated the bewildering complexity of arguments about Redemption, its long delay, and the overwhelming joy of attainment in a similar way:

Imagine a man fallen into a pit: if he had been saved immediately, he might well have supposed that he could have devised his own escape . . . if he had been left in total darkness, he might have thought he could have escaped with the help of a light . . . if he had light but no ladder, he might have thought that he could have escaped with the help of a ladder, or a rope, or other aids. All these aids—ladder, light, time—were supplied before Christ came, to show man that all his own efforts, however assisted, were vain.[31]

These 'imaginations' did not lead, at least not in theology, to new knowledge, but they led to a firmer grasp and warmer embracing of old truths. In theology, the role of imagination, properly directed, was to increase the warmth of reception. A favourite pair of concepts which Grosseteste used in this connection was *aspectus mentis* and *affectus mentis*[32] The first of

---

[30] *Hex.* VIII. iv. 1, p. 222. See Alexander Murray, 'Confession as a Historical source', in *The Writing of History in the Middle Ages*, ed. R. H. C. Davis and J. M. Wallace-Hadrill, Oxford, 1981, 279–80, for some illuminating remarks on the importance of Imagination in Grosseteste's directions on Confession.

[31] *De Cessatione Legalium*, I. viii. 6–7.

[32] This dual character of knowledge in Grosseteste's thought has been dealt with by several scholars, notably by McEvoy 1982, pp. 107, 135, 138, 257–8, 331, where other

these concepts referred to the mind's grasp of the bare formulae of truth, the second to the intensity of commitment. Grosseteste had no use for the one without the other. We may know that God exists, but unless this knowledge is accompanied by a movement towards God, it is quite empty. It is like knowing the name of a land and nothing else; it adds nothing to the substance of our thought. Full knowledge requires that the act of embracing the truth (*affectus*) should be added to the state of recognizing the truth (*aspectus*). To make this jump, a vivid realization of the truth, inspired by the imagination, is needed. This applies to all knowledge whatsoever—theological, moral, scientific: it is only by making the truth a part of ourselves that it becomes fully known; and only when it is thus fully known can it lead to further discoveries.

6. Grosseteste's scholarly vision

The figure which tentatively emerges from these fragmentary observations is that of a man of unusual independence and originality. In the context of contemporary scholastic thought, his independence verges on the reckless. He did not normally make use of existing collections of sources, and then proceed to compare, analyse, dissipate their confusions, solve their contradictions, and thus, standing on the shoulders of the past, see further than his predecessors. He made a new start, read widely, and collected his own store of material in large quantities. He allowed his mind to play round his reading, looking closely at the points which interested him, gaining new perceptions. His conclusions were often expressed with doubts and hesitations, and readers were left to make such use of them as they could.[33]

So far as I know, he never mentioned any of his masters, or the circumstances or place of his own studies, or the scholars who had recently made contributions to the subject. His references to the great scholastic writers of the twelfth century are very few. He mentions St Bernard fairly often; St Anselm

references will be found. A full account of knowledge would also have to consider the final stage of wisdom, arrived at by the purification of both the *affectus* and *aspectus mentis*, which provides the final safeguard against *falsa imaginatio*. On this see *Hex.* I. v. 2, p. 55; I. viii. 5, p. 61; and I. xix. 1, p. 78.

[33] See below, p. 164, for the theory of initial resistance leading to a conviction of the truth.

less often but sometimes on important issues; Hugh of St Victor only as a commentator on Denys the Areopagite. Peter Lombard is mentioned scarcely at all, though he certainly knew Peter Lombard's *Sentences* and he used his commentaries on the Psalms and Pauline Epistles in his Oxford lectures between 1225 and 1235.[34] He mentions no later Parisian teacher. If we reject his authorship of the *Summa Theologiae* which Fr. Callus attributed to him, his use of the *Sentences* amounts to very little. Everywhere he preferred to go back himself to the ancient sources without any intermediate aids.

Like all his contemporaries, he quoted his sources extensively, indeed too abundantly and without any severe precision of aim. But he had collected most of them for himself in the course of his own reading. Hence he was often unusually precise in indicating the book and chapter of his source; and, at other times, his quotations were free versions of an original that had become part of his own thought. This combination of range and imagination helped to make him one of the most original and awkward men of his time.

He was not by nature a systematic thinker any more than he was by nature a tidy organizer of material from the past. His strength lay in discovering areas of knowledge to which he could make a new contribution. Having done this, he was content to leave it to others to go further if they could, while he passed on to the next problem. At times, however, he was extraordinarily persistent in searching for all the works of an author who excited his interest, and in pursuing the ramifications of a problem that caught his attention.

His greatest single scholarly effort was directed towards making the works of Denys the Areopagite more accessible and intelligible to the Latin world. The quality in these works which captivated him and justified the effort will concern us later.

---

[34] Among the books which he owned was a copy of Peter Lombard on the Psalms with glosses by a later master called Herlwin, who is probably the master of that name who taught in Paris in the late twelfth century. This volume has survived in Pembroke College, Cambridge MS 7. It has a note stating that Grosseteste pledged it to the monks of Bury St Edmunds for their copy of Basil's *Hexaëmeron*. It is clear that he never reclaimed it, and it may be significant that it has none of his own marginal annotations, which are a common feature in his books. There is a description of the MS by B. Smalley in *Cambridge Historical Journal*, vi, 1938, pp. 103–13, but Dr Smalley is chiefly concerned with the biblical glosses on ff. 133–267, which did not form part of the original volume.

We are concerned here only with the originality of his programme of research, unparalleled in its time in its completeness
and breadth of conception. He took a complete body of
difficult, little studied, imperfectly translated Greek texts, and
sought the best Greek manuscripts and all existing Latin translations. From this material he produced a new text, and provided it with a commentary which was partly linguistic and
partly theological. He compared the readings of the Greek
manuscripts and their Latin versions; he distinguished between
Greek and Latin verbal usages; and he added paraphrases of
difficult passages and elaborations of points which especially
interested him; and he infused into the whole a warmth of
general agreement and like-mindedness.

The whole undertaking provided a study in depth of a single
author's whole body of writing. It forms a striking contrast to
the general scholastic indifference to the context of disparate
texts brought together to be used as starting points or stages in
an argument. In the details of its method and the scope of its
plan, his edition of Denys's works was a profoundly imaginative
enterprise. To accomplish it, Grosseteste brought together and
directed the efforts of a group of helpers who in their linguistic
skills and unity of purpose could not have been found anywhere
else in Europe.

He employed a similar method for other texts also, notably
the complete corpus of John of Damascus's works and the *Ethics*
of Aristotle. Next to Denys, it was on the *Ethics* that he lavished
the greatest efforts of his team, in translating the text, in as-
sembling and translating its ancient commentaries, and in providing the whole with the elements of a new commentary on
the same lines as that which he had provided on Denys. Aristotle was not an author as congenial to him as Denys; but the
subject—the constitution and operations of the passions and
powers of the soul—was one that had engaged him from his
earliest days as a scientist and physician.

These great enterprises were only possible for Grosseteste in
his old age and will be discussed later. In his younger poorer
days, he concentrated his attention on problems to which he
could make an original contribution on his own. Taking a small
selection in chronological order, we find him tackling such
problems as the reason why Saturn, the planet which travels

fastest and should therefore be hottest, is in fact the coldest of the planets; the various types of water in nature and in symbol; the precise extent of the Christian's obligation to obey the precepts of the Jewish Law, and the exact moment when the Law ceased to be obligatory; the timing of the Incarnation. These are a few of the problems which he chose for full and independent enquiry. They were all directed towards a more exact understanding of the system of the universe in its natural and supernatural operations. Most of his thoughts on these and other subjects had very little effect on his scholastic contemporaries outside his own small circle of friends and helpers. They would for the most part have been forgotten if he had not left his books and notes to the library of the Oxford Franciscans. Here they were an object of curiosity—mainly respectful, but not generally influential—to successive generations of Oxford scholars for a hundred years after his death. Then a change of intellectual climate brought them into the central controversies of the day, and men found, or thought they found, that *Lincolniensis* had anticipated some of their most hazardous thoughts.

We now know him, or can know him, better than any other Englishman of his time; but our knowledge owes little or nothing to his contemporary scholastic influence. This is another way in which he differs from the successful masters of his day. A successful university teacher generally influences his contemporaries most powerfully, and owes his later influence to an uninterrupted stream of continuing study. Grosseteste's influence on his contemporaries appears to have been at best fragmentary, and his intellectual reputation, like the survival of many of his works, chiefly arose from his rediscovery in the fourteenth century. The peculiar pattern of survival helps to underline his aloofness from the main stream of the contemporary schools. His independence and rude strength were uncomfortable qualities in a scholastic setting. To what forces, apart from those of a remarkable personality, did they owe their formation? It is to this question that we must now turn.

3

Two Patterns of Education

Two areas of ambiguity have now been identified which require further study. The first of these is defined by the widely
differing judgements on Grosseteste's character and achievements presented by his contemporaries and by later generations
of historians; the second by the contrast between his habits of
thought and those of his most successful scholastic contemporaries. But there is a third which now requires to be
sketched. It lies in the ambiguities in his education and later
career. In this area, the question which needs to be answered
is whether he differs from the majority of successful scholar-
bishops of his day, and, if so, in what ways and for what reasons.
In its simplest form this question may be put in this way: was
he the product of a provincial or of a European education?

There can be no doubt which of these two was considered
the more desirable throughout the whole of the twelfth century.
Intellectually, and in the prospects which it opened up, an
education in the European schools went far beyond anything
that England could offer. It would seem to have been available
to able men of almost all levels of society, and it was an essential
feature of the portrait of Grosseteste drawn by Fr. Callus and
his collaborators in the memorial volume of 1955 that he too
had spent his early years as a student and teacher in the schools
of Paris, or at least in schools in Oxford which had a strongly
Parisian orientation. It was only on this assumption that he
could be placed firmly in the main stream of contemporary
scholastic thought.

The general pattern of this education was quite well defined:
after an elementary education in a local school or under a
family tutor, a young man would go abroad, generally to Paris
but occasionally to other foreign schools of high repute, for the

advanced study of grammar, logic and the other liberal arts. This course of study would occupy roughly the same period of years as the studies of a modern undergraduate and graduate student, perhaps seven years in all from the age of about seventeen to twenty-four. Of course this ideal curriculum was subject to interruptions and disappointments of every kind: the death of parents or patrons, the drying-up of resources, the hazards of ill-health, debauchery, lack of ability or lack of persistence. But many managed to stay the course, and they had good reasons for their persistence.

For the first time in European history students and teachers at Paris and Bologna enjoyed the intoxicating experience of participating in the work of an academic community engaged in solving problems of universal importance, clarifying the principles of the Christian religion, of human behaviour, and of correct reasoning, and then of adapting these principles to the organization of society. The students had the stimulus of belonging to a cosmopolitan body of men of varied backgrounds and turbulent instincts, and future importance. The masters had the stimulus of critical pupils and the daily discipline of expounding difficult subjects and solving intricate problems. And they all had the satisfaction of adding to a growing body of important knowledge. The books which the masters wrote have left a vivid impression of their teaching, and it is still possible from the imperfect records that remain to trace the development of increasingly refined distinctions from one course of lectures to the next. The remarkable developments of this time in government and society, in theology and law, and in the application of rational discourse to ordinary life, would not have taken the form they did if the schools of Paris and Bologna had not existed.

After a period of studying and teaching which might last from two or three years to five or ten, the successful student would return to England as a young master of arts seeking employment in an ecclesiastical or lay household. His hope would be that his usefulness, helped by the interest of a patron, would soon bring a permanent endowment in the form of a benefice. If all went well, he would have achieved this aim by the age of thirty, and he would begin planning a further period of study—in Paris or Bologna, in theology or canon law—which would fit him for the highest offices in ecclesiastical and secular government. This period of study also might last some six or seven years, and then he would be fitted for any office from archdeacon to pope. This was the pattern; and, though the ranks got thinner as the difficulties grew and the length of time got more extended, we can find many men following this general path of intellectual study and practical usefulness. The list of men from England and Wales in Grosseteste's youth who owed their success in life to more or less extended periods of foreign study along these general lines included Gerald of Wales, Edmund of Abingdon, Alexander Nequam, William de Montibus, Abbot Samson of Bury St Edmunds, John Blund, Thomas of Marlborough, Simon of Sywell, Master Honorius, Stephen Langton.

Naturally there were great differences in the details of their careers. Some were lucky in their patrons, in the weight of their family influence, and in the posts which fell vacant at the right time; others were unlucky. Two of the men I have mentioned became archbishops, three became abbots, four became archdeacons, one rose no higher than chancellor of Lincoln. But they were all successful men; they had all studied, most of them had taught, in Paris; and their position in the world was based on their success in the schools.

These men started from widely different social backgrounds. At the top of the social ladder there were the men like Gerald of Wales whose family connections gave them the expectation of reaching the highest positions in the Church and exerting a memorable influence on events. But even those who socially had everything in their favour found it useful to study abroad. They knew what they were doing when they went to study in the schools of Paris: they were learning the language of government at the highest level, and promotion came to them more quickly and easily as a result. Those who started with fewest advantages had to wait a long time for promotion, but even they had generally reached a steady platform of success by the time they were forty. Those who had not succeeded by then had to think of joining a religious order. They might not have a vocation for the religious life, but it would give them scope for their talents and an assured future for their old age: Samson succumbed to the monastic life when he was thirty-one;

Thomas of Marlborough at about the same age; Alexander Nequam when he was forty. No doubt, there were important differences in the considerations which led each of these men into monasteries instead of into the hierarchy of the secular Church; but they all sought to fulfil their potentialities as scholar-administrators along the route that offered most chance of satisfaction or service or worldly success according to their temperament. Whether they became bishops or abbots, or only archdeacons or priors, their careers were based on their success in the schools of Paris or Bologna. They sought to make their up-to-date technical learning the foundation for a wide influence in the world.

Another feature that all these men had in common, besides their unusual skill in performing the academic exercises of the day, was that they all had some resources on which they could draw to get them started in life. By far the best resource was a wealthy and well-connected family. Failing this, an able man with only modest wealth and family support could succeed if he had a powerful patron, who might be a distant relative or a magnate whom his family served. A young man with no resources and no patron could scarcely have made the journey to a foreign city; certainly he could not have studied in it with the necessary intensity for five years or more. With a little money, a determined and able young man might survive the rigours of life in a strange land and study to some purpose; but, having survived, he could not hope to get a livelihood in the Church without the influence of a family connection or the good will of a patron. So he might better have stayed at home.

How low in the social scale could a young man be and still make good in the competitive world of the great schools? Of the men I have mentioned, the humblest in social background was Abbot Samson, but even he was not wholly unendowed. He had a small patrimony, insufficient indeed to support him during his years in Paris but enough to start him on his road.[1] He had no patron, but he was lucky in Paris to find a charitable benefactor, a seller of holy water, who kept him alive in the schools. So he survived his studious years and learnt to love the scholastic life; but all this counted for little when he got home.

[1] For Samson's social background and career see *The Chronicle of Jocelin of Brakelond*, ed. and trans. by H. E. Butler, Oxford, 1949, pp. 43-4.

He still had to fight to get a small benefice which would give him security and allow him a further period of study. He fought hard, but he fought in vain. He risked his life to serve the monks of Bury St Edmunds in their lawsuits, he showed extraordinary resourcefulness and vigour in their service, and he hoped to receive a benefice as his reward. The monastery had many benefices. But it also had many applicants; all of them (it would seem) more powerfully supported than Samson, despite his great merits. Samson would have loved to follow the career of learning; but for this he needed a benefice. He was also a practical man, and he wished to turn his learning to good effect in the service of the Church. As a practical man, he recognized the signs of failure. He saw that he could never achieve success in the world in competition with men who had more powerful friends and relations. So he early turned to the only available alternative: he entered the monastery. Fourteen years later he became abbot, and he ruled with notable success for nearly thirty years. The monastery benefited from his scholastic and governmental skills; and without them he would never have got to the top. It was not the summit of his earlier dreams, but it made him one of the leading magnates of the kingdom. Yet, among his intimates, he used to say that he would never have become a monk if he could have got a benefice worth £3 a year.

Of all the Englishmen of the day who rose to the eminence of prelacy via the schools of Paris, Samson was the one whose lowly social position put his success most conspicuously at risk. There must have been many more who did not succeed and who fell into poverty and obscurity. We are apt to forget them because they left no records. We are also apt to forget the very many men who saw the risks and did not attempt to follow this path to success. The rise of Englishmen to fame and influence in the twelfth and early thirteenth century through years of study in foreign schools is so easily intelligible and so abundantly documented that there is a strong tendency to attribute this course to all suitable men about whose education nothing is known. But there was an alternative.

II. THE ENGLISH ALTERNATIVE

For every student who went abroad there were probably several hundred who, reluctantly or not, stayed in England and had to be content with the education they could find at home. What kind of men were they? What kind of schools were available for them? What could they learn?

The answers to all these questions must be ill-defined because we have to make room for many different types of men, of school, and of curriculum. But some outlines can be traced which broadly separate both socially and intellectually the men who stayed at home from those who went abroad.

1. The social environment

First, as to the men. We have seen that those who went abroad to study needed some resources to go; but (even more important) they needed the support of powerful family connections or patrons when they returned. No doubt there were some who took the risk and succeeded without these advantages; but they are hard to find. So, in seeking the men who stayed at home for their education we may conveniently start with those who were too poor to go abroad, or too ill-connected socially to profit from the highest skills when they returned. Not for them the higher offices in the Church. The highest aims of literate men not favoured by family connections or patrons could only be a parochial benefice, or membership of a local religious community, or a modest employment in local courts or in the household of a local magnate. The demand for men in all these employments grew rapidly throughout the twelfth century. The widespread building of new parish churches, the demand for vicars to perform parochial duties on behalf of the monastic houses who engrossed the rectories of parish churches, the increasing size and number of clerical staffs attached to the households of all classes and types of local magnates, probably too a growing demand for masses for the dead, all added to the general demand for literacy at a relatively low level.

Merging with this lowest class of seekers after education, there was a less rapidly growing, but important educational demand from men who belonged to families in that middle station which first makes its presence felt in numerous documents in the twelfth century. Their families had small estates in one or more counties, and among their possessions there would be one or two parish churches to be distributed among clerical members of the family. These were men who neither grovelled nor aimed high; they were satisfied with a competent prosperity. And to them must be added the dynasties of hereditary rectors of parish churches who formed a respectable clerical local aristocracy in England till the end of the century. Altogether, the large and miscellaneous class of clergy belonging to this wide stratum of society provided some of the most independent intellects in English society. Since they made no claim to the higher appointments in the Church, they could follow their own interests in history or science without troubling themselves to seek an equipment for high office in the great schools of Europe.

These men of middle rank and independent resources—indifferent to social promotion, or lacking the connections which would give them access to it—performed a great service to those below them in the social scale. They acted as an aristocracy of the unprivileged; and they helped to define, and opened the way to, intellectual goals at which even the most unprivileged could aim. It is to this group of men, as I shall suggest, that Grosseteste, himself unprivileged, owed most. The case for looking on him in this light will need to be established in such detail as the nature of the evidence allows. But, before attempting this, it will be an advantage to have as clear an idea as possible of the advantages and disadvantages of a purely English local education in the last quarter of the twelfth century: what opportunities did it offer? in what circumstances was it available? what were the intellectual and material rewards of such an education?

We must first note that the growth in the demand for literate men in types of employment suitable for those from the lower and middle ranks of society brought about a vast expansion in the number of schools throughout the twelfth century.[2] By the end of the century, even the smallest towns seem to have had

[2] The history of English schools in the twelfth century has to be put together from a large body of charters, saints' lives, miracle collections, legal records, and chronicles. The early efforts in this field, especially of A. F. Leach, are too uncritical to be satisfactory. A good beginning in the light of modern scholarship has been made by N. Orme, *English Schools in the Middle Ages*, 1973, pp. 293-325. Orme lists the places and evidence for thirty-five schools in the twelfth century. A full count could increase this number; and, given the extreme unlikelihood of the survival of evidence with little or no legal or finance interest, this total may be no more than 5% of the schools that existed.

at least one school and there were several schools in all the larger towns. At the summit of this provincial system, in the last decade of the century, Oxford emerged as the one scholastic centre in England which was capable of drawing students from abroad, even if only from scholastically backward areas like northern Germany or Hungary.[3]

The records of these schools are extremely fragmentary, for they were only preserved when they became the property of a religious community, or the subject of litigation, or the scene of a miracle. But, even within these limitations, the documents are sufficiently abundant to show that there was competition among masters to teach in them and that there was profit to be had in owning them.[4] From an early period in the twelfth century we see masters being summoned, or seeking a summons, to take over schools in quite small towns. We see other masters, without a summons and at the risk of eviction, setting up a school wherever there seemed to be an opening. We see masters who had hoped for better things—a position in a royal court or a chance of teaching in Paris—having to be satisfied with a school in a small English town like Oxford, or in a very small one like Dunstable. We see such masters on the look-out for a chance to move to a better place: from Dunstable to St Albans or from Oxford to Paris. We see the king giving monopolies for teaching within a town to religious houses, and we see struggles between monopoly and free enterprise which generally end in a compromise under the general jurisdiction of the diocesan bishop. But, above all, we see the number of schools continuing to grow throughout the twelfth century.

At its lowest level the scholastic scene must have been immensely varied and chaotic in operation; but it gradually settled down along a few recognizable lines. In the first place,

---

[3] The earliest known foreign students in Oxford are a clerk from Hungary who was supported by Richard I in 1193 and 1194 by payments made by the sheriff of Oxford, and two brothers from Friesland who studied canon and Roman law from about 1195 to 1200. (See *HUO* i. 18-19).

[4] A charter of Robert Chesney, Bishop of Lincoln 1148-66 (*English Episcopal Acta: Lincoln 1967-1185*, ed. D. M. Smith, 1980, no. 134), tells in brief the whole story of competition between masters, and shows the efforts of owners of scholastic monopolies to control and profit from the demand for schools. It may be remarked that the general aim of monopolists, in this and all other cases of a similar type, was not to prevent the setting up of schools, but to obtain a fee from the teachers who had to be licensed by the monopolist, in this case the canons of Huntingdon.

the ownership of well-established schools, like the ownership of parish churches, fell increasingly into ecclesiastical hands. There were obvious reasons for this: schools, like parish churches, provided a convenient form of endowment for religious communities, and especially for communities of Augustinian canons whose sites and properties generally lay in towns. Also, teachers and pupils alike were normally clergy, and as such amenable to ecclesiastical jurisdiction; and the substance of the teaching was in the last resort subject to the authority of the bishop. Consequently, although schools often seem to have come into existence as a result of individual enterprise, we generally hear about them only at the moment when they were granted to a religious body.

No doubt the physical appearance of the schools varied from a single classroom or a room in a vicarage to some more substantial accommodation. But even the greatest were not elaborate organizations. All cathedrals had schools attached to them. But no English cathedral school in the twelfth century had anything like the size and prestige of the schools of Milan cathedral in the eleventh century, where there were many classes and pupils serving the needs of a large, ancient and sophisticated urban community. Even a hundred years later, England could offer no social or literate environment of anything like this size and complexity. The best description of the physical setting of an English cathedral school comes from St Paul's in London. Here, in about 1120, there were three masters, each with his class at the west end of the cathedral. One of them was a canon, who alone had lands and tithes for his support. He had the custody of all the books of the cathedral and the keys to the chests in which they were kept, and he was clearly the head master; the other two were teachers without benefices. We hear of a somewhat similar organization at Salisbury; and there is no reason to think that the other cathedrals had anything much more elaborate. No doubt by the end of the century cathedral schools were no longer satisfied with accommodation at the west end or in the transept of the church, but we know nothing about their new quarters.[5]

[5] For the situation of the schools of Milan and their place in the community in the period c.1075–1120, see Landulfus de S. Paulo, *Historia Mediolanensis*, MGH, *Scriptores*, xx, 1868, pp. 70–1. For the arrangements at St Paul's see *Early Charters of the Cathedral*

But the great majority of schools for secular clergy were not attached to cathedrals. Even when they belonged to religious houses, they were self-supporting units which existed as a source of profit to their owners and teachers. The arrangements which we find described at Derby in a charter of about 1170 outlines a pattern which must have been very general.[6] The school consisted of a house containing a hall, which was used as a schoolroom, with chambers for the master and boarders; and attached to the house were several outhouses, including an oven, the use of which produced an income to support poor scholars. This set-up of a master, with an usher in the larger schools, and a variable number of pupils, partly lodging together, became well established in the twelfth century. It was flexible and adaptable to all educational needs from those of a small town school to the schools which combined to form the University of Oxford from the thirteenth century onwards. It is impossible to estimate accurately how many such schools there may have been in England by 1200, but we shall probably be in the right order of magnitude if we think of several hundred scattered all over England providing reasonably profitable employment for a similar number of masters.

If the school belonged to a religious community, as it did at Derby, the owner appointed a master for life or for a fixed number of years, probably at a fixed rent, and left him to make individual bargains with his pupils or their parents. It was a simple system which left no records, and it is only by chance that we can see it in action. Most clearly we see it in the life of Samson abbot of Bury St Edmunds when the son of his former schoolmaster asked for the vicarage of a church which belonged to the Abbey. Samson had a whole drawerful of papal pro-

of St Paul, London, ed. M. Gibbs, Camden Series, 3rd series, no. 58, 1939, charters 273-4. In *c.*1127 the master received a grant of the tithes of two estates, to which more were added by the bishop in the 1190s (ibid. 216–17). At Salisbury, in 1139, King Stephen gave the church at Odiham, a valuable piece of royal patronage, *ad opus magistri scole*. Examples, both of them, of the gradual build-up of English scholastic endowments.

    [6] The evidence comes from a charter of 1161–82 in the *Cartulary of Darley Abbey*, ed. R. R. Darlington, 2 vols., 1945, i. 80–1: Walkelin of Derby (a royal moneyer) and his wife Goda notify the king and bishop of Chester that they have given their house in Derby with all the buildings on the site to the Augustinian canons of Darley: 'secundum hanc dispositionem scilicet quod aula sit in scola clericorum et thalami sint in hospitium magistri et clericorum in perpetuum.' It is not clear that the grant took effect but the physical layout of a school with its hall, bed-chambers, and outhouses is clear.

visions which gave their nominees a prior right to vacant benefices, but he granted this one before them all: 'When I was a
poor clerk, your father, Master William of Diss, gave me ad-
mission to his school and the chance of learning without contract or fee; so, for God's sake, I give you what you ask.'[7]

The individual 'contract and fee' in return for the opportunity to learn: this was the simple system which must have
assured a livelihood for many schoolmasters in all parts of the
country. What did they teach?

2. The intellectual environment

To begin with, what did they *not* teach? It is highly unlikely
that there was any school in England, even at the end of the
twelfth century, where a student could find teaching in theology or canon law at a level comparable to what he could find
at Paris or Bologna. In Oxford, there were indeed teachers in
both subjects who had studied and taught abroad. Alexander
Nequam who lectured on theology in Oxford from about 1190
to 1197 had spent several years in the Parisian schools and he
was well acquainted with the works and methods of the chief
masters. And in canon law during these years there were three
masters in Oxford who had taught in Paris. But the level of a
master's teaching depends more on the ability, outlook and
circumstances of his pupils than on the methods of his teachers.
The meagre record of the teaching of all these masters in Oxford
suggests a steep decline from the rigour and technical complexity of the products of the great foreign schools. The decline
in technicality brought some compensations. Alexander
Nequam's theological writings have an independence and
spontaneity which makes them agreeable to read, and his recollections of his days in Oxford leave a pleasing impression of
clerical society in a small provincial town.[8] Similarly, the records of the Oxford masters in canon law during the same
decade show a close attention to local problems, to local pro-

[7] Jocelin of Brakelond, op. cit. , p. 44.

[8] For an account of Nequam's life and works, see R. W. Hunt, *The Schools and the
Cloister: The Life and Writings of Alexander Nequam (1157-1217)*, ed. M. Gibson, Oxford,
1984. The most famous anecdote relating to his Oxford days concerns his insistence on
lecturing on the Feast of the Immaculate Conception. He was always ill when the day
came and his colleagues remonstrated with him and persuaded him to desist.

cedures and the peculiarities of local custom. No doubt, this was what students—most of whom were already familiar with local courts—needed; but observers capable of comparing the teaching in Oxford with that of Bologna or Paris mocked the intellectual gaucherie of the Oxford system.[9] The contrast is strongly reminiscent of a similar contrast which, almost exactly eight hundred years later, foreign observers of historical teaching in Oxford noticed when they compared the severe disciplines of the German universities with the general discussions and essays which formed the main discipline of students in the universities of Oxford and Cambridge. In technical skills, the decline was steep; balanced, in the eyes of insular practitioners at least, by some benefits in humane values.[10]

Oxford in the last ten years of the twelfth century came much nearer than any other English town to providing the level of scholastic teaching that Englishmen had been seeking in foreign schools for the last hundred years. But it was still not good enough for those who could manage to go abroad. Even Edmund of Abingdon, who had been at school in Oxford, went to Paris for his serious studies in 1192. But if the English schools, and the English scene generally, did not offer students the finest edge of scholastic sharpness or the latest forms of legal and theological argument, they offered some advantages denied to the frequenters of the Parisian or Bolognese schools. The immense success of the great European schools was partly due to their having developed stereotyped methods of enquiry, which they applied to a limited range of sources. Naturally, they concentrated on the kinds of questions and the areas of knowledge which could be dealt with by the techniques in which they

[9] See *HUO* i. 16–20. Also S. Kuttner and E. Rathbone, 'Anglo-Norman Canonists in the Twelfth Century', *Traditio*, vii, 1949–51, 323–7 (to which must be added Kuttner's *Retractationes* in his *Gratian and the Schools of Law, 1140–1234*, 1984, pp. 26–34); Jane E. Sayers, *Papal Judges Delegate in the Province of Canterbury, 1198–1254*, 1971, pp. 47–54; R. W. Southern, 'Master Vacarius and the Beginning of an English Academic Tradition', *Medieval Learning and Literature: Essays presented to R. W. Hunt*, ed. J. J. G. Alexander and M. T. Gibson, 1976, pp. 257–86. With all submission to the great authority of Stephan Kuttner, I do not think he pays enough attention to the actual situation in Oxford or to the evidence for the limitations and local orientation of English canon law teaching in this period.

[10] The best foreign observer was P. Frédéricq, *De l'enseignement supérieur de l'histoire en Écosse et en Angleterre: notes et impressions de voyage*, 1885. The views of the Oxford tutors, now buried in their local *Magazine*, will perhaps be given a wider publicity in some future volume of *HUO*.

were pre-eminent. This hardening of an academic curriculum is a common feature of all successful academic systems: it can be seen today, and it could be seen in Europe in the late twelfth century. The great European schools were at the height of their fame in 1200, but there were already critics who found their procedures stultifying, their questions too abundant in too limited a field, and their answers diminishing in importance.[11]

These were not criticisms that could be made about the English schools. They might not take their students far, but they left them their freedom and offered some new prospects. I have mentioned that the limitations of Oxford as a centre of specialized teaching encouraged a more discursive treatment of themes which would have been more rigorously explored in Paris. It may now be added that lack of specialization, which limits progress along pre-ordained lines, can liberate both teachers and students. A schoolmaster working on his own in a small town lacked the daily stimulus of critical pupils, learned companions, and difficult intellectual problems to be solved as a matter of daily routine. But he had one precious advantage. He had freedom to follow his interests wherever they led. He could study books outside the syllabus of the schools. He could express his ideas without regard to the rules of scholastic dispute. If he was lucky enough to be in or near a cathedral city or great monastery, he might have access to a library with ancient copies of rare texts, such as existed in Malmesbury, Hereford, Worcester and several other places. His life was less tied to scholastic routine. His hold on the means of life might be tenuous. If he was without a benefice, he would have to rely on drawing an income from his pupils or from writing letters and charters for a local magnate, or representing them in their lawsuits, or attending them in their illnesses, or drawing horoscopes of their children, or warning them of dangerous conjunctions of the planets. His life would be precarious, but free in a way that no master in a great school could be.

These are the two patterns of scholarly life at the end of the twelfth century. The first was by far the more powerful in its results and intellectually more coherent in its contents. The men who followed this route left a literature which had an immediate and fundamental influence on European life and

---

[11] I hope I may have a chance to say more about these criticisms elsewhere.

thought. The second is more individual, more widely scattered, and less immediately powerful. The men who followed this route have left a large number of historical, devotional and scientific writings, in which insular influences are strongly marked. It is a body of literature which had little immediate influence on the contemporary scene or on the development of society, and it has not yet received the sympathetic study which it deserves.[12]

To which of these two classes did Grosseteste belong? To the privileged and influential élite, who filled the higher positions in the Church? As a learned bishop he would appear most naturally to belong to this category, but there are difficulties in placing him in it. Or did he belong to the class of the relatively poor and unprivileged representatives of an insular tradition? In order to answer this question, we must first go back to the meagre records of his education and career before he burst into the full light of contemporary publicity by becoming bishop of Lincoln in 1235.

[12] On this subject in general, see my paper 'The Place of England in the twelfth-century Renaissance', *Medieval Humanism and other Studies*, 1970, pp. 158-80; also R. M. Thomson's criticisms in his 'England and the Twelfth-century Renaissance', *Past and Present*, ci, 1983, 3-21.

4

Outlines of a Provincial Career

I. EARLY AND MIDDLE YEARS

THE earliest surviving contemporary evidence for Grosseteste's career comes from a time when he was in his early twenties, and it is compatible with his having followed either of the two courses described above. Like nearly every other literate clerk, whether he came straight from a local school or had just returned from Paris or Bologna, he had to make himself useful to some magnate who could employ and reward him. The only clerks exempt from this necessity were men whose family connections gave them an assurance of a benefice and a position in society. Grosseteste did not belong to this class. He was of humble, perhaps very humble, birth: that was the one thing about him on which such varied observers as Matthew Paris, the canons of Lincoln, Richard Earl of Clare, and Grosseteste himself, were agreed.[1] So, like most other men, he had to find an employer and a patron.

He chose the bishop of Lincoln for his first attempt. As we shall see, he probably already had a connection with the town, and had perhaps gone to school there at the expense of its leading citizen. Then, at a date between 1189 and April 1192,

---

[1] Matthew Paris, *Hist. Angl.* ii. 376: 'ex humillima stirpe procreatus'. He also reports the bitter regret of the canons of Lincoln that they had elected a bishop *de tam humili* (*Chron. Maj.* iii. 528). The Franciscan responsible for the early part of the Lanercost Chronicle reports the rude question of Richard Earl of Clare who asked Grosseteste how he, a man of humble birth, could have acquired so much courtesy; he also gives Grosseteste's dignified reply 'humili de patre et matre sum natus.' Grosseteste's further explanation, that he had learnt courtesy from the really great men with whom he had lived since his youth, would have been an important biographical detail, if he had not added that the men he referred to were all in the Bible. Evidently he could hold his own in talking to an earl. (*Lanercost Chronicle*, p. 44; see, for its authorship, A. G. Little, 1943, p. 48). Grosseteste's biographer, Richard of Bardney (*Anglia Sacra*, ii. 334), elaborates and perhaps exaggerates his humble birth: 'Pauperibus trabeatus avis, puer iste parentis post obitum panem mendicat ore suum.' For this source, and the story it tells, see below, pp. 75–82.

we find his name at the bottom of a long list of witnesses to a charter of Hugh, bishop of Lincoln, confirming the possessions of the monks of St Andrew in Northampton.[2] In common with most of those whose names come before his in the list, he is given the title of 'Master'. That is to say, like the others, he had not only been to school, but he had reached a standard of proficiency which entitled him to teach. Perhaps he had had his own school or had helped his master as a second master: more likely the latter, for he must have been a young master when he witnessed this charter. Our estimate of his age is conjectural, based on his being still vigorous enough in 1250 to undertake a long and extremely controversial visit to the papal court at Lyons. It is hard to imagine that a man much over eighty could have accomplished this feat of endurance. Every year that we push back the date of his birth before 1170 adds a further improbability to the chronology of his career. If we date the charter as late as possible, in 1191 or early in 1192, and place Grosseteste's birth in 1169 or 1170, he would have been a master of twenty-one or twenty-two: a possible age for a young master from a local school, but scarcely for a man from Paris.

Most of the witnesses whose names preceded Grosseteste's were members of the household of the bishop of Lincoln. At least two of them had studied in Paris. Probably all of them were hoping for promotion, and several achieved it without waiting long: Master William de Montibus, recently returned from Paris, would soon be chancellor of Lincoln; Master Roger of Rolleston would soon be archdeacon of Leicester; and almost at once Master Robert of Hardres would be archdeacon of Huntingdon; Master Simon of Sywell had to wait several years, dividing his time between administration in the diocese and teaching in Oxford, before becoming treasurer of Lichfield. But they all achieved a respectable eminence without too long a delay. In all probability, Master Robert Grosseteste, though he came at the bottom of the list, had similar hopes. If so, they came to nothing. He may have remained on the fringe of the

---

[2] BL MS Royal 11 B ix, ff. 24ᵛ-5. The charter can be dated before April 1192 because among the witnesses is Mr Robert de Hardrei without a further title: he had become archdeacon of Huntingdon before 4 April 1192. But the charter may belong to any earlier year after 1189. (See Greenway, 1977, pp. 27, 165.)

bishop's household for some time, but he never appears again in any known charter of Bishop Hugh or his officials. Indeed, he does not appear again in any document connected with the diocese of Lincoln for over thirty years. Nevertheless, his time in Lincoln was not wasted: he managed to get a testimonial which anyone would be glad to have.

The testimonial was written by Gerald of Wales. Gerald had gone to Lincoln, probably at some date between autumn 1194 and summer 1195, when he was prevented by the imminent outbreak of war from going to Paris for a further period of theological study.[3] Presumably, he met Grosseteste and was greatly impressed by him, for he wrote a letter recommending him to William de Vere, bishop of Hereford. It would appear that Grosseteste had already been accepted by William de Vere for work in his household, but Gerald wrote to emphasize his claim to high consideration. The terms in which he wrote could scarcely have been more flattering:

I know that he will be a great support to you in various kinds of business and legal decisions, and in providing cures to restore and preserve your health, for he has reliable skill in both these branches of learning, which in these days are most highly rewarded. Besides, he has a solid foundation of the liberal arts and wide reading, which he adorns with the highest standards of conduct.[4]

A deep knowledge of law and medicine are not quite the areas of excellence one would expect to find picked out for special commendation. We think of Grosseteste as a natural scientist and theologian. But in 1195 he would not yet have studied theology; and his interest in medicine is frequently shown in the imagery and symbolism of his later writings.[5] As for law,

---

[3] For this incident, see Giraldus Cambrensis, *De Rebus a se gestis*, in *Opera*, ed. J. S. Brewer, RS, 1861, i. 93. The war scare which caused Gerald to give up his plan of studying in Paris and to turn to Lincoln must have been in the interval between the truce of Verneuil in July 1194 and the outbreak of full-scale warfare in January 1196. Many contemporaries looked on Richard I's occupation of Vaudreuil in the summer of 1195 as the real beginning of the war, but the period before this event would have been filled with rumours sufficient to cause Gerald to seek a quieter haven than France. For the situation in these months, see F. M. Powicke, *The Loss of Normandy*, 1913, pp. 156–8.

[4] *Opera*, i. 249.

[5] In addition to his knowledge of the human body displayed in several passages (see below, pp. 177–9, 196–7), his frequent association of pastoral care with medical knowledge—in itself a fairly commonplace theme—is sufficiently detailed to suggest a

although it was for him the least congenial of all studies, all men engaged in administration had to be familiar with the work of the courts, and we have plenty of evidence that Grosseteste satisfied this requirement. Besides, like all writers of testimonials, Gerald no doubt picked out those accomplishments which would appeal most strongly to the future employer.

Whether his commendation helped to establish Grosseteste in William de Vere's household can never be known, but there is ample evidence that he quickly became an active administrator in the diocese of Hereford. During the next few years, he witnessed several of the bishop's charters, and he might reasonably have looked forward to early promotion.[6] But then the calamity befell him which was most to be feared by a rising young man: on Christmas Eve 1198 the bishop, his patron, died before he had provided Grosseteste with a benefice. The bishopric was then vacant for nearly two years, and during this time the main part of the administration would have been in the hands of royal officials; the household of Bishop de Vere would have been disbanded, and the new bishop, Giles of Braose, when he was finally appointed, would bring his own men with him. As a result, Grosseteste disappears from view. During the next twenty years, we have only one recollection of his own, and only one document which mentions him. The *recollection* shows that, like many who were engaged in ecclesiastical administration, he was in exile in France during at least some part of the period when England was under papal interdict and the king was an excommunicate.[7] The *document* is

familiarity with medical practice (see *Dicta* 101, 90 and 35, in Brown, 1690, pp. 262, 266, and 279).

[6] He regularly witnessed the charters of the bishop to the priory of St Guthlac, Hereford, in the second or third place among his clerks (Balliol College, Oxford, MS 271, ff. 21^v, 73^v, 97^v, 106^v).

[7] This recollection forms part of the report which Matthew Paris received from John of St Giles about Grosseteste's death-bed conversations (*Chron. Maj.* v. 404). It clearly refers to a time before Stephen Langton's return to England in July 1213, and probably to a period after 1210. The dying Grosseteste had been denouncing Innocent IV's support of the usurers of Cahors, and he recalled the better days when he had seen and heard Eustace, abbot of Flaye, James of Vitry, Archbishop Stephen Langton during his exile, and Master Robert Curzon, preaching the ejection of Cahorsin usurers *a partibus Franciae*. But where did this campaign take place? All the evidence we have of the activities of the Cahorsins at this time (apart from a single Cahorsin usurer in London) points to the Mediterranean and Atlantic coasts and the southern half of France: La Rochelle, Marseilles, Montpellier, St Giles, Toulouse, Carcassonne, Cahors, and the region of Quercy. There is no evidence that they reached Paris till the end of

a judgement which Hugh Foliot, archdeacon of Shropshire, acting as a papal judge-delegate together with Grosseteste and another official in the diocese of Hereford, delivered in a dispute between the monks of Worcester and a small local landowner, probably between 1213 and 1216.[8]

The appearance of Grosseteste in this company suggests that he may have continued to work in the diocese of Hereford, and more particularly in the archdeaconry of Shropshire, after the death of Bishop de Vere. This possibility is particularly attractive, because he next re-emerges from obscurity when Hugh Foliot, who had been archdeacon of Shropshire since the 1190s, became bishop of Hereford in October 1219. Between 1200 and 1219, Hereford had had two bishops with whom Grosseteste had no known connection. But almost immediately after the appointment of Hugh Foliot we have evidence that he was once more active in diocesan administration. At some time before August 1220 he was in trouble with the royal justices for having heard a plea about secular property in an ecclesiastical court in Shropshire.[9] And, at a date after October 1219 which cannot yet be more accurately determined, he witnessed a charter of Bishop Hugh Foliot announcing the institution of a parson to a church also in Shropshire.[10] This re-emergence under a new

the thirteenth century. The campaign may have been inspired by the growing power and influence of the Cahorsins in the south as a result of the aid they had given to the crusade of Simon de Montfort against the Albigensians in 1209-12. How Grosseteste came to be involved in it remains at present unknown. It evidently left a sufficiently deep impression on him to elicit the single piece of autobiographical recollection which we possess—and that on his death-bed forty years later. Whatever the circumstances, the story as we know it at present does nothing to support (as is often imagined) the view that he was teaching in Paris during these years. For details, see Y. Renouard, 'Les Cahorsins, hommes d'affaires Français du XIIIe siècle', *TRHS*, 5th series, xi, 1961, pp. 43-67.

[8] For the text of the document and its date, see R. R. Darlington, *The Cartulary of Worcester Cathedral Priory*, Pipe Roll Society, 1968, pp. 72-3.

[9] *Curia Regis Rolls*, ix, 1952, pp. 171, 328. The royal justices heard the case in August 1220, so the alleged offence must have taken place several months earlier. Grosseteste and his two co-defendants were not present in court and the sheriff reported that they had no lay fee on which distraint could be made: the bishop of Hereford was, therefore, ordered to distrain them to be present on Michaelmas day in five weeks' time. When the case was reopened, they were still absent and the sheriff was ordered to enforce their presence in February 1221. At this point, the affair disappears from sight.

[10] This charter of Bishop Hugh Foliot announces the institution of a parson of Culmington (Shropshire) on the presentation of Osbert, abbot of Haughmond in the same county. To judge from his position in the witness list, in which he comes above the bishop's official, Grosseteste was at this time high in the bishop's household.

bishop, who had for many years been archdeacon of Shropshire, together with the solitary document relating to Grosseteste's activity in Shropshire probably between 1213 and 1216,
lends weight to the possibility that after the death of Bishop de
Vere he joined the household of the archdeacon of Shropshire,
whose colleague he must have been during de Vere's lifetime,
and that he continued for some time to serve him after he
became bishop of Hereford.

I mention these humble circumstances and possibilities
partly to indicate the kind of life that seems most likely for a
man without family connections or an important patron; but
partly also to correct a common fallacy. It is often supposed
that able and intellectual men—especially if they are commonly
given the title of *Magister*—must have been engaged in teaching, preferably in some well-known school, and that only men
so engaged could have continued to think seriously about intellectual subjects. This supposition is quite contrary to common sense and common experience. No man could make a
living in the schools unless he either had an established school,
or a continuous stream of private wealthy pupils, or a cathedral
canonry which required or enabled him to teach. Until the
friars came, it was extremely difficult for men to teach in the
higher branches of learning over long periods of time: if they
had benefices or positions in a large household, their duties
frequently removed them from the schools; and if they had no
other source of income, the academic life was a precarious one
and could only be intermittently engaged in by any but the
most famous and sought-after masters.[11] Since the famous are
the men we know most about, their success has encouraged a
false view of the opportunities open to the less famous.

This does not mean that a man who had to seek his living in
the service of men greater than himself would never teach. The
administrative life was seldom a full-time occupation. It might
require lengthy absences from England, especially for journeys
to the papal court. But, despite such interruptions, there is
widespread evidence that scholars who held middle-range pos-

(Cartulary of Haughmond Abbey, Shrewsbury Borough Library MS 1, f. 52, in-
accurately transcribed in *Trans. Shropshire Archaeological Soc.* i, 1878, p. 182).

[11] For more details on this point, see my paper 'The schools of Paris and the school
of Chartres', *Renaissance and Renewal in the Twelfth Century*, ed. R. L. Benson and G.
Constable, Cambridge, Mass., 1982, 125–32.

itions in the clerical hierarchy as archdeacons, deans, canons or simple members of a great household often combined those duties with periods of study and teaching in the schools. On general grounds it is likely that he taught at least intermittently; but whom, or where, or at what level he taught, are questions which escape all conjecture. It would not be surprising to find that he spent periods of several months at a time teaching in Oxford, or in Hereford, or for that matter in Shrewsbury. If we are right about the circumstances of his life, he would teach wherever and whenever he found it most profitable and convenient for himself, for his potential pupils, and for his employer.

This state of affairs, however, changed rapidly after 1220, and the change in Grosseteste's fortunes, which had been far from brilliant up to this point, may be connected with a revolution at the top level of English administration which took place between 1221 and 1224. The circumstances will have to be examined when we come to consider an unduly neglected source of information about Grosseteste.[12] But, for the present, it will suffice to note that, for whatever reason, he quite quickly changed from being a nonentity so far as the public was concerned to being a man of consequence and rising fame.

Leaving this gap for the moment unfilled, we come to the turning-point in Grosseteste's whole career in 1225. In this year, the episcopal register of Hugh of Wells, bishop of Lincoln, states that the bishop has given the rectory of Abbotsley (in the county of Huntingdon, midway between Bedford and Cambridge) to Master Robert Grosseteste, a clerk in deacon's orders.[13]

This is an entry of decisive importance from several points of view. In the first place, so far as we know, it was Grosseteste's first benefice, and it was a substantial one. With this gift, there-

[12] See below, p. 80.

[13] *Rotuli Hugonis de Welles*, ed. F. N. Davis, Canterbury and York Society, 1908, iii. 48. The bishop's mandate was dated 25 April 1225, but it could not become effective till 6 May, when the benefice would fall into the bishop's gift by the failure of an unknown patron to make a presentation within six months of the benefice's becoming vacant on 5 November 1224. The presentation was therefore highly speculative and Grosseteste received it subject to the non-appearance of a lawful claimant. The bishop had lost no time and was evidently in a hurry to do something for him. This haste has a bearing on Grosseteste's alleged presentation to Clifton which I examine below, p. 79.

fore, he passed from the ever-present risk of penury and un-
employment to the comfortable enjoyment of a life-long
income. He was no longer dependent on patronage or pupils.
He was free to exercise his talents as he wished. And, since his
parish was only a day's ride from Oxford, and he might have a
curate, he could spend much time in the schools without neglecting his parishioners.

Another important point in this entry is its statement that
he was only in deacon's orders. This strengthens the likelihood
that Abbotsley was his first benefice. When he was a bishop he
made himself notorious for his insistence that all holders of
parochial benefices should be priests.[14] Of course, he might not
have lived up to his own principles, but he was not a man to
be fierce in principle and lukewarm in action: with him, action
followed thought more closely and vigorously than with most
men. So, in the absence of definite evidence to the contrary,
we may assume that Abbotsley was his first benefice, obtained
at the ripe age of about fifty-five.

His being only in deacon's orders in 1225 also suggests that
he had not yet started publicly lecturing on theology. Once
more, not everyone obeyed the rule that doctors in theology
should be priests; but once more Grosseteste was not generally
favourable to laxity. On both counts, therefore, 1225 looks like
the start of a new era in his life.

II. THE OXFORD YEARS

From 1225, and probably somewhat earlier, until 1235, Grosseteste's life was intimately and continuously associated with Oxford. For the first time we can trace his career and development,
if not in great detail, at least with some approach to intimacy
and without the huge gaps and uncertainties which fill his first
fifty years and more. These ten years were in many ways the
most important and fruitful years of his life. By 1225 he had
completed the greater part of his scientific thinking and writing.
In the years which followed, we find him teaching and writing
on the Bible and studying the Fathers.[15] It was this change of

---

[14] See his Statutes for Lincoln diocese, Powicke and Cheney, i. 273 (c. 30); and
Chron. Maj. v. 279 for the attempts of many holding benefices in his diocese to obtain
papal dispensation from this requirement, which he strictly enforced.

[15] See below, chapter 6, for the grounds for these statements.

studies which led to his growing interest in Greek and his growing sympathy with the thought of Greek theologians. It was in these years too that he produced the series of theological writings which show him in the full vigour and variety of his intellectual effort; and at the mid-point in the period, in 1230, he experienced, if not a religious conversion, at least a new commitment to Christian life and pastoral work.

Although we can be sure that a large part of his time in these years was spent in Oxford, it is not until 23 June 1234 that we have a precisely dated and unambiguous official document which connects him with the Oxford schools. This document is a royal mandate directing him, together with Master Robert Bacon OP, and the chancellor of the university, to supervise the arrest of all prostitutes in Oxford who had disobeyed a royal order to leave the town.[16] It is clear that the king regarded these three men as peculiarly qualified for this hopeless task. The choice of the chancellor speaks for itself. Grosseteste and Robert Bacon were probably chosen because they were the current lecturers in theology to the Franciscans and Dominicans respectively, the religious orders whose influence was rapidly growing at the royal court at this time.[17] In less than a year after this, Grosseteste—and, once more he must have had the king's approval—was a bishop.

How had the man, whom we last saw in royal documents in 1220 engaged in disputes with royal officials over local ecclesiastical administration, reached this surprising eminence?

To answer this question, we may begin by going back to 1225 when he got the benefice of Abbotsley and probably became a priest. The ten years after this date can be divided into two roughly equal parts. For the first five years Grosseteste was a theological lecturer in the secular schools of the university, and his success brought him to the highest position among the masters. I have argued elsewhere that it was in these years that he was elected as chancellor of the university by the corporate body of masters in defiance of the bishop of Lincoln in whose hands the power of nomination strictly lay; but the manoeuvre was only partly successful, for the bishop countered

---

[16] *Close Rolls, 1231–4*, p. 568.
[17] *Chron. Maj.* iii. 251 (an addition by Matthew Paris to Roger of Wendover's account of the Parliament of October 1233).

the move by allowing Grosseteste the power of chancellor without the name.[18] We know too little about the incident to see
far into its causes and motives, but it is clear that the masters
of the university, like corporate bodies of all kinds in towns and
trade guilds, and in universities elsewhere, were beginning to
assert their independent authority, and Grosseteste may have
sympathized with this movement.

By 1230 he was certainly the most distinguished master of
the schools in Oxford. He was beginning to break new ground
in theology, and attracting growing attention by his sermons
and lectures. We happen to have a manuscript which throws a
brilliant light on his rising reputation. It is a manuscript which
came into the possession of the monks of Durham as a gift from
Bertrand de Middleton, who was prior from 1244 to 1258.[19]
But the manuscript had been written earlier, certainly before
1232, and it had had earlier owners. We can be quite sure of
this because the man who owned the manuscript in that year—
and even he may not have been its first owner—scribbled in
the margins several notes about travelling expenses between
London and South Wales, loans, small purchases of the cathedral chapter of Llandaff and (most surprising of all) the
details of an elaborate penance imposed on the writer on 27
February 1232. His name is unknown, but he was clearly a
wealthy man, for the minutely detailed penance included an
obligation to feed a hundred poor persons for seven years. The
owner of the volume was, therefore, not only wealthy, but
capable of committing spectacular sins and paying for them.
His knowledge of the finances of the canons of Llandaff, his
record of journeys, purchases, and small loans, suggest that he
was employed in the household of the bishop of Llandaff and
he must have passed through Oxford on his travels between
South Wales and London. The probability is that on one of
these visits he bought the manuscript with its record of Grosseteste's lectures and sermons. Five quires contain Grosseteste's

---

[18] *HUO* i. 27–36.

[19] Durham Cathedral MS A iii 12, a composite volume made up of several disparate
parts which seem to have been bound together from an early date. The folios with
Grosseteste's comments on the Psalms and Sermons are ff. 2–17, 78–87, 104–127. The
marginal notes of expenses, journeys, income of canons of Llandaff, and the penance
of the owner are on ff. 121–2, 130, and 137ᵛ. There is an illustration of one of its pages
in *HUO* i, facing p. 244. The contents of the volume are discussed below, pp. 113–16.

notes on the Psalter, some of them in more than one version, interspersed with sermons, and thickly annotated. They are all anonymous, with the exception of three sermons of Jordan of Saxony and one of Master Roger of Salisbury;[20] but Grosseteste's authorship of most of them is beyond dispute because he later included large sections of the material in the collection of his *Dicta*, which I have already mentioned.

Professor Harrison Thomson, who first pointed out the importance of this manuscript, thought that these pages were written in Grosseteste's own hand. This is a mistake, as later scholars have pointed out.[21] But they were certainly written by someone who had access to Grosseteste's notes. They are not *reportationes* made by an auditor at his lectures, for they reproduce the identical words of the later *Dicta*, which a listener could not have done. So they must come from Grosseteste's own material. Yet the copy was clearly not made under his guidance, for it is full of absurd errors and misunderstandings. So it seems probable that it was made by an outsider, perhaps without Grosseteste's knowledge. Furthermore, the extracts contain *two* versions of large parts of the lecture notes, which seem to belong to different stages in their development—perhaps lectures in successive years.

Whatever the precise process of transmission may have been, the existence of this volume shows Grossteste as a theological lecturer and preacher in the Oxford schools, probably in the years shortly before 1230. It is a unique record of teaching and preaching in Oxford at this time, the earliest record we have which comes to us straight from the schools. It shows Grosseteste at the height of his academic influence, when the record of his words was eagerly seized, annotated and passed from one owner to another until it ended up in the library at Durham.

[20] These sermons are on ff. 88-103 in the same hand as the preceding section with Grosseteste's comments on the Psalms. Jordan's sermon of 11 November is the only one with its authorship recorded in the text; his two others of 6 December (perhaps also in Oxford) and 27 December (probably in London) have their authorship noted in the margin. For Jordan's visit to England and the text of the sermons, see A. G. Little, 'Three Sermons of Fr. Jordan of Saxony, the Successor of St Dominic, preached in England AD 1229', *EHR* liv, 1939, 1-19. For Master Roger of Salisbury, see *BRUO*, iii, 1632: it is likely that his sermon also was preached in Oxford in 1229 on 17 June. See Little, loc. cit. p. 4. Fr. Jordan's three sermons with many others are also found in Canterbury Cathedral MS D 7. (See T. Kaeppelli, *Archivum Fratrum Praedicatorum*, xxvi, 1956, 161-91.)

[21] See especially R. W. Hunt in Callus, 1955, pp. 139-40.

In the academic year 1229-30 an event took place which was destined to have a decisive influence on his life. I have mentioned that, among Grosseteste's comments on the Psalms, the manuscript also contains three sermons of Fr. Jordan of Saxony, St Dominic's successor as master general of the Order of Preachers. The sermons were preached during a visit which he paid to the Dominicans in England in 1229-30, and at least one of them was preached at Oxford to an academic audience. The date was the Feast of St Martin, 11 November 1229. The substance was an attack on academic pride and a call to pastoral commitment: 'To be called Master is not in itself evil; but to wish to be called Master is the height of pride.' This was the message of the sermon. The fact that it was preserved among Grosseteste's notes might be an accident. But we know that Jordan of Saxony's message made a deep impression on him, for after Grosseteste became a bishop he wrote to Jordan recalling the frequent conversations they had had in Oxford at the time of his visit and asking him to attach to his household the friar John of St Giles to help him in his pastoral work. This was the friar who attended him on his death-bed and reported his dying words, and the request was made in words of fervent friendship and devotion for which nothing in Grosseteste's earlier writings has prepared us.[22]

Grosseteste was not the only Oxford master to be influenced by Jordan's visit. His colleague, Master Robert Bacon, the other leading theological lecturer in Oxford at the time, became a Dominican, and Grosseteste's pupil Adam Rufus became a Franciscan at about the same time. Grosseteste himself did not go so far. Perhaps he was too old to change; perhaps his new commitment to pastoral work was qualified by his commitment to learning. Besides, we know that he did not wholly approve the Franciscan dependence on begging: he thought that the beguines of the Rhineland, who worked with their hands, had chosen the better part.[23] He did not give up everything, but he divested himself of academic eminence and devoted his learning to the young and impecunious community of Franciscans in

[22] *Ep.* no. 40; and cf. *Chron. Maj.* v. 400, 705.
[23] On Robert Bacon see *BRUO* i. 87 and B. Smalley, 'Robert Bacon and the early Dominican school at Oxford', *TRHS* xxx, 1948, 1-19. For Adam Rufus, see below, p. 123. For his opinion of the beguines, see Thomas of Eccleston, p. 99.

Oxford. This was probably in 1230 or 1231. In 1232, he went further: he resigned the archdeaconry of Leicester, which he had held since 1229, and gave up all his other revenues except his prebend in Lincoln cathedral. As he explained to his sister and to his friend Adam Marsh, he had given up wealth and its cares, and even the pastoral work for which he was ill-equipped, to give his mind to spiritual truth.[24] For the next few years until he became a bishop he could devote himself to broadening his theological base and teaching a very mixed collection of pupils.

The decade from 1225 to 1235 is thus fairly securely documented. But we are still in the dark about the time and circumstances which brought Grosseteste to Oxford. The only light we have on this comes from a source which has been too readily dismissed as useless. To this we may now turn.

III. THE MESSAGE OF A DESPISED SOURCE

The source is a *Life* of Grosseteste, written in 1502 by Richard, a monk of the Benedictine abbey of Bardney, about ten miles from Lincoln. It was written for the then bishop of Lincoln, Dr William Smith, and it is the only substantial medieval biography of Grosseteste.[25] Almost no one has taken it seriously except Professor J. C. Russell.[26] He deserves much credit for this, but even he has not sufficiently enquired why it deserves better treatment than it has generally received. Seen through modern eyes, it could scarcely have less claim to respect: it is late in date; it is poetic and rhetorical in form; it attributes to Grosseteste some of the marvels which were later transferred to Roger Bacon—the making of a brazen head which could answer difficult questions, and possession of a wonderful horse which took him to Rome in the course of a night. Its disqualifications leap to the eye.

It contains marvels which are wholly incredible. But, if marvels are held to be sufficient to condemn all its other facts, the same criterion would condemn many ancient and medieval

---

[24] *Ep.*. nos. 8 and 9; also Greenway, p. 34; and for *Ep.* 8, below, pp. 191-2
[25] The Life is printed in Henry Wharton, *Anglia Sacra*, 1691, ii. 325-41.
[26] See J. C. Russell, 'Richard of Bardney's account of Robert Grosseteste's early and middle life', *Medievalia et Humanistica*, ii, 1943, 45-55.

chronicles. Then, it contains many facts which are unsupported by any other source. But, where so little is known, almost any fact is likely to be unsupported. We can only ask whether it is likely. Without making any excessive claims for a writer who had to pick up his information wherever it could be found, Richard of Bardney's account must be considered as a serious attempt to collect all that could be known about one of the most distinguished bishops of Lincoln for the instruction of one of his most literate and humane successors. He reported everything. Some of his details are beyond belief marvellous, but others, whether right or wrong, are distinctly unromantic. He gives us the only coherent account of Grosseteste's education we possess. The fact that he contradicts nearly everything we have been encouraged to believe about his early connection with Paris and Oxford is perhaps no longer to be counted against him, especially since—writing for a bishop who was an Oxford scholar and founder of an Oxford college—he is unlikely to have omitted anything that could have reflected any glory on Oxford.

The story that he tells of Grosseteste's career until a date which may be located some time after 1220 is as follows.

He was born in a village called Stow and brought up in desperate poverty by his widowed mother. He was still a boy when she died; and after her death he drifted to Lincoln, begging his bread. He begged at the door of the mayor, who at first drove him off, but then befriended him. Under his patronage he went to school in Lincoln and made great progress in grammar. Then he went to the schools of Cambridge to study logic and rhetoric. Later, he began to be known for his amazing scientific knowledge, especially of the natures of all birds, beasts and plants, and their medical uses. He was employed by an elderly bishop of Salisbury to go to Rome on his behalf, a journey which he achieved in a single night on his marvellous horse. After this he went to Oxford; and when his wonderful brazen head was accidentally broken, he abandoned his scientific studies and turned to theology. In this he was encouraged by the king, whose secretary he had become, and he was supported by the bishop of Lincoln who gave him a benefice at Clifton.

At this point we reach the stage in Grosseteste's career which is more fully known from other sources, and we may stop to ask what value, if any, can be attached to what Richard of Bardney has told us so far.

Apart from the magic horse and brazen head, the main details which are known from no other source are the name of his birthplace, the circumstances of his early life, his begging at Lincoln, the charity of the mayor, his schooling in Lincoln and Cambridge, his work for the bishop of Salisbury, his journey to Rome, the patronage of the bishop of Lincoln, the name of his first benefice. They may be wrong. But if they are wrong, there is no principle of romance and no urge to please a patron that can account for them. Besides, several of the details make prosaic additions to what we know from other sources.

We know that he was born in Suffolk; Richard of Bardney omits the county but he alone mentions the village, Stow. There are three Stows in Suffolk: Stowmarket, Stow Langtoft and West Stow, all near Bury St Edmunds. The last two especially catch the eye because they were both villages owned by the monks of Bury St Edmunds, with whom Grosseteste seems to have been on friendly terms later in his career.[27] This familiarity, which nothing in his later life can explain, would be intelligible if he had been born on one of their manors.

We know from other sources that his origins were widely recognized as remarkably humble. On this point Richard of Bardney supplies details, which may well contain a large element of popular romance elaborating a well-known fact. But, even when we have made a large allowance for this, there remain some details which have a good deal to be said for them. For instance, it cannot strictly be true that as a boy he begged at the door of the *mayor* of Lincoln because there was no mayor until about 1205.[28] But the first mayor, Adam of Wigford had long been a wealthy citizen of the town, and among other charitable acts he is known to have supported a handicapped child in his household.[29] The only question is whether it is more likely that the young Grosseteste was also an object of his

---

[27] His borrowing St Basil's *Hexaëmeron* from the monks (see above, p. 46 n.) also indicates some degree of familiarity with Bury St Edmunds. For the connection between Stow Langtoft and West Stow and the monastery, see R. H. C. Davis, *The Kalendar of Abbot Samson of Bury St Edmunds*, Camden Series, R. Hist. Soc., 1954, pp. xix, 34, 36.

[28] Francis Hill, *Medieval Lincoln*, 1965, pp. 194–5, 382–3.

[29] Ibid., p. 111.

charity, or that Richard of Bardney (or his source) gratuitously invented this incident.

Then, too, it is only from Richard of Bardney that we know of Grosseteste's early schooling in Lincoln. On this point his testimony has been accepted without a murmur. But when he tells that Grosseteste went from Lincoln to Cambridge for more advanced study, no one has taken him seriously because we expect him to have aimed higher. Cambridge was certainly no summit of academic ambition; but it must have been emerging as a town with more than average opportunities for higher study, sufficient anyhow to attract some masters from Oxford during the closure of the Oxford schools from 1209 to 1214. It is entirely credible that already by about 1185 it was a place which could excite the ambition of a poor youth.

When we come to Grosseteste's career after his school days, there are more unconfirmed details. We do not know that he worked for a bishop of Salisbury, but we do know that bishops of Lincoln and Hereford had both failed to give him the security he sought, and masters in this position had often to take temporary work wherever they could find it. As for the studies which qualified him for employment in an episcopal household, Richard of Bardney has details which deserve attention. Like Gerald of Wales, he attaches special importance to his knowledge and practice of medicine: 'He studied and made known whatever virtues are hidden in trees, shrubs, flowers, herbs and seeds. He knew all the natures of beasts and of every reptile and creeping thing, and found out the songs of birds, with which he soothed the sufferings of the sick and brought them help.'[30] Grosseteste's works have many details which display his widely ranging interest in just those facts of nature which Richard of Bardney mentions—the natures of plants, trees, beasts, birds, diseases and medicines. And yet these were not the subjects which later readers, who were generally interested in problems of physics, astronomy, or theology, chiefly quoted

[30] Richard of Bardney, c. xix: 'Quicquid in arboribus, virgultis, floribus, herbis / Seminibusque latet, praecinit iste studens. / Omnes naturas pecudum cognovit, et omnis / Reptilis, et vermis omnis; et omnis avis / Invenit voces, quibus allevare solebat / Aegrorum morbos, subsidiumque dabat.' The word *praecinit* in this passage may be just a poetic flourish, but it may imply that he wrote something on the subject to be sung—similar perhaps to his long didactic poem, the *Château d'Amour*—suitable for a noble household. An interest in the songs of birds fits also with the love of music for which he was famous long after his death.

from his works. Apart from Richard of Bardney, only Gerald of Wales mentions his interest in medicine. So, late though the source is, we seem to be taken back to some primitive stratum of information.

Grosseteste's long wait for a benefice is another point in favour of Richard of Bardney's account, though the details which he gives are certainly distorted. He says that Grosseteste's first benefice was given him by the bishop of Lincoln, and he gives the name of the parish—Clifton.[31] We have no other evidence for this, and it is probable that the presentation, if it was ever made, was frustrated. Clifton was a place where this could easily happen. It was a village of small land-holders with a poorly endowed church about ten miles from the parish of Abbotsley, which the bishop gave him in 1225. The presentation to Clifton was the subject of recurring litigation throughout the first thirty years of the thirteenth century. In 1219 it was shared between two land-holders, probably the descendants of litigants who were already disputing the right of presentation in the royal court in 1201; and in 1230, the abbess of Stamford and another land-holder were in the royal court on the same business.[32] In the midst of these disputes, it may well have happened that a vacancy gave the bishop an opportunity to try to nominate his own candidate. It was only, as we have seen, through the failure of the rightful patron to exercise his right of presentation to Abbotsley that Grosseteste finally succeeded in getting a benefice; so an earlier unsuccessful initiative is by no means improbable. The alternative is that Richard of Bardney or his source invented a wholly pointless incident. Whatever the truth may be, at least he was right in saying that the bishop of Lincoln gave Grosseteste his first benefice: perhaps Clifton which failed, then Abbotsley.

He seems to be right on another point which aroused the incredulity even of his advocate, Professor Russell. Richard of Bardney says that Grosseteste became a priest when he began

---

[31] Ibid., c. xxii.

[32] The troubled history of the benefice at this time can be traced in the bishops' registers of Lincoln (Canterbury and York Society, vols. i (1909), iii (1907), iv (1908), x (1913). See esp. *Rotuli Hugonis de Welles*: i. 93, ii. 79, iii. 23; *Rotuli Roberti Grosseteste*, p. 22, gives a survey of events going back to 1215. See also *Curia Regis Rolls*, i. 436-7; ii. 69, for the dispute in 1201; viii, pp. xiii, xiv, for 1219.

to study theology and received a prebend.[33] Since we know
that he was still a deacon when he got Abbotsley in 1225,
Russell thinks this must be mistaken, on the grounds that he
had long been a theologian and presumably had received earlier benefices. But there are good reasons for thinking that his
receiving a benefice, becoming a priest, and starting to lecture
in theology are closely related in time and in motivation. So,
despite the unlikely chronology, it seems that Richard of Bardney was following a sound source.

The king's favour and influence in getting him this pre-
ferment and re-orienting his studies is another point on which
we have only the testimony of Richard of Bardney.[34] But once
more, it cannot lightly be brushed aside. Grosseteste's rapid
rise after long obscurity seems to require a belated impulse from
some outside source. Where this impulse came from cannot be
demonstrated; but it is noticeable that the beginning of his
rise from obscurity coincided with an almost forgotten but
momentous political revolution. In the years between 1221 and
1223, a group of bishops, including the bishops of Salisbury
and Lincoln, and led by the archbishop of Canterbury, Stephen
Langton, brought about the release of the young king from the
control of the guardians who had governed the country since
his accession. To achieve this end, it was necessary to get a
pronouncement from the pope that, despite his youth, the king
was fit to govern. Secrecy and speed were essential. They sent
messengers to Rome, who brought back a papal declaration
dated April 1223 that the fifteen-year-old king was old enough
to rule on his own.[35] At once the castles and bailiwicks in the
hands of the king's guardians were transferred to the control of
the archbishop (four castles), the bishop of Salisbury (five
castles), and Lincoln (one castle). The king issued his first
orders in his own name in December 1223.[36] Was the change in

[33] Richard of Bardney, c. xxi.
[34] Ibid., c. xxi.
[35] The nature of the revolution is admirably explained and its details summarized
in Powicke, *Henry III and the Lord Edward*, Oxford, 1947, i. 52–68. The reorganization
of royal government, in which the papal declaration of 1223 played a vital part, was a
long continuing process which lasted from the death of the regent, William Marshal,
in 1219 to the expulsion of Fawkes de Breauté and the confirmation of the Charters in
1225. During this period the role of Stephen Langton and the bishops was of the
greatest importance in bringing in a new and more insular balance of power.
[36] For those letters, see *Patent Rolls of the Reign of Henry III*, i, 1901, p. 417, and *Rotuli
Litterarum Clausarum (1204–27)*, 1833, i. 578.

Grosseteste's fortunes connected with this ecclesiastically organized political revolution? If he had performed some notable
service—if, even without a magic horse, he had gone to Rome
for the vital papal letters—we would have a foundation for the
account which Richard of Bardney gives of the king's interest
in his promotion, as well as an explanation of the new phase in
his career quite different from all that had gone before.

In what may seem one of his wildest flights of fantasy, Richard of Bardney associates the turning-point in Grosseteste's
career with his friendship with the young king. He was, he says,
'the king's friend; he sat at his table among his friends and he
acted as his secretary and then he became the keeper of his
secret seal.'[37] I do not know that any historian of royal administration has so much as mentioned this statement; certainly
none has treated it seriously. And yet it fits curiously well
with the circumstances of the moment when the pope declared
Henry fit to rule. Every great man had his secret seal for making
known his private will. King John had one, and he had made
much use of it outside the ordinary routine of chancery and
exchequer business. It was just the thing that the liberated
youth would want. Yet the accepted view is that he had to
wait till 1230, seven years after the papal declaration of his
independence, before he got it. The intervening years are very
obscure, and there are no documents to prove the point one
way or the other. But the story can scarcely be an invention of
Richard of Bardney's time, for by 1500 the Keeper of the Privy
Seal and the king's Secretary were distinct officers, and the
former presided over a very great and formal office of state. In
the thirteenth century however, the two names 'Secretary' and
'Keeper of the Privy Seal' were used interchangeably: they
expressed, not an office but a relationship with the king, ill-
defined, ill- documented, standing outside the normal routines
of administration.[38] The combination of the two offices in Richard of Bardney's account points back to a time when the
king was just beginning to have the means for expressing his

[37] Richard of Bardney, c. 23: 'Secretarius hic regi, custosque sigilli postea privati,
rege iubente, fuit.'

[38] For the combination of the positions of secretary and keeper of the privy seal in
the thirteenth century, see L. B. Dibden, 'Secretaries in the thirteenth and fourteenth
centuries', *EHR* xxv, 1910, 432–40; and for the origins of the privy seal, T. F. Tout,
Chapters in the Administrative History of Medieval England, 1920, i. 151–7, 206–8.

private will beyond the reach of the established offices of the kingdom: it may precisely represent the situation of the young Henry III in 1223.

These are speculations which cannot be pressed too far. But, at least they suggest that Richard of Bardney had access to sources of a period much earlier than his own day. Moreover, his account of Grosseteste's friendship with the young king gains some support from the affectionate tone of their later letters and from Grosseteste's remarkable familiarity with the families and officials who were connected with the royal court in the 1220s.[39] And, taking his account of Grosseteste's life as a whole, it has the merit of detaching him from the last vestiges of the all-too-smooth progress through the stages of an international scholarly career, which is contrary to all that we know of him. It associates him with a struggle appropriate to a poor man without a patron, who rose in the world late in life by a combination of lucky circumstances and great abilities. It is in this light that we may now turn to investigate the elements of his intellectual equipment. As a preparatory step, we must examine the resources and traditions of learning which were available to him.

[39] For his relations with the inner circle of the king's friends and officials, see below, pp. 192 (Richard Marshal), 246 (Simon de Montfort), 254 and 257 (William Raleigh). For his relations with the king, the letters preserved in Grosseteste's correspondence show their friendly familiarity, esp. *Ep.* nos. 101-4.

5

The English Scientific Tradition

IF, at least provisionally, we cut Grosseteste off from the Parisian schools, and delay his appearance in the Oxford schools till he is past middle age, and if we place the schools of Oxford and of every other English town far behind those of Paris in intellectual brilliance and refinement of method, we are left with a situation which is full of interest for Grosseteste's development. We must imagine a long struggle against lack of recognition, without a steady endowment, by a man either engaged in business—legal, perhaps medical, possibly astrological—in an ecclesiastical household, or teaching a motley collection of pupils, in circumstances which may have been conducive to intellectual individuality but were unfavourable to a steady output of learned work. We may imagine him also more dependent on the resources of an English tradition of scholarship than on the newer scholastic tradition of the Continental schools.

We have already noted that an Englishman who was cut off from the central European tradition of scholastic training paid a heavy penalty in diminished opportunities for intellectual debate and for rising to great position; also that there were compensations in the form of greater variety and opportunities for individual development. What form did these compensations take, and where were they to be found? Certainly not chiefly in the schools; rather, in the thoughts and interests of schoolmasters in their leisure hours. But most of all, they arose from the circumstances of life in monasteries, courts, and cathedral or collegiate chapters. In these communities, the common life raised problems to be solved, provoked subjects for discussion, and provided meeting places and libraries where talented men could meet, talk, and find a body of learned literature greater than that which any individual could hope to possess.

Fruitful ideas are generally in some way attached to the needs of everyday life, and the varied needs of monasteries, cathedrals and courts stimulated a considerable and many-sided literature in England in the twelfth century. This is true also of other parts of Europe, but the English productions have a distinctive blend of scientific, governmental, historical and imaginative interest. This blend was partly derived from the inherited tradition of Anglo-Saxon scholarship, and partly reflected the relative freedom of the native tradition from the new fashions of thought inspired by the great European schools. Of course, it was impossible, with so much movement between England and the Continent, for any literate person to remain quite uninfluenced by developments in scholastic thought abroad. But the means for pursuing these lines of thought with the intensity of effort and debate necessary for success were lacking; when they were transported into a provincial environment they quickly lost their edge. By contrast, the long-continuing native tradition showed a remarkable power of survival and development: of survival, because the monastic institutions of Anglo-Saxon England remained intact; of development, because the pre-Conquest interest in astronomy, chronology and natural science rapidly acquired new sources and new uses.

This tenacity was also helped by an undercurrent of positive hostility to the new forms of scholastic thought. Broadly speaking, there were three main types of hostility to scholastic thought in the twelfth century.

The first type of hostility was monastic in origin and religious in principle. It rejected scholastic theology because it did not spring from a life of religion but from the problems of secular society; because it was a problem-solving theology, rather than a theology of worship; because it encouraged worldly young men to have a good conceit of themselves and gave them a false assurance in answering theological questions in the hope of rising to positions of wealth and power, to the neglect of the humbler, slower, devotional theology of monastic life. The earliest powerful and self-conscious expression of this objection came from the old centres of monasticism in the Rhineland, most notably in the person of Rupert of Deutz.[1] But wherever there were monasteries, even monasteries hospitable to the new forms of scholastic thought, there were likely to be in them some defenders of an older kind of theology which concentrated more on elucidating the symbolism of the Bible than on dissecting and reorganizing the concepts of the Fathers.

The second form of hostility was directed against the scholastic neglect of literature and literary exercises. The main centres of this objection were the schools of northern France, not far from those which were producing the most precocious examples of early scholasticism: very roughly one might look on this division as a conflict of interests between the schools of the areas of the Loire and the Seine.[2] This literary and humane objection has a great future but it scarcely enters into the scope of our present enquiry.

The third form of hostility was directed against the scholastic cultivation of the sciences of concepts and definitions, to the neglect of the sciences of *things*—the natural sciences. The main voices of this objection came from Englishmen, most notably Adelard of Bath and Daniel of Morley, who rejected the procedures and aims of the greatest European schools on specifically scientific grounds. The lives of these two men cover the whole century. They have a special importance both in filling out the general picture of English intellectual effort, and in providing a foundation for Grosseteste's scientific work. Everything about them—their position in society, their careers, their subjects of study, their sources, and their aims—contribute towards understanding Grosseteste.

Adelard of Bath

The first of these exemplary figures, Adelard of Bath, was—to judge from his name and social position—one of those men of mixed English and Norman descent who were largely responsible for the survival of a pre-Conquest English learned

---

[1] On Rupert of Deutz's attitude to the new theology, see G. R. Evans, *Old Arts and New Theology: The Beginnings of Theology as an Academic Discipline*, 1980, 57–79; and John H. van Enghen, *Rupert of Deutz*, 1983, pp. 181–220.

[2] This type of anti-scholastic sentiment has had full justice done to it by many scholars, but by none with more vigour and sympathy than C. H. Haskins, *The Renaissance of the Twelfth Century*, 1927; and half a century earlier, in a book now largely out-dated in detail but still impressive, R. L. Poole, *Illustrations of Medieval Thought and Learning*, 1884, 2nd edn., 1920.

tradition.[3] In the earliest years of the twelfth century, or even slightly earlier, Adelard had followed the Continental trail, taking a small group of pupils to Laon, the most flourishing cathedral school of northern France at that time. Having got there and heard the most successful masters of the day, Master Anselm and his brother Ralph, he abandoned his pupils in Laon and went south to Italy and the Mediterranean in search of a different kind of knowledge. To his abandoned pupils, he gave this explanation: 'I left you in Laon, so that I could give my full attention to the work done by the Arabs, while you no less zealously imbibed the changing opinions of the French'; and later in the same letter, 'It is difficult for me to discuss the nature of animals with you, because I learnt from my masters, the Arabs, to follow the light of reason, while you are led by the bridle of authority; for what other word than "bridle" can I use to describe authority?'[4]

There are some words here of lasting importance; but the nature of their importance needs to be seen in its contemporary setting. Adelard did not intend to make a general pejorative judgement on authority as opposed to reason, or on theology as opposed to science. He simply contrasted two fields of study which differed in three respects: in subject matter, in method, and in sources. In subject-matter, the great emphasis of Laon and later of Paris was on grammar, logic and analytical theology: by contrast, Adelard wanted to study the natural sciences. In method and sources, the great advances of the northern French schools came from a minute comparison of a fairly limited range of ancient authorities, from which there emerged newly refined concepts and new groupings of concepts. *Per contra*, Adelard wanted to study the nature of things in the universe, and for this study appealed to 'reason' in contrast to authority. It would be easy to exaggerate, easy also to mock, the extent of Adelard's newly discovered 'reason', but at least

[3] The most recent general account of Adelard's life and work is by Marshall Clagett in *Dictionary of Scientific Biography*, ed. C. C. Gillespie, 1970, i. 61–4. The account by C. H. Haskins, *Studies in the History of Medieval Science* (1924, 2nd edn. with corrections 1926), 20–42, is still valuable. The edition of Adelard's later works by C. Burnett will put the whole subject of his influence in England on a firm foundation. Meanwhile, the most important autobiographical notes are in his *Quaestiones Naturales*, ed. M. Müller, *BGPMA* xxxi. 2, p. 4, and *De eodem et diverso*, ed. H. Willner, *BGPMA* iv. 1, 1903, pp. 21, 34, 49.

[4] *Quaestiones Naturales*, p. 11.

it meant that, alongside the ancient books and commentaries on the sciences, the student was from the beginning confronted with calculations of the altitude and movements of planets, measurements of angles, and precise observations of times. Adelard's own works show him slowly struggling out of the generalized philosophical tradition of Platonic science into a new world of calculation. They provide evidence of his increasing confidence in dealing with calculations which are almost totally absent from the scholastic methods which he abandoned.

With regard to sources, it must not be thought that students of grammar, logic and theology were necessarily hostile to new sources: in Adelard's own lifetime, some newly translated pages of John of Damascus provided welcome help in the definition of the Trinity, and Aristotle's *Sophistici Elenchi* were quickly absorbed into the school teaching on logic. Nevertheless, in general, the students of grammar, logic, theology and law had plenty to keep them busy in analysing and comparing old sources without feeling any great urge to seek new ones. Individual masters might be temperamentally addicted to novelty; but the corporate receptivity to new sources in these schools was sluggish, and for their main purpose rightly so.

It was in a quite different spirit that Adelard sought new sources. He did not seek to fill gaps in a body of knowledge already almost complete: he sought to revive old and forgotten sciences. The sources for these sciences were the phenomena themselves, and the guides to understanding these phenomena were ancient Greek scientific works, largely unknown in the West and chiefly to be found on the frontiers of the Latin world in Arabic translations or in Greek. The study of the phenomena themselves and of the ancient accounts of them had to go on side by side—neither could be understood without the other. The sources constantly demanded attention to the phenomena; and the phenomena were chaotic and meaningless without a guide. In the natural sciences, the dialogue was between things and books. By contrast, in grammar, logic, theology and law, the dialogue was between one book and another; they confirmed, completed, or contradicted each other, and only very occasionally required to be completed by observation of the world outside the sources.

These simple contrasts were Adelard's starting-point, and

they forced him to break away from the schools of northern France and seek new materials on the frontiers of the Arab world, in southern Italy and in the newly founded principality of Antioch. These were the places where western Christians, Greeks, and Muslims met, and where he could make contact with the continuing scientific thought of ancient Greece. When he returned from his travels, he brought with him to England perhaps some new material, but certainly a mind receptive to new methods of treating geometry and astronomy.

Before we look more deeply into the nature and inspiration of Adelard's revolt against the scholastic thought of the most famous of contemporary schools, we may briefly consider the case of our second rebel about seventy years later. By 1170, the school of Laon had long been eclipsed by the far greater intellectual pre-eminence of the schools of Paris. These schools carried to a much higher level of achievement the main methods and interests of Laon. Among the Englishmen who took the by now well-established route to Paris was a young man, Daniel of Morley.

Daniel of Morley

Daniel belonged to the class which had the resources to go abroad to study, without the incentive to follow those studies which led most directly to high office.[5] He came from a Norfolk landed family of modest standing, sufficiently well endowed to have a family benefice to which he could return when his studies were finished. Provided that he was content with this, he could follow his own inclinations in his studies. If he had wished to rise higher, he would have done well to study theology or law. But he was satisfied with what he had. He was a local man through and through; having no ambition, he was free to look beyond ambition.

His own words tell us why he rejected the studies which were transforming Europe :

[5] All of Daniel's known connections are with Norfolk, in which county he held the rectory of Flitcham mear Holkham till about 1205, acting frequently as a royal justice and in other capacities in local affairs. His name is almost invariably given as Daniel de Merlai in the records, and his more distant connections seem to be with a family from Morlaix in Calvados, Normandy, an area which supplied several families to England in the time of Henry I. The villages of Morley St Botolph and Morley St Peter in Norfolk probably preserve the English form of his name and point to the area in which the family had its main possessions.

I found brutish men in the schools, who assumed an appearance of grave authority. On the benches in front of them, they had heavy tomes containing the teachings of Ulpian in golden letters. In their hands they held pencils poised to mark their books reverently with asterisks and obelisks. They sat as silent as statues; and this was well, for they seemed wise only by being silent; when they spoke, their words were infantile.[6]

Evidently, therefore, Daniel found himself in a class studying in the *Digest* the deeper questions of Roman Law, the hand-maid of canon law. He was disgusted with what he saw. He had no desire to become like these men, poring over texts and content to acquire no more than a nodding acquaintance with the natural sciences—the sciences which, besides their great practical advantages, threw light directly on the Scriptures. So he went off to Toledo, where the wisest philosophers of the world were to be heard, and where the teaching of the Arabs, 'wholly devoted to the natural sciences', could be studied.[7]

It will be seen that there is a distinct similarity between Daniel's criticism of the teaching at Paris in about 1170 and Adelard's criticism of the teaching at Laon sixty or seventy years earlier. Daniel introduced a different motive for studying the natural sciences from that of Adelard, namely the help they could give in interpreting the Bible—the oldest motive of all in western Christendom. But this did not prevent his sharing Adelard's enthusiasm for the study of astronomy for astrological purposes. What they both objected to was the bookishness of the scholastic system, the exclusive concentration on the analysis of a limited range of authorities, and the neglect of the world of natural phenomena. They both sought release from these limitations by contact with Arabic learning, and that meant in practice a renewed contact with the stream of Greek scientific learning which had never found a home in the Latin world.

Like Adelard before him, Daniel later returned to England.

[6] Daniel of Morley, *Liber de naturis inferiorum et superiorum*, ed. G. Maurach, *Mittellateinisches Jahrbuch*, xiv, 1979, pp. 204–53.

[7] The words of this emphatic statement deserve careful study: 'Cum hoc, inquam, in hunc modum [*i. e. the manner of study in Paris described above*] se habere deprehenderem, ne et ego simile damnum incurrerem, artes quae scripturas illuminant non in transitu salutandas vel sub compendio pretereundas mecum sollicita deliberatione tractabam. Sed quoniam doctrina Arabum, quae in quadrivio fere tota existit, maxime his diebus apud Toletum celebratur, illuc ut sapientiores mundi philosophos audirem festinanter properavi' (ibid. , p. 6).

He brought with him a precious collection of books on a wider range of natural sciences than those which had attracted Adelard. The available texts of ancient sciences had expanded very greatly since Adelard had broken through the barriers of Western learning. But the price to be paid was the same as before. Daniel, like Adelard, forfeited any claim he might have had to the highest offices in the Church. Both men preferred their intellectual interests to their careers. On his return to England Adelard seems to have settled down in Wiltshire. Probably he held some small position in the royal government, for in 1130 he had a local tax exemption, which was a common perquisite of men in the royal service.[8] Daniel too settled down to a long obscurity in his family benefice in Norfolk. He sat on local inquests and acted as a local justice, and died in about 1210. Perhaps he was married. If so, he was the last of his line of married rectors, for his successor left the benefice to a local monastery.[9]

Alfred of Shareshill

To these two examples of men who combined a provincial career with a deeply committed interest in science, we may add a third—Alfred of Shareshill. He has a special interest for us because he was more nearly Grosseteste's contemporary and introduced into England some hitherto unknown sources which Grosseteste certainly used.

The details of Alfred's career are almost entirely unknown. His name implies that he came from the village of Shareshill in Staffordshire, and his whole life, so far as we can trace it, was connected with this county and the diocese of Lichfield in which

---

[8] *Pipe Roll 31 Henry I*, ed. J. Hunter, 1833 (repr. ed. C. Johnson, 1929), p. 22. On the official position which this entry suggests, see R. L. Poole, *The Exchequer in the Twelfth Century*, Oxford, 1912, pp. 56-7.

[9] J. C. Russell, *Isis*, xviii, 1932-3, pp. 14-25, has traced the references to Daniel of Morley in the Pipe Rolls and *Curia Regis* Rolls from *c.*1180 to *c.*1205, and it is very likely that these refer to our scholar: the dates fit and the records are coherent. Further references can be found in the *Feet of Fines* and in the charters of Flitcham in *Hist. MSS Commission, Various Collections*, iv. 313, 316-17, nos. 703-37. Daniel was rector of Flitcham in Norfolk and active in local affairs; but shortly after 1205 he was succeeded by John of Morley, who is described as rector and patron of the church. John, who seems to have taken some kind of monastic vow, gave the rectory and its glebe to his projected priory. The plan was finally carried out after his death and the clerical dynasty came to an end.

it lay.[10] It is evident from his works that he spent some years in Spain studying the scientific works which were available there, and he learnt enough Arabic to understand and translate into Latin the Arabic versions of Greek texts. One of the works which he translated was a pseudo-Aristotelian work on the nature of plants, which he sent to a certain Master Roger who was a canon of Hereford.[11] Partly, no doubt, on account of its (false) attribution to Aristotle, but even more for the unusual interest of its subject-matter, it had a very wide circulation in the later Middle Ages. It was certainly used by Grosseteste, for several of his speculations about the differences between plants and animals—their life, their food, their souls, their powers of reproduction, and so on—can be traced back to hints in Alfred's translation. From every point of view, it was a notable work, not least because both the Greek and Arabic texts are now lost, and Alfred's translation was the only form in which this work circulated under Aristotle's name almost to the present day.

We are not, however, at present concerned with Alfred's considerable contribution to the scientific knowledge of Western Europe, but only with the circumstances and obscurity of his life. He was clearly well known to his scholarly contemporaries in England, and he had very close connections with Alexander Nequam during the time when Alexander was teaching at Oxford in the 1190s.[12] But we know of no school to

[10] His name is variously mutilated in the sources, but there seems no doubt that the Staffordshire village of Shareshill, ten miles from Lichfield, lies behind all the variants, and a canonry at Lichfield is the only benefice which he is known to have held. The most recent studies of his life and writings are by J. K. Otto in *Viator*, iii, 1972, 275-9; and vii, 1976, 197-209. Apart from the internal evidence of his works, the only document in which he appears is a charter of Ralph Neville, dean of Lichfield 1214-22 in BL MS Harleian 4799, ff. 59ᵛ-62, an enormous interpolated document which needs further study. His works and translations were the most widely studied of all the works of English scientists before Grosseteste. J. C. Russell's article on 'Hereford and Arabic Science in England, c.1175-1200' in *Isis*, xviii, 1932, was the early study which pointed in the right direction.

[11] For some brief but illuminating remarks on the history of the *De Plantis* with a translation of the text, see E. S. Forster in the *Works of Aristotle*, ed W. D. Ross, vol. vi, *Opuscula*, Oxford, 1913. Alfred's dedication of this work to Roger (of Hereford) is printed in *Nicolai Damasceni De Plantis*, ed. E. H. F. Meyer, 1841.

[12] Alfred's main work *De Motu Cordis* was dedicated to 'Magister magnus Alexander Nequam', with the statement that it had been undertaken chiefly at Alexander's instigation. Since Alexander is addressed simply as 'magister' and not as canon or abbot, the work presumably dates from the years before c.1197 when he left Oxford to become a canon of Cirencester.

which Alfred himself was attached, and his position in society remains an almost complete mystery. We know of no official position which he held; and such advancement as he achieved seems to have been in his native county of Staffordshire. Almost certainly he ended his life as a canon of Lichfield, the diocese in which he was born. As with Adelard and Daniel of Morley, the price of a long intellectual outreach was a restricted and unknown life. When he sent his translation of the *De Plantis* to Roger of Hereford he wrote as one torn between the highest aspirations and the lowest expectation of recognition, quoting Empedocles (a name he had learnt from Aristotle's scientific works) on the blessedness of despising affluence and desiring future felicity and mental illumination, and concluding with an appeal for a fair hearing: 'Do not judge this work by its size, but consider the difficulty of the subject matter, and the labour of translating it from the florid style which is customary in Arabic. Pray read it carefully.'[13] We see here the provincial innovator pleading for attention—'do not be deceived by the modest appearance of the gift or its donor'—the plea of men whose work has brought them no glory in the world.

II. SCOPE AND LIMITS OF SCIENTIFIC THOUGHT

All these men were sufficiently wealthy to have gone to any of the great European schools, and sufficiently talented to have profited from the elaborate intellectual disciplines which they offered. Yet they chose instead to go to the frontiers of Christendom to seek a different kind of knowledge. They abandoned the hope of proficiency in a great new system of knowledge and the expectation of great positions in society. Adelard of Bath and Daniel of Morley were conscious of what they were renouncing and why they renounced it. It was a momentous decision. They were opting out of the greatest of all contemporary enterprises—the enterprise of extracting a coherent body of knowledge from the Bible, the Fathers, the Councils and decrees of popes, from the grammarians and logicians of

---

[13] Meyer, op. cit., 1; 'In quo quidem opusculo non sedule quantitatem velim ut consideres, sed tantam rerum difficultatem miro quodam verborum compendio comprehensam, quantocumque sudore ex tam fluido loquendi genere, quod apud Arabes est, expressa sit, attentius, si libet, inspicias.'

the Latin world. What did they object to? What did they seek to put in its place?

Adelard of Bath and Daniel of Morley give their own answers to these two questions, and though we could have wished for some fuller explanations, we must begin with what they tell us. Adelard claimed to prefer the 'reason' of the Arabs to the 'authority' of the schools of Laon; and to this he added his preference for the 'solidity' of what he could learn from the Arabs to the 'fluctuating opinions' of the French schools. Daniel's protest was against the brutish dullness of poring over the minutiae of texts instead of seeking knowledge of the natural sciences. In one way or another, they both sought knowlege of *things* rather than of *books*, of nature rather than concepts, and (if we follow Adelard) knowledge which came from reason rather than authority.

On the surface, these complaints seem singularly ill-judged. So far as 'authority' was concerned, the natural sciences depended on the authority of ancient writers quite as much as the theological, legal and grammatical-logical studies of Laon and Paris. And, as for 'reason', there was certainly more scope for reasoning in scholastic studies than in the sciences of the Arabs. We have only to turn to discussions on almost any Biblical text, and compare them with discussions about the operations of the brain or the heart, to be convinced of this. Nor is it difficult to find the explanation. A text like 'Thou shalt not kill' had to be set in the context of several other texts, some of which allowed killing on certain conditions, while others examined the principle on which the general prohibition was based. The prohibition also had its setting in actual experience, and in a hierarchy of divine commands. So any discussion of the text was an immensely intricate exercise in rational discrimination. In contrast to this, the operations of brain or heart were known only from accounts by authors whose sources of information were extremely obscure, and whose facts could scarcely be tested. The grounds of discussion were therefore quite different in the two cases: in the first, they were full and well prepared; in the latter, they were sketchy and uncertain.

So far as method was concerned, therefore, all the advantages were heavily weighted in favour of the scholastic disciplines. The real advantage, which Adelard and Daniel were seeking by their long journeys and the sacrifice of their careers, was a knowledge of nature which they could not find at home.

This statement of their aims at once invites another criticism. It is false to suggest that scholastic thought was indifferent to nature. Quite the contrary: one of the greatest scholastic achievements of the twelfth century was to enlarge, and to enlarge very greatly, the operation of nature both in thought and in experience. In almost every area of life, events that in earlier centuries had been ascribed to supernatural causes, which required to be dealt with by supernatural processes, were given a natural origin and a natural remedy. Even in such essentially supernatural events as baptism, the eucharist, and penance, the supernatural element had been carefully distinguished from the natural components which fell within the scope of human regulation. The general tendency of scholastic thought was everywhere to enlarge the scope of nature.

And yet, the nature which had been enlarged by twelfth-century scholastic thought was quite different from the nature which Adelard and Daniel and other travellers went to find in Spain, Sicily, and still further afield. Scholastic nature was a highly intellectualized concept, almost or entirely synonymous with reason. It did nothing to promote the study of the actual operations of the natural world, except in human behaviour and in the sciences of the mind. In this context, the phenomena of the natural world presented themselves mainly as temptations or obstacles to be overcome. Men who were trained in the scholastic tradition studied the natural world mainly with a view to tracing the limitations within which human minds and wills had to operate. They classified temptations, and provided remedies and penalties which would help to free reason from the constraints of the passions, and from the pressures of the external world. They approached the phenomena of nature like mariners exploring a hostile coast, not with a view to landing and surveying the country, but with a view to providing navigational signs and precautions against shipwreck. They were regulators, not explorers.

But the men with whom we are concerned were explorers. They wanted to understand the things of nature, not the concept of nature. And the difference between their view of nature and that of scholastic thought also entailed a difference in their view of the role of authorities and reason in their pursuit of knowledge. Certainly, nearly everything they knew about nature came from ancient books, like everything that theologians knew about theology, but their methods of using this knowledge were different. The sciences gave less opportunity for dialectic, and more for observation, however fragmentary and ill-conducted. The star catalogues of the Arabs, and the measurements of angles attached to the new translations of Euclid, were not simply visual aids to understanding a written text, like the diagrams of syllogisms in Boethius's treatises on logic: they were representations of the reality from which the written text was one step further removed. To understand the text it was necessary to understand the diagrams and calculations; and to understand them it was necessary to look at the sky.

The readers of these new scientific translations had as yet very little idea of the method of scientific enquiry. That was to come later; and to this development Grosseteste was to make an important contribution. But from the beginning it was clear that a method was required different from the intensive study of texts along the lines which Adelard had observed at Laon and Daniel at Paris. It was not so much the texts which needed careful study, as the figures and diagrams; and not so much the figures and diagrams, as the things which they represented. It was necessary to wait for a clear night, to take an astrolabe, and go out and measure angles of elevation and note the position of the stars; and then return to the tables made by astronomers in Toledo; and then discover the number of hours and minutes by which the Toledo tables needed to be adjusted for the latitude (or was it longitude or both?) of London or Chester. These things needed to be puzzled out, and this could only be done by frequent reference to a general plan of the heavens. The reasoning which guided these operations followed different lines from those commonly practised in the schools. It was reasoning which was more fragmentary, and yet, as Adelard justly observed, less a matter of opinion. Its practical application lay in astrological prediction. This was more hazardous than the dialectic of the schools. Yet, in principle, it was more capable of verification, because what was predicted could be verified in this world, whereas the statements of theology could only be verified in eternity.

Scientific study was of course not new in the twelfth century. It was in fact much older than scholasticism. But it had not moved forward for several centuries. At the beginning of the century, the works of Bede and Isidore of Seville still filled a large part of the scientific horizon and met most of the scientific needs of the day. Bede was the still unsurpassed master of the chronological sciences, which were based on astronomy and concerned with the movements of sun and moon through the heavens. Isidore of Seville was still the master of all the natural knowledge of created things—beasts, reptiles, birds, fishes, plants and stones—inherited from the ancient world through Pliny's *Natural History* and other encyclopaedias. In England, these two branches of scientific knowledge, drawing on the same old sources, continued to be prominent throughout the twelfth century, and a brief account of their development down to the time when Grosseteste received them from his predecessors will provide an introduction to understanding what he made of them. We may begin with the natures of earthly creatures, and then consider the stars.

1. The natures of earthly things

The commonest way in which the natures of things were known to Englishmen in the twelfth century was not from schoolbooks but from a variety of illustrated books—herbals, bestiaries, lapidaries. Of course, it was not only Englishmen who knew nature chiefly from these sources, but England seems to have been peculiarly rich in such books and to have continued to produce and export them throughout the twelfth century. The real importance of these volumes as repositories of scientific information has been largely missed because their illustrations are remarkably beautiful, and this has caused them to be looked on as the medieval equivalent of coffee-table books. Even M. R. James, who did more than anyone to bring these works out of obscurity and to establish their sources and provenance, was chiefly interested in their artistic merits: 'But for its pictures,' he wrote of one of the most complete examples of its kind, 'I do not think that this book could have gained or kept any popularity. Its literary merit is *nil*, and its scientific value (even when it has been most extensively purged of fable and reinforced with soberer stuff) sadly meagre.'[14]

This is misleading. These books were compilations of the learning of the past, drawn from the most venerable writers of antiquity, about a large part of the created universe. They were encyclopaedias of all that was known about the physical world, and the moral, medical and allegorical significance of all God's creatures in the service of Man. The illustrations were aids for identifying the subjects, a means of ready reference to the characteristics of each species. Certainly these books were not made to be studied in the schools, for they did not deal with a school subject; but they were made for study, not casual entertainment. Their main substance was old, but considerable efforts were made, chiefly in England, to add descriptions and moralizations from up-to-date authors like Gerald of Wales and Peter of Cornwall.[15]

The bestiaries were the most important branch of this literature. Of these, some forty English manuscripts have survived, the majority of the twelfth century, and they show that scholarly men were at work on them, adding new items and extending their subject-matter to include trees, stones, birds, fishes, seas and rivers, mountains and lakes, until a single volume could provide a complete view of the main creatures and features of the physical world with an allegorical interpretation of their natures.[16] We do not know whether Grosseteste owned such a volume, but it is certain that he was deeply influenced by this body of knowledge.

There were other sources in which a similar body of information could be found, notably Isidore's *Etymologies*, Pliny's *Natural History*, and Bede's *De Natura Rerum*. Grosseteste made extensive use of the first of these works. Pliny had been too well pillaged by Isidore to enjoy a wide circulation, but a new

[14] M. R. James, *The Bestiary* (with reproduction of CUL MS Ii. 4. 26), Roxburghe Club, 1928, pp. 1–2. Despite his misjudgement about the scientific value of the bestiaries, James's work, and especially his classification and location of MSS, is of fundamental importance for the study of the English tradition.

[15] The growing ambitions of compilers in their enlargements of these volumes are well described by James especially in connection with the late twelfth-century MSS BL Harl. 4751, Royal 12 F xiii, and Bodleian MS Bodley 764, which have the additions mentioned above.

[16] These additions are found in Gonville and Caius College, Cambridge, MS 109, in St John's College, Oxford, MSS 61 and 178, and in University College, Oxford, MS 120.

abbreviation of his work was made in about 1170 by Robert of Cricklade, prior of St Frideswide's in Oxford, and dedicated to King Henry II.[17] Although it had little success, it showed that there was still an interest in gathering information about the natural world from this much plundered compilation.

Another indication of general interest in the properties and allegorical meanings of natural objects is the unexpected popularity in England in the late twelfth century of the ninth-century compilation by Rabanus Maurus, De Naturis Rerum.[18] This work added vast quantities of allegorical interpretations to the facts reported by Pliny and Isidore; and, we know that Grosseteste possessed a copy.[19]

These were the main sources of information about the creatures and objects of the natural world before about 1190. Most of them aimed at giving not only information but interpretations. They expressed a view of the universe which Grosseteste made the starting-point of his theology: the view that the natural world is a mirror of the mind of the Creator and a repository of warnings, precepts and examples useful for human life.

As an area of study, the greatest weakness of the natural science displayed in these sources was the absence of new ma-

[17] The abbreviation survives in three manuscripts, BL Royal 15 C xiv, Eton College 134, and Hereford Cathedral P. 4. viii. It is analysed with excerpts by K. Rück, SB München, 1902, 195-285. Its two prefaces, one to King Henry II, the other to students in monasteries and schools (pr. by Rück, pp. 265-6), describe its aims: it is intended as a guide to the natural history of the inhabited world, its peoples, animals, fishes, trees, herbs, stones, and gems, with their medicinal uses and virtues. In brief, it is a work of general usefulness for non-experts. Rück in his book Die Geographie und Ethnographie des Naturalis Historia des Plinius (Munich, 1903) points out the important place of England, and especially Anglo-Saxon England, in the transmission of the text of Pliny. Another abbreviation of Pliny by an otherwise unknown English scholar, Retinaldus, is preserved in Balliol College, Oxford, MS 146A and in Wolfenbüttel MS Extrav. 160, 'both written in England'. (See L. D. Reynolds on the transmission of Pliny's Natural History in Texts and Transmission: A Survey of the Latin Classics, ed. L. D. Reynolds, Oxford, 1983, pp. 314-15.)

[18] Dr R. W. Hunt pointed out its unusual popularity in England in the twelfth and early thirteenth centuries are evidenced by surviving copies in BL MS Royal 12 G xiv (from St Albans), Corpus Christi College, Cambridge, MS 11, St John's College, Oxford, MSS 5 (from Reading), and 88, New College, Oxford, MS 159, Trinity College, Oxford, MS 64 (from Gloucester), and Worcester Cathedral MS F. 21. (Bodleian Library Record, iv, 1953, p. 253.)

[19] His copy has not survived, but a thirteenth-century MS which belonged to the Oxford Franciscans contains corrections from a liber episcopi, which in this context can only mean Robert Grosseteste. For the marginalia found in this MS, Laud misc. 746, see above, p. 40 n., and for its provenance, Callus, 1955, p. 126.

terial. The compilations might grow in their range of subjects, their organization might be improved, and a few details added from ancient sources which had not been fully exploited by earlier compilers. But there was no real movement. This may seem strange, since the whole world was open to observation. But observation is unproductive without some system of enquiry or guidance for the observer, and these were lacking. The only notable new observations from real life, so far as I know, came from Gerald of Wales. Gerald was a man who took great pride and pleasure in what he had seen while he was in Ireland with Prince John in 1185. He recorded these details in his *Topography* of Ireland, and he added traditional details and spiritual interpretations to his observations. But, above all, he observed. For instance, he says that he saw as many eagles in Ireland as you would see hawks anywhere else. Here was a genuine observation. But when he came to describe the creatures he had seen he was apt to fall back on the stock of traditional knowledge preserved in the bestiaries—for instance, the ability of eagles to look at the sun, their longevity, and their habit of flying upwards till they scorched their wings.[20] To these 'facts' he added spiritual interpretations which were also to be found in bestiaries: their ability to look at the sun represented the grace given to contemplatives to see God's nature, and so on. He quickly found it easier to add new interpretations than to supply new facts, and in the later editions of his work he greatly enlarged the number of interpretations without adding to the number of observations. Archbishop Baldwin of Canterbury especially admired those additions and asked Gerald if he had any authority for them. The author proudly claimed them as his own, and the archbishop was suitably impressed.[21]

We should think more highly of him if he had trusted his eyes more; but his preference for adding symbolic inventions rather than observed details is important. It shows that it was much more difficult, and seemed much less useful, to see things correctly than to invent moral interpretations of things imperfectly seen. It also shows that allegorical interpretation was

[20] *Topographia Hibernica*, i, c. 13, in *Giraldi Cambrensis Opera*, RS, v, 1867, pp. 39-45, where the proliferation of allegorical interpretations between the date of the first recension *c.*1186 and of the last about twenty years later can be clearly observed.

[21] *De Rebus a se gestis*, i, c. 20, *Opera*, i, 1861, pp. 79-80.

the main purpose of studying nature. Gerald had started well as an observer during his visit to Ireland in 1185-6; but later, as he fell increasingly under the influence of the Parisian theologians, he seems to have lost the power or will to make original observations. He became absorbed in his lawsuits, and he lost the brightness of his early inspiration.[22] The interest, therefore, of Gerald's elaborations, and Archbishop Baldwin's reception of them, lies in revealing the small amount of encouragement there was to add new observations to the body of natural knowledge. The whole emphasis, at least in the official and cosmopolitan circles in which Gerald moved during most of his later years, lay in the multiplication of spiritual interpretations which could be used by preachers and moralists.

This tendency not only discouraged new observations, but distorted observations when they were made. We can see this in Gerald's account of a bird almost unknown to traditional science. In Ireland he saw ospreys, a bird only briefly mentioned in Pliny and Isidore, and not at all in Rabanus Maurus's encyclopaedic work. Gerald described how he had often watched the bird fishing.[23] It hovered over a stream until it saw a fish. At once it dived into the water, guiding itself with one foot while with the other it seized the fish. Then it rose from the water, retracting its free claw while the other held its prey. This was well observed. But at this point interpretation took over. Gerald got the impression that the two feet were differently formed—the one open and menacing, the other closed and peaceful; and in later editions he added an interpretation of this supposed contrast, comparing the osprey's irregular construction to the devil beckoning with one hand while he used the other to destroy his victim.

Here we have an example of observation quickly leading to a symbolic interpretation which discouraged further observation. Another example of the search for new scientific knowledge being swamped by the search for spiritual significance can be found in the work of Gerald's younger contemporary Alexander Nequam. His *De Naturis Rerum* contains no new scientific thoughts or observations; it is a huge collection of spiritual

interpretations of natural phenomena taken from a large number of sources, including the very recent work of Gerald himself.
Nequam had evidently thought deeply about the allegories of
nature and he was willing to use new information when he
could find it, but his search for allegory did not stimulate a
search for the facts on which it was based. He was content to
enlarge Gerald's account of ospreys by comparing their brilliant display and predatory habits with the attractive appearance of the rich in flattering the poor in order to plunder
them.[24] This had a fine contemporary relevance for preachers,
but it was not a scientific advance. Indeed, in this whole area
of natural science, the scholarly efforts of the late twelfth century were concentrated rather on making scientific knowledge
available for edification than on finding more facts of nature.
As Nequam himself wrote in his preface, his purpose in describing the natures of things was not to explore nature but to
ascend from the study of natural properties to their Creator: 'I
do not wish the reader to think that I am investigating the
natures of things in order to write a philosophical or physical
work: I am writing a moral (that is to say, allegorical) treatise.'[25]

This statement is an accurate expression of the aim of most
students of the natures of earthly things at the end of the twelfth
century. On a foundation of ancient knowledge which had
scarcely changed, a towering structure of moral and spiritual
significance had been built. Their aim was to add to the super-
structure, not to enlarge the foundations.

2. The Stars

We now turn to the other main branch of twelfth-century
science in its English context: astronomy, which had its basis
in arithmetic and geometry, and its practical application in
astrology. Here the development is substantially different
from that which we have just observed in the study of natural
objects:[26] the role of symbolism is much reduced, the practical

---

[24] Alexander Neckam (*sic* for Nequam), *De Naturis Rerum*, ed. Thomas Wright, RS,
1863, p. 108.

[25] Ibid., pp. 2–3.

[26] The most useful survey of the new literature which became available in the twelfth
century is M.-T. d'Alverny, 'Translations and Translators', in Benson and Constable,
1982, 421–62.

applications are more extensive and urgent, and the flow of new material and of new scientific techniques is much more rapid and revolutionary.

Nearly everything that was known about astronomy in England in the early twelfth century came from a few ancient sources. There are several handsome manuscripts of the period from 1070 to 1120 from Peterborough, Thorney, Crowland and other Old English monasteries which preserve impressive records of this body of knowledge.[27] They demonstrate both its continuing interest and its lack of development since the days of Bede. The reason for the continuing interest was the same as Bede's—the establishing of a firm chronology and the needs of the liturgical calendar. For these purposes, a simple and definite body of knowledge about the movements of the sun through the zodiac, and of the moon in relation to the sun, was essential. This area of study continued to elicit a steady stream of works on the calendar down to the time of Grosseteste and Roger Bacon, who both wrote treatises on *Computus*—that is to say, on the calculations necessary for chronology. The subject retained all its ancient importance, because the need for calendars can never be outgrown. But, apart from the growing discrepancy between astronomical time and the ecclesiastical calendar, which became conspicuous in the thirteenth century and was ultimately to lead to the reform of Pope Gregory XIII in 1582, there were no significant new problems relating to the calendar to be solved.

The case was quite different in the other great area of astronomical prediction, which was concerned, not with the regularities of the calendar, but with plagues, famines, wars, earthquakes and other natural dangers and disasters which were thought to arise from conjunctions of the planets. Almost no one doubted that useful predictions of these events were theoretically possible. But they required vastly more complicated calculations of all planetary movements than predicting the date of Easter. These more elaborate predictions

[27] These manuscripts are now very well known, but for our present purpose I may refer to an account I gave of them in *Medieval Humanism and other Studies*, 1970, 165–8. This body of knowledge was not yet outmoded at the end of the twelfth century, as can be seen in a *réchauffé* of it in an English MS described by H. Beber, 'An Illustrated Medieval School-book of Bede's *De Natura Rerum*', *Journal of the J. Walters Art Gallery*, xix, Baltimore, 1956–7, pp. 19–20, 65–7.

had not been much practised in Western Europe before the twelfth century, partly because there was no instrument for making sufficiently accurate measurements of planetary movements, partly because—mainly owing to the influence of St Augustine[28]—astrological predictions were theologically under a cloud. These were mutually supporting disabilities, and they both disappeared at the same time, in the first quarter of the twelfth century.

The technical disability disappeared with the possession of an instrument which made precise observations of the position of heavenly objects possible—the astrolabe. The first Englishman—and one of the first Europeans—to own one was Walcher, prior of Malvern, who already had an astrolabe in 1092. From this beginning, and perhaps from this source, its use spread to several scholars in the general area of Worcester, Hereford, Malvern and Bristol during the next thirty years.[29] At the same time, despite St Augustine's strong and frequently expressed antipathy, the theological objection to astrology crumbled. For Augustine, consulting the stars for information about future events was on the same level as consulting the entrails of animals: they were practices, not only irrational in themselves, but an affront to divine Providence and human liberty. Besides, he argued, they did not work, as anyone could see who compared the varying fortunes of twins born under the same stars. These views, which seemed decisive so long as they could not be challenged in practice, looked different to men with an astrolabe in their hands. In the first place, it was clearly absurd to equate the movements of celestial bodies, which ordered the days and years and poured down light and life on living creatures, with the obscene probings of steaming entrails. And, as for the twins of identical birth but differing careers, who could foretell what differences of planetary influence a more accurate measurement of the moment of birth might reveal? Worse contradictions than this were being regularly resolved by careful analysis in the schools. No doubt there were knotty problems which would not easily be resolved, but the

---

[28] See Augustine, *De diversis quaestionibus*, PL 40, 28-9; *De Doctrina Christiana*, ii. 22, PL 34, 51-2.

[29] Once more, it may suffice at present to refer to my remarks in *Medieval Humanism*, pp. 168-71.

twelfth century was a period of hope, and the attitude to astrology changed quite quickly and fundamentally in the middle years of the century. Thereafter, and for a long time to come, the forces favouring an expansion of astrology with a view to its practical usefulness were too strong to be resisted.

I have already mentioned some of the Englishmen who took a leading part in this expansion. Adelard of Bath was one of the first to bring Arabic star-tables into England. Then, from about 1120 onwards, he and a group of scientists working chiefly in the areas of Worcester, Malvern and Hereford proceeded to translate, extend and adapt these tables to the latitude of English towns. These men were followed by others whose names and works have gradually been brought to light in the last sixty years by the efforts of many scholars, notably C. H. Haskins and Mlle d'Alverny.[30] The twelfth century scholars mainly responsible for those developments after Adelard of Bath—Robert of Ketton, Robert of Chester, Roger of Hereford, Daniel of Morley, Alfred of Shareshill—came from widely scattered parts of England, but an unusually high concentration of effort has been found in the area of Worcester and Hereford, with centres of study in monasteries, cathedral chapters and secular courts. These studies could not easily be fitted into any scholastic curriculum, but their chronological and liturgical uses still gave them a place in monastic studies; and their predictive possibilities, besides appealing to monks like everyone else, were of special interest in the courts of magnates. The nature of this interest may be judged from the dedication of an astronomical work to Robert, earl of Leicester, in about 1140:

Philosophers have defined astronomy as 'the science of the laws and natures of the stars'; but some of them, without abandoning this definition, have gone further and defined it as 'the system of movements and conjunction of the fixed stars and planets by which it is possible to know not only the present, but the past and the future.'[31]

---

[30] See M.-T. d'Alverny's survey mentioned above, n. 26.

[31] From the preface addressed to Robert, earl of Leicester, by Raymond of Marseille in his treatise on the astrolabe in BL MS Royal 12 E xxv, f. 172ᵛ. Mlle d'Alverny drew attention to the importance of this work (op. cit. , pp. 447, 458), and she and E. Poulle are preparing an edition. Raymond's connection with England is otherwise unrecorded, but it should be noted that the epithet 'of Marseille' is no more than a modern editorial convenience to denote that his astronomical table is based on Marseille. On his work, see also E. Poulle, 'Le Traité d'astrolabe de R. de Marseille', *Studi Medievali*, 3rd ser., v, 1964, 866–900; also Haskins, *Medieval Science*, pp. 96–8.

It was the last of these possibilities which chiefly commended the study to such people as the earl of Leicester. At the time when he received this work, he—like every other important English baron—had to take great risks in deciding to support one or other of the two claimants to the crown, King Stephen or the Empress Matilda. The earl of Leicester got his choices right. He supported King Stephen during almost the whole reign. Then at the last minute he made the leap to the other side. Was he helped in these decisions by a knowledge of the stars? We shall never know; but he needed all the knowledge he could get in committing his own life and limbs, the fortunes of his family, and the future of all his descendants to an act of feudal treachery. Who would not seek the help of the stars in matters of such moment, when everyone agreed that even the simple operation of bleeding was more efficaciously performed under some stellar influences than others? We have only to look at the English chronicles of the late twelfth century to see that men of all ranks in society expected great things of this new source of knowledge.

Prophecy was everywhere in the air as a means of foreseeing events and averting calamities. Prophecies came from all kinds of sources—from dreams, from visions, from the Bible, from the prophecies of Merlin; but intellectually by far the best supported predictions came from the stars. This appears very clearly in Daniel of Morley's account of his reception when he returned to England after studying the works of the Arabic philosophers in Toledo. His old friend John of Oxford, whose long years of labour in the king's service had earned him the bishopric of Norwich, questioned him about the knowledge which he had acquired in Toledo and especially about astronomy. Daniel gave an optimistic account of its wider possibilities:

Since the astronomer knows about future events, he can repel or avoid disasters such as civil wars or famine, earthquakes, conflagrations, floods, and general pestilences of men and beasts. Even if he cannot altogether escape them, he can prepare for them in advance, which will make them more tolerable than they are to those who are overtaken unawares. I interject this [*he adds*] to refute the errors of those who malign the studies of astronomers.[32]

---

[32] Daniel of Morley, op. cit. , p. 239.

The maligners of astronomy were by this time in full retreat, and most men were only too willing to listen to what the astronomers could tell them. The year 1184 provides evidence of this Europe-wide interest and of the English contribution towards satisfying it. It had become clear to students of astronomy that a threatening series of dangerous planetary conjunctions was to be expected in 1186. From places as far apart as Cordova and Chester experts started to make calculations to find the exact time, the likely severity, and if possible the nature of the dangers ahead. Alongside calculations and predictions made in Cordova and Toledo, there circulated two English efforts, the first by William, a clerk of the constable of Chester castle, the second by Anselm, a monk of Worcester.[33] It is noteworthy that by far the most extensive and detailed measurements of the impending conjunctions are those of the astrologer of the constable of Chester.

As the anticipated crisis approached, the archbishop of Canterbury ordained a three-day fast throughout his Province. What happened? There was a violent hailstorm in Kent and floods in Wales. In October 1187 Jerusalem fell. Too late! If it had fallen a year earlier it could have been hailed as the vindication of the astrologers' science. In the event, the enemies of astrology held that nothing significant had happened. Gervase, the monastic chronicler in Canterbury, who hated the archbishop, joyfully reported that an abundance of corn and general prosperity had confounded the prophets, and that the only tempests had been those which the archbishop himself created within his own Church.[34]

This kind of disappointment was to dog the footsteps of the astrologers for the rest of the Middle Ages. But science never suffers from mere lack of success. Failure only proves the need for still greater minuteness of observation and accuracy of calculation. This was the position in Grosseteste's youth. So far,

---

[33] Roger of Howden, observing affairs from his rectory at Howden in Yorkshire, and still in touch with royal officials with whom he had worked during his years in the service of Henry II, added to his Chronicle the texts which were available to him. See *Gesta Regis Henrici secundi Benedicti abbatis*, ed. W. Stubbs, RS 1867, i. 324–8; and, for his later edition, *Chronica Rogeri de Hoveden*, ed. W. Stubbs, RS, 1869, ii. 290–6. For Howden and his Chronicle, see David Corner, 'The *Gesta Regis Henrici Secundi* and *Chronica* of Roger, Parson of Howden', *Bulletin of the Institute of Historical Research*, lvi, London, 1983, 125–44.

[34] Gervase of Canterbury, *Opera Historica*, ed. W. Stubbs, RS, 1879, i. 335.

astrology had scored no resounding success, but there was still plenty of hope and scope for improved techniques of investigation and greater subtlety of interpretation. The air was thick with predictions. The young Grosseteste certainly shared the common belief in the efficacy of astrology. The earliest piece of hand-writing, which can with some confidence be ascribed to him, is an inscription on a diagram which pin-points the conjunctions of Mars and Saturn and of Saturn and Jupiter in 1216.[35] These were the same conjunctions that had alarmed Europe in 1186; so no doubt astrologers were warning their patrons of evils to be expected from this new threat, as the clerk of the constable of Chester and others had done thirty years earlier. Among them in 1216, it would seem, was Grosseteste. By this date, he was deeply involved in scientific learning in both the branches which I have described above: the knowledge of natural objects, no doubt especially those necessary in medicine; and the movements of the heavens, essential for predictions of all kinds—calendarial, medical and astrological. So far as we know, he was the first Englishman who was able to command this whole field of knowledge with its growing bulk of Greek and Arabic texts, without needing to seek it in distant parts of Europe. In 1216 he was in mid-career and the greater part of his own writing still lay in the future. It makes a convenient point at which to turn to trace the main stages of his intellectual development on foundations laid largely by his English predecessors.

[35] Bodleian, Savile MS 21, f. 158. See Thomson, pp. 30-3 with plate. Hunt in Callus, 1955, 133-4, gives cautious support to the identification with Grosseteste's hand. Our knowledge of Grosseteste's confidence in the influence of the stars does not, however, depend on this identification: see his *De artibus liberalibus* (an early work), Baur, pp. 5-7, and *De impressionibus aeris*, ibid., pp. 42-51.

II

GROSSETESTE'S THOUGHTS ON NATURE, MAN, AND GOD

6

Towards a Chronology of
Grosseteste's Thought

I HAD hoped that it would be unnecessary to discuss the detailed chronology of Grosseteste's writings. Each of them requires a more intricate argument than is easily compatible with
the discussion of the larger problems of environment, personality, intellectual outlook and influence, which are the main
subject of this volume. But several of the conclusions to which
these general discussions point would be placed in jeopardy
without the support of a detailed chronology of some important
turning-points, not only in his life, but more especially in the
development of his thought. I make no attempt to provide a
complete chronology of all his works, but only to provide a
sufficient basis for the more general considerations which
follow.

Like everything else connected with Grosseteste, the chronology of his thought is beset with peculiar difficulties. There are
problems about the authenticity of works, preserved for the
most part in manuscript written a hundred years or more after
his death from sources that no longer exist; problems in relating
his scientific and his theological thoughts; and further problems
in relating his writings and his life. Besides all these sources of
difficulty, he is more than usually reticent about mentioning
contemporary events or personal experiences. The most reliable
dates are those which mark the years when translations from
Arabic or Greek of works which he quotes became available in
the West; but they are rare and not easy to interpret. The date
1217, as the year when Michael Scot completed his translation
of Al-Bitruji's *De Sphera* has been meticulously preserved;[1] and
there are reasons for thinking that his translations of Averroes

[1] See below, p. 130

were not generally available before 1230.[2] But when we ask whether Grosseteste could have used these works in some earlier form, and still more when we ask when he could first have used a translation of Aristotle's *De Animalibus*, conjecture begins to play a large part in any calculation.[3]

In view of these difficulties, it may be profitable to begin by concentrating on the period from 1225 to 1232, the earliest period of Grosseteste's life for which a fairly substantial body of contemporary evidence survives. During these years, there is clear evidence that he lectured on theology in the University of Oxford; that, in or shortly after 1230, he gave up his position in the schools to become *lector* to the Oxford Franciscans; and that, towards the end of 1232, he gave up his archdeaconry of Leicester, which he had held since 1229, and all other posts of authority and emolument, to follow more closely the Franciscan pattern of intellectual and spiritual life. Between 1225 and 1230, and perhaps as late as 1232, he had been a fully fledged university teacher, administrator, and pastoral guide in the highest faculty of the university. It was certainly not a light combination of duties. It implied a considerable re-orientation of study and activity, and we may begin by considering what evidence we have of his work as a theologian during this period.

I. GROSSETESTE'S EARLY THEOLOGICAL DEVELOPMENT

The evidence for his intellectual pursuits during these years consists, in the first place, of a few letters, the earliest of his that survive. One of these, which can be dated 1220 to 1229, con-

[2] This subject has been extensively studied, most thoroughly by R. de Vaux, 'La Première Entrée d'Averroès chez les latins', *Revue des sciences philosophiques et théologiques*, xxii, 1933, 193–245. The most important testimony for our purpose is that of Roger Bacon, who seems to refer to a precise event—perhaps even to the physical presence of Michael Scot, 'qui, annis Domini 1230 transactis, apparuit deferens librorum Aristotelis partes aliquas de Naturalibus et Metaphysicis cum expositionibus authenticis' (Bacon, *Op. Maius*, i.55; iii. 55). It has become customary to decry details like this in Bacon's works (see Haskins 1924, 284), but a distinction should be drawn between his judgements and his experiences: the statement I have quoted belongs to the latter and I see no reason why it should not be right. But this does not exclude the possibility that Grosseteste had earlier knowledge of parts of the translation.

[3] Michael Scot introduced this work to the West. It has generally been assumed that his translation was done at about the same time as his translation of Al-Bitruji in 1217. But there is evidence that he was active several years earlier. Besides, there were passages of the *De Animalibus* in circulation as early as 1210: see *David de Dinanto quaternulorum fragmenta*, ed. Marian Kurdzialek, *Studia Medievistyczne*, 3, Warsaw, 1963.

tains a long discourse on God as 'first form' and on the nature of angels. I have discussed its contents above, and noted its exclusive dependence on St Augustine. Also we may notice that in discussing angels he makes no reference to the work of Denys the Areopagite—a significant indication of the relatively primitive state of his theological reading at that time. Another letter, written in 1232, contains a violent plea for sterner treatment of the Jews who had been expelled from his archdeaconry. This will require some comment later, but we may note its hard and inflexible application of theological doctrine to practical life. Then a third and the most attractive of these letters, addressed to his sister in November 1232, contains an explanation of his retirement from the cares of practical authority to concentrate on intellectual and spiritual things.

Besides these letters there are two philosophical- theological treatises *On Truth* and *On Free Will* which probably belong to the years of transition from secular to theological studies. But the most important record of his developing theological thought is a commentary on the Psalms, which would have formed a central part of his duties as lecturer in theology. The record survives in several different forms and can be divided into three phases, which probably cover the whole period from about 1225 to 1230 or slightly later. The dates will require to be justified; but first we may distinguish the phases.

1. Phase 1: comments on Psalms 1 to 54

The record of the first phase is preserved in a primitive state in the Durham Cathedral manuscript A. III. 12, which has been described above.[4] Among its contents, in a somewhat disordered state, are Grosseteste's comments on Psalms 1 to 54, sometimes in more than one version. The comments are very selective. That is to say, they do not form a continuous series, but are disquisitions on widely separated verses, seldom more than one or two in any single Psalm and often omitting whole Psalms without comment. In the main they concentrate on natural objects such as trees, leaves, hills, the heart or eye, which gave

---

[4] Durham MS A. III. 12 ff. 2–17, 104–22ᵛ; Eton MS 8 ff. 1–38ᵃ. Besides comments on the Psalms, these pages in both MSS contain extraneous material, apparently by Grosseteste. For the Durham MS, see above, pp. 72–3.

scope for a scientific description in which some spiritual significance could be detected. In addition, there are comments on
matters of moral theology—poverty, anger, envy, pride, and
so on. They show a strong interest in details, but a complete lack
of interest in the continuous text of the Psalms or in systematic
theology. They are the notes of a man with something to say
about a limited number of subjects, drawing on a body of
scientific information often derived from Rabanus or Isidore,
with a sprinkling of more advanced knowledge from the new
Aristotelian and Arabic sources reproduced in substance but
not mentioned by name. The named sources are chiefly theological: most frequently Augustine and Gregory the Great,
and a few others—Jerome, Cassiodorus, Chrysostom—make an
occasional appearance.

Grosseteste's comments are anonymous in this manuscript,
and his authorship and the completeness of the record might
be in doubt but for two circumstances. The first, which guarantees the authorship, is that in later life, when he made a selection
of his *Dicta*, he drew copiously on these comments.[5] The second,
which guarantees the completeness of the record, is that the
manuscripts which contain the whole of his commentary present, with very few exceptions, only the same material as the
Durham manuscript as far as Psalm 54.[6]

Further, that these comments had their origin in lectures
given in the Oxford schools is guaranteed partly by the Oxford
connections of the manuscript itself; partly by Grosseteste's own
description of his *Dicta* as having been gathered from his sayings
in the schools; and partly by a chance reference to the schools
in one of the comments, where in speaking of pride, he illustrates his remarks by a reference to the scornful laugh with
which a contender in the schools shows contempt for his
opponent:

There are those who, when they cannot express their contempt in

[5] Out of a total of 147 *Dicta*, thirty-eight are found among the comments on the
Psalms in the Durham MS; and twelve of them are found twice, generally in different
versions. For detailed references, see Thomson 1940, pp. 214–32.

[6] The two main manuscripts (substantially identical in contents) are Eton College
MS 8, and Bologna, Archiginnasio A. 893. There are also extracts in Vatican MS
Ottobon. lat. 185, which I have not seen. The Eton MS contains seven *Dicta* which
are not in Durham, and the Durham MS six which are not in Eton, out of a the total
number of forty-five *Dicta* which had their origin in the Commentary on the Psalms.

words, make use of a gesture to diminish the reputation of someone else—for instance, when a student is opposing or replying, a fellow-student will cackle or laugh, or signify by a blank stare, or by sinking his head in his hood, or in some similar way, that what is being said is of no account and not worth serious attention.[7]

Here we have a clear reference to the full paraphernalia of the scholastic dispute, and incidentally to a common academic habit at all times, meticulously (as was his habit) observed by Grosseteste. I know of no earlier reference to the schools in Grosseteste's works.

Of course, these scattered comments would not in themselves suffice for a course of lectures. We may suppose that, like many another lecturer on a subject that was new to him, Grosseteste had a few original ideas to contribute, but for the rest had to fall back on common material which he did not bother to preserve among his notes. It must be admitted that even those which he thought worthy of preservation show little sign of theological profundity; but they have a liveliness, a sense of immediate response to congenial topics, and a vivid realization of the structure of physical objects, which justify his wish to preserve them.

We know that these comments cannot be later than 1231, when the manuscript was certainly in existence. But may they not be very much earlier? May they not belong to the early years of the century, or at least to the years immediately following the reopening of the Oxford schools in 1214? The record does not support such a suggestion, for this reason: two later manuscripts survive which contain the whole of the Durham material followed by the continuation of Grosseteste's comments from the point where it ends (Psalm 55) to Psalm 100.[8] If the Durham material went back to a much earlier date than the rest of the commentary we should expect some signs of a new beginning or change of method at the point where the

[7] 'Quidam enim cum non possunt verbo, aliquo nutu vicem verbi supplente, bonum alterius diminuunt, utpote cum aliquis scolaris opponit vel respondet, conscolaris assidens cachinno vel risu vel aliquo nutu signat et innuit alterius oppositionem vel responsionem nullam esse; et quandoque ipsa faciei immobilitate et in caputio submersione innuit quod alterius oppositio vel responsio non est digna attenta auditione.' (Durham MS ff. 6ᵃ and 86ᵇ; Eton MS f. 9ᵈ; *Dicta* no. 128, printed in Brown 1690, ii. 287.)

[8] For these MSS see n. 6 above. There is a valuable account of the Eton MS by M. R. James in *JTS*, 23, 1922, 181-5.

Durham material stops; but we find neither. For the next ten Psalms everything continues as before. After this, changes set in which become very considerable as the commentary advances. But each new step is prepared for by the previous stage. At no point do we have the impression of a commentator returning to his subject after a long interval. What we observe is a process of continuous development, at first slow and uncertain, then rapid and decisive.

But, it may be objected, even though there is a continuous development throughout the commentary, may not the whole work be much earlier than 1230? We shall consider this question when we come to the end. Meanwhile a brief characterization of the development after the end of the material in the Durham manuscript will display the rhythm of change as it gathers momentum.

2. Phase 2: comments on Psalms 55 to 79

This stage of the commentary shows a slow and at first uncertain evolution.[9] The changes which occur are shown partly in the increasing length and completeness of the commentary, partly in a diminishing interest in isolated physical objects requiring scientific descriptions, partly in the increasing attention to the theological and devotional contents of the Psalms, and finally in the appearance of a new source which announces a large extension of the material at Grosseteste's disposal.

The increasing length and completeness of the commentary can be indicated very briefly. Between Psalms 54 and 63, no Psalm has more than a single comment and four Psalms have none at all; between Psalms 64 and 73, the number of comments on each Psalm rises to an average of four, and only two Psalms have none; between Psalms 74 and 79, there are comments on nearly every verse. The total length of the commentary expands accordingly: the comments on Psalms 65 to 79 occupy as much space as those on all the previous sixty-four Psalms. Meanwhile, the earlier concentration on physical objects has disappeared: the last comment on a physical object which Grosseteste selected for his *Dicta* was an allegorization of Corn in his comment

[9] My account is based on Eton MS 8, ff. 38–73ᵈ.

on Ps. 64. 4.[10] This did not mean that natural science and allegory had lost their interest; but henceforth such comments were part of a wider theological exposition—they were not spasmodic and isolated points of interest.

Finally, the new source, which first appears in the course of an exceptionally long theological survey of Psalm 79, is the Greek theologian Gregory of Nazianzus. His appearance marks a decisive step forward, which introduces the third phase of Grosseteste's theological thought.

3. Phase 3: comments on Psalms 80 to 100

After Psalm 79 every Psalm is dealt with fully, with comments on its structure and relationship to its neighbours.[11] The sources mainly quoted are still the old ones; but alongside them, in increasing bulk after a spasmodic start, there are references to Gregory of Nazianzus, Basil, Athanasius, and above all Cyril and Theodoret. M. R. James, who first drew attention to this new wealth of Greek material, judged, no doubt rightly, that the appearance of these names did not imply that Grosseteste possessed copies of their separate works, but only a Greek *catena* on the Psalms made up of quotations from them.[12] Alongside this *catena*, Grosseteste had access to some other volumes which begin to make their appearance in his commentary: a Greek text of the Psalms, and a copy of some part of Origen's *Hexapla* which displayed the various Greek translations in parallel columns. He does not yet appear to have been able to read them unaided. His remarks on the texts display only an elementary interest in the relationship between Greek and Latin.[13] But elementary though they are, his linguistic notes and his increasing reliance on Cyril and other Greek theologians all indicate that a great new force had come into his intellectual life.

[10] *Dictum* 97; Eton MS f. 40b-c.

[11] Eton MS ff. 74-203.

[12] *Catenae* of extracts from the Greek Fathers on various books of the Bible formed an important part of Byzantine theological literature from the seventh century onwards. The volume to which Grosseteste had access has not been identified.

[13] M. R. James, loc. cit. p. 184, was mistaken in thinking that Grosseteste's comment on a confusion in a text of Cyril ('forte exemplum falsum est et corruptum') suggested that he 'was himself translating the words of Cyril that lay before him': he was only detecting a geographical error. In fact, all his textual remarks have a close similarity with those found in his commentary on Jerome's Introduction to the Vulgate (see below, pp. 183-5), and show him at an elementary stage in learning Greek.

These new sources are not just so much additional intellectual baggage: they are the bearers of a new inspiration, and their appearance accompanies and promotes a growing confidence and range in his theological observations. For the first time, the commentary begins to contain passages which introduce some of the central ideas of his later theology. And yet it is important to note that, exciting though the appearance of new Greek sources may be, the old Latin ones—with Augustine far ahead of all the rest and with Gregory very strongly represented—retain their vast predominance right to the end of the commentary. Indeed, his growing exploitation of sources which he had used from the beginning of his commentary is even more evident than his appeal to new ones. For example, Psalm 83 is quite short—it has only thirteen verses. But in expounding it, he quoted eight passages from six different works of Augustine, eight from Gregory's *Moralia*, and one each from Rabanus, Bernard, John of Damascus, and Aristotle's *De Animalibus*. This is the mixture as before, but in much larger doses. The additional Greek sources are significant in indicating the direction of his development, but their appearances are relatively infrequent. What we are witnessing, therefore, in his comments on these later Psalms is not just the appearance of some new sources. Much more, we see a growing confidence, a widening range of theological speculation, and a new mastery in handling his sources.

We must finally ask at what date Grosseteste's commentary arrived at its final stage of development. There is one statement which gives a clue to his position when he was writing his final comments on Psalm 100. In commenting on verse 7 ('He who speaks evil will not abide in my sight') he writes:

This is well said. For us, who are placed in a position of authority (*nobis autem qui in gradu regiminis constituti sunt*), even a frivolous word becomes pernicious. As Bernard said, 'For the laity, a joke is a joke; but in the mouth of a priest, it is blasphemy'.[14]

It is the phrase 'We who are placed *in gradu regiminis*' which arrests our attention. In what position was Grosseteste when he wrote these words? He could scarcely have used them after

---

[14] Eton MS 8, f. 202ᵈ. For further details of his comments on this Psalm, see below, p. 180.

1232 when he had given up all his positions of *regimen*. And by 1235 when he became a bishop, he had too solemn a sense of the uniqueness of the episcopal authority to use a phrase which implied that he shared this position with some of his hearers. The only time when his remark would have been wholly appropriate was when he was an archdeacon lecturing in theology to a mature audience in the university schools. His comments on Psalm 100, with which he concludes his commentary, express an inflexible commitment to the regulation of the whole Christian community which, as we shall see, is exemplified in his actions as archdeacon of Leicester from 1229 to 1232.

He never continued his lectures beyond this point. Psalm 100, as Grosseteste interpreted it, contained a resumé of the virtues and vices of practical life:

As Cyril says, this Psalm describes the perfect conduct of life and teaches the perfection of holiness, which consists, not only in shunning evil and doing good, but also in fighting evil and destroying it both in ourselves and others, and in promoting good not only in ourselves but, to the extent of our power, in others also . . . This perfection of conduct has three parts: our conduct as individuals; our conduct in a family; and our conduct as citizens among fellow-citizens. We can consider all three of these parts in expounding this Psalm.[15]

The exposition which follows occupies no less than twelve folio pages and brings the Eton manuscript to a close. This represents a fullness of treatment vastly different from the scattered notes with which the commentary began. It brought the work to a natural climax and provided a suitable ending as he prepared himself to turn to a more contemplative way of life. The whole course of his comments from beginning to end, with their faltering start and gathering confidence, could have covered a period of five to seven years. During these years Grosseteste was deeply engaged on a bold plan of theological reading. He no doubt also gave other lectures on the Bible and perhaps wrote other treatises; but his lectures on the Psalms would seem to have been the ones which he took most care to preserve. They contain the record of his earliest progress as a theologian, and, having established them in their Oxford setting, we can turn back to his works of the years before 1225.

[15] Eton MS, f. 198ᵃ. The exposition ends on f. 204ᵇ. For the final words, see below, p. 180.

II. GROSSETESTE'S EARLIER SCIENTIFIC WRITINGS

That Grosseteste was a scientist before he was a theologian scarcely needs to be argued. Common sense as well as common practice would suggest as much. There is besides ample evidence that at least some of his scientific writings are earlier than c.1225 when we have our earliest view of him as a theologian. I am going to argue that, not only *some*, but *most* of his scientific writings belong to the thirty years before 1225. I shall suggest that one work, which he later revised, may be as early as c.1195, when he would have been about twenty-five years old; and that all his most substantial scientific works, except for those which are more metaphysical than strictly scientific, belong to the period of his life before 1225. I shall attempt to establish the general truth of these conclusions in the pages which follow. It is not impossible, or even unlikely, that Grosseteste continued to produce some scientific work while he was mainly engaged in theological study and lecturing after 1225. But in view of all his other occupations in these years, I think it unlikely that he could have had time for much scientific work, and I am sorry to find myself disagreeing on this point with the latest and most authoritative account of the chronology of his scientific writings by Professor McEvoy.[16] According to his calculations, the following works are to be assigned to the period from 1225 to 1233:

1225–8	*De luce*
1225–30	*Computus correctorius*
c.1226–8	*De fluxu et refluxu maris*
1228–30	Commentary on *Posterior Analytics*
1228–32	Commentary on *Physics*
c.1230	*De differenciis localibus*
	De motu supercaelestium
	De lineis
	De natura locorum
1230–3	*De iride*
	De colore

[16] McEvoy 1983. Despite my dissent from several of his chronological conclusions, I wish to record my debt to this magisterial survey of the contents and sources of Grosseteste's scientific works; as also to the series of comments in Dales 1961, 1962, 1977, and in his editions now in process of publication.

De calore solis
De operationibus solis[17]

These works comprise well over half of Grosseteste's complete corpus of scientific writings, and by far the most important part of them. They are works of very varying length; but three of them are substantial, and of these the two Commentaries on Aristotle are among the most significant scientific works of the thirteenth century. Of the smaller works, several express his most original ideas, and they could not have been written without intense concentration. If we add to these his Commentary on the Psalms, with all that it implies in theological reading, lecturing, reaching out towards an understanding of Greek theology and Greek language—not to mention his involvement in university affairs, in preaching, in the duties of an archdeacon, and finally in whatever experience of conversion led him to change from the secular schools to the Franciscans—we may reasonably doubt whether such a combination of activities can be envisaged as possible.

It is true that the date of writing a work is not necessarily the date at which most of the thinking necessary for composition was done. But this consideration can give very little help in supporting McEvoy's dates. None of these works gives the impression of being a mere record of earlier conclusions. They all appear to be works of a man fully engaged on the problems he is writing about; and it is on this basis that McEvoy has allocated them to these dates.

It may also be said that the proposed dates are more fluid than they seem when set out in the uncompromising form of a chronological table. Each date depends on the weighing of probabilities, and perhaps no rigid objections could be raised to minor reshuffles which would put some works rather earlier and others rather later than the dates assigned to them in this list. I shall in fact argue that most of these works are to be dated earlier and others later than the dates assigned to them by McEvoy. But there is something more at stake than a simple reshuffle of works to squeeze them into the available space. The principles which lie behind the proposed chronology of scientific works require examination.

[17] Ibid., p. 655.

One reason for McEvoy's dating some of these works so late in the 1220s is his belief that Grosseteste was scientifically so immature in the early 1220s that his more mature works (especially the two great Commentaries) need to be dated as late as possible in the decade to give him time to develop. But he also wishes to see Grosseteste's scientific development completed before he turned to theology. McEvoy's words with reference to the group of treatises dated 1230-3 in the list are significant here: 'they derived from a single inspiration and probably followed each other fairly rapidly, closing the series of Grosseteste's scientific opuscules with éclat before he turned his attention to other interests (mostly of a theological nature).'[18] The combination of these two principles is largely responsible for the great congestion of scientific works between 1225 and 1233: they must be late enough to allow for his scientific development, but early enough to allow time for his theology, which on this basis cannot be accommodated before about 1233.

All McEvoy's judgements are the result of deep thought and a long familiarity with the material, and none of them can be lightly rejected. Nor is it necessary to reject the principle that the scientific works mainly preceded the theological. But the scientific works need to be given a much wider chronological extension. This is what I shall attempt, and I think it will lead to a different view of Grosseteste's development than is implied in McEvoy's chronology.

As a start, I shall comment on individual works and consider the grounds for their inclusion among the works of the years 1225-30; and I shall suggest that some should be rejected altogether, and others dated either earlier or later.

1. Works to be considered for rejection

DE FLUXU ET REFLUXU MARIS[19]

This is an interesting work and by no means unworthy of Grosseteste, but its inclusion in the list leads to difficulties both of doctrine and chronology. Professor Dales, who began by

---

[18] Ibid., p. 635.

[19] For the text, see Dales 1966. The attribution to Mr. A. Exon. is in Assisi, Bibl. Comunale, MS 138; there is a reproduction of it in Dales's edition.

accepting Grosseteste's authorship, later rejected it largely on grounds of doctrinal incongruity, which McEvoy disputes.[20] I find Dales's arguments persuasive; but I am even more strongly persuaded by an early ascription of the work to another almost unknown writer, because little-known writers do not easily get the credit for writing works in competition with greater names. Moreover, while all the attributions to Grosseteste are of the fourteenth century or later, it is a mid-thirteenth century note which describes the work as *a magistro A Exon in scolis suis determinata*. This has the merit of being circumstantial and also of pointing to a known master of the Oxford schools.

Who was he? Dales and Callus have both suggested Adam Marsh. But there is another candidate with better credentials. Grosseteste had a favourite pupil Adam, who is variously described as 'Rufus' or 'of Exeter' or (sometimes, perhaps by assimilation) 'of Oxford'. It was to him that Grosseteste addressed his long letter on God as *prima forma* and on the nature of angels. He joined the Franciscans in about 1230 and soon left for the mission field, dying in Italy on his way. Grosseteste condoled with the Franciscans on his departure and lamented the early death of his 'dearest disciple and special friend', whose learning he praised.[21] The attribution fits the man; his close connection with Grosseteste is vouched for by Grosseteste himself. So we have an early and circumstantial attribution to a pupil of Grosseteste, who was active in Oxford at the right time. It would be hard to find a clearer case for accepting an early attribution against the evidence of later manuscripts. On this and other grounds listed by Dales, I think his rejection is right.

The removal of this work simplifies the chronology of these years a little. The removal of the next will do more.

[20] See Dales 1966 (in favour) and 1977 (against); against this rejection, McEvoy 1983, p. 630. Fr. Callus (1955) also pronounces against its authenticity and in favour of the attribution to Adam Marsh. McEvoy's strongest argument for the work's authenticity is that 'the doctrine of light is better developed by the *De fluxu* than by any preceding work of Grosseteste'. But the argument, which seems to be based on Grosseteste's remarks in his Commentary on *Post. Anal.*, ed. Rossi, pp. 385-9, does not point in the direction of the theory expounded in his *De luce* (see below, pp. 136-9).

[21] The details of Adam's life are collected in *BRUO* i. 660-1 under 'Exeter, Adam of'. Apart from Grosseteste's letters, nos. 1, 2, and 38, the main source of our knowledge is Eccleston, pp. 16-18.

DE GENERATIONE STELLARUM[22]

It is agreed that this work is to be dated between 1220 and 1225. So it does not impinge on the period of Grosseteste's theological activity. But it raises difficulties of a different kind: it contains crudities of thought which, if they are Grosseteste's, make necessary a later date for his more mature scientific writings, and this leads to the unnatural congestion of the years after 1225. On any system of chronology it is difficult to fit it into the sequence of Grosseteste's works. It quotes a wide range of Aristotle's scientific works which it would have been difficult for anyone to assemble before about 1220. Yet its lack of subtlety in argument and its contradiction of some of Grosseteste's doctrines place it so far apart from his other scientific works that its acceptance imposes a view of his late development that is, to say the least, very disturbing. In McEvoy's words: 'The dominant impression left by a perusal of this work is one of astonishment that an intelligent reader could at once know so much and understand so little of the Aristotle he has been studying.'[23] And this is Grosseteste at fifty! Dales is equally unflattering:

Methodologically it has little to recommend it . . . two aspects of this work should be especially noted for comparison with Grosseteste's later works: the crudity of its discussion of color, completely dependent on Aristotle, and the belaboring of the assertion, derived from Aristotle, that there are degrees of transparency. This second point Grosseteste takes for granted in his later works and even makes it an essential part of his theories of color and heat.[24]

Whatever may be thought about the doctrine, the differences of approach and ability seem to me decisive. A scholar may change his views. But what he will not change is his mind. The brash assertiveness and syllogistic rigidity of its arguments form a contrast at every point to the subtlety and tentative quality of Grosseteste's mind. To be convinced of this, it is only necessary to compare the treatment of the nature of stars in this work with Grosseteste's treatment of the same theme in his *Hexaëmeron*. In the former we find: 'Everything which is col-

---

[22] Printed in Baur, pp. 32–6. Dated by Dales *c.*1220, by McEvoy 1217/20–1225. For discussions, see Dales 1961, p. 383; McEvoy 1983, pp. 622–4.

[23] McEvoy 1983, p. 622.

[24] Dales 1961, p. 383.

oured is a mixture; stars are coloured; therefore stars are mixed bodies.' But in the *Hexaëmeron*: 'Many have sought most diligently, but I do not know whether any have found the truth; or if they have found it, I do not know any who have demonstrated its truth by a true and certain argument.'[25]

It may be argued that these words were written twelve years later and in different circumstances, but I do not believe that the man who wrote the first could ever have written the second.

So we must turn to the foundation on which the attribution to Grosseteste is based. It is not found in any early manuscript or in any surviving English collection of his works, but in one Czech and three Italian manuscripts of the fourteenth and fifteenth centuries. These manuscripts are clearly related in their contents, and their connections deserve a closer study. Meanwhile, it may be said that they illustrate a desire, which became widespread in the fourteenth century, to make as complete a collection as possible of Grosseteste's writings. The collectors had good sources; but they had no way of distinguishing genuine works from others which were associated with them. I think that its attribution to Grosseteste is another example of the familiar process of judging the authorship of a work by the company in which it was found.

Its inclusion in the Grosseteste canon has been a large obstacle to any reasonable interpretation of his intellectual development. It presented him as a late learner and even later thinker; as one who was learned before he had learnt to think; and as one who was dogmatic at fifty, before he became the searcher for truth who reveals himself in all his well-attested works. Its rejection will allow us to see the same mind at work from an early age, and to ask whether some of his scientific work may not be much earlier than has been generally allowed. This brings us to the next topic.

2. Works to be considered for earlier dating

DE COMETIS[26]

The occasion for writing this little work was the appearance of a comet, and scholars have concluded that the comet was Halley's. It used to be thought, on the basis of the present

---

[25] For the first passage, see Baur, p. 33; for the second, *Hex.* III. vi. 1, p. 106.
[26] For the text see Baur, pp. 36–41; and for further discussion, below, pp. 147–50.

periodicity of the comet, that this required a date 1228-9.[27] But it is now known that the recurrences of the comet took place at rather longer intervals during the Middle Ages and that the true date of its reappearance was 1221-2, at which date it is well attested in English chronicles. Consequently, McEvoy has attributed the work to 1222-4.[28]

The difficulty with this date is twofold. First, in this work, Grosseteste is ignorant of the long discussion on comets in Aristotle's *Meteorologica*, where a view of their nature is expounded which is widely different from that which he adopts.[29] That he should disagree with Aristotle would not be surprising, but that he should disagree in silence can only mean that he did not know the work. Yet it had been known in England for more than twenty years.[30] It would be surprising if a man of Grosseteste's known avidity for new knowledge had remained so long in ignorance of this work in the area of his special interest. Besides, in his work, Grosseteste explicitly recites and answers the views of others, presumably those with whom he had discussed the question, and none of them shows any acquaintance with Aristotle's views. So this late date raises a difficulty not only about Grosseteste's knowledge, but also about the knowledge of a wider group of scholars.

But Halley's was not the only comet reported in English chronicles. In 1197 the Tewkesbury and Worcester Chronicles reported a comet which appeared throughout the whole winter of 1196-7.[31] These two chronicles drew their information from another local source now lost. In 1197 Grosseteste was employed in the area from which these reports come. He was in the household of the bishop of Hereford, and Hereford was the most active centre of astronomical studies in England at that

---

[27] For earlier estimates of the date of the work based on a mistaken periodicity of Halley's comet, see Thomson 1933, p. 25, and Dales, 1961. For a complete survey of the comet's appearances, see J. G. Porter, 'Catalogue of Cometary Orbits', *Memoirs of the British Astronomical Association*, xxxix. 3, 1961, p. 90; with a supplement, ibid. xl. 2, 1966, p. 16. The medieval periodicity was about seventy-nine years.

[28] McEvoy 1983, pp. 624-7.

[29] *Meteorologica*, I, 6-7.

[30] It is quoted by Alfred of Shareshill in his *De motu cordis*, which he sent to Alexander Nequam probably while he was still a master in Oxford, before *c.*1197 (see Baeumker 1923, p. 39).

[31] *Ann. Mon.* i. 55; iv. 389. It is clear from the structure of the annals that the comet was conspicuous in the early months of 1197, and that the annalists of Tewkesbury and Worcester had another local annal as their source.

time. It seems at least possible that this comet inspired the discussions from which Grosseteste's treatise arose. The early date would explain the lack of knowledge of Aristotle's *Meteorologica* and the general vagueness of doctrinal background in the work. The work does not appear in any of the general collections of Grosseteste's works which were put together in the fourteenth century. It survives only in widely varying forms in a few manuscripts with no obvious interconnections.[32] These may all be symptoms of its having its origin before he began keeping the writings which he later bequeathed to the Oxford Franciscans.

An early date can be no more than a suggestion, but it is supported by another earlier dating which imposes itself in a much more peremptory fashion. I refer to the dating of the various versions of Grosseteste's *Computus*.

COMPUTUS, I, II, AND III

The three versions of this work on the calendar are dated by McEvoy:[33]

I   1215–20
II   1225–30
III 1244

The first thing to say about this chronology is that, through no fault of McEvoy's, it is wholly misleading. The error begins with the recension dated 1244 by its discoverer S. H. Thomson. He reported that the work was dated 1244, and in support of this assertion he quoted the following sentence in it: 'Since the birth of our Lord, 1200 years and more, *namely 44*, have elapsed, in which number there are ten hundreds and ten twenties.'[34]

What Thomson did not mention was that the words *scilicet 44*, which turned 1200 into 1244, were a marginal addition. They may refer to the date at which the work was copied; but they cannot have been written by Grosseteste, for they

---

[32] For the very confused textual history, see Thomson 1933, pp. 19–21, and 1957, pp. 36–7.

[33] McEvoy 1983, pp. 618–22.

[34] Trinity College Dublin, MS 441, f. 104^v: 'sed a nativitate domini elapse sunt 1200 anni et eo [*margin* scilicet 44] amplius, in quo numero sunt decies centum et decies 20, et ita per 10 dies recessit iam solliticium hiemale a nativitate domini'. For an incomplete report, see Thomson 1941, p. 97.

contradict the calculation in the text: 'ten hundreds and ten twenties' = 1200. All that Grosseteste tells us is that the work is later than 1200, and by implication earlier than 1220.

This mistake of Thomson led to another. Believing that the date of the recension he had discovered was 1244, he naturally thought that it was a revision of the *second recension*. But it does not take long to discover that it is a revision of the *first*, and comes before the second recension. So the whole sequence needs to be revised; and as soon as this has been done the various pieces fall into a new shape.

It becomes clear that the first recension is a very elementary work with a strong literary and ecclesiastical bias.[35] Scientifically it is less advanced than work on the same subject which was being produced in Hereford by 1200.[36] The main authority it quotes is Gerlandus, a computist of the early twelfth century who was widely regarded as outmoded by about 1170. The other main writers referred to are Dionysius Exiguus, who had been a mainstay of the subject since the time of Bede, and John Beleth, the writer of a mid-twelfth century work on the liturgical calendar.[37] For the rest, there are many quotations from Ovid, several mnemonic verses on the number of days in each month, the behaviour of nones and ides in March, May, July and October, and similar subjects. No doubt some of this material would be found in any *Computus*, but Grosseteste's first recension is very markedly directed towards the elementary instruction of priests who needed to know about calendars for practical purposes. It is not for scientifically interested and well-informed students of technical chronology.

Even as an elementary book Grosseteste was soon dissatisfied with it. He made his second recension in order to correct the mistakes, obscurities and omissions in the first.[38] I have not studied it sufficiently closely to comment on its improvements

[35] This version, like its first revision in the Dublin MS, survives in a single manuscript, Bodleian Library, MS Bodl. 679, ff. 65–75.

[36] For the computistic works associated with Hereford, see Haskins 1924, pp. 85–8, 124–6; Russell 1932, 14–16, 20–1.

[37] MS Bodl. 679, ff. 68ᵛ, 70. For Gerlandus being outmoded by *c*.1170, see Haskins 1924, p. 86 n. 21. The reference to John Beleth's *Summa de divinis officiis* assumes that it will be available to the reader: f. 70, 'In summa magistri Joh. Beleth plenius invenies'.

[38] The reader of the new recension, he writes, will here find the earlier omissions and defects corrected: 'Quae vel dimissa sunt in alio tractatu, vel minus lucide, vel aliter dicta quam ibi, hic repperi possunt' (Trinity College Dublin, MS 441, f. 104ᵛ).

in detail, but one of them was on a subject which was giving scientific chronologers a great deal of trouble in the early thirteenth century—namely the increasing deviation of the ecclesiastical calendar from the natural seasons of the year. This was a point which Grosseteste had omitted in his first edition, and he added a passage to explain how the deviation had come about and why it was increasing. He explained that the astronomical year was shorter than the calendar year to the extent of one day in every hundred and twenty years. Consequently by 1200 the festivals had been displaced by ten days since the birth of Christ: this was the point which the calculation noted above ($10 \times 100 + 10 \times 20 = 1200$) was intended to demonstrate. He quoted no sources to support this variation, but the passage shows that—in contrast to the first recension— Grosseteste was now taking an interest in serious astronomical problems. Nevertheless, in spite of these improvements, the work in its second recension was still an elementary one. It may have been written not long after 1200.

By the time that he produced his third edition he had moved on a long way in his scientific interests; and he set about giving his treatise a more solid scientific basis which would make it suitable for advanced students. This recension, known as the *computus correctorius*, is the only one which has been printed, and it must now be reckoned the last.[39] It brings the work for the first time fully abreast of contemporary science. The names of Dionysius Exiguus, Gerlandus and John Beleth have disappeared; and they have been replaced by a series of new names—Ptolemy, Thabit, Arzarchel, Abrachis, Albategni, and (as an afterthought) Albatrangius. Names, of course, do not necessarily mean that Grosseteste had read their books, but he had at least studied Ptolemy's *Almagest* and made use of the astronomical tables of Toledo, perhaps also those of Paris. Besides, the difference in intellectual atmosphere between this recension and the two earlier ones is very conspicuous: this last recension (unlike the first or even the second) was the work of someone swimming vigorously in the tide of modern scientific knowledge, and undertaking independent measurements and calculations. For example, he now modifies the explanation he had given in the second recension of the divergence between

[39] Steele 1926, pp. 212–68.

the seasons and the calendar. In the second recension he had said that the advance was one day in 120 years; but now he writes that Albategni had discovered that the true year was shorter than Abrachis and the computists had thought. The result was that the calendar was now known to have fallen behind the seasons to the extent of one day in every 100 (not 120) years. So the error was greater than had been supposed— twelve (not ten) days by 1200. And this, he goes on to say, 'agrees with what we have found *per experimentum nostri temporis*'.[40]

Grosseteste, then, has clearly taken a great step forward since his earlier recensions. What dates are we to assign to them? As for the first, a date before 1200, and perhaps even before 1195, seems likely. It reveals a Grosseteste who was as yet untouched by contemporary science: such a man as Giraldus Cambrensis described in about 1195, a scholar with a good literary background and all-round accomplishments on the eve of his association with the diocese of Hereford. The second, hitherto called 'III', belongs to the early years of the thirteenth century, certainly before 1220, probably before 1210. As for the third, hitherto called 'II', our only guide is its statement that 'Alpetrangius' (Al-Bitruji) had *recently* discovered a way of explaining the retrogressions and irregularities in the movements of the planets without recourse to the eccentrics and epicycles of Ptolemy. This statement is correct, and we must ask when it could have been written. Al-Bitruji's work *De Sphera* (which is certainly the work referred to) would seem to have been written after 1185, and Grosseteste was adding—perhaps as an afterthought—a piece of information which had only recently come to his notice and which, as McEvoy has noted, he had not yet assimilated. It may be that he had not even seen the work, but had only heard about it. The fact that he mentioned it at all has generally been taken to mean that he was writing after 1217, when Michael Scot completed his Latin translation of it.[41] This too may be correct; but it is a mistake to suppose that scholars never heard of any new discoveries until they

[40] Ibid. p. 215.

[41] The dating formulas at the end of Michael Scot's translation are not consistent with regard to the year; but *Friday* and *18 August* are constant, and 1217 is the only year which fits this conjunction. See F. J. Carmody, *Michael Scot's Translation of Al Bitruji's 'De motibus celorum'*, University of California Press, 1952.

had been translated into Latin. It may sometimes, perhaps generally, have happened that translations were made because news of the original had created a demand. At all events, Grosseteste's knowledge of this particular work does not point to a careful study of the complete text, and we may date the final edition of his *Computus* at any time between 1215 and 1220 without violence to the facts so far as we know them.

As a crude approximation, I would suggest as the dates of the three recensions *c*.1195, *c*.1205, and *c*.1215–20. If this were accepted it would carry the continuous development of Grosseteste's scientific interests back to his early years; and this would help to solve the problem of what he was doing intellectually during his undocumented years between the ages of 25 and 50. It would also mark the stages of his development in scientific knowledge and maturity during this whole period.

THE COMMENTARY ON ARISTOTLE'S *POSTERIOR ANALYTICS*

Without doubt this is Grosseteste's major work on philosophy and science. Several different dates have been proposed by modern scholars. Fr. Callus proposed the first decade of the thirteenth century, A. C. Crombie a date shortly after 1220, Dales 1227–9, and now McEvoy, 1228–30.[42] Two of the main general considerations advanced in favour of a late date appear to me invalid—namely the immaturity of Grosseteste's scientific thought in the early 1220s, and the need to place this Commentary after the *De fluxu et refluxu maris*. If these are removed, there seems no reason why it should not belong to the years 1220–5 where Crombie placed it. This would have the further advantage of admitting the testimony of Nicholas Trivet, which McEvoy rejected with reluctance, that Grosseteste wrote the Commentary when he was a Master in Arts.[43]

To be honest, I attach no importance to Trivet's testimony, though I approve its tendency. If he had said that Grosseteste composed the work when he was a theological lecturer, it would—though difficult to believe—have been another matter. But, writing in Oxford in about 1320, it was natural for Trivet

---

[42] Callus 1955, 12–13; Crombie 1953, 46–7; Dales 1961, 395–6; McEvoy 1983, 636–41.

[43] Nicholas Trivet, *Annales*, ed. T. Hog, 1845, p. 243.

to think that a commentator on the *Posterior Analytics* must have been a lecturer in Arts. I think he is right as to the time, but the work does not seem to have any close connection with a lecture course. It has all the qualities and shortcomings which we shall later notice in his other comprehensive work *De Sphera*: it is very full on some subjects which are not central to the main argument, and sketchy on others which are.[44] Although he goes through the text chapter by chapter, there are only two chapters on which, for no obvious reason, he provides a sentence by sentence commentary. Elsewhere he provides a free interpretation of the argument and sums it up as he goes along in two series of *conclusiones* expressed in his own words. These *conclusiones*, growing one from another, are reminiscent of the theorems of Euclid, whom he clearly prefers to Aristotle as an exponent of scientific reasoning.

The conclusion that it was written before he became deeply involved in theology, and therefore not later than 1225, is also suggested by the very primitive knowledge of Greek which he displays in it. As we shall see, one of the early features of his theological work is his growing interest in and knowledge of Greek. When Grosseteste's interest is aroused, he shows his alertness at every opportunity. But he shows no alertness to Greek in discussing the *Posterior Analytics*. Although he observed that the Latin text had obscurities and corruptions, he expressed no curiosity about the Greek text. Even when he noted that Aristotle wrote *aliqua contingunt ex aliis* when he meant *sequuntur ex*, and *credere* when he meant *scire*; or when he commented on his peculiar use of *utique*, he did not speculate on the Greek origin of these phrases: he wrote almost as if Aristotle was responsible for the Latin.[45] Nevertheless he knew a little—a very little—about Greek grammar. In explaining Aristotle's view that 'to relax' implied change, Grosseteste remarks that this might arise from the fact that the Greek infinitive sometimes signifies 'beginning to do something'. True enough. But Grosseteste seems to think that *any* form of the Greek infinitive 'to relax' may sometimes mean 'to begin to relax'. Elsewhere he makes the sound suggestion that the translator perhaps used the feminine form *recta* instead of the neuter *rectum* for 'right-

[44] See below, pp. 142-6.
[45] For these linguistic points, see Rossi, pp. 102-3, 110, 263.

angle' because the Greek word could have been feminine. Right again. But Grosseteste clearly did not know the Greek word, for he could only put forward his idea as an hypothesis.[46] So the general position is that at the time when he wrote his commentary on the *Posterior Analytics* Grosseteste had not yet begun any serious study of Greek, still less had he been alerted to the importance of Greek for clearing up obscurities in the text.

The manner and style of the commentary suggest that it was either written before Grosseteste's arrival in Oxford, or that it was a free interpretation of a difficult book not yet incorporated in the syllabus of the schools. As a survey of a new and complicated work, it might have been made for a group of men familiar with Euclid, to whom the text of the *Posterior Analytics* was available but not yet assimilated. Grosseteste was free to dwell on points which interested him, to recast the argument in his own way, and to express his criticisms of Aristotle without reserve. He speaks with the freedom of a scholar among friends, without the constraints of a lecturer instructing students; and the most interesting things he has to say are not so much explanations of the text as excursions from it. Everywhere there is a variety of interest and method which makes the work the best reflection of his mind before he turned to theology.

THE COMMENTARY ON ARISTOTLE'S *PHYSICS*[47]

This is a work that cannot be fitted into any single chronological slot. Unlike the Commentary on the Psalms which shows a progressive development in which each step leads to the next, the *Physics* commentary is made up of three discontinuous parts. To judge from its sources, the commentary on Books 1–4 could have been written at about the same time as the commentary on the *Posterior Analytics*. But the comments on Books 7–8 are closely related to the *Hexaëmeron*, and those on Book 5 to the *De colore*. These connections suggest a date 1232–5 for the com-

---

[46] Rossi, p. 349. By the time that he wrote his comments on Aristotle's *Ethics*, he knew that this conjecture was right and he could supply the Greek word: ' "Rectam"enim hic vocat Aristoteles angulum rectum, quia "gonia", quod est angulus in graeco feminini generis est.' (H. P. F. Mercken, *The Greek Commentaries on the Nicomachaean Ethics of Aristotle in the Latin Translation of Robert Grosseteste*, i, 1973, p. 122.)

[47] For the text, see Dales 1963 and his comments, especially pp. ix–xviii; also McEvoy 1983, pp. 643–4.

ments on these Books.[48] Book 6 stands by itself and could be
later than either of the other parts: its peculiar feature is that
it is entirely occupied with a comparison between Proclus's and
Grosseteste's division of Aristotle's conclusions in this Book.
When Grosseteste became familiar with Proclus's work is
wholly unknown, but it is more likely to be late than early.
Moreover, since Grosseteste can compare his own treatment of
Book 6 with that of Proclus, it would seem that he had already
made a commentary on it which has not survived. This is a
further indication that the three parts of the commentary as
they now survive did not form part of a single work, but were
put together from different fragments by some later hand. To
define their dates would require closer study, and all that can
be said provisionally is that the commentary on Books 1–4 may
belong to the period before 1225; that on Books 5, 7–8 to the
period from 1232 to 1235; and that the comments on Book 6 in
their present form probably belong to a still later date.

III. GROSSETESTE'S LATER SCIENTIFIC WRITINGS

In considering Grosseteste's commentary on the *Physics*, we
have touched on work which may straddle two distinct periods
of his life—the period before he lectured in the schools on
theology, and the period when he had withdrawn to the Franciscans—that is to say, before 1225, and after 1230/2. This
division draws attention to works which may be later than the
dates ascribed to them by McEvoy. It is to them that we now
turn.

McEvoy's chronology of scientific works assigns eight treatises to the years 1230 to 1233. Several of them are short, but
they are full of vitality and ideas which, if not quite new, are
expressed with a new vigour and breadth. McEvoy looks on
these works as 'closing the series of Grosseteste's scientific opuscules with éclat before he turned his attention to other interests

---

[48] In contrast to the comments on Books 1–4, those on Books 7–8 both quote
Averroes—a fairly sure indication of a date after about 1230. On Book 5 Grosseteste
does not quote Averroes, but he expounds a doctrine of light and colour in words
which show a close relationship with his late treatise *De colore*, which *does* quote
Averroes. Books 1–4 of the *Physics* were always looked on as a distinct entity, and it
would not be surprising if Grosseteste made a separate commentary on them at an
earlier date.

(mostly of a theological nature)'.[49] If these words had been written about the series of works which culminated in the commentary on the *Posterior Analytics* or possibly on the first four books of the Physics, I would have no criticism to make. But they can scarcely be right when applied to works written as late as 1230-2. In the first place, on any possible chronology, Grosseteste had already been deeply engaged in theology for several years before 1230. And more important, the breadth of vision of these later works seems not to *precede*, but to arise out of his theology: it is the result of a struggle to bring his science and theology into a single field of knowledge. This I believe to be the true perspective of his final phase both as scientist and theologian. He had come to see that there was no gap between the physics of Creation and the theology of Creation, any more than there was a gap between the process of Creation and the process of Redemption. They all formed one field of knowledge because they all formed a single field of divine activity and intention. The light which shone on the natural world had the same source as the light which shone in Revelation and Redemption, and the expression of this centrality of light was to be found above all in the Bible. Indeed, it was his study of the Bible which convinced him that light was not only the most satisfying of all natural phenomena, but also the emanation from the divine nature which at the first moment of Creation penetrated and gave form to the whole universe. The Bible, fortified by Augustine, Gregory and the Greek Fathers had brought Grosseteste to this view when he still had twenty years of life in which his vision could be worked out in detail. It is, I think, a mistake to hurry the last phase of his science in order to leave him time to turn to theology. It was theology which brought him to it.

This ordering of his development not only leaves him with time on his hands after 1232; it also exposes the sense in which he can be said to have been scientifically immature ten or twelve years earlier. In the early 1220s, what he suffered from was not immaturity of scientific reasoning, such as the *De generatione stellarum* displays, nor from backwardness in obtaining new information, such as a late date for the *De cometis* would suggest. He suffered from a lack of a theological perspective.

[49] McEvoy 1983, p. 635.

The result of this was that, although by 1220 he could appreciate the geometrical perfection of light and associate its properties with, those of sound, he could not yet see it as the link between God and the universe. It was in this sense that his science was still incomplete. This completeness came from the study of theology in the vital years after 1225.

It would prolong these notes and perform no useful purpose to go through the last groups of scientific treatises, dated in McEvoy's list from 1230 to 1233, with this theological dimension in mind. I believe that most of them are likely to be later than the dates he gives them; but, more important than their dates, is their place in Grosseteste's development. The problem and perhaps part of its solution may be illustrated by the history of a single work which McEvoy dates as early as 1225-28: the treatise *De luce*.[50]

DE LUCE

This short work contains the fullest expression of Grosseteste's final view of the role of Light in the universe. Here light is described as the *prima forma corporalis* of Creation; it diffuses itself in all directions to the extreme limits of the universe in the first moment of time; it carries with it as its inseparable concomitant the matter of the whole universe; then from the furthest boundary of the outermost sphere it returns through the celestial spheres to the terrestrial, where it produces the four elements of fire, air, earth, and water. In brief, light is the splendour and perfection of all embodied things (*species et perfectio corporum omnium*).

Certainly we have here one of the most lucid and brilliantly conceived pieces of writing of Grosseteste's later years. Yet, it must also be observed that, like much else that he wrote, it tails away into a rather chaotic and unintelligible sequel in its final paragraphs. Having at last seen his way through a perplexing central problem, Grosseteste was still left with a wide range of problems not yet fully resolved. Nevertheless, the comprehensive clarity of the central core of the argument is beyond doubt.

By what date, and through what stages, had he reached this

[50] Ibid., pp. 648-54. Text in Baur, pp. 51-9.

clarity? It is common ground that the two other works in which this central idea is stated, though in a more fragmentary way, are the commentary on Genesis 1: 1–2: 17 in his *Hexaëmeron*, and his commentary on Ecclesiasticus 43: 1–5 (generally known as the *De operationibus solis*).[51] To these we may add that Grosseteste also touched on the theme towards the end of his commentary on the Psalms.[52] Our only question is, what do these texts suggest about the date of *De luce*? Although the role of light in the universe is most fully developed in the *De luce*, McEvoy believes that the *Hexaëmeron* and *De operationibus solis* are later than *De luce*, and that their more fragmentary treatment of the problem is due not to Grosseteste's thought being less developed than in the *De Luce* but to their having different and, on this subject, more limited purposes. In principle, this is not impossible. But, so far as the *Hexaëmeron* is concerned, it is hard to see why a full-scale work on Creation should not have provided the opportunity, indeed necessity, for a full account of the role of light in Creation if the idea had been fully worked out when it was written. If the *De luce* had already been written, we might have expected some passages from it to have been quoted or summarized in the *Hexaëmeron*. Grosseteste had no aversion to repeating himself; he more than once repeated or recalled passages from his commentary on the Psalms in the *Hexaëmeron*.[53] But, on the subject of light, the *Hexaëmeron* is always more confused and incomplete than *De luce*. It describes light as *corporalis*, but not as the *prima forma corporalis*; as *naturaliter sui generativa*, but not as the bearer of matter through the universe; nor is it related to the creation of the elements.[54] In short, unless we have strong reasons for thinking otherwise, we must conclude that the *Hexaëmeron* is earlier than the *De Luce*.

The case of the *De operationibus solis* is different, partly because its scope might well have inhibited a complete statement of the role of light in the universe, and partly because in the little that

---

[51] They have been edited with exemplary thoroughness by Dales and Gieber 1983 and McEvoy 1974.

[52] The passage occurs in commenting on Ps. 96: 11, *Lux orta est iusto*. McEvoy 1974, p. 73, quotes a fragment of this text.

[53] See, for example, *Hex.* v. xxi. 2 (p. 180), where a substantial portion of his comment on Ps. 55: 4 (Durham MS f. 121ᵃ) on the sun is repeated verbatim.

[54] On these points, see *Hex.* ii. x, pp. 97–8; iv. xii. 2, p. 122; viii. iii. 1, p. 220; and on the elements iii. vi. 1, p. 106, and iii. xvi. 3–4, pp. 117–18.

it says on the subject it certainly expresses a view of light
nearer to the *De luce* than the *Hexaëmeron*. But there is one
insuperable—as it seems to me, although McEvoy interprets it
otherwise—objection to the view that the *De operationibus solis*
is later than *De luce*. Quite simply, the *De operationibus solis*
expresses in a tentative form ('*Forte* lux est prima forma') the
doctrine of light which is discussed and then definitively expressed ('Lux est ergo prima forma corporalis') in the *De luce*;
and the whole argument of the *De luce* is based on this formula.
The obvious explanation is that, in the *De operationibus solis*, the
new idea was just emerging, and that, in the *De luce*, it was
proved and exploited. McEvoy dissents: 'it is my opinion that
the word "perhaps" (*forte*) indicates, not uncertainty, but a
kind of self-consciousness: the theory in question was Grosseteste's own and he did not wish to advance it as though it were
a universally accepted truth.'[55]

There are two grounds for doubting whether this explanation
is correct. The first is that tentative expressions are very common in Grosseteste's works: there are several examples in the
De operationibus solis itself, and they are certainly intended to
convey a real uncertainty and not a kind of self-conscious modesty.[56] And secondly, in the *De luce* he certainly thought he had
proved his thesis, and he had no inhibition in stating it. There
was no reason why he should be reticent at a later date unless
he had changed his mind—a possibility which McEvoy rightly
denies. A more natural interpretation of the evidence, from
every point of view, would suggest a development from the
Commentary on the Psalms, to the *Hexaëmeron*, to the *De operationibus solis*, to the *De luce*. In this sequence the development
from the first fragmentary formulations to the fully formed and
clearly expressed statement is steady and consistent. McEvoy's
reversal of this sequence seems chiefly to arise from an attempt
to bring Grosseteste's scientific development, including its
metaphysical extension in his theory of light, to completion
before beginning his theology. This aim, combined with the
belief that Grosseteste's science was still immature in the early
1220s, required the crowding together of his scientific works in

[55] McEvoy 1983, pp. 650–1.
[56] For similar expressions in this work, see McEvoy 1974, p. 62 l. 7, p. 68 l. 5, p. 69
l. 9, p. 76 ll. 7–9, p. 77 l. 6, p. 83 ll. 4 and 12, p. 86 l. 8, p. 89 l. 6.

the years 1225-33. It also required that his theology should be
delayed to an implausibly late date.

I do not claim, in this sketch of his development, to have
solved all the difficulties, nor to have assigned all his works to
the appropriate moment of his career. But I think that some
progress has been made, and that this progress is consolidated
by shifting the *De luce* forward from *c.*1225 to a later date which
I would hesitate to designate with any precision. In view of the
great complexity of the question, it is reassuring that Fr. Gieben
takes a similar view and dates the *De luce c.*1241 or later.[57] I
can express no view about the precise date, but the sequence
suggested by this date seems to me entirely right.

IV. A SKELETON CHRONOLOGY

The foregoing considerations would lead to a time-table for
the works which have been discussed, roughly as follows :

Computus I	*c.*1195
De Cometis	*c.*1200
Computus II (formerly *III*)	*c.*1205
Computus III (formerly *II*)	*c.*1215-20
Commentary on *Posterior Analytics*	*c.*1220-5
Commentary on *Physics* I-IV	*c.*1220-5
Commentary on *Psalms*	1225-30
Commentary on *Physics* V, VII-VIII	*c.*1232-5
Commentary on *Physics* VI	?
De Luce	*c.*1235-40

The *De generatione stellarum* and *De fluxu et refluxu maris* disappear
from the list.

All these dates are in varying degrees conjectural and they
are liable to be modified, some perhaps drastically, by further
study. But I think that the main lines of development are fairly
clear: a long period of scientific development from about 1195
till the early 1220s; followed by years of strenuous reading
and theological teaching and writing till 1235; and, thereafter,
continued scientific and theological speculation, with an increased emphasis on pastoral work in his active life; and, in his

---

[57] As reported by McEvoy, ibid., p. 648.

intellectual life, large-scale, ambitiously planned, and elaborately organised works of translation, especially of the *Hierarchies* of Denys and the *Ethics* of Aristotle, till the end of his life.

This will be the background of the chapters which follow.

7

Grosseteste's Scientific Vision

IF the arguments which have been advanced so far are acceptable, it will appear that the greater part of Grosseteste's scientific work had been completed by 1225, with the exception of those developments, mainly with regard to the place of light in the physical and spiritual constitution of the universe, which are to be associated with his theology. Further, it would seem likely that his scientific development was only loosely associated with any scholastic centre, though in its origins and inspiration it was probably more closely connected with Hereford than with any other place, and his Commentaries on the *Posterior Analytics* and *Physics*, may have been stimulated by his association with the schools of Oxford in the years after 1220.

It is entirely in keeping with his general background that the earliest piece of handwriting which can reasonably be ascribed to him should be the inscription, mentioned above (p. 107), regarding the conjunctions of Mars and Saturn, and Saturn and Jupiter, in 1216. Grosseteste certainly shared the common belief of his contemporaries in the importance of planetary influences on human life; but it is worth noting that the hand which wrote the calculations on the diagrams did not make any conjectures about their significance. This may be pure chance; but it bears out the impression left by all his writings on astronomy that, though astrological prediction may have been the aim, Grosseteste's own interests and expertise lay in the mathematical and physical problems of astronomical events, rather than in their interpretation.

We know that in his later years, after he had turned to the study of theology, he developed reservations about the efficacy of astrology. In this he was probably influenced by Augustine, whom he took as his main guide in his new studies. There is no sign that he ever rejected the theory of planetary influences, which implied the possibility of prediction and forewarning.

But in his last years, when he himself assumed the role of a seer, he had moved far away from astrology to a different kind of prediction altogether.

We may divide the main body of his scientific work into three main areas of interest: astronomy, things and events in the natural world, and the general principles of scientific knowledge. His commentary on the *Posterior Analytics* is especially rich in material on all three; and several of these themes are revived in his later theological works, especially in his *Hexaëmeron*, which easily lent itself to reflections on nature. But despite his own frequent mixing of these themes, it will be convenient if we begin by separating them, starting with astronomy, and going on to the nature of things and the general principles of scientific thought expressed in his *magnum opus*, his commentary on the *Posterior Analytics*.

I. GROSSETESTE'S VIEW OF THE HEAVENS

His astronomical enquiries can be approached from two different starting-points—either from the only comprehensive treatise which he wrote on the subject, or from his numerous small notes or essays on particular problems, such as the causes of rainbows, comets, and eclipses. We will start with his single comprehensive treatise, *De Sphera*, for it helps to throw light on the way in which he approached the whole subject.[1]

DE SPHERA

The *De Sphera* aims at providing a brief outline of a large subject for beginners. Yet even in such an elementary book the peculiar characteristics of his mind are everywhere apparent. They make the work less useful as a textbook, but add greatly to its liveliness and its ability to stimulate the interest of the reader. These points can best be appreciated by comparing his outline with an almost exactly contemporary work by another Englishman, John of Halifax or Holywood (*de Sacrobosco*, as it will be convenient to call him), who probably wrote in Paris, and covered the same ground at similar length.[2]

The aim of both these books was to give a general account of

---

[1] For the text, see Baur, pp. 10-32.
[2] See Lynn Thorndike, *The Sphere of Sacrobosco and its Commentators*, Chicago, 1949, pp. 76-117.

the whole organization of the heavens from the circle of the fixed stars down through the orbits of the seven planets to the circles of the four elements with earth at the centre.

Fundamentally, the general view of the system had not changed since Bede wrote his *De Natura Rerum* five hundred years earlier. But it was necessary to bring Bede's work up to date by introducing the student to eccentricities in the movements of the planets in relation to the fixed stars, which needed to be understood as a preliminary to the more precise measurements of contemporary astronomy. The main work which needed to be taken into account in doing this was the *Almagest* of Ptolemy, as well as some of the other works of Arabic writers which had recently become available in Latin. Grosseteste was certainly well equipped to do all this; but he was extraordinarily reticent about his authorities. He mentions Ptolemy's *Almagest* at only one point, and then simply to point out that Thabit ben Qurra had shown *per certa experimenta* that the movement of the fixed stars differed from the account given by Ptolemy.[3] This sounds grudging: but it is more interesting than that. It shows something about Grosseteste's mind in its scientific phase: indifferent to the slogging parade of authorities, but, in a single throw-away comment, revealing that he had a critical knowledge of them. It implied, further, that if Thabit could show experimentally that Ptolemy was wrong, so could Grosseteste; so, with care, could anyone. Ptolemy had summed up the observations of the centuries before him; then, on one point, Thabit had added a new 'experience'. The process might go on indefinitely. Established doctrine was important because it summed up the results of the great stream of experience through the centuries; but experience was decisive on details, and Grosseteste hoped to make his own additions to the stream.

Generally, of course, experience only confirmed established doctrine; but in doing this it made a contribution, if not to the subject, at least to the vividness of the student's understanding of it. For instance, in proving that the earth is not flat but spherical, he says that this could be known by experience because (if it were flat) the horizon would be at the same point in the heavens for everyone no matter where they

[3] Baur, p. 25.

were.[4] There was no need to say more; but to make the point more vivid he proceeded to give a long account of an experiment, no doubt taken from one of his Arabic sources. At the city of 'Arim' in India (he relates), the Pole star is on the horizon; if you go further north, the Pole rises in the heavens till it is overhead; this could only happen if the world is round. Similarly, if you go east or west, the stars rise either earlier or later. Similarly with lunar eclipses: those which happen in the evening at Arim will be at midnight further east; and will not be seen at all further west. These were 'experiences' which anyone could verify; the universality of the law is not changed but becomes more vivid, more operative in the mind, by verification. The explanation is somewhat laborious, but it shows the mind of a man who takes pleasure, not in generalities, but in individual situations which reveal general laws.

Grosseteste's strong preference for the visible and the concrete is evident in the number of times he begins a new section with an appeal to a visual image: 'Let us imagine', he keeps repeating, 'a semi-circle', 'a circle', 'a straight line','the zodiac', or 'each path in the zodiac'.[5] These are the phrases with which he punctuates the steps in his argument. Then he will sometimes engage in some fairly rash speculation, such as that the southern hemisphere must be uninhabited because the sun's course south of the equator brings it too close to the earth's surface to permit life in those parts.[6] And finally, he ends with a long and elaborately illustrated account of the movements of the moon in relation to the sun and the earth: far too much, one might think, for a general account of the whole system. The reason for this curious imbalance was probably Grosseteste's own special interest in eclipses. Certainly, eclipses are events of great interest for astrologers; but this was not the reason for Grosseteste's interest in them. He was interested in the geometrical shapes of the shadows cast by the earth and the moon, and the evidence they provided for the texture and spherical shape of the moon, and the behaviour of light. Here, as everywhere in his writings, he took up the subjects to which he could make a contribution; and he allowed his personal interests to shape his

[4] Ibid., p. 13.
[5] Ibid., pp. 11, 13, 14, 15 (bis), 20, 22, 25, 26.
[6] Ibid., p. 23.

work, even in what was no more than an elementary textbook. We shall see a similar tendency more fully and brilliantly displayed when we consider his commentary on Aristotle's *Posterior Analytics*.

A man who approached the task of writing a textbook in this spirit was likely to produce a book of unusual interest but of only limited usefulness in the schools—especially in schools conducted with an eye to imparting well-organized information and separating established truth from debatable points. It is not, therefore, surprising that, like most of his works, to judge from the distribution of surviving manuscripts, this treatise had only limited success in the thirteenth-century schools. It grew in popularity only with the growth of Grosseteste's general reputation from the mid-fourteenth century onwards when his personal style and the general tendency of his work came to be appreciated.

As a school textbook it could not compete in popularity with Sacrobosco's work on the same subject. The two works were written at roughly the same time and certainly at the same stage in the development of the subject.[7] But Sacrobosco's work soon became the commonest textbook on astronomy in the schools of Europe, including Oxford, and it fully deserved its success. It covered the subject fully yet succinctly, with a reasonable amount of detail and with a sufficient number of references to authorities to inspire confidence. It is not indeed an easy book to follow; it needed a master to explain and fill it out. Perhaps this was one of its attractions: it gave the master plenty to do. There is no 'let us imagine' in John de Sacrobosco, and there are no appeals to common experience or common eyesight. Where Grosseteste says 'You have only to look at the heavens to see that their movements are circular', his rival more obscurely observes, 'that the heavens are round is proved

---

[7] Hard evidence about the dates of both works is virtually non-existent. In sources and style both would fit most naturally into the first quarter of the thirteenth century. There is no evidence that either author borrowed from or was influenced by the other. McEvoy 1982, p. 506, says of Grosseteste's work that it 'was probably composed within a few years of 1215'. Less happily in 1983 this has become 'the work need not have been composed more than a few years after 1215'. I think that *c.*1215 is as good a date as we can get on present evidence. In view of Grosseteste's quotation of Thabit against Ptolemy, it may be noted that Thabit's work is found in the Bodleian Savile MS 21, ff. 150–5, in close association with the astronomical calculations for 1216 which seem to be in Grosseteste's hand.

by three arguments from similitude, convenience, and necessity':[8] a marvellous opportunity here for the lecturer to eluci-
date the obscurity of Sacrobosco's explanation. Sacrobosco's
work was pre-eminently suitable as a handbook for masters
who needed a basis for their lectures. It suited their procedures.
So it is not surprising that the later medieval statutes of Oxford
University laid down that the Arts student should spend eight
days studying it, naturally with the help of a master's commentaries, of which several have survived.[9] The Oxford statutes
did not mention Grosseteste's work.

Indeed, it is hard to know how Grosseteste's book would
have fitted into a school programme. It is a book for the study
rather than for the lecture room. One can imagine it stimulating the interest of pupils and leading them to the study
of the works of Alfraganus, Thabit, or the *Theorica Planetarum*
of Gerard of Sabbinetta, or Ptolemy himself. These were works
with which Grosseteste seems to have been familiar. It was
from them and from contemporary English students of the
subject that he had picked up his own astronomical knowledge,
and he probably expected the younger generation to do
likewise.

There are sufficient indications in the *De Sphera* that Grosseteste was a man with a preference for clear visual experiences
which confirmed, extended or corrected the general system of
medieval doctrine. His combination of experience and doctrine
cannot easily be accommodated in a textbook: it is better adapted to the writing of short essays on points of detail which
have not been sufficiently dealt with in the received body of
doctrine. This was the mode of writing in which he excelled.

About a dozen essays have survived which contain the main
evidence both of his limitations and opportunities in adding to
the scientific doctrines of the past. Nearly all of them are related
to the phenomena of the heavenly bodies, and it will suffice as
an illustration of his mind and method if we examine one of
them—his little treatise on comets.

[8] See Baur, p. 13, for Grosseteste's 'quod coelum sit sphaericum, patet per ap-
parentiam nobis in visu'; Thorndike, op. cit., p. 80, for Sacrobosco's 'quod celum sit
rotundum triplex est ratio: similitudo, commoditas, necessitas'.

[9] *Statuta Antiqua Universitatis Oxoniensis*, ed. S. Gibson, 1931, p. 33. The *Tractatus de
Sphera* appears several times in the Statutes, generally without an author's name; but
when an author is named, it is always Sacrobosco.

DE COMETIS[10]

This is not one of his more important works. In fact, it is rather confused and obscure in its argument, and it is preserved in several mixed-up forms which suggest that its text was never firmly established. But it has several points of great interest: first, it begins with a statement about his method of enquiry which is highly characteristic; then, it is on a subject which bridges the two main areas of science, the science of the heavens and the sciences of the sub-lunar world; and finally, if the suggestion I have made above is acceptable, it is one of the earliest of his scientific writings.

The statement of his method of enquiry is contained in the first two sentences, which describe the two foundations of this work: an immediate experience and a body of doctrine. The experience comes first: 'The recent appearance of a comet was the occasion of my applying my mind to the nature of comets, and what came to my mind on the subject I have taken care to put into writing for common use.'[11] But then, behind experience and leading it to knowledge, comes doctrine: 'I say at the very beginning that those who consider and experience events and form their own opinion from their experiences without any depth of doctrine (*absque profunditate rationum*) necessarily fall into erroneous opinions.'

From this starting-point Grosseteste goes on immediately to criticize three current views about the nature of comets. These may be broadly distinguished by saying that the first explained them as the effect of the reflection of the sun's rays from stars; the second saw them as conflagrations in the heavens caused by many rays being focused on the same point; and the third looked on them as temporary aggregations of stars. Grosseteste has already told us the grounds of his general criticism of these opinions: they are the views of men who have observed a phenomenon and attempted to explain it with insufficient knowledge of the doctrine necessary for a true explanation. In the present case, this insufficiency showed itself in two forms.

[10] Printed in Baur, pp. 36-41, and (on the basis of the superior MSS. Florence Bibl. Marucelliana Cod. C. 163, Bibl. Riccordiana Cod. 885, and Madrid Bibl. Nat. lat. 3314) by S. H. Thomson, *Isis*, xix, 1933, 19-25, with supplement in *Med. et Hum.*, xi, 1957, 36-7. For discussion of its date, see above, pp. 125-7.

[11] These are the first words in the text printed by Thomson 1933; they are omitted in the reworkings of the text printed by Baur.

First, in ignorance of the principles of celestial natures: since these are unchanging, it is wrong to attribute to them eccentricities of behaviour or changes of composition. Second, in ignorance of the geometrical principles of reflection, which would quickly show that comets could not have their origin in reflected light.

Having disposed of the current opinions, Grosseteste makes a bold attempt to give an explanation which will take account of the basic difficulty raised by comets. The difficulty is that comets cannot properly be looked on as celestial phenomena since they are clearly unstable: their appearance is unpredictable; they are visible only for a short time; and, even during this time, their appearance varies; sometimes their tails point in one direction, sometimes in another, sometimes they are invisible; sometimes they are bright, sometimes dull. Everything about them suggests instability; but stability is the essential quality of all things celestial. And yet they have one essential symptom of a celestial origin: they move with the daily movement of the spheres. How is this dual character to be accounted for? I will quote only one sentence of Grosseteste's argument which contains the key to his solution: 'It is clear therefore that a comet is sublimated fire separated from its terrestrial nature and assimilated to the celestial nature.'[12] In other words (so far as I can understand this complex statement) comets consist of the element of fire, in its pure state. Consequently, they have a terrestrial origin, for fire is one of the four elements of the sub-lunar world. But they exhibit fire without the taint of combination with other elements; so they belong to the highest of the terrestrial spheres, and—whether as a result of the tendency of fire to rise or from some other cause— they have strayed into the celestial sphere of unchanging being. They are hybrids between earth and heaven, and they reflect in a debilitated state the influence of the celestial planet under which they were formed.

I must leave the implications of this theory and the manner in which Grosseteste works it out to those more learned in these matters than I am. I shall comment on only three points. In the first place, it is very remarkable that on so recondite a

[12] Thomson 1933, p. 24; Baur, p. 38, where the word 'trica' is used for 'cometa' of Thomson's text.

question Grosseteste mentions no author on the subject. The three opinions which he outlines and rejects are given without names attached to them. They are simply the views of those who have 'considered' or 'experienced' one or other aspect of the comet's behaviour without a full knowledge of the necessary doctrines of astronomy or mathematics. In view of his introductory sentence about the appearance of a comet having prompted his thoughts on the subject, it is hard to resist the conclusion that the rejected opinions were those of colleagues or companions who likewise had speculated about the thing they had seen without having read any work which dealt with the subject.

Secondly, the *De Cometis* shows us Grosseteste, perhaps at the start of his scientific career, already asserting the two foundations of scientific knowledge: experience and doctrine. The experience on this occasion was the appearance of a comet— an event not likely to be experienced again for a long time. On other occasions, and for other treatises, he would base his argument on experiences of greater frequency, such as lunar eclipses, or on everyday experiences such as rainbows and the refraction of light. His 'experiences' are never, I think, contrived or set up as 'experiments'. They are observations of events that happen in nature. To this extent he belongs to a pre-experimental age; but in his emphasis on close observation, combined with general doctrine about celestial and terrestrial spheres and the mathematical rules of reflection as the foundation of scientific argument, he is in a different world from his older contemporaries, Alexander Nequam and Gerald of Wales; nearer to Daniel of Morley and Alfred of Shareshill; and perhaps nearer still to astronomers in the diocese of Hereford with whom he consorted after 1195.

Thirdly, it is noticeable in this work that one of Grosseteste's main concerns was to safeguard the astrological status of comets as transmitters of influences from celestial bodies. He did this by insisting on their dual character: they were of terrestrial origin, but set in the sphere of celestial bodies; consequently they transmitted the influence of the planet under which they were formed in a disordered way, which caused illness in individuals, and disorders in communities and in nature. The theoretical leap may seem hazardous, but it could be justified by the universal experience of disasters associated with the appearance of comets. So Grosseteste might claim to have followed the double principle of all scientific reasoning, careful observation combined with a rigorous attention to doctrine.

It is an interesting, and not irrelevant, question to ask what he would have made of Aristotle's account of the subject if he had known it. According to Aristotle, comets were caused by dry, hot exhalations rising until they came in contact with the rotating heavenly sphere, which by friction caused them to burst into flame. Sometimes the fire was short-lived, but sometimes, when the exhalation was of the right consistency, it was lasting and became a comet with a streaming tail. This was a much simpler and mechanically superior explanation to Grosseteste's; but it reduced the contact of the comet with the celestial spheres to a merely surface friction. On astrological grounds, it is likely that Grosseteste, at least in his earlier years, would have thought Aristotle's account defective and would have preferred his own, despite its ambiguities.

II. THE *POSTERIOR ANALYTICS* AND THE NATURAL WORLD

Grosseteste's special contribution to the thought of his time lay in the equal weight which he gave to observation and to the doctrine appropriate to each of the natural sciences. His emphasis on observation may reflect his peculiarly independent personality. But he also found in Aristotle's *Posterior Analytics* a theoretical account of the roles of observation and general reasoning in building up a body of scientific knowledge, which made a deep impression on him. It is quite possible that Grosseteste was the first medieval thinker to appreciate the nature and importance of this work, and his commentary on the text is the piece of scientific writing which best displays the range of his interests and talents. To understand its place in his life, we must look first at the way in which his predecessors had used it, and then at what he made of it.

1. The entry of the *Posterior Analytics* into Western thought

The *Posterior Analytics* had been made available to the West in a Latin translation by James of Venice in about 1140, but it had only very slowly made its way forward into general circulation by the end of the twelfth century.[13] There were two reasons for this slow progress: first, the intrinsic difficulties of the work, and secondly, a lack of interest in the problems which it discussed.

The intrinsic difficulties were of several different kinds. First, the extreme difficulty of the questions which Aristotle attempted to answer: how can we know, and what can we know, about the structure of events which we experience in the world around us? What degree of certainty can we achieve in what we know? And how can we organize our knowledge systematically? He was, as a recent commentator has remarked, trying to do for all branches of scientific knowledge what Euclid did for geometry alone: that is to say, he was preparing the ground for a critique of demonstrative knowledge in every area of science from biology to physics, and from psychology to ethics.[14] It was an enterprise of overwhelming difficulty, and one on which—to quote again the same recent commentator— Aristotle's treatise left a mass of 'tangled obscurities through which the two main doctrines of the *Posterior Analytics* fitfully gleam'.[15]

In addition to these general difficulties, the work had special difficulties for twelfth-century Western readers. John of Salisbury, who was as well qualified as anyone in the century to understand it, put the difficulties in a nutshell: 'There are', he wrote, 'as many obstacles to understanding this work as there are chapters in it—and you are lucky if there are not more obstacles than chapters.'[16] He tried to explain why everyone found it more difficult than Aristotle's other works, and he mentioned several possible causes—the confusion caused by an unusual number of scribal errors; faults introduced in the transmission of the text; confusions even in the mind of the author himself who, in drawing his illustrations from different disciplines, had failed to order his thoughts with his accustomed lucidity.

[13] For the translation by James of Venice, see L. Minio-Paluello, 'Iacobus Veneticus Grecus', *Traditio*, viii, 1952, 265-304 (repr. in the author's *Opuscula: The Latin Aristotle*, 1972, 189-228). For its dissemination after this date, see L. Minio-Paluello and B. G. Dod (edd.), *Aristoteles Latinus*, iv, 1968: *Analytica Posteriora*, pp. xx-xli.

[14] On these points I have found the remarks of Jonathan Barnes, *Aristotle's* Posterior Analytics (with translation and Commentary), Oxford, 1975, extremely helpful.

[15] Ibid., p. xii.

[16] *Metalogicon*, iv, c. 6 (ed. C. C. J. Webb, 1929, p. 171).

But there was another more fundamental reason why every-one in the twelfth century found the work especially difficult: the problem which dominated the whole work, the problem of how we know about the natural world, was not a problem in the twelfth century. The theory of knowledge which lay at the root of all scholastic effort was this: God had made man with full knowledge of the nature of all created things, and with a sufficient immediate knowledge of God for all human needs. A large part of this knowledge had been distorted, blurred or darkened as a result of the Fall; but something remained, and much of what had been lost had been recovered by God's subsequent revelations in the Bible, and by the long-continued efforts of men of superior intellectual power during the supreme centuries of human history from about the fourth century BC to the fourth century AD, when intellect and Revelation had combined most powerfully to restore the diminished knowledge of mankind.[17]

It followed from this view of the restoration of human know-ledge after the Fall that the main task of modern scholars was not to make new discoveries, but to recollect, restore and or-ganize old knowledge, and make it serviceable for the present. The problem was not 'How do we know?', for to know was inherent in man's nature. It was not even 'How do we restore what was lost by the corruption of man's nature?', for this task had largely been already accomplished. The problem was, 'How can we rediscover and make easily available the records of old knowledge and put the whole together in a useable form?' In this task, observation of physical phenomena could play only a small part.

The problems in the *Posterior Analytics*, therefore, scarcely existed for twelfth-century scholastic thinkers, and Aristotle's solutions seemed both unnecessary and unconvincing. The idea that new knowledge of genuine importance could be obtained by collecting, arranging, and examining the miscellaneous data of sense impressions was implausible on several grounds. In the first place, the senses are notoriously unreliable. Secondly, the

---

[17] The most succinct and widely disseminated twelfth-century outline of the growth of human knowledge is in Hugh of St Victor's *Didascalicon* of *c.*1130, ed. C. H. Buttimer, Washington, 1939, and translated with an excellent commentary by Jerome Taylor, Columbia Univ. Press, New York, 1961.

great minds of the past had long ago extracted from the fluctuating mass of sense impressions the main constant categories
such as *genera* and *species* in the natural world, and justice,
faith, hope and love in the spiritual world. These categories
represented the essential nature of things, and their refinement
depended more on improved definitions than on further observations. It seemed highly unlikely that the shifting and unreliable impressions of the senses could make serious additions
to the certain and systematic body of knowledge which was the
aim of all serious enquiry.

This combination of obstacles accounts for the general neglect of the *Posterior Analytics* for more than fifty years after
its introduction in the West, and for the superficiality of the
occasional comments on it which scholars were moved to make.
John of Salisbury, who was the only writer of the century to
describe the work in the context of contemporary thought, had
some notion of the difficulty of introducing it into the schools
of his day. He was well aware that in this work Aristotle attempted to extend the area of logic from the structure of argument to the rules appropriate to the study of the physical
universe. But he knew that this lay beyond the scope of the
contemporary schools:

This book deals with the most difficult branch of argument, the art of
demonstration (i. e. of demonstrating the truth of general laws of
nature). But this has fallen into disuse among us, except by mathe-
maticians, and even among them it is used only by geometers; and
their discipline is rarely found except in one region of Spain and in
the neighbouring parts of Africa, where geometry is studied for the
sake of astronomy, as it is also in Egypt and among the peoples of
Arabia.[18]

This is a very striking comment, made in about 1160, by a
scholar who knew from long experience the range of scholastic
learning pursued in Paris in the middle years of the twelfth
century. But even by the time that John of Salisbury was writing, his words about the areas to which the study of geometry
was confined were no longer true. Adelard of Bath had brought
the combination of geometry and astronomy from the frontiers
of Europe to England; Raymond was engaged in their study

[18] *Metalogicon*, iv. 6 (p. 171).

at Marseille; and there were no doubt other places where practitioners could be found. But these studies had not entered the central stream of scholastic teaching, and it took many years for the importance of the *Posterior Analytics* to be appreciated.

The very slow progress of the work as an intellectual tool can be illustrated in the early years of the thirteenth century from the use that Alexander Nequam made of it. Like John of Salisbury, he felt the fascination of this strange and difficult work. He looked on it partly as a collection of logical puzzles disturbing the traditional study of logic, partly as a haphazard collection of scientific curiosities ripe for moralization. He noted that it had caused a shift in some of the logical doctrines taught in Paris;[19] and he seized on one of Aristotle's scientific illustrations for moralization. Since the illustration reappears in Grosseteste's commentary, it will prepare the ground for a useful comparison if we notice now the use that Nequam made of it.

Aristotle had mentioned that distant stars twinkled and near ones did not. In the *Posterior Analytics* he was not concerned with the truth of this statement or its causes, but only with the two contrasting forms of argument arising from it: from effect to cause ('they twinkle; therefore they are distant), *or* from cause to effect ('they are distant; therefore they twinkle'). Nequam picked up the illustration; but he was interested neither in the logical contrast nor in the scientific cause; he was interested only in the allegorical significance. His words illustrate the main tendency of English scientific thought at the end of the twelfth century, and they bring us close to Grosseteste's own scientific starting-point. With suitable abbreviation—in their fullness they are very long—they deserve to be quoted, if only to show the subordination of scientific facts to the spiritual reality which they denoted:

The scintillating brightness of the stars brings grateful comfort to mortals by night. Similarly, in the night of this life, sweet comfort comes from those whose deeds shine in the presence of God and men. The stars are placed on high to give light to many. Similarly, spiritual men, the lights of this world, are useful to many, if they are in high positions . . . Stars twinkle, as Aristotle says in his *Posterior Analytics*, because they are very far distant from the earth. Other stars do not

---

[19] *De Naturis Rerum*, pp. 291, 293–4, 299.

twinkle, because they are near. The same effect can be seen in a candle which does not twinkle when it is near, but only when it is far away. Similarly, the minds of the faithful who are far removed from earthly desires are radiant with the light of grace.[20]

There is here not much science and even less logic. The form of the argument, which was Aristotle's only reason for mentioning the matter, gets no attention at all. The scientific reason for twinkling at a distance and not twinkling when near is also left unexplained. Nequam does not ask why scintillation happens, but only what spiritually it means. And yet, in parenthesis, there is one genuine observation—whether Nequam's or borrowed we cannot tell; but it is not Aristotle's—he notices that a candle in the distance twinkles, but nearby it does not. This small observation brings us a little nearer to scientific 'experience', and to Grosseteste.

2. Grosseteste and the problems of Nature

As soon as we turn to Grosseteste's commentary, written perhaps no more than ten, and certainly not more than twenty, years later than Nequam's remarks, we recognize a new scientific consciousness and complexity. He is more aware of the diversity of problems discussed in the *Posterior Analytics* and of its logical structure and general intention. He summarized its argument correctly and in his own words. When he came to the passage on twinkling and non-twinkling stars, he at once commented on the difference between arguments 'quia' and 'propter quid'.[21] Nevertheless his main interest, and his main areas of originality, lay in examining the scientific content of Aristotle's illustrations. Unlike Nequam, he did not (in this work at least) concern himself with the allegorical significance of these illustrative details: he gave his whole mind to ex-

[20] Ibid., pp. 37-8. In another place, Nequam quotes the *Post. Anal.*, as a source of scientific information. See p. 142: 'Pisces non respirant, ut ex doctrina Posteriorum Analecticorum liquet.' There is in fact no mention of the respiration of fish in *Post. Anal.*, and this is not Aristotle's doctrine in those works (e.g. *De Partibus Animalium*, iv. 13) where he discusses the problem. Nequam's statement, therefore, is an illustration of the distorted way in which the ideas of works not yet fully available in translation circulated in the early thirteenth century.

[21] Robertus Grosseteste, *Commentarius in Posteriorum Analyticorum Libros*, ed. Pietro Rossi, Florence, 1981, p. 189.

amining the physical causes of the alleged phenomena; and
these discussions which form incrustations, so to speak, on the
main course of Aristotle's argument provide an admirable observation post from which we can observe the range of Grosseteste's interests and the character of his scientific vision.

His most illuminating discussions—that is to say, those in
which he draws on his own knowledge and his own special
studies—are concerned with phenomena of nature which are
mentioned by Aristotle merely as illustrations of his argument:
the scintillation of stars; the origin of sound; the origin of rain;
the causes of thunder, of the flooding of the Nile, of the falling
of leaves in autumn; and the relation between horns, teeth and
stomachs in horned animals. On all of these subjects he either
contradicts, or finds something to add to Aristotle. The grounds
of his dissent and the nature of his additions provide a lively
guide to the geography of his mind.

THE SCINTILLATION OF STARS

We have already noticed the problem and Alexander
Nequam's response to it. Grosseteste explored it more deeply
and his explanation can be summarized thus. The eye will
always strive to see things as clearly as possible; but objects
appear smaller as their distance from the eye increases; consequently the eye has to strain harder to distinguish its features;
this straining sets up a tremor which gives an appearance of
twinkling.[22]

Briefly, therefore, Grosseteste transfers the cause of the twinkling from the star to the eye, and makes it depend on the
narrowing angle of vision as the distance increases. The explanation may be wrong; but it is recognizably scientific in
isolating a significant variant and associating it with the sense
of strain which everyone experiences in concentrating the eye
on a distant object.

This is not only scientific in principle; it also seems to be
significantly different from anything which Grosseteste found
in his sources. In the *Posterior Analytics* he would have found no
explanation at all. Elsewhere, however, in his *De Caelo*, Aristotle
did attempt an explanation of the twinkling phenomenon, and

[22] Rossi, pp. 190–1.

this was a work in which Grosseteste had a very strong
interest.[23] In the *De Caelo* Aristotle attributed the twinkling of
distant stars to their great distance from the observer 'whose
visual ray, being excessively prolonged, becomes weak and
wavering'.[24] So here we have a physiological explanation somewhat similar to Grosseteste's. But Grosseteste differs on one
essential point. Aristotle thought that the 'visual ray' became
weakened by excessive length. Grosseteste attributed the weak-
ening, not to the length of the 'visual ray', but to the diminishing angle of vision. Clearly, there are here two different
presuppositions about the nature of the space between the observer and the distant stars. Aristotle's 'weakened visual ray'
implies either that there are obstacles in space (perhaps dust
or some other impurity) which progressively diminish the
strength of the visual ray, or that the impetus of the visual ray
generated by the observer diminishes with distance. Grosseteste's insistence on the diminishing *size* of the visible object
implies that space is wholly translucent—and this in fact seems
to have been his opinion about space above the sphere of the
moon. Also, perhaps more important, Grosseteste's explanation
follows a line of thought that was congenial to him. He had
thought much about the geometry of light, angles of vision,
reflection, refraction and similar subjects, and he preferred
Euclid to Aristotle as a guide to scientific thought. So the
straining of the eye to see as the angle of vision becomes smaller
made an instinctive appeal to him.

THE ORIGIN OF SOUND

It is on the origin of sound that he makes his most original
suggestion, and the way in which his suggestion arises from
a remark of Aristotle's provides a good example both of his
dependence on Aristotle for stimulation and his independence
in developing his own views. The passage in Aristotle from

[23] The credit for the discovery that Grosseteste translated the *De Caelo* and Simplicius's Commentary on it belongs to D. J. Allen, 'Medieval versions of Aristotle—*De
Caelo* and the Commentary of Simplicius', *MARS* ii, 1950, 81–120. McEvoy 1982, pp.
477–8, sums up the present state of knowledge on the subject. We do not know when
Grosseteste first became acquainted with the *De Caelo*, but his serious work on it
certainly belongs to a later period in his life, and it is unlikely that he knew it when he
commented on the *Posterior Analytics*.

[24] *De Caelo*, 290ᵃ 18.

which his suggestion arose was the origin of several of Grosseteste's speculations.[25] Aristotle had remarked that widely different events could have the same type of cause. For example,
an echo, a reflected image, and a rainbow, are all different
forms of repercussion. This was a remark which stirred Grosseteste's interest at several different levels. It appealed to his
geometrical interest in the measurement of angles. Then, at a
deeper level, it appealed to his sense of the unity of nature in
all its parts. And deeper still, all forms of repercussion seemed
to him to exhibit the operation of the primary matter of the
universe: light.

Aristotle had said that echoes, reflections and rainbows
are 'identical in genus' but 'different in species'. He did not
elaborate the ways in which these different phenomena were
similar, but Grosseteste attempted an explanation. He said that
reflected images and rainbows are two different effects of light
falling on solid surfaces, the first on impenetrable surfaces from
which the light rebounds, the second on transparent surfaces
which deflect the beams of light according to geometrical rules
which can be demonstrated. But this explanation still left echoes
unexplained: what form of repercussion do they exhibit?
Grosseteste's explanation is very extraordinary. He says that
sound is also an effect of light—not of light falling on a surface,
but of light which is imprisoned in pockets of rarefied air within
all corporeal bodies. When a body is disturbed by a blow, these
pockets (or atoms as we may almost call them) are dislodged
from their customary inertia and continue to reverberate until
they return to their original state. This reverberation causes the
noise we hear. An echo is produced when the original sound is
obstructed by a solid body in which it sets up a similar ex-
citation of pockets of light within it; this agitation makes a
corresponding sound which we hear as an echo.

Grosseteste seems here almost to be touching the fringe of a
modern view of matter. But all that concerns us here is his
willingness to go beyond Aristotle in attempting to understand
the uniformities of nature. Here as everywhere he shows a
strong urge to find explanations for physical occurrences which

[25] Rossi, pp. 386-7. The passage in *Post. Anal.* is ii, c. 15 (98ª23-34). See also
Grosseteste's *De generatione sonorum*, Baur, pp. 7-10.

will embrace a variety of observed facts and give them a place in a general view of the universe.

THE FLOODING OF THE NILE

The same tendency is well exemplified in the next problem which Aristotle mentioned in the same section of the *Posterior Analytics*. The passage runs as follows:

Other connections—that is, other than the forms of repercussion just mentioned—differ in that the 'middles' (or causes) are subordinate one to another. For example: Why does the Nile rise towards the end of the month? Because, towards its close, the month is more stormy. Why is the month more stormy towards its close? Because the moon is waning. Here the one cause is subordinate to the other.[26]

Grosseteste evidently—and rightly—felt that scientifically this is very feeble, and he proceeded to give a remarkably complete explanation of an event in nature which had seemed to scholars of the generation before his own to be one of the insoluble problems of the universe.[27] He based his explanation on several sources that had only recently been available, and he used them with the confidence of one who believed that the foundations of the problem had at last been uncovered. 'I say', he wrote, 'that it is the humidifying influence of the moon, which augments the amount of moisture in the air and in the water. This humidity is fortified by the warming influence of the sun, which rarefies the waters and causes them to expand.'[28]

The combined influences of sun and moon thus bring about the flooding of the Nile. In addition, he mentions contributory causes, such as high winds whipping up the waves and obstructing the mouth of the river with sand-banks. But in the end he returns to an emphatic statement of a single original cause in the movements of the heavens: 'the causal order is this: the heavens move the seasons and the seasons move the things of nature.'

In this explanation, two points are clear. First, Grosseteste

---

[26] *Post. Anal.* ii. 15 (98ᵃ29–34).

[27] John of Salisbury, *Policraticus*, vii. 3 (ed. C. C. J. Webb, ii. 98–9), mentions tides, the source of the Nile, and the lunar influence on the rise and decline of humours in animals among the *dubitabilia* which are susceptible of no explanation either by faith or reason or sense.

[28] Rossi, pp. 387–9.

gives a fuller and more coherent account of the causes of the
Nile's flooding than Aristotle; and, second, his account lays
great emphasis on the movements of the heavens, and particularly on the complementary influences of the moon (which
increases the amount of humidity in the water and atmosphere)
and the sun (which causes this increased humidity to expand).
As for the stormy weather which Aristotle emphasized, this is
only a secondary cause for Grosseteste, but he examines it in
greater detail and discovers two separate effects in high waves
and the creation of sandbanks which contribute to the flooding.

This is only one of several examples of his close attention to
detail, and of his dissatisfaction with Aristotle's account of a
scientific problem leading him to further enquiry.

THE CAUSE OF THUNDER

A similar dissatisfaction prompted his investigation of the cause
of thunder. Aristotle had said that thunder is the noise of fire
being quenched by water in the clouds.[29] Grosseteste was not
satisfied with this because, as he observed, when fire is quenched, it does not in fact make a noise like thunder. So he
proceeds to give an account of what happened step by step. He
follows Aristotle in his account of moist air rising from the earth
till it reaches an area of hot air where a combination of heat
and pressure sets it on fire. But then his account diverges from
Aristotle's. He agrees that the fire is extinguished by the surrounding moisture; but it is not this that makes the noise. The
noise comes from the expansion (or in Grosseteste's phrase,
rarefication) of the air when it is heated. This causes it to force
its way through the surrounding vapour with an explosive force
which produces the roar of thunder.[30]

BIOLOGICAL REFLECTIONS

At another point, Grosseteste takes up Aristotle's brief account
of the connection between three superficially unrelated
phenomena in animals: having horns, having only one row of
teeth, and having a third stomach.[31] On this subject, he makes
use of Aristotle's treatise on the *Parts of Animals*, but he also

[29] *Post. Anal.* ii. 8 (93^b 77-13), ii. 9 (94^a 3-10), ii. 11 (94^b 32-4).
[30] Rossi, pp. 342-3.
[31] *Post. Anal.* ii. 14, 98^a 16-19.

adds something which is not found in Aristotle's works. He follows Aristotle in thinking that animals with horns have only one row of teeth because their horns used up the material needed for a second row of teeth; and they have a third stomach because, requiring more machinery for adequate mastication, they need an additional stomach to store the food for further chewing. This leads him to further reflections on the economy of nature in making provision for different methods of defence which necessitate economies elsewhere in the system: hinds, camels and oxen, all have only one row of teeth and a third stomach, but only oxen have horns; the others rely on different modes of defence—hinds on extra speed, camels on extra weight and size—and their systems are adjusted to their environment and digestion in different ways. For example, the camel has a hard upper plate instead of teeth which allows it to eat hard spiky food. Therefore, if we wish to give a scientific account of the phenomenon 'having horns', we may say that 'having horns goes with *not* having upper teeth, but having some other aid to digestion instead of teeth'. Equally, 'lacking upper teeth' may be explained as 'having horns or some other aid for defence instead of horns'. Or we may say that 'having horns' is the cause of not having teeth in the upper mandible; and not having teeth in the upper mandible is the cause of having an extra stomach.[32]

Most, perhaps all, of the scientific details in these observations could be found scattered throughout Aristotle's works. What Grosseteste adds is his own sense of the providential economy of nature in the adaptation of the organisms of living creatures to their needs and environment—ideas which point forward to the scientific thought of later centuries.

FALLING LEAVES

Aristotle dealt with this subject at some length in connection with the problem whether the existence of an effect logically entails the existence of a cause precisely commensurate with the effect.[33] He rejected the universal character of deciduous

[32] Rossi, pp. 381-3, where references will also be found to Aristotle, *De Partibus Animalium*, iii. 2, 662[b] 23 ff., and iii. 14, 674[a] 27 ff.

[33] *Post. Anal.* ii. 16, 98[b] 5-20; ii. 17, 99[a] 23-9. This principle was later to have great practical importance for Grosseteste in discussing the prime cause of the decay of Christendom (see below, pp. 277-81).

trees (namely, 'the possession of broad leaves') as too general an explanation of their leaves' falling; and he proposed as a sufficient cause 'the congealing of sap at the junction of leaf-stalk and stem' or 'something of the sort'. In commenting on this, Grosseteste appears (as always) to be more interested in scientific explanation than in the logical problem which it illustrated.[34] He rejected Aristotle's suggestion that it was the *congealing* or thickening of sap which caused the leaves to fall: on the contrary, it was the *drying up*, or rarefication, of the sap that caused their fall. His argument was that the thinness of the sap, which led to the drying up, was an essential feature of broad-leaved deciduous trees, for it was only by being thin that the sap could reach the extremities of the large leaves. Consequently, there was a necessary connection between the type of sap, the size of leaf and the fact that they were deciduous. Aristotle, he remarked, erred in thinking that it was the thickening or congealing which caused the leaves to fall. But he pointed out that there was a special case in which the congealing which Aristotle postulated actually took place: this was when the petals of flowers, which protect the nascent fruit, fall when the sap congeals to form the fruit. 'Aristotle did not understand this', he added.

Grosseteste also said a word in favour of the 'broad-leafed' explanation which Aristotle had rejected as too general an explanation of their falling: their broadness (he explained) adds to their weight and wind resistance, and can therefore be a contributory cause of their fall when the sap becomes thin.[35]

These remarks on the superficially unimportant subject of why leaves fall illustrate the very complex nature of Grosseteste's thought about the natural world. It is a highly intricate combination of observation and doctrine, of induction and deduction. Moreover it is closely related to his practical experience of the world: the man who will later teach the countess of Lincoln how to calculate her stock of seed corn is here at work in the observation of trees in the orchard; the believer in the economy of nature is active in observing the role of the flower in protecting the fruit. And all these features are brought together, as we shall see, in interpreting the spiritual sig-

[34] Rossi, pp. 392-8.
[35] Rossi, p. 398, ll. 167-71.

nificance of natural processes in the Psalms. This wholeness in his thought becomes most evident when he turns to theology, but it was always there. The main principle of his theology had been learnt in his science.

THE INITIAL IRRIGATION OF THE EARTH

When Grosseteste came to the passage in the *Posterior Analytics* where Aristotle speaks of the everlasting cyclical process of coming-into-being and ceasing-to-be as exemplified in rain falling, earth moistening, dew rising, cloud forming, rain falling and so on, he was quick to pick up the error.[36] Whatever the philosopher might say about this endless process, in truth the earth was first moistened not by rain but by subterranean springs and moisture drawn from the sea by secret passages, which irrigate the whole. So the process had a starting-point which did not require any previous unending sequence of rain, etc. It started with sea-water penetrating the earth and then rising up through the earth, so that dew formed and evaporated to make the clouds from which rain fell. It was thus that the cyclical process as we know it began. There is no need to postulate an endless cycle.

Grosseteste was impatient with those who thought that Aristotle's general view of the universe was compatible with Christianity. In particular he was always ready to condemn Aristotle's doctrine of the eternity of the world, which underlay his account of an endless cycle of rain and evaporation: on this point, as on others, the Book of Genesis preserved the true scientific explanation. But, despite his impatience with Aristotle's errors and shortcomings,[37] he comes closer to the exploratory spirit of Aristotle than Aquinas, who treated him too little as a tentative enquirer and too much as an organizer of accurate truth. What Grosseteste found in Aristotle often sparked off a train of thought of his own. His comment on the

[36] *Post. Anal.* ii. 12, 96ᵃ 1–7. For Grosseteste's comments, see Rossi, pp. 361–3, and *Hex.* i., viii. 2–4 (pp. 58–61); x. i. 9 (pp. 289–90).

[37] In addition to his criticisms of Aristotle's scientific and theological errors, he also criticizes his too great brevity (pp. 107, 109), his confusions ('more suo perturbans ordinem', p. 8), his deliberate obfuscations ('more suo occultandi gratia', p. 269; 'exemplum illud aliquid habet obscuritatis et dubitationis', p. 262). Complaints about Aristotle's obscurity are very common at this period (for examples, see Callus 1943, p. 263), but Grosseteste's are better documented and more precise than most.

first sentence of the *Posterior Analytics* provides a striking example of Aristotle's inflammatory influence on him, and it also gives us an insight into his own ideal of teaching and learning. Aristotle's first sentence runs thus: 'All knowledge is acquired by doctrine and intellectual discipline . . . based on pre-existing knowledge.' On this, Grosseteste comments:

I say that knowledge of principles is not acquired by doctrine, because we learn only that which, when we first receive it, seems to us doubtful or false. Then, after we have doubted or held a contrary opinion, it manifests itself to us as the truth . . . To speak more truly, what teaches us is not what we outwardly hear or read, but what inwardly illuminates the mind and shows it the truth.[38]

Learning, for Grosseteste, required an active participation of the mind in doubting, denying, and receiving illumination. It was to this activity that Aristotle stirred him, especially when he disagreed. He had no share of Aristotle's systematic power; yet his investigating zeal—tentative, uneven and wrong though it often is—responded to a similar spirit in Aristotle.

3. Grosseteste's account of scientific knowledge

In all his additions and corrections Grosseteste shows himself, like Nequam, more stimulated by Aristotle's illustrations than by the forms of argument which they illustrated. Aristotle's lightest word was enough to set him scurrying to present the case more clearly, and to develop the scientific explanation more fully. Grosseteste's view of knowledge differed widely from Aristotle's; but in practice he came very close to Aristotle,

[38] The first sentence of the *Post. Anal.* in the Latin version quoted by Grosseteste reads, 'Omnis scientia acquisita per doctrinam et disciplinam, non dico sensitivam sed intellectivam, aggenerata [*or* aggregata] est ex pre-existente cognitione.' Grosseteste's comment reads: 'Et dico quod scientia principiorum non est acquisita per doctrinam, quia non docemur vel addiscimus nisi illud quod cum primo concipimus est nobis dubium vel apparet falsum, et post dubitationem vel contrariam opinionem manifestatur nobis eius veritas. Nec solum illud voco doctrinam quod ab ore doctoris audimus, sed scripturam etiam loco doctoris accipio; et, si verius dicamus, nec qui exterius sonat docet nec littera scripture exterius visa docet, sed solum movent hec duo et excitant; sed verus doctor est qui interius mentem illuminat et veritatem ostendit.' (Rossi, p. 94.) Wycliffe, with his usual flair for picking out significant passages in Grosseteste and sharpening their impact, quotes this passage as follows: 'magister et signa eius non sunt nisi instrumenta quedam per accidens moventia, sed est interius verus doctor, qui mentem illuminat et veritatem ostendit' (*De Veritate S. Scripturae*, i. 202: for this aspect of Grosseteste's influence, see below, pp. 303-7).

and clearly learnt much from him about the way in which knowledge about the natural world is to be sought.

For instance, he differed from Aristotle on the necessity of sense impressions as the basis for knowledge: after describing Aristotle's position on this question, he roundly declared:

Nevertheless, I say that it is possible to have some knowledge without the help of the senses, for in the divine mind all knowledge, not only of universals but also of all particulars, exists eternally . . . and intelligences which have received illumination from that source of light see all knowable things, both universal and particular . . . and this would be the case with all human beings, if they were not weighed down under the load of the corrupt body.[39]

In principle, therefore, the senses are not necessary for knowledge. But in practice, in man's fallen state, they are needed to provide hints of that knowledge which mankind has lost, and to point the way towards its restoration:

It is not in sensation that we know; but it is as a result of sensation that knowledge of the universal comes to us [*coaccidit in nobis*]. This knowledge comes to us *via* the senses, but not *from* the senses [*non gratia sensus*].[40]

There can be no scientific method for testing Grosseteste's view of divine illumination, for it is only experienced as an interior effect. But the procedure he describes has the great merit of encouraging the widest possible use of the senses in the process of knowing: they are the tools that make knowledge possible. They are like a walking stick for a lame man: it is not the cause of his ability to walk, but a *sine qua non* of his doing so.

This view of the senses allowed Grosseteste to follow Aristotle, and yet to reconstruct his arguments and illustrations in his own terms. He was especially successful in interpreting the final chapter of the *Posterior Analytics* which brings the whole argument to the test of practical experience. In this chapter, Aristotle, having completed his study of the various forms of valid demonstration, asks a final question: how can we obtain the primary knowledge necessary for such demonstrations? This knowledge cannot be innate; for, if it were, the question of how

---

[39] Rossi, pp. 212–16 (on *Post. Anal.* i. 18, 81ª 37–ᵇ 9).
[40] Rossi, p. 269: Grosseteste is here commenting on *Post. Anal.* i. 31, 87ᵇ 27–39.

we can get it would not arise. Nor can it be acquired from pre-existing knowledge, for this would imply the existence of innate knowledge. So it must come from a capacity in the mind for recognizing the general truths which fit, and which alone fit, the evidence of the senses. The evidence of the senses, says Aristotle, rising to his greatest imaginative height, is like a stream of defeated soldiers fleeing from a battlefield without order and without direction; suddenly, one man stops and turns to face the enemy; then another stops beside him, and another, and another, until the original order of the army is recreated.[41] Pictorially, this represents the mysterious process whereby the incoherent flow of sense impressions takes shape and becomes a replica of an external order, of which these impressions are the fugitive effects.

The supreme test of Grosseteste's understanding of the *Posterior Analytics* is to ask what he made of this. So far as we know, no previous reader in the West had made anything of it, for the reason which I have already mentioned: since reason and revelation were the only (and sufficient) restorers of the image of truth, which had been shattered at the Fall, there was no need to call in the senses.[42] But Grosseteste understood the passage brilliantly—though not quite as Aristotle intended, for a mistranslation in the Latin version put him on the wrong track.[43] Yet he turned even this misunderstanding to good account and gave the text an original twist of his own. He took the passage to mean that, as a result of the overthrow of man's natural powers through sin, the higher faculties of reason, memory and imagination collapsed, but they were saved from complete ruin because the humblest faculty, sense perception, stood firm. With this faculty as their *point d'appui*, the higher

---

[41] *Post. Anal.* ii. 19, 100ᵃ 11-13.

[42] John of Salisbury, the only scholar known to have discussed the passage at some length before Grosseteste (*Metalogicon*, iv. 9, 12, 13, 20, ed. Webb, pp. 174-5, 178, 186-7), seems entirely to have missed the point. His main emphasis was on the deceitfulness of the senses and the need for a wide range of authorities both secular and sacred: 'Qui naturam animae diligentius investigare voluerint, non modo Platonis, Aristotelis, Ciceronis, et veterum philosophorum scripta revolvant, sed et Patrum qui veritatem fidelius expresserunt.' (Webb, p. 187.)

[43] James of Venice, the author of the Latin translation of the *Post. Anal.*, or his copyists misunderstood the essential phrase in Aristotle's simile, οἷον ἐν μάχῃ τροπῆς, 'like a rout in battle', and translated it 'sicut in machinae eversione', 'like the overthrow of a *machina*' (a word often used of the whole system of the universe) (*Post. Anal.* ii. 19, 100ᵃ 12; *Aristoteles Latinus*, iv, ed. Minio-Paluello and Dod, p. 106 and n.).

faculties could gradually return to their function of building up the true image of the universe which they had lost in their general ruin. So the senses after all, the weakest part of human nature, the part which men shared with the animals, were the saviours of the whole system of human knowledge:

Since sense perception, the weakest of all human powers, apprehending only corruptible individual things, survives, imagination stands, memory stands, and finally understanding, which is the noblest of human powers capable of apprehending the incorruptible, universal, first essences, stands![44]

Weak and unreliable though they were, their survival allowed the grander parts of the fabric of human knowledge to be restored to something approaching the original state which had been intuitively present to Man before the Fall.

This is not quite what Aristotle intended, but it is a noble vindication of the place of the senses in human knowledge. As so often happens in Grosseteste's scientific insights, we have here not only the outline of a scientific method extending from the first fragmentary observations of the senses to the generalities of scientific laws, but also the first inkling of a transition from science to religion: 'God chose the weak things of the world that he might put to shame the things that are strong' (I Cor. 1: 27). Grosseteste does not here quote this or any other biblical text; he keeps strictly within the limits of the natural world. But as we come to the end of his commentary on the *Posterior Analytics*, the transition is not far away.

Before we go on to this transition one further observation is necessary to complete the picture of Grosseteste's view of scientific knowledge. Granted that sense impressions are the sources from which scientific knowledge is obtained, what is the power in the soul which makes it possible to grasp the permanent causes and co-ordinating principles in natural events? Aristotle said that the faculty which made scientific knowledge possible was *νοῦς*, which in the Latin translation was *intellectus*.[45] *Nous* and *intellectus* were words well known to all students of Plato's *Timaeus*: they stood for the active principle of *mind* in the universe. In other contexts, they were words also used to mean the

[44] Rossi, p. 405.
[45] *Post. Anal.* i. 33, 88ᵇ 35; Minio-Paluello and Dod, p. 65.

power by which we understand, or to denote the accomplished understanding of general truths. But, in *this* context, Aristotle meant the power of grasping intuitively the underlying structure of a physical event.[46] We do not know that any reader of the Latin translation before Grosseteste understood this. But it is quite clear that Grosseteste did. At one point he wrote: '*Here* I use the word *intellectus* to mean the power of apprehending things from within, and without a "middle term".'[47] That is to say, intuitively. And elsewhere he describes the process in greater detail, taking as his starting point the faculty of mind which James of Venice translated as *sollertia*.[48] This gave Grosseteste the opportunity he needed:

Sollertia is the penetrating power in virtue of which the mind's eye does not rest on the outer surface of an object, but penetrates to something below the visual image. For instance, when the mind's eye falls on a coloured surface, it does not rest there, but descends to the physical structure of which the colour is an effect. It then penetrates this structure until it detects the elemental qualities of which the structure is itself an effect.[49]

One cannot read these words without a thrill of recognition: is not this the way in which a historian comes to recognize the significance of any historical event? However insignificant it may seem, the event spontaneously discloses a large area of intelligibility, making that which only a few moments before had seemed impenetrably confused suddenly appears a scene of order. What Grosseteste here describes is an experience of all enquirers who begin with the observation of particular events and aim at grasping the coherence which lies beneath the surface.

This process of enlightenment has almost nothing in common with the scholastic method. It is a method of discovery, initiated by an observer looking at individual events and seeking to discover their nature and causes. It relies for its success on a mysterious faculty of the mind which eludes definition.

[46] See the note of W. D. Ross, *Aristotle's* Prior *and* Posterior Analytics, 1969, pp. 606-7.

[47] Rossi, p. 406: 'Voco autem hic "intellectum" virtutem animae apprehensivam res apprehensibiles deintus absque medio.'

[48] *Post. Anal.* i. 34, 89ᵇ 10; Aristotle's word was ἀγχινοία; for the Latin translation, see Minio-Paluello and Dod, op. cit. , p. 67.

[49] Rossi, p. 281; and see p. 286 for further remarks of Grosseteste on the same theme.

Whether this faculty is a power of recalling a divine illumination or an inherent power of intuition is immaterial: whichever it may be, it opens up a limitless possibility of new knowledge quite independent of statements by earlier writers and only to be tested by further observations of which the greater part are still in the future. All this is widely different from the scholastic programme of advancing knowledge by the elucidation of earlier writings, by the analysis and refinement of their concepts, and the better organization of the accumulated knowledge of the past. It is different in method; different in the environment which it requires; different too in the end to which it points. It does not require the collaboration of many men, but the persistent observations of individuals. It does not lead to order and consolidation, but to change and disarray.

There is no reason to believe that this contrast was apparent to Grosseteste; still less that he foresaw the immense consequences which lay ahead. Here, as in many other ways, he differed greatly from Roger Bacon: he had no vision of great developments in the future. His independence of mind came naturally from his isolation from the traditions of the great schools, from his provincial circumstances, from his Augustinian view of knowledge as a kind of illumination, and from his own rude strength. This combination makes him a solitary figure, often tentative and uncertain in his conclusions, but very sure of the ground on which he stood, even when his reflections led him far from the beaten track and brought him to disconcerting conclusions.

8

From Science to Theology

I. GROSSETESTE'S CHANGE OF DIRECTION

WE have already found reasons for thinking that Grosseteste's circumstances and prospects changed abruptly during the years between 1220 and 1225; and that this change was completed by his obtaining a valuable benefice in the diocese of Lincoln in 1225; by his ordination as a priest in that year or shortly afterwards; by a change in his main interest from science to theology; and by his becoming a lecturer in theology in the university of Oxford. For the next ten years, his life was intimately associated with Oxford. These ten years were divided into two roughly equal parts: the first five years when he was a leading lecturer in the secular schools of the university; and the second five years when he had abandoned this position to become lecturer to the community of Franciscans outside the city walls, a change of life which culminated in 1232 when he renounced all his sources of income except his prebend at Lincoln.[1] He himself saw this as the final act in a religious conversion, in obedience to the Biblical precept, 'Whosoever does not renounce all that he hath, cannot be my disciple'.[2] It was an act which brought him into full association with the Franciscans. Nevertheless, he had reservations about the Franciscan practice of begging instead of earning a livelihood.[3] His ideal still remained that of a scholar. He cut himself free from administration to concentrate his mind: 'Unless the mind shields itself from external desires, it will not penetrate to inner truths'.[4]

[1] See above, pp. 69-75.
[2] *Ep.* no. 8, p. 44.
[3] Thomas of Eccleston, *De Adventu Fratrum Minorum in Angliam*, ed. A. G. Little, Manchester, 1951, pp. 98-9.
[4] His explanation of his action is expressed in a series of quotations from Gregory, *Moralia in Job*, v. xi. 20; v. xxix. 51; v. xxxi. 57. For the way in which this combination may have been made, see below, pp. 191-2.

His break with the world of ecclesiastical promotion marked a moment of increasingly intense dedication to theological and pastoral problems, and his emergence as a man· with a fully developed theological vision. It also marked the climax of several years of steady work and theological preparation. It is with the work of these years of transition and theological preparation that we are now concerned.

It was of course not at all unusual for a man to change from Arts to Theology: that was part of the common process of scholastic development. What was unusual in Grosseteste's case was his advanced age: he was not simply following a routine, but turning to a new way of life. How did he go about it? There are two sides to the question: first of all, what was there in Oxford to guide or shape his course? Secondly, what assets did he bring to the subject, how could he use them, what deficiencies needed to be remedied?

The question of what there was in Oxford can be briefly answered. It is in the highest degree unlikely that there was any statute or formal document laying down the conditions which had to be met before a man might lecture in theology; but there must have been some conventions to be observed. Even in Paris, the statutory requirements were vague; but Robert Curzon, as papal legate in northern France, had laid it down in 1215 that no one might give public lectures on theology in Paris until he had heard lectures on the subject for five years.[5] This did not apply to Oxford, but even a scholar of Grosseteste's seniority would have needed the goodwill and approval of the other masters, and perhaps also of the bishop of Lincoln.[6] We do not know who the other masters were, but we can be reasonably sure that there were one or two theological lecturers in Oxford by 1225. They were not men of any name or fame. The only notable lecturer, Edmund of Abingdon, had left in 1222; but those who remained would at least have established a practice of lecturing on books of the Bible, certainly on the Psalms and Pauline Epistles, probably on Gen-

---

[5] *Chartularium Universitatis Parisiensis*, i. 79. For the development of theology in Oxford, see *HUO* i. 471–88.

[6] The control of the bishop of Lincoln seems to have been lax. In May 1246 Grosseteste obtained from Innocent IV authority to refuse to allow anyone to teach in Oxford in any faculty who had not been examined and approved by him, 'several persons having presumed to do so'. *CPR* i. 225.

esis, perhaps (following Alexander Nequam's example) on some of the books attributed to Solomon, such as Proverbs and the Song of Songs. A lecturer (again following the example of Alexander Nequam) might have given an outline of theology, though not yet in the form of lectures on the *Sentences* of Peter Lombard. Grosseteste would have needed to establish good relations with them; and, if I am right in thinking that the whole body of masters broke through the strict requirements of the legatine constitutions of 1214 and elected him as their chancellor at some date before 1230, it is clear that he was a dominant figure among the masters by this date.

A more difficult and important question is how Grosseteste saw his role as a theologian. No one could have started on a new course of study at his advanced age without taking stock of his assets and liabilities. He must have asked himself what qualifications he brought to his task, and what he lacked. We do not know how he framed these questions; but, rather surprisingly, his surviving works give us a remarkably clear idea of how in practice he answered them. His assets were a scientific method of enquiry and a body of scientific knowledge; his deficiencies were his lack of wide theological reading and ignorance of Greek and Hebrew. On both counts his position was highly unusual. Equally unusual were the ways in which he set about exploiting his assets and filling the gaps in his equipment. We may consider them one by one:

II. GROSSETESTE'S THEOLOGICAL ASSETS

1. His scientific method

Grosseteste liked to begin his scientific enquiries with the observation and careful study of natural phenomena such as eclipses, comets, falling leaves, etc. , and to explain them with the help of the great textbooks on the subject. His explanations allowed an equal weight to his own observations and the doctrine of the authoritative writings of the past, but in the end no doctrine was so authoritative that it might not be overturned by new observations. Observation was, therefore, primary; but Grosseteste insisted that observers frequently went wrong through their ignorance of the doctrine of their subject, which led them to jump to superficial conclusions.

In science, the fundamental materials are the objects and events of the natural world. The ultimate source of knowledge of these is observation; the works of the great past masters are nothing but a reservoir of the accumulated observations of the past codified by the greatest of them, Aristotle, Ptolemy, and so on. How could this method be applied to theology? As a starting-point, we may say that, for Grosseteste, what nature is to science, the Bible is to theology. The Bible and nothing else. There is a difference of emphasis here between Grosseteste and his scholastic contemporaries. In scholastic thought, the line which separated the primary authority of the Bible from the authority of patristic writers, conciliar definitions, and papal decisions was blurred, because, despite the admitted primacy of the Bible, most questions were discussed on the basis of texts which were non-biblical.[7] It was out of their conflicting statements that a systematic body of theology was created. This was not at all Grosseteste's method. Just as his best scientific thoughts arose from the close examination of an individual event, so in theology his best thoughts came from the close study of individual biblical texts from which he extracted a general truth that in some way went beyond what he found in earlier writers. In his theology, therefore, as in his science, he brought the *vis penetrativa* of his mind to bear on the basic material to reach the general truths which had been ad-umbrated but not exhausted by earlier writers. This reaching out to something beyond the findings of earlier writers did not imply a desire to contradict them. It might do no more than add a personal or vivid note to what they had written; but it kept open the possibility of new discovery.

After he became bishop of Lincoln, he wrote a letter to the

---

[7] That is to say, non-biblical in the strict sense. But Hugh of St Victor included authoritative Christian writers, Augustine, Jerome, Gregory, Bede, and others, in his list of New Testament writers, giving them a comparable position to that of the 'holy writers' (Job, Psalms, Song of Songs, etc.) of the Old Testament. Each Testament, in his view, had a threefold division: in the Old, the Law, the Prophets, and the 'holy writers' such as Solomon; in the New, the Gospels, Apostles, and the Fathers. I quote from the record of Hugh's lectures in Bodleian Library MS Laud. misc., 344, f. 42^v, for which see B. Bischoff, 'Aus der Schule Hugos von St Viktor', *Mittelalterliche Studien*, ii, 1967, 181–6 (reprinted from *Geisteswelt des Mittelalters: Studien u. Texte M. Grabmann gewidmet*, 1935, i. 246–50).

theology lecturers of Oxford which has always been recognized
as an important expression of his view of the primacy of the
Bible; but I do not think that the intransigence of the claim
which he is making has been fully realized.[8] He admonishes
the masters to keep the morning hours free for lectures on the
Bible and not to allow lectures on other texts to intrude into
those hours, which were of capital importance for masters and
students alike.

At first sight this appears a fairly trivial subject: a mere
matter of academic timetable—a subject which often causes a
lot more trouble than it deserves. But the matter did not seem
trivial to Grosseteste. He saw it as a question of profound
importance. He argued that the foundations of a discipline, like
those of a building, must consist of stones capable of bearing
the weight of the whole structure: they must be *lapides vere
fundamentales*, and those could be none other than the Law
and Prophets of the Old Testament, and the writings of the
Evangelists and Apostles of the New Testament.

So, the question of timetables is subsumed under the much
more important issue of fundamentals. Grosseteste stresses the
word again and again. No less than nine times in a relatively
short letter he repeats the word *fundamentalis*—a word, incidentally, for which there seems to be no earlier Latin authority than this letter. The fundamental source demands the
fundamental hours of the day: Grosseteste found biblical authority for this: 'There is a time for everything . . . a time for
planting and a time for plucking up that which is planted . . .
a time for laying foundations and a time for building.' I paraphrase his words:

You must make sure that only foundation stones are laid in the
foundations: to mix up these foundations with lesser stones, and to let
them intrude on the foundation hours is contrary to the doctrine of
Holy Scripture, contrary to the natural order of things, and manifestly
a departure from the practice of our Fathers and predecessors, and
even from that of the regent masters of theology in Paris.[9]

Is this mere extravagance on Grosseteste's part, or is it a serious
expression of his considered view? Grosseteste certainly saw this

[8] *Ep.* no. 123.
[9] Ibid. pp. 346–7. The texture of the argument which I have briefly reproduced is
very dense and wholly supported by biblical authorities.

mixing up of fundamental texts with texts of lesser weight in a very vivid light. His words have the note of strong evangelical fervour; but it would be quite mistaken to give them a modern evangelical meaning. He had no desire to discard the authoritative interpreters of Scripture. Just as Aristotle was an essential aid to the understanding of natural science, so the Fathers were essential aids for understanding the Bible. But, in both subjects, he wanted to keep the foundations clear of debris of all kinds, so that they could support the building of doctrine and practice as only they could do. This was the method which he brought with him from the natural sciences.

2. His scientific knowledge

Besides a method, he also brought a body of knowledge which (he was persuaded) could have great importance for the study of the Bible. Among all the writings available for human study, the Bible was unique in this: it came from the mind of God. Consequently, it had the divine prerogative of being able to convey truth not only in the language of man-made words, but also in the language of God-made things. For instance, when the Book of Numbers described how Moses raised up a brazen serpent in the wilderness which cured those who looked at it from the deadly bites of serpents, this was more than the description of a historical event. It was a theological statement about God and Man, and about past, present and future, all reflected in the image of the brazen serpent which represented the crucified Christ, who would save those who believed in him. This is an example of God's use of things as a means of conveying truths unknown to those who experienced the event. But if this view of the language of things in Scripture is accepted, it is capable of almost infinite extension. Nearly every object and incident in the Old Testament may have a meaning over and above the meaning of the words. These possibilities had been very fully exploited in the writings of the Fathers and in the encyclopaedic works of the early Middle Ages. They had become a fixed and, as it seemed, permanent feature of Christian thought. But their range had not been much, if at all, extended in scholastic theology. The efforts of the schools

had been concentrated on the tasks of consolidation, clarification, and definition.

There was wisdom in this restraint. Nevertheless, it left a
puzzle. If God spoke through the things which He had created,
there was a clear duty to pursue the message of created things
to the utmost. And not only in the Bible, but in nature too. In
the Bible, all things—lions, serpents, rocks, seas, sheep—had
meanings which could only be discovered by knowing both the
mind of God and the natural characteristics of all created
things. And these creatures also had lessons for mankind quite
independent of their biblical context: every reader of Bestiaries,
Lapidaries, Herbals, was familiar with this fact. Here was a
field of enquiry with important possibilities for the study of the
Bible and of the divine plan of the universe. It stood wide open
for a man who had spent many years deeply immersed in the
study of astronomy and medicine, and all their contributory
sciences of animals, plants, physics, geometry and the nature
of all created things. When Grosseteste first started to teach
theology, he seems to have thought that the best contribution
he could make was to bring his extensive scientific knowledge
to bear on the study of the Bible, and to enlarge the understanding of Scripture by exploring the content of its natural
symbols.

The evidence for this lies in the Durham manuscript containing his comments on the Psalter described above. In these
comments he skips from one natural object mentioned in the
Psalms to the next, bringing his scientific knowledge to bear
on them, and attempting to penetrate more deeply into their
spiritual meaning by closely observing their natural
characteristics.

The first Psalm gave him an immediate opportunity. It begins by saying that the just man is like a tree planted by the
waterside: it will bring forth fruit in due season, and its leaves
will not fall. Grosseteste could scarcely have had a better start:
trees, leaves, fruit were all subjects he had studied in nature
and in the latest works of Aristotle. As we have seen, he had
sharply corrected Aristotle on the subject of falling leaves. Now
he had an opportunity to place his knowledge at the service of
theology. The leaves, he says, are the words of God, which the
just man does not let fall. The image is apt because the structure

of the leaf mimics in shape and function the structure of the organs of speech: the stalk, the windpipe; the leaf, the tongue; the sap, the words of God; the water, whence the sap arises, God. In the just man, the sap flows because he speaks the word of God; his leaf does not fall because the word does not dry up; he may justly be said to have been planted by the waterside because he listens to God and does His will. But in the unjust man, the sap dries up; the word of God is not spoken; the leaf falls to the ground; he is separated from God and from the water of life.

This was not a revolutionary theology, but it gave a new life to an old image. So Grosseteste went on through the Psalms, enlarging the images of the Psalmist by a deeper study of the natural objects on which they were based. With this aim he commented at length on mountains (Ps. 2: 6), morning and night (5: 4), tears (6: 7), lions (7: 7), the moon (8: 4), asps (13: 2), the eye (24: 15), the heart (32: 15), and so on. He was often able to bring new science to enliven verses whose meaning had faded through long exposure to common use.

His method in these comments remained what it had been in his comments on natural phenomena in the *Posterior Analytics*. He let his mental eye rest on the physical objects mentioned in the Psalms, taking them in the order in which they came in the text. He noted their peculiarities of structure and behaviour: among many other things, he distinguished the different types of hills, pointed or rounded, volcanic or spongy, cloud-covered or exposed to the sun, rich in streams or dry. He described— once more using some recent scientific knowledge—the inter-related functions of heart and lungs, blood and air; the composition and medicinal properties of tears; the physical attributes of day and night; the role of the sun in the heavens, giving light not only to the earth but to the stars, and regulating all their movements. From these scientific observations, he went on to expound the spiritual functions represented by these distinctions.

Many theologians in the generation before Grosseteste had made lists of natural objects and their spiritual meanings in the Bible; but I do not think that anyone else had tried to explore, with the help of recent knowledge, the scientific foundation of these spiritual realities. In his explanations he was an innovator. But the results in fact were disappointing, and, if he had stopped here, he would not have made a reputation as a theologian: he was attempting to give new life to an old habit of exegesis, which despite the liveliness and penetration of some of his observations remained obstinately comatose. It may have been the realisation of this fact that caused him to experiment with new kinds of symbolic exposition. He made diagrams to illustrate the different ways in which 'shield' (the 'shield of goodwill','the shield of faith', the 'shield of the heart') was used in the Bible to express spiritual truths; and a further diagram to show the irradiation of virtues in the universe.[10] He began also to extend the range of his comments to explore new aspects of the relationship between the physical universe and the activities of the spirit. The following brief examples will illustrate the gradual enlargement of his theological thinking.

The first comes from an essay on the Sun based on a very obscure verse, Ps. 55: 4, *Ab altitudine diei timebo*. 'The day', he explains, 'is the sun giving light to the earth':

The sun dwells longer in the summer constellations than in the winter ones. The summer constellations are the works of contemplation, in which the fervour of charity is warmer and the light of intelligence clearer. The winter ones are the works of the active life, in which charity is cooler and the light of intelligence dimmer.[11]

The next is a comment on Ps. 59: 5, 'You have given us the wine of compunction to drink':

Good wine gives nourishment and health to the body; it clarifies the blood and opens the veins and purifies them; it expels the dark melancholy generated from the heart; it makes the soul forget its

[10] The 'shield' and irradiation diagrams are in Durham MS ff. 14ᵛ and 15. It seems quite certain that they are copied from Grosseteste's own drawings, for *Dictum* 95 is unintelligible without the drawing which accompanies it in this manuscript (and, so far as I know, in no other manuscript, except on a loose leaf in Eton MS). This drawing has also a special interest as the earliest known example of a diagram of the Trinity which became very common in the later Middle Ages: it seems possible that Grosseteste invented it: for some early examples (but none as early as the Durham MS), see Michael Evans, 'An illustrated fragment of Peraldus's *Summa* of vice: Harleian MS 3244', *Journal of the Warburg and Courtauld Institutes*, xlv, 1982, figs. 3–6.

[11] *Dicta*, no. 105, on Ps. 55. 4, Durham MS f. 121ᵃ⁻ᵇ, Eton MS, f. 30ᵇ⁻ᵈ. See also Grosseteste's *De Sphera*, caps. 2–3 (Baur, pp. 16–21) for a scientific account of the summer and winter progress of the sun through the zodiac, and *Hex.* ii. ix. 4 for the symbolism of action and contemplation in darkness and light.

gloom and gives it joy and comfort; it gives the soul a happy boldness in undertaking subtle and difficult enquiries.[12]

By a happy coincidence the practical application of this doctrine can be found exemplified in a penance of a daily glass of good wine which Grosseteste imposed on a sullen friar.

Then later, in commenting on Ps 81: 6, 'Ye are gods', he made a brief excursion into a subject which was to occupy him very deeply after he had studied the works of Ps.-Denys—the 'deification' for which Man had been created. But this first sketch was inspired by Boethius's *Consolation of Philosophy* before he knew Ps.-Denys, and his exposition is expressed in the language of geometry and of idealist logic. He begins with Boethius's long discussion on blessedness which concludes with the statement that God and blessedness are one and the selfsame thing. To this Grosseteste adds:

Nothing can be concluded more truly or firmly or more worthy of God. To this, following the practice of geometers who are accustomed to add corollaries to their demonstrations by way of corroboration, I will add: if men become blessed by participation in blessedness, and if blessedness is divine, then clearly the greatest blessedness is in attaining divinity. Similarly, to be just is to attain justice; to be wise is to attain wisdom; so to be blessed is to obtain divinity, and 'to be gods'.[13]

While he was thus beginning to extend the range of his 'mystical' theology, he was also writing short essays on states of mind such as pride, humility, and justice. These are mixed up with his allegorizations of natural objects in his earliest comments on the Psalms. And, towards the end of his period as a lecturer in the secular schools—among the latest additions

---

[12] *Dicta*, no. 73. This is not in the Durham MS but in the continuation of the commentary in Eton College MS 8, f. 39^{b–d}. The recollection of the penance which he imposed is preserved in Eccleston, p. 92: 'He said to a Friar Preacher, three things are necessary for health: food, sleep, and jollity. He also prescribed as a penance for a melancholic friar that he should drink a full cup of the best wine, saying "My dearest brother, if you had such a penance frequently, you would have a better conscience." ' For further references, see Thomson 1940, p. 224; and for the medical source of the doctrine, see below, p. 197.

[13] The chapter in the *Consolation of Philosophy* on which this argument is based is iii. 9, which in Grosseteste's copy in Trinity College, Oxford, MS 17, is liberally sprinkled

with his symbol Θ, which means *De beata vita*: the interlocking of Man with God. For his use of this manuscript as a theological source, see below, pp. 196–7.

to the Durham manuscript—we find signs of a growing interest in the pastoral problems of the Church expressed in rough and powerful eloquence. Most notably, in a sequence of thoughts which formed a draft for one of his *Dicta*, we find such phrases as these—'the lives of shepherds are book and mirror for their flocks'; 'pastors who batten on the miseries of others will ask for food and it will not be given them'; 'just as it would be ridiculous and damnable for someone ignorant of medicine to receive pay for curing diseases, so it is for a pastor who knows nothing about the cure of souls.'[14] In words like these we can trace the emerging outline of the later bishop; and, later still, a main part of his appeal to Wycliffe and the Lollards.

These are the thoughts which were shaping themselves in Grosseteste's mind in about 1230. And, at about the same time, in his final words on Ps. 100, which we have already noticed as the culmination of his lectures in the schools, he gave a general view of religious life in society, which consisted not only in doing good and avoiding evil, but also—and here comes a note which will dominate Grosseteste's life when he becomes a bishop—in destroying evil both in oneself and in everyone else so far as possible. The final verse of the Psalm reads: 'I shall soon destroy all the ungodly that are in the land, that I may root out all evil-doers from the City of God.' On this Grosseteste comments:

This verse is especially important for prelates and for the good life in the community . . . By the word of God, and by judicial power, and in every possible way, sinners and the workers of iniquity are to be driven from the City of God, that is from the Church and from the society of men living under the law of God. It is not possible to drive out *all* sinners. Nevertheless, prelates, and whoever else holds power ordained by God, and every faithful believer in his own sphere, ought to aim with all his power at the eradication and destruction of all sinners, just as a farmer aims at destroying the weeds among his growing corn.[15]

[14] See Durham MS, f. 78ᵈ–79ᵃ, a sermon on 1 Timothy 4: 12, *Exemplum esto fidelium*, which was revised to become *Dictum* no. 35, in which form it became well known in the late fourteenth century.

[15] Eton MS 8, ff. 198ᵃ–204ᵇ; for the passage quoted, see f. 203ᵇ. It reads as follows: 'Iste quoque versus specialiter congruit prelatis et omni etiam recte conversanti inter concives, ut "in matutino", hoc est "velociter", cum omni studio in luce dilectionis et divinae legis interficiat gladio verbi Dei et potestate indiciaria et modis aliis quibus potest omnes peccatores, ut omnes videlicet de civitate Dei, hoc est de ecclesia et de

I have already remarked that Grosseteste probably wrote these last words in about 1230. Almost everything of lasting value that he had to say about theology still lay in the future. But he had reached a stage at which he could look forward with confidence to his work as a theologian. He had come a long way from his earliest comments on the Psalms. He had already had some opportunity as archdeacon for translating into practice his rules for the *perfecta conversatio inter concives* with which he concluded his commentary. As bishop he was to have much more. The intervening five years were to produce his earliest mature theology; but before going further, we must turn back to his work of preparation.

III. GROSSETESTE'S THEOLOGICAL DEFICIENCIES AND THEIR REMEDY

It would appear that he was conscious of two main deficiencies in his theological equipment: ignorance of the languages necessary for studying the Bible, and lack of extensive reading in the Fathers. At the time when he was making his comments on the Psalms and giving his lectures on the Bible, he was engaged in remedying these defects—by learning Greek and by reading Patristic and a few later texts with profound attention. The two activities need to be examined separately.

1. The origin of his Greek studies

We have noticed that, when he wrote his commentary on the *Posterior Analytics*, he knew a little Greek—enough to comment, not quite accurately, on the use of the infinitive in Greek, and to speculate about the gender of the Greek word for 'right-angle'. But he showed no interest in Greek as an aid in solving some of the difficulties in the text. For understanding what Aristotle meant, he was content with the Latin translation.

societate hominum sub una Dei lege viventium disperdat omnes operantes iniquitatem. Licet enim non possit hoc adimplere ut videlicet omnes mali omne parte ea qua ulli sunt auferantur de ecclesia et societate bonorum vel correcti vel iuste condempnati, tamen quilibet prelatus et quaelibet potestas a Deo ordinata et quilibet fidelis pro portione sua hoc debet intendere et ad hoc conari pro toto posse ut omnes peccatores interficiantur et disperdantur sicut intendit agricola omnes carduos sarculo prescindere de medio crescentis tritici.'

What was it that altered this attitude and made learning
Greek and translating Greek texts one of the main occupations
of the last twenty or thirty years of his life? There seems no
doubt that the change was connected with his change from
science to theology, and there was a reason for this. In the
sciences, the fundamental material is not what is written in
books, but what is found in nature. However important Aristotle and other authorities might be in providing the doctrines
necessary for understanding nature, there was no compelling
need to go back to their original language to get to the heart
of the matter: even their wisest words were not the 'lapides
fundamentales' of the subject. But in studying theology the
situation was quite different. The words of the Bible *were* the
fundamental material. A translation was already one step removed from the foundation: to get back to the original was to
get back to the foundation. On this point, he had the testimony
of Augustine: 'for the books of the New Testament especially,
where the Latin versions are uncertain, reference must be made
to the Greek'; and (for the Old Testament), 'for men of Latin
tongue, Hebrew and Greek are chiefly necessary.'[16] Many men
had read these words and many scholars in the twelfth century
had made some effort to follow Augustine's precept. Dr Smalley
has shown that several biblical commentators in the twelfth
century—notably two Englishmen, Andrew of St Victor and
Herbert of Bosham—sought the aid of Jewish scholars in their
efforts to get back to the original Hebrew of the Old Testament.[17] But it was more difficult to find Greek speakers who
could give similar help with the New Testament and with the
Septuagint version of the Old, and it is unlikely that many felt
a strong urge to make the necessary effort.[18]

It was entirely in keeping with Grosseteste's habits of con-

---

[16] Augustine, *De Doctrina Christiana*, ii. 34 (ed. W. M. Green, CSEL 80, 1963).

[17] Beryl Smalley, *The Study of the Bible in the Middle Ages*, 2nd edn., 1952, 149–73; 'A
commentary on the *Hebraica* by Herbert of Bosham', *RTAM* 18, 1951, 29–65.

[18] Peter Comestor, in his *Historia Scholastica*, quite often refers to Greek etymologies
of place-names etc. , but he shows no further interest in the language. There are,
however, signs of growing interest in the early thirteenth century. In particular, Alexander of Hales's *Exoticon* (Bodleian Library MS Auct. F. 6. 8, ff. 9–13, continued in
MS Digby 92, ff. 96–107), which aimed at explaining Greek words necessary for the
study of the Bible, may be contemporary with Grosseteste's first steps in the language
described below. If so, it shows a similar stirring of interest—with this difference, that
Grosseteste went on to get a working knowledge of Greek.

centration on details that he should have taken the problem more seriously than his contemporaries. There is no sign of this interest in his earliest comments on the Psalms; but in his comments on the later Psalms, from 80 to 100, they are more frequent; and in his commentary on Jerome's introduction to the Vulgate, his use of Greek in explaining the etymology of words used in the Bible has become almost obsessive.[19] Grosseteste took his pupils through this introduction in a very schoolmasterly way, sentence by sentence, enlarging on Jerome's account of peoples and places. Here, as nowhere else in his works, we see Grosseteste as the conscientious teacher of beginners. But he never repressed his own predilections, and they came out in his comments on the names of places and people with a Greek derivation. Whenever Jerome mentioned the name of a person or place, Grosseteste would begin by looking up the etymology given by Isidore and Pliny. He reported what they said, and then he added whatever new material he had been able to collect from his recent theological reading, especially from Augustine's *City of God* and *Confessions*, and from Jerome's *Letters* and treatise 'on Hebrew names'. But most significantly he added information derived from his own study of Greek. For instance, when his text mentioned Egypt, he reported what Isidore said about the origin of the name, and then he added: 'Egypt is the land flooded by the Nile. It is called Egypt from the Greek which means "approaching the river": *Eggizo*, I approach; *potamos*, river. Another etymology is: *aygas pionas*, having fat goats'.[20]

On Athens, Grosseteste is especially copious, and his remarks

[19] Grosseteste's commentary on Jerome's introduction to the Bible is only found as an introductory section of his *Hexaëmeron*, with which it is printed by Dales and Gieben, 1982, pp. 17–48. In style, however, and in the type of audience which it addresses, this introductory section is quite different from the work which follows. It is unashamedly elementary in its sentence-by-sentence explanation of the text, in its purely grammatical and unspeculative content, and in its statement (p. 41, sect. 112) that he is now going to go back to explain points of only slight difficulty *propter aliquos simpliciores*. This same thought is repeated (p. 44, sect. 139), where he speaks of things which require explanation *propter minores*. These distinctions imply an audience which included pupils in need of elementary instruction. The *Hexaëmeron* differs from the introduction in almost every way: it is very broad and speculative in its treatment of the text of Genesis 1–2; and it makes no concessions to elementary pupils, or to pupils of any kind. The combination of the lectures on Jerome's Introduction with the *Hexaëmeron* appears to be a factitious union of two disparate works originally intended for different audiences.

[20] *Hex.*, p. 21.

on the name must have come from someone who had been
there and could report on the beliefs of the natives. 'Athens as
some say', he writes, 'comes from *a*, "without", and *thanatos*,
"death", because it is the home of immortal wisdom.' Then,
after a long passage on the origin of Athens from Augustine's
City of God, he continues with a further addition of his own:
'According to the Greeks, the interpretation of the name
"Athens" is "a gathering of intellect" from *athrein nun*, for
Athene is the goddess of wisdom; or from *non lactendo* [ἀτιθήνη],
"without a wet-nurse", because Athene, according to legend,
was born without a mother from the head of Jove.'[21]

In addition to these endless etymologies, Grosseteste made
observations about the Greek language which demonstrate the
seriousness of his study and his beginnings as a textual critic.

For instance, there is a passage in which Jerome mentioned
three sources of knowledge, giving them their Latin names,
doctrina, *ratio*, and *usus*, with their Greek equivalents. The manuscripts of the Vulgate in Grosseteste's time invariably gave the
Latin words followed by a meaningless jumble of penstrokes
representing Greek words which were no longer intelligible.
Grosseteste found this situation a challenge to his critical acumen. He looked at as many manuscripts as he could get hold
of. In all of them he found a similar array of random shapes.
But in some of them he could make out the third word. This is
how he reported his discovery:

All the manuscripts which I have so far been able to find have the
Greek words in a form so corrupt that I cannot read them. In some
manuscripts, however, the last word appears to be πειραν, which
serves well enough, for *peiran* is experimental knowledge. *Doctrina* in
Greek is *didaskalia* or *dogma*, and *ratio* is *logos*, but these do not seem to
correspond with the pen marks in the texts which I have so far seen.
If Jerome wrote some words other than these, I confess I cannot guess
what they were.[22]

These observations represent the muddy source which was
to grow into a great river of new knowledge during the next
twenty years. In themselves, they are more of a tribute to
Grosseteste's critical acumen than to his knowledge of Greek,

but he has obviously made considerable progress since his commentary on the *Posterior Analytics*. He now has some knowledge
of Greek vocabulary. Perhaps he had a dictionary. Almost
certainly, he had a teacher, who had been in Athens and could
tell him something about the beliefs of the inhabitants and their
habits of spelling and speaking, their pronunciation, and their
use of the circumflex.[23] But, above all, he had the incentive to
find out more.

The existence in England at this time of a man familiar with
Athens, who could teach Greek, is a reminder that the 1220s
were a time remarkably propitious for this study. The fall of
Constantinople in 1204 and the colonization of parts of the
Byzantine Empire by Latin settlers had brought Greeks and
Latins together in many new ways, and in greater numbers
than ever before. The Latin administrations of Constantinople,
Athens and Nicaea offered employment to Latin clerks, who
had a chance to converse with Greek scholars, collect Greek
manuscripts, and learn something about Greek habits which
books could not tell them. It was almost certainly from a man
with this background that Grosseteste learnt to take his first
steps in Greek, and we can even name him with some confidence. Among the English clerks who had sought employment
in one of the new Latin principalities, there was one Master
John of Basingstoke, who had spent some years in the Latin
Duchy of Athens. He returned to England at a time which we
cannot exactly determine, bringing with him some Greek books
and reports of others which he had seen. When Grosseteste
became a bishop, one of his first acts, within months of his
election in 1235, was to make John of Basingstoke archdeacon
of Leicester.[24] Grosseteste was extremely fastidious in his ecclesiastical appointments, and we can be sure that in 1235 he
had already known John for some considerable time and had
found him serviceable. If the hypothesis that John of Basingstoke was his teacher in Greek is correct, he made possible
a great deal of Grosseteste's later work and thought, and he

---

[23] Ibid., pp. 30–5.
[24] Grosseteste was consecrated on 17 June 1235, and John of Basingstoke was acting
as archdeacon throughout his first year. He also succeeded Grosseteste in his prebend
of Leicester St Margaret, which Grosseteste had retained when he gave up his other
offices in 1232 and only relinquished when he became bishop. See D. E. Greenway,
Fasti Ecclesiae Anglicanae: Lincoln, 1977, pp. 34, 77.

was suitably rewarded.[25] As Grosseteste's knowledge grew, so his conception of its purpose developed. He began to see that it is impossible to study a text carefully without studying it in its original language. This applied in the first place to the Bible, and Grosseteste certainly had some knowledge of the Septuagint and the New Testament in Greek by about 1230. Beyond this there stretched the further prospect of a better understanding of Greek theology. There is some evidence that he was already seeking Greek texts for this purpose between 1230 and 1235.

To this end, he brought together helpers to translate, comment on, and make new texts available in the West. By the time he became a bishop he was poised to use his episcopal wealth to enlarge the scope of Christian learning and to direct the efforts of men to whom a fleeting political situation had given a knowledge of Greek more extensive than had been seen in England since the time of Theodore of Tarsus. This large enterprise cannot be understood in isolation. It must be seen in the context of his own wider theological horizon, opening out from his theological reading in the 1220s. To this reading we must now turn.

2. His programme of reading

It would have been very understandable if he had sought to enlarge his theological knowledge in the first place by working through the organized selections of materials and discussions about them which had been made in the twelfth century. And it is very strange that he did not do this. After all, these works were among the most impressive achievements of the Middle Ages, and their authors—Anselm of Laon, Abelard, the author of the *Summa sententiarum*, Peter Lombard, Peter Comester, Robert of Melun, Peter the Chanter, Stephen Langton, Prepositinus, to mention only the most obvious—established a tradition of theology based on carefully selected texts which has a permanent place in the development of European thought. But Grosseteste did not follow them. His neglect of his

---

[25] For the details, some of them perhaps legendary, of John of Basingstoke's early life and discovery of the *Testaments of the Twelve Patriarchs* in Athens, and for his association with Grosseteste, see Matth. Paris, *Chron. Maj.* v. 284–7.

great scholastic predecessors cannot have been accidental. It may partly have arisen from his English provincial environment which had separated him from this development. But also his scientific habit of concentration on precise problems, on observed phenomena, and on fundamental texts, probably influenced his approach to theology. He went first to the Bible, then to its main expositors—Augustine, Jerome, Gregory, Ambrose, Bede, John Chrysostom, John of Damascus, Origen. To this list he admitted a few others, Rabanus Maurus for his symbolism, St Anselm and St Bernard for their spirituality, and last of all Denys the Areopagite for his antiquity and his broad view of the relationship between all parts of Creation and its Creator. It is noticeable that the only twelfth-century scholastic writer on his reading list was Hugh of St Victor, and he appears only as a commentator on Denys.[26]

These were the writers on whom he mainly relied to enlarge his field of vision. But he did not forget the texts of his earlier secular and scientific studies. When we examine the Index of his theological reading we shall find that he re-read or recollected familiar secular texts for their theological content. Among the works which he re-read for this purpose we can confidently place Boethius's *Consolation of Philosophy*, Seneca's letters, and Aristotle *On Animals*; among those which he recollected but did not re-read we can place Ptolemy's *Almagest*, Hippocrates's *Aphorisms*, the *Metaphysics* of Algazel and of Avicenna, the *Optics* of Alhasen, and Calcidius's Commentary on Plato's *Timaeus*. A strange collection of baggage indeed for someone setting out to be a theologian, and one which perhaps no one but Grosseteste could have carried. The use he made of them all must be considered in some detail if we are to understand the structure of his mind and thought.

We may begin by noting the intense concentration with which he studied his chosen authors. This is demonstrated in the most vivid way in some of the surviving volumes which he possessed. Among them, the most impressive is the copy of

[26] The foundations of our knowledge of Grosseteste's library and the system of annotation associated with it were laid by R. W. Hunt in his two articles, 'The Library of Robert Grosseteste', in Callus 1955, pp. 121–45; and 'Manuscripts containing the Indexing Symbols of Robert Grosseteste', *Bodleian Library Record*, iv, 1953, 241–55. Like everyone else who has studied the subject I am deeply indebted to these pioneering studies.

Augustine's *City of God* and Gregory's *Moralia in Job*, both of them works of great length and complexity of content.[27] Another, equally impressive in its own way, is his copy of Boethius's *Consolation of Philosophy*.[28] This too is annotated in his own hand. In the first of these volumes, he supplied chapter references for the biblical quotations—no easy matter since there were hundreds of them and the text never provided more than an indication of the book from which they came. In both volumes, he corrected the text. But, most strikingly, he indexed these works throughout with an astonishing abundance of symbols to draw attention to about four hundred different subjects. These symbols give the volumes in which the system was used an incomparably bizarre appearance. As an example, I reproduce on the opposite page the symbols in the margin of a single short chapter of the *City of God* (xi. 2), about 500 words in length; and I attach to each of the marginal symbols the explanation which we owe to the chance survival of a key to them in a manuscript now in Lyons.[29]

Although the list gives only a small selection of the whole, it presents a number of features which immediately arrest the attention. In the first place, this brief chapter of Augustine suggested to Grosseteste a very unusual list of topics: sleep, dreams, imagination, are, to say the least, curious intruders in a list which begins with prayer and God's omnipotence and ends with the road to heaven. They make it clear that Grosse-

---

[27] Bodleian Library, MS Bodley 198. The manuscript is described (with a plate) by Hunt, in Callus, op. cit., 121, 133, and in *Manuscripts at Oxford: An Exhibition in memory of R. W. Hunt (1908–1978)*, Bodleian Library, Oxford, 1980, No. 10, pp. 58–9.

[28] Trinity College, Oxford, MS 17.

[29] The key to Grosseteste's indexing symbols survives in Lyons, Bibliothèque Municipale, MS 414, ff. 16ᵛ–32ʳ with the title 'Tabula Magistri Roberti Lincolniensis episcopi cum additione fratris Adae de Marisco, secundum distinctiones ix, quarum prima est de deo.' The nine *distinctiones* are: *De Deo, De Verbo, De Creaturis, De Ordine Ecclesiae, De Sacra Scriptura, De Vitiis* (2 parts), *De Futuris, De Anima et virtutibus eius*. The detailed bibliography breaks off in the middle of *De Vitiis*, part 1. It is quite unclear how extensive Adam Marsh's 'additio' was: it may have been no more than the appendix of 60–70 subjects without symbols which follows the main list, which preserves (as I shall suggest) the Index at an early stage in its development, certainly not later than about 1230. Professor R. H. Rouse has found what seems to be a much later form in Paris, Bibliothèque Nationale, MS n. a. l. 540, and a full account of the development of the system, probably under the inspiration of Adam Marsh, must await investigation of this manuscript and the other manuscripts (partly listed by Hunt, art. cit.) in which the symbols are found. I am greatly indebted to the librarian at Lyons for supplying me with a microfilm of the essential pages of MS 414.

teste had not forgotten his scientific reading in turning to theology, and the complete list of symbols confirms that his theology will be much concerned with the natural world.

The symbols (MS Bodl. 198, f. 45ᵛ)	**Their meaning** (MS Lyons 414, ff. 17ʳ–19ʳ)
⌐	on prayer
⊬	on God's omnipotence
∧	on God's wisdom
ع⋯з	on the Creation of the World
⊤	on sleep and dreams
✿	on imagination
⟩	on the dignity of Man
⊹	on reason and understanding
·|·	on faith
✳	on the divine humanity
⟁	on the road to heaven

The large number of subjects which Grosseteste found in this short passage of Augustine shows that he was not making a *florilegium*, a collection of notable passages, such as many other medieval scholars made. He was making something like a modern index, to which he could refer on many miscellaneous topics. There are many aspects of the plan which are difficult to understand, and cannot be described here. But there are a few questions which we must attempt to answer if we are to understand the mind of Grosseteste: what was the plan? when did he make it? how could it be used? What light does it throw on his development as a theologian?

IV. GROSSETESTE'S THEOLOGICAL INDEX

1. The nature of the plan

The plan consisted of three parts. First, his collection of texts was annotated with about four hundred symbols like those reproduced above. Secondly, he had a subject index arranged systematically in nine sections, each with about fifty separate subjects, and each subject with its distinctive symbol. Thirdly and most important, he had a bibliography, listing under each subject the authors and the places in their works where the appropriate symbols would be found.

This certainly represents an immensely ambitious plan of reading and indexing for a single scholar. On the surface, too, it seems impenetrably complicated; and so it would be to anyone unfamiliar with the books and symbols which covered their margins. But for Grosseteste, who had read the books, invented the symbols, and understood the arrangement of subjects in the index, it was not really difficult to use, provided that it was strictly adhered to, easily accessible, and kept up to date. It seems likely that these conditions for continued usefulness fairly quickly ceased to be met; but there are also reasons for thinking that the plan played an important role in Grosseteste's early theological development.

2. When did he make it?

There are several indications that the plan, as preserved in Lyons MS 414, was completed by about 1230. The main reason for thinking this is that it does not quote books which he is known to have studied, and been deeply influenced by, not long after this date. For example, in his index he quoted only the first nine homilies of St Basil's *Hexaëmeron*. These alone had been translated into Latin. But when he wrote his own *Hexaëmeron*, certainly before 1235, he quotes all eleven of Basil's homilies, beside the complementary work of Gregory of Nyssa, which is not quoted at all in the Index. The works attributed to Denys the Areopagite are a similar case: in his Index the only work for which he gives precise references is the *Celestial Hierarchy* with the commentary of Hugh of St Victor. But by 1235 Grosseteste knew Denys's other works and was interested in a new translation.[30] A similar situation exists with regard to the works of John of Damascus: in the Index he quotes only his 'Sentences', but at a later date he was active in translating his other works. And finally, the Index does not contain the other Greek theologians who were first mentioned in his later lectures on the Psalms.

Altogether, therefore, it seems reasonable to regard the Index, as we now have it, as a record of Grosseteste's reading between about 1220/5 and 1230 when he was preparing himself as a theologian and giving his early theological lectures.

3. How could it be used?

I have already mentioned the letter which he wrote to his sister at the end of 1232, telling her that he had renounced all his sources of income except his prebend at Lincoln, and that he had done this in obedience to the command of Scripture: 'Whoever does not give up all that he possesses, cannot be my disciple.'[31] To support his explanation, he wove together into a single sentence three separated passages in Gregory's *Moralia* on the peace of a man freed from worldly cares who can contemplate inner truths hidden from those engaged in business. It seems unlikely that he could have remembered the exact

---

[30] The index includes one general reference, without specifying the exact book, to the *Ecclesiastical Hierarchy* on baptism. I suspect that here, as with a single general reference to St Bernard on the Song of Songs, Grosseteste had either not yet studied the work carefully or did not possess it, for his references to all other works are notably precise. His interest in a new translation is evident in *De Cess. Leg.* III. i. 14: on this, see the forthcoming edition by Dales and King.

[31] *Ep.* no. 8.

words of these passages without looking at the texts. But how could he have found them, buried as they were in separate chapters of a vast work? One possibility is that he looked up *Contemplation* in his Index. Here all three passages were listed with several others. It would then be a simple matter to go to his copy and find the appropriate symbol in the margins. In fact, we can do the same, and once we have the clue we can find in a few minutes in his own manuscript the three passages which Grosseteste used.[32]

There are other examples of quotations in Grosseteste's letters of the period 1229 to 1232, when he was archdeacon of Leicester, which point to a similar use of the Index. For example, he had intended to go on a pilgrimage to Rome or perhaps Jerusalem, and he had got leave of absence for this purpose from the canons of Lincoln. But then disorders were reported in Italy, and the bishop of Lincoln and his fellow archdeacons urged him to stay at home. He hated changing a resolution; but he finally agreed and wrote a long letter excusing himself from the charge of inconstancy and quoting three of Seneca's letters in his defence. If we look up *Stability and Constancy* in the Index we find a mutilated list of references to Seneca containing two of the three letters, and the third was perhaps also there originally.[33] Then too there are traces of his use of the Index in two letters which he wrote to Richard Marshal when he succeeded to the earldom of Pembroke in 1231.[34] His two treatises *De Veritate* and *De libero arbitrio* also show clear signs of its use.[35] Further, we can find evidence of the use of the Index in some of his *Dicta*, and one of them—on the qualities of a just judge—

[32] The relevant passages in MS Bodl. 198 are on ff. 127ᵈ, 129ᵈ, and 130ᵇ.

[33] See *Ep.* no. 3 quoting Seneca's letters nos. 23, 35, 67. The entry in the Index (f. 26ᵛ) *De stabilitate et constanca* has been partly cut away, but the numbers 35 and 67 are still visible.

[34] *Ep.* nos. 6 and 7 are to Richard Marshal with extensive quotations on humility and the divine Wisdom, which can be related to the Index entries *De sapientia Dei* (f. 20) and to the marginal symbols in MS Bodl. 198.

[35] The sources quoted in *De libero arbitrio* (first recension) are strikingly close to the references in the Index under 'Free Will' to Cicero's *De divinatione* and *De natura deorum*, Seneca's *Letters*, *De beneficiis*, and *De naturalibus quaestionibus*, and especially Boethius's *De consolatione philosophiae*. The marginal notes in Grosseteste's copy of Boethius are also closely associated with the passages quoted. The second recension of the *De Libero Arbitrio* largely reproduces these quotations but with some later additions not found in the Index. In the *De Veritate* about twenty quotations from ten works of Augustine are related to references in the Index.

is little more than a succession of quotations, which could be gathered by referring to this title in his Index.[36] Altogether, therefore, there is evidence that the Index with its associated symbols was useful as a working tool during the years before and shortly after 1230. Yet its importance was probably short-lived: it was too unwieldy and too troublesome to keep up-to-date to repay the labour spent on it. It looks like one of those ambitious projects which a determined beginner in a new subject embarks on, and then outgrows. This would account for the unfinished state in which the Index has been preserved, and the disconcerting difficulty in linking Grosseteste's quotations in his later works with his Index. It seems certain that Grosseteste's disciple, that arch-enthusiast Adam Marsh, later developed the Index and communicated his enthusiasm for a time to the Oxford Franciscans after Grosseteste had left them. [37] But there is little reason for thinking that Grosseteste continued to add to it or to use it extensively after about 1230.

It would seem, therefore that the importance of this plan of indexing and retrieval, was merely temporary. It shows how a remarkable man, coming late into the central area of theology from a position outside the main scholastic stream, could equip himself by his own efforts and with little outside assistance to take a leading place among the theological lecturers of Oxford university—a university which had indeed no great tradition behind it, but a considerable future not far ahead. It was the expedient of a powerful outsider, and its usefulness for him was exhausted when he had achieved the mastery which he sought.

But if for Grosseteste its importance was short-lived, for us it has some information which we are glad to have.

V. GROSSETESTE'S THEOLOGICAL DEVELOPMENT

The interest of the plan as a whole lies in providing us with his theological starting-point. It defines the range of subjects which he thought relevant to his theology—in particular the wide range of questions about the natural world, human behaviour

[36] *Dictum* no. 103, *De iusto iudice* (Durham MS, f. 119; Eton MS 8, ff. 31ᵛ-32; printed in Brown 1690, pp. 274-6).

[37] For its later use among the Franciscans, see Hunt 1953, and R. H. and M. A. Rouse, *Preachers, Florilegia and Sermons: Studies in the Manipulus Florum of Thomas of Ireland*, Toronto, 1979, p. 18.

and biology, and the stars. It also draws our attention to the authors who were most influential in his early theological development, and—even more significant—those whom he found most congenial in developing the kind of theology to which he was increasingly drawn.

These are matters which deserve some elaboration. It is not often that we can mark the steps of intellectual growth in a man of Grosseteste's power and independence of mind. The Index and its associated texts give us the opportunity of following in some detail his development from scientist to theologian, moving under his own power and following his own genius. At the risk of some tedium, we must at least trace the outlines of the process.

It will be helpful to start with a list of the writers referred to in his Index, giving the number of subjects on which he found something of interest in each of them, with a rough calculation of the total number of his references to their works.

The number of subjects fully annotated in our surviving list is 197, and the complete list of references is about 6,000.[38] The authors were divided into two classes: first, the main theological sources—the Bible in a section by itself; then, the Fathers and a small selection of their medieval successors—in the central list; then, in a marginal list, the secular sources—rather oddly including the Lateran Council of 1179.[39] To provide a point of comparison, I also list the number of quotations from each of these authors in Peter Lombard's *Sentences*.

I have set out the repellent statistics in some detail because they contain an important message about the ways in which Grosseteste set about utilising his scientific knowledge for theological purposes and extending his reading of the Fathers to produce an original theological vision. In deciphering this message, it will be convenient to begin by examining his use of secular and scientific sources, and then proceed to his theological sources and the way he developed them.

---

[38] The number of references can only be approximate and it would be a waste of time to count them too diligently because a single reference to a section or chapter of a work may include several occurrences of the symbol in the margins of the text. The number of marginal symbols will, therefore, generally be greater than the number of references.

[39] I omit a few unimportant authors. For a complete list (except for the omission of the *Aphorisms* of Hippocrates) see R. W. Hunt in Callus, 1955, pp. 141-5.

Author	Number of subjects	Number of references	Peter Lombard's *Sentences*: number of quotations
1. Main List			
Augustine	181	3,000	581
Gregory	157	1,257	41
Jerome	96	488	88
Bernard	75	244	—
John of Damascus	74	280	26
John Chrysostom	64	111	14
St Anselm	48	124	—
Rabanus	34	84	—
Denys the Areopagite	25	36	—
Ambrose	17	33	71
Bede	16	48	21
Isidore of Seville	15	24	6
Basil	13	27	—
Origen	5	14	10
2. Marginal List			
Seneca	58	333	
Aristotle			
On Animals	29	68	
Metaphysics	17	18	
On Sleep	3	3	
On Death	1	1	
Boethius			
Consolation of Philosophy	27	50	
Preface to Ptolemy's *Almagest*	6	6	
Avicenna's *Metaphysics*	3	3	
Hippocrates' *Aphorisms*	2	2	
Algazel's *Metaphysics*	1	1	
Alhazen's *Optics*	1	1	
Calcidius on Plato's *Timaeus*	1	1	

1. The secular sources and their use

First we should note that the secular sources form an unusual mixture: there are a few texts long current in the schools of western Europe, and a larger number of texts only recently

translated from Greek or Arabic. Further, a few of these sources
are quoted quite frequently (Boethius; Seneca; Aristotle *On
Animals* and *Metaphysics*); but others are quoted only once or
twice, and then on the most unlikely subjects: Aristotle's *De
Animalibus*, on education, the laws of war, just kingship, honouring one's parents; his *Metaphysics*, on electing prelates, jus-
tification and grace, and concupiscence;[40] Alhazen's *Optics*, on
the dignity of the human condition;[41] the preface to Ptolemy's
Almagest, on humility, poverty, riches and envy;[42] Calcidius's
commentary on the *Timaeus*, on friendship;[43] the *Aphorisms* of
Hippocrates, on fasting and old age;[44] Avicenna's *Metaphysics*,
on prayer.[45]

It is inconceivable that Grosseteste re-read Calcidius,
Alhazen, Hippocrates and Avicenna to collect this bizarre
handful of quotations. We can only suppose that he used his
memory of earlier reading to recall passages which had struck
him as illuminating. But the references to Boethius, Seneca and
Aristotle are much too frequent and detailed to be accounted
for in this way: he must have re-read them with his theological
programme in mind. In the case of Boethius we can prove that
this is what he did, for the copy which he annotated for his
Index has survived with his symbols and annotations added in
his own hand.

This volume provides a vivid testimony to his habits of work.
Its margins are freely decorated with symbols drawing attention to such subjects as Providence, Fate, Free will, God's
foreknowledge and human blessedness. In addition, he noted

[40] Grosseteste's copy of *De Animalibus* was Michael Scot's translation in 19 Books,
similar to that in Merton College, Oxford, MS 278: Bks. 1-8 contain the *Historia
Animalium*; Bks. 11-14 the *De Partibus Animalium*; Bks. 15-19 the *De Generatione Animalium*
(Bks. 9-10 are a miscellany and are not referred to in Grosseteste's Index).

[41] The single reference is to Bk. 2. 2. I have not been able to identify the passage,
but several are possible. For the text, see *Opticae Thesaurus Alhazeni Arabis libri septem*,
ed. F. Risner, Basel, 1572.

[42] This 'preface' is not by Ptolemy; there is a copy in Bodleian MS Laud misc. 644,
f. 210^{r-v}, giving a brief account of Ptolemy's life and thought, and mentioning all the
subjects referred to in Grosseteste's Index.

[43] The reference is to the first sentence in Calcidius's preface.

[44] The references are to *Aphorisms* 1. 5 and 1. 13. The former is especially relevant:
'Omne enim peccatum, quantumcumque sit magnum, sit maius in tenuis dietibus
quam in grassioribus' (Venice, 1493, p. 6; for a different text, see I. Müller-Rohlfsen,
Die lateinische Ravennatische Übersetzung der Hippocratischen Aphorismen, Hamburg, 1979).

[45] Avicenna, *Liber de Philosophia Prima*, ed. S. van Riet, ii, 1980, p. 537.

relevant passages in several works of Augustine.[46] It seems clear from these notes that he was deeply engaged in studying Augustine while annotating Boethius, but perhaps he had not yet got very far in this study for nearly a third of his references are to a single chapter of the *Enchiridion*. It is also clear that he had not yet got far in Greek, for though he was assiduous in correcting Boethius's Latin text, he passed over glaring corruptions in the Greek words without remark. In this volume we see Grosseteste at an early stage in his shift from the liberal arts to theology; and we can observe how he shaped the subject-matter to his new purposes. The annotation of the *Consolation of Philosophy* can be linked with his work *On Free Will*; and, in commenting on the Psalms, his argument about blessedness and 'deification'was inspired by one of the most heavily annotated chapters (iii. 10) in Boethius. His *Dictum* about the virtue of wine in banishing the gloom and timidity of the mind may reasonably be linked with the passage which he noted in Hippocrates on the evils of a low diet; and his study of Aristotle on the procreation of animals, seems to lie behind this passage in praise of the study of sexual intercourse in his *Dicta*:

The body of a man is better and nobler than any tree; and that of a woman is better and nobler than the earth. And the seed from a man's body from which a man is generated is better and nobler than any other kind of sowing. Therefore the seed from the body of a man falling into the body of a woman to procreate children is—barring the defilement of carnal concupiscence—better and nobler than any kind of seed falling into the ground. Consequently, good, pure and honest meditation on this is better and more honourable than meditation on the procreation of trees, provided it is not contaminated by concupiscence or corruption. And the same may be said about the organs of generation, which are not to be thought shameful.[47]

These words belong to a different world from that of most contemporary comments on sexuality, and they illustrate the influence of his scientific studies on his theology. Nevertheless, the general balance of the books he indexed, and the way in which he made use of his scientific sources, leave no doubt that

---

[46] The works referred to are *De Musica, De Trinitate, De beata vita, De libero arbitrio, Confessiones, De Quaestionibus LXXXIII, Enchiridion.* No other author besides Augustine is mentioned except, at the last sentence, Seneca.

[47] *Dicta*, no. 29. I translate a fragment of the text from Bodleian MSS Bodl. 830, f. 27, and Laud misc. 374 f. 35^{r-v}.

he was engaged on a thorough reorientation of his manner of thought, as well as his way of life.

2. The theological sources and their development

LATIN SOURCES

It will be seen at once, from the list set out above, that Grosseteste's order of preference in his theological reading was very different from Peter Lombard's. Augustine alone has a similar predominance in both lists. But the choice of Augustine's works is different: the *City of God*, which is only slightly represented in Lombard, is overwhelmingly the most important of Augustine's works for Grosseteste; and his surviving copy of this work with its vast array of indexing symbols fully testifies to the intense concentration with which he had read it. On nearly every subject in his Index Grosseteste found something of interest in Augustine which deserved a reference. Then, Gregory the Great, who comes a poor fourth in Lombard, is far ahead of all other authors except Augustine in Grosseteste's list: he dominates the whole field of moral conduct and biblical symbolism. Here again the survival of Grosseteste's copy of the *Moralia in Job* demonstrates the intensity of his reading of this text, which is more frequently quoted in the Index than any other work except the *City of God*.

These are the two foundations of Grosseteste's theology. But the high place of Bernard and Anselm is also noteworthy, especially in view of the total absence of any other twelfth-century writers, except Hugh of St Victor on Denys the Areopagite. Grosseteste seems to have possessed a quite complete collection of Anselm's works of the kind which was becoming fairly common in the early thirteenth century—a collection which contained derivative works like the *De Similitudinibus*, to which he frequently referred. His collection of St Bernard's works was much less complete: it does not seem to have contained the sermons on the *Song of Songs*, to which he makes only one vague reference; but he made up for this deficiency by his large number of references to the *De Consideratione*, and he also had a selection of Bernard's letters, to which he quite frequently referred. If Augustine and Gregory provided the general background to his theology, Anselm's *Cur Deus Homo* and Bernard's *De Consideratione* provided models at two high points in his thinking: Anselm on the Incarnation, and Bernard on the government of the Church.

GREEK SOURCES

For his future development, however, the most important feature of the Index is the large place that the Greek theologians, John Chrysostom, John of Damascus, Denys the Aeropagite, and Basil, had begun to take even before he knew their works in Greek or in any approach to completeness. Chrysostom, who makes a large display in the Index, has a disappointing future in Grosseteste's later work. But the three others, John of Damascus, Denys the Areopagite and Basil have a future which requires a brief explanation. None of them were newcomers to the Western world in the 1220s, but Grosseteste used them more extensively in his Index, and will use them more in the future, than any earlier medieval theologian.

John of Damascus

John of Damascus is the Greek most frequently quoted, despite the fact that the only work which Grosseteste knew at this time was his *De Fide Orthodoxa*. This work had been translated in the mid- twelfth century by Burgundio of Pisa in time to be used in Peter Lombard's *Sentences*.[48] Lombard, however, used only that small part of the work which dealt with the doctrine of the Trinity, and all later Latin writers before Grosseteste seem to have copied Lombard in this limitation. Grosseteste by contrast quoted the work from beginning to end on all manner of questions: the Creation of the world, the dignity of the human condition, the cardinal virtues, counsel, goodwill, free will, the election of prelates, baptism, the perfection of Holy Scripture, the manner of expounding Scripture, how prophecy is to be received by us, teaching and learning, what sin is, the source of evil, and many other subjects. He found in John of Damascus a writer who shared his interest in the natural world and especially in the structure of the human soul, its perceptions, its

---

[48] See Peter Lombard, *Sententiae*, I. i, p. 124* (*Spicilegium Bonaventurianum*, iv, 1971); also Joannes Damascenus, *De Fide Orthodoxa*, ed. E. M. Buytaert, Franciscan Institute Publications, No. 8, New York, 1955.

imaginative faculty, and its power of perceiving the laws that lie behind appearances.

When he made his Index, Grosseteste was dependent on Burgundio's translation, but he soon found his way to the Greek text and began comparing the varying recensions. These showed him that Burgundio had used a defective text which left out much matter about the stars, the seas and the winds. The note which he wrote when he made this discovery provides a key to one of the reasons for his attraction to John of Damascus:

These two chapters are omitted in some copies of the Greek text, perhaps because they did not seem very germane to the subject-matter of theology. But those who are truly wise think that a knowledge of all truth is useful for understanding and expounding theology. Therefore, having found these chapters in the Greek exemplar, we are unwilling to omit them, believing as a certainty that so great an author would not have included them in this book unless he had known that they would have some value for the study of Holy Scripture.[49]

By the time he wrote these words, Grosseteste was deeply engaged in the work of correcting the existing translation of *De Fide Orthodoxa* and making the first Latin translation of John of Damascus's *Logic, De Centum Heresibus, Elementarium Dogmatum*, and his comment on the hymn 'Holy, Holy, Holy'.[50] In 1230, all this work lay in the future, but the basis had been laid in the years when he discovered Greek theologians who had views similar to his own about the natural world and its importance for theology.

Denys the Areopagite

Denys the Areopagite had presented a bewildering problem to Western scholars before the time of Grosseteste. On the surface, his credentials were impeccable. It was universally agreed that the writer of the works which went under his name was the Athenian convert of St Paul, who had later become bishop of Paris and died a martyr's death evangelizing Gaul. His shrine

---

[49] Magdalen Coll., Oxford, MS 192, f. 166ᵛ. For the two missing chapters, see Buytaert, op. cit. , caps. 22-3.

[50] Thomson 1940, pp. 46-52, lists the MSS of these translations, of which only the *De logica* has been published (ed. O. A. Colligan, Franciscan Institute Publications, No. 6, New York, 1953).

near Paris was the religious centre of Capetian France. His writings were believed to be the earliest Christian writings outside the Bible.

His position, therefore, as a link with the Apostolic Age was unchallenged. The monks of St Denis and the kings of France who wished to glorify their patron saint, and theologians everywhere who wished to find their roots in Apostolic teaching, had every reason to promote the study of Denys's writings.[51] And yet, despite their labours, they had failed to stimulate interest in them. The reasons are not far to seek. Try as they might to torture the Greek into intelligible Latin, the language of these writings remained obscure, their doctrinal content was imprecise, and what was intelligible seemed perilously like heresy. They presented none of the clear statements of doctrine which could be used in the twelfth-century schools. They were too elusive and contorted in their piety to serve the purposes of public or private devotion. The calm and lucid mind of Hugh of St Victor had been able to extract from the most obviously useful and least puzzling of Denys's works a full account of the nine orders of angels. This filled a gap in the spiritual cosmology of Christendom; but even here the main doctrine of angels had already been satisfactorily elucidated for the Latin world by Gregory the Great, who transmitted the Dionysian hierarchy with only one alteration.[52] So the twelfth century continued to be indifferent to Denys's works.

The story of Grosseteste's discovery of Denys's works follows a similar pattern to his discovery of John of Damascus. Little though he knew of Denys's work, he found that it illuminated subjects which went far beyond the matter indicated by its title—such subjects as the essence and simplicity of God, the cardinal virtues, contemplation, the unity of a multitude, silence, free will, the election of prelates, the perfection of Holy Scripture, prophecy and how it is to be received by us, teaching and learning, sin and the Fall, justice and pride. This wide

[51] For the translations and revival of interest in the works of Ps.-Denys before Grosseteste, see G. Théry 'Documents concernant Jean Sarrazin, reviseur de la traduction Érigénienne du *Corpus Dionysiacum*', *AHDLMA* xviii, 1951, 45–87; H. F. Dondaine, *Le Corpus dionysien de l'université de Paris au XIIIᵉ siècle*, 1953.

[52] Gregory the Great, in his *Homilia in Evangelia*, 33. 7, presents the same order as Ps.-Denys with the single difference that he reverses his positions of Virtues and Principalities.

range of references to the single work of Denys which he had studied before 1230 suggests that he already found in him, as in John of Damascus, a congenial spirit, and his later work abundantly confirms this impression. His reading of the *Celestial Hierarchy* stimulated him to further research into the whole body of Denys's works. Already before 1235 he was interested in, and perhaps organizing, a new translation of Denys's works; and after 1235, when he had the resources of the bishopric of Lincoln at his disposal, he was able to seek the best Greek texts, to compare them with the three existing Latin translations, to note their variants and improve their renderings, and finally to provide the whole Dionysian *corpus* with a commentary gathered from all available ancient sources.[53] As a sustained and many-sided scholarly enterprise, it was unparalleled in his own day and not often equalled at any time. In this work, Grosseteste was a pioneer of a new kind of co-operative effort which the broadening intellectual activity of the thirteenth century brought into existence. The most productive scholars began to need the help of teams of assistants, and he was one of the earliest directors of such a team—alone among them in not having the organization of a religious Order behind him.

Such an expenditure of effort and resources prompts the question, what was it that moved Grosseteste to so great an undertaking at a time when his life was already filled with every kind of vexation and administrative drudgery? Partly, no doubt, it provided a welcome relief from the endless business of his diocese. Partly, too, it gave him an opportunity for that large and far-sighted use of his episcopal resources which was perhaps the main enjoyment that his position gave him. But, chiefly, Denys's works satisfied many of his deepest instincts. They provided the fullest account in Christian literature of the multifarious gradations of Being flowing out from God and carrying the imprint of the divine nature through all the subordinate orders of ministering spirits and earthly agents. They satisfied Grosseteste's instinct for seeing order in a vast array of details, and they allowed him to make his own contribution to this order in developing his view of Light as the agent which

---

[53] See R. Barbour, 'A manuscript of Ps.-Dionysius *Areopagita* copied for Robert Grosseteste', *BLR* vi, 1958, 49-16, for a brilliantly illuminating account of Grosseteste's efforts in collecting material for translating and commenting on the works of Ps.-Denys.

carried the divine unity throughout the universe, penetrating the whole from the unchanging One to the manifold diversity of created beings. And, besides all this, Denys linked together the Greek and Latin Churches, the Apostolic age and the present day, Platonism and Christianity. In this last, he helped to resolve a troublesome contradiction in Grosseteste's thought: Grosseteste was a natural Platonist who distrusted Plato. Denys provided a Platonism rooted in the Bible and in the Apostolic age—a Platonism that was wholly Christian. This was what Grosseteste as a scientist, philosopher and theologian most desired: the unity of God and Creation stamped with the authority of the earliest Church. He found it in Denys.

Basil the Great

The third Greek theologian who opened new prospects in theology was St Basil. His works make only a modest contribution to Grosseteste's Index: only twenty-five references on thirteen subjects. All these references are to a single work—Basil's Homilies on the Six Days of Creation. Once more, the subjects on which Grosseteste found material of interest for his Index are quite surprising. None has any special reference to the Creation: nearly half are on 'the manner of expounding the Scriptures' and 'learning and teaching'; and the others are on such varied subjects as 'chastity', 'honouring one's father and mother', 'the prohibition of public spectacles',[54] 'preachers and preaching', and so on. It would appear, therefore, that he read the work with his eyes open for thoughts on all kinds of subjects which interested him, but without, at that time, any great expectation of enlightenment on the subject of Creation.

In this lack of expectation, he would simply have been following in the footsteps of earlier readers in the West. Basil's homilies had long been known in the early Latin translation of Eustathius, which Grosseteste used in making his Index. But twelfth-century Latin writers on Creation had not made much use of them. Their homiletic form did not lend itself to imparting precise views or facts about Creation which could be useful to philosophical writers like Abelard, Thierry of Chartres, and Clarembald of Arras; and the substance of Basil's

[54] The references to this subject are of some interest in view of Grosseteste's later prohibition of miracle plays, for which see below, p. 261

work had anyhow been incorporated in Ambrose's *Hexaëmeron*. Grosseteste stood in this tradition when he made his Index. But a few years later, when he wrote his own *Hexaëmeron*, after he had left the secular schools to devote himself to teaching the Franciscans, his attitude to Basil had completely changed—a change which we will follow in the next chapter, when we come to consider his theological maturity.

9

Grosseteste's Theological Vision

I. A THEOLOGY OF CREATION

By 1230 Grosseteste had cut his theological teeth, a quarter of a century after his more conventionally educated contemporaries. He had given several courses of lectures on the Psalms, and he had thought sufficiently well of the mixture of science and symbolism, and the growing emphasis on the pastoral care and government of the Church, which he had developed in these lectures, to preserve parts of them with some care. Probably he had also lectured on Jerome's introduction to the Bible and used his growing knowledge of Greek to explain the names of places and characteristics of peoples. These comments also he had thought worth preserving. Fragments of his lectures on the Epistles have also survived which may go back to his earliest days as a lecturer. Besides, he had preached as a theologian in the university, and he had become an archdeacon. Perhaps also he had been elected chancellor by his colleagues on what must have been a somewhat turbulent occasion. Altogether, he had emerged as a man of weight and independence. He was now a local theologian of some note, and he had begun to display an unusual range of learning; but he had not yet shown any real power of theological thought, and, apart from some tentative ideas in his later lectures on the Psalms, he had made little original use of the reading on which he had been engaged for the past few years.

But he had several authors on his hands, ripe, so to speak, for development. Among them Basil the Great occupied a modest place. At the time when the Index was made, the prospects for Basil as a formative influence in Grosseteste's thought did not seem bright. But not long after 1230—perhaps as early as 1232–3—a great change had taken place. At about this date Grosseteste himself wrote a *Hexaëmeron*. There is some reason for thinking that it may have been the earliest of the three theological works written between 1230 and 1235 in which he developed his own distinctive style. It was a style which we may briefly describe as scientific and symbolic in method, Greek in sympathy, pastoral in approach. His science continues to be shown in his interest in natural phenomena and in his habit of selecting detailed problems for intensive consideration, often with only tentative conclusions. His symbolic leanings are shown in his readiness to view every object in the universe as a symbol of spiritual truth. His Greek sympathies are apparent in the large place which he gives to Greek writers in all these treatises, and in his readiness to adopt their opinions and follow their suggestions. His pastoral intention is shown in the pastoral applications which he gave to his theoretical considerations, recondite though they often were.

From all these points of view Basil's *Hexaëmeron* now appeared as a model to be followed. Like Grosseteste, Basil had a strong interest in miscellaneous scientific details and their symbolic significance. He too saw light as a specially significant link between the Creator and the created universe. When Basil spoke of nature, he wished not only to convey knowledge, but to share an experience. He told his audience, 'You must not only study, but participate.' He compared them to spectators at the games, who were required to sit with bare heads so that they shared the sweat of the players and thus became more than spectators. This was how they were to participate in theology. They were to 'contemplate the universe and see God speaking about himself'. When they looked at the stars, they were to stand in the presence of the author of the universe.[1] Grosseteste expressed similar thoughts: knowledge is not enough in itself; it has value only when it becomes a lively experience, a participation; *aspectus* must be accompanied by *affectus*; *cognitio* must be completed by *amor*; the permanent part of the Old Testament law must be practised not outwardly only, but with heart-felt assent—only then could it impart life. This theme worked its way into every part of Grosseteste's thinking and preaching.

The style, too, of Basil's homilies was an inspiration to the

---

[1] See *Eustathius: Ancienne version latin des neuf homélies sur l'*Hexaëmeron *de Basile de Césarée*, ed. E. Amand de Mendieta and S. Y. Rudberg, Berlin, 1958, VI. 1. 1, p. 69.

lecturer who had now committed himself to a Franciscan ideal of life and teaching. In his *Hexaëmeron*, Basil spoke to ordinary people, not just to the clergy. His work was cast in the form of mid-day discourses, somewhere between sermons and lectures. At the beginning of one of them, he says, 'You have come here once more to contemplate the marvels of the second day of Creation. Many of you are artisans earning your living by manual labour, so I must be brief and not keep you too long from your work.'[2] This was the kind of audience which the friars saw as pre-eminently their own. Basil aimed at being intelligible to all so far as possible: this also was Grosseteste's aim. Neither he nor Basil could help being learned, but their common aim was not so much to increase knowledge as to draw the hearts of their hearers to God.

As always in this phase of his life, when his interest was aroused, Grosseteste began looking beyond the Latin text to the original Greek. When he wrote his *Hexaëmeron*, he chiefly used the old Latin translation of Basil's work;, but on one occasion at least he had clearly looked at the Greek hoping to clear up an obscurity. He quoted Basil in a version which he had either made himself or caused to be made for him—not with much success, for he confessed that he was still baffled by what he read: 'It is perhaps not possible for anyone, certainly not for me to express what Basil here seeks to convey [he was speaking of the eternal ideas in the divine mind]. . . I am a child in spiritual interpretations and can only speak as a stammerer; but on this subject I cannot speak at all. I must return to more familiar subjects.'[3]

This passage, which comes almost at the beginning of his *Hexaëmeron*, is the first indication we have of the new phase in Grosseteste's studies when he began to seek not just etymologies, but a fuller understanding of the text by going to the original. In doing this he discovered (as he also discovered in studying John of Damascus) that the translator had sometimes omitted important passages in the original: Eustathius's translation contained only the first nine of the eleven homilies in the com-

---

[2] Eustathius, III. 1. 5, p. 31.

[3] *Hex.*, I. xii. 4 (pp. 68–9). Grosseteste here quotes a passage from Basil's *Hexaëmeron* I. 5. 1, in which one sentence differs substantially from Eustathius's translation. Grosseteste's version is not much more intelligible, but it seems to show some contact with the Greek text.

plete text, and Grosseteste either translated the omitted homilies or had them translated, for he certainly used them.[4] He
also discovered that Basil's brother, Gregory of Nyssa, had
written another work *On the Creation of Man* to fill a large gap
in Basil's homilies. This was another work which Grosseteste
had not possessed when he made his Index; but he used it now.
He found in it one passage which was especially congenial to
him, and he appropriated it without mentioning its source: 'I
wish the reader to know that if I write anything not to be found
in the words of our authorities, I put it forward not definitively
but "as an exercise for my hearers, following the footprints of
truth conjecturally and tentatively".'[5] The final phrase here is
a quotation from Gregory of Nyssa. This was an image after
his own heart, and he repeated it in his *De Cessatione Legalium*
naming the source:

It should be noticed that the holy writers often intend to indicate
what was *possible* rather than to assert what *was*, and many of their
statements are about possibilities rather than certainties. Even when
they seem to us to speak assertively as about absolute truth, they often
propound things as an exercise. As Gregory of Nyssa says, 'We put
forward what comes into our mind not definitively but as an exercise
for our attentive hearers.'[6]

Passages such as this reinforced Grosseteste's natural inclination
to stretch out beyond the limits of the known to the area of
conjecture. Basil and Gregory of Nyssa authorized this practice
in the study of Holy Scripture, and they provided an invaluable
support at the moment when he was launching out into independent theological speculation. This was, I think, the chief
contribution which Basil and his brother made to Grosseteste's
thought. They gave him an example of freedom in discussing
biblical texts and opened the way to a theory of inspiration
which justified the relaxed and informal kind of theology which
Grosseteste found most congenial. He came to see that the Holy
Spirit did not always inspire the sacred writers in the same
way: sometimes they were inspired to express views of possible
truths rather than certainties; sometimes the Holy Spirit might

---

[4] See Dales and Gieben, introduction to *Hex.*, pp. xxiv–xxv.
[5] *Hex.* IV. i. 4 (p. 123).
[6] *De Cess. Leg.* IV. iii. 5.

leave even St Peter and St Paul to their own devices, to provoke
the discovery of some new truth through error:

Although we ought always to try to reconcile contradictions, it may
not always be possible, because, just as the spirit of prophecy is not
always present in the prophets, so perhaps the Holy Spirit did not
always inspire the words even of these two saints (Peter and Paul),
but left them to their own opinions so that their disagreement might
produce some useful fruit for us.[7]

This view of varying levels of inspiration, which Grosseteste
developed from Gregory of Nyssa and from contact with Greek
theology, has very wide implications, which Grosseteste only
touched on. But he saw enough to recognize that the contradictions and discords in the *discors concordia* (as he calls it) of
Holy Scripture, and consequently of Christian doctrine, had
a deeper source and a more positive role than most of his
contemporaries would have appreciated. Of course he saw that
in the end there was no room for outright contradictions; but
he also saw that the harmony of the celestial music contained
discords for which there might be no immediate resolution, and
that tentative and hypothetical conclusions had a role in the
search for truth which was not allowed for in scholastic
procedures.

It was not surprising, therefore, that Grosseteste found it a
congenial task to elaborate the hints dropped by Basil. At one
point, Basil remarked that the first words of Genesis, 'In the
beginning', have a variety of meanings. Grosseteste followed
this up with avidity.[8] He had long been interested in these
words because he saw in them irrefutable evidence that Aristotle's view of the eternity of the world was erroneous: 'With
the hammer of these words Moses crushed the philosophers
who assert with Aristotle that the world has no beginning.'[9] He
could now luxuriate in the intricacies of the formidable phrase,
and he illustrated the different kinds of 'beginning' with Biblical and philosophical examples until he could think of no
more. Then he gave up and left the field to others:

[7] *De Cess. Leg.* IV. iii. 3. The whole discussion in part IV of *De Cess. Leg.* on the
concors discordia per has duas fistulas (Augustine versus Jerome on the one hand; Peter
versus Paul on the other) should be read in this connection.
[8] *Hex.* I. viii. 1–10, pp. 58–67.
[9] *Hex.* I. viii. 4, p. 61.

In all these ways, and perhaps in other ways which are hidden from me, these words 'In the beginning' indicate how God in the beginning created heaven and earth.[10]

Here, as in many other places in Grosseteste's writing, we have the sensation of an endless pursuit in which all can join. Or again, when Basil remarked on the suitability of the month of March (Nisan) as the best time for the Creation, Grosseteste was able to supply further arguments: it was at the equinox when the sun shines with greatest effect on every part of the world; it was at the most temperate moment of the year; and the spring equinox was better than the autumn for Creation, because it was a time of generation and growth rather than of decay and death.[11]

Basil's mixture of science and theology encouraged him to use his scientific knowledge in the service of biblical exegesis, and it brought theology into close touch with natural causes. In these matters, Grosseteste was no dogmatist. When Basil differed from Latin scholars in his speculations about the existence of a firmament above the firmament of the fixed stars, Grosseteste placidly set out the various theories and concluded with the remark that it was not his business to try to settle an issue which had puzzled better men.[12] For his own part, he would only add that, if a firmament *did* exist above the firmament of the fixed stars, it would certainly not rotate like the other spheres. Why not? Because the rotation of the starry spheres was ordained—like everything else in the universe—for the good of mankind in distributing the heavenly influence equally over the whole human race.[13] But the influence of any sphere beyond the stars, whether it rotated or not, would be entirely uniform. Therefore its rotation could bring no benefit to the dwellers on earth; therefore, if it exists, it does not rotate.

This modest addendum to an inconclusive discussion is a

---

[10] *Hex.* I. viii. 10 (p. 67): 'Tot igitur modis, et forte aliquibus qui me latent aliis, dicto "principio" creavit Deus celum et terram "in principio".'

[11] *Hex.* I. x. 2 (pp. 65–6).

[12] *Hex.* I. xvii. 1 (p. 75): 'Horum autem auctorum [viz. Josephus and Gregory of Nyssa] controversiam non est meum determinare, sed si celum istud primum sit aliud a firmamento secundo die creato, videtur quod illud sit immobile.'

[13] 13. 'Cum enim omnia propter hominem sint . . . motus celorum non erit nisi propter generationem hominum et eorum que hic inferius ministrant homini' (loc. cit., pp. 75–6). Cf. *De Cess. Leg.* II. ii. 2: 'Nulli dubium quin omnia sint facta propter hominem et propter hominem secundum optimum statum hominis.'

good deal less modest than it pretends to be. After all, it lays down a principle of staggering magnitude, that *everything* in the universe—not just crops and animals, but stars and their rotations, and whatever sphere there may be beyond the stars— all exist for the good of mankind. This was a principle which Grosseteste had already enunciated as one of the topics of his theological Index: 'Quod omnia propter hominem'. We know from his Index what the foundation of this principle was: it was a single—but no doubt in his view sufficient—sentence in Deuteronomy 4: 19, which stated that all the stars of heaven were created to minister to all the peoples of the earth. In less fundamental sources, Grosseteste could find only four supporting texts in Gregory's *Moralia*, John Chrysostom's *De Reparatione Lapsi*, John of Damascus's *Sentences*, and a single passage in Aristotle *On Animals*. Of these, we can identify only the first with certainty;[14] and we may think that they provided only weak supports for a principle so far-reaching as the unqualified centrality of Man in the order of created beings. But here we see Grosseteste using the principle as a guide to the construction of the universe; and we shall soon see that he was prepared to strike out boldly in developing its consequences.

II. THE CENTRALITY OF MAN

The centrality of man in the universe was a commonplace of Christian thought. It is implicit in the words (Genesis 1: 26) 'Let them have dominion over the fish of the sea, and over the birds of the air, and over the cattle, and over all the earth, and over every creeping thing that creeps upon the earth.' But this is a limited sovereignty over other creatures for practical purposes. The doctrine takes on a larger dimension if everything in the universe has a symbolic value, for symbols can only be useful for mankind: angels, having immediate access to truth, could have no use for symbols. So, if all created things have a

---

[14] Grosseteste's list of authorities for 'Quod omnia propter hominum' is found in Lyons MS 414, f. 23ᵛ with the appropriate symbol ⊙ : a microcosm within the macrocosm. We can identify the passage in Gregory's *Moralia* from his manuscript of this work, Bodley MS 198, where the symbol appears in the margin of f. 130ᵈ against the passage 'caelum et terra . . . pro eorum usu . . . perseverant' (Bk. 5, c. 34; *PL* 75, 713 D).

symbolic value, the centrality of man stretches further than
practical dominion over other creatures. Ants and lions, and
all other creatures of no obvious human utility, become the
instructors of mankind; and to investigate their natures becomes a scientific duty if the maximum amount of instruction
is to be extracted from them.

This was Grosseteste's plan in his earliest lectures on the
Psalms, when he took each natural object mentioned by the
Psalmist and gave it a universal setting in the symbolism of the
universe. If he abandoned that task before he reached the end
of the Psalms, this was not because he lost faith in the universal
symbolism of nature. He may simply have thought that he had
exhausted the symbolic interpretations of his stock of scientific
knowledge. Or perhaps, with his now considerable body of
theological reading, he wanted to discuss other theological
problems: the place of Man in the universe; the relationship
between God and Man and all created things; the laws of the
Old and New Testaments; the entry of God into the universe
in Christ. These were the main problems with which Grosseteste
was concerned in his mature theology of the years between
1230 and 1235.

The 'omnia propter hominem' entry in his Index contains
an early hint of the direction in which his mind was moving.
He took a further step when he came to consider the creation
of Man as described in Genesis 1: 26: 'Let us make Man in our
image and after our likeness.' Every commentator on Genesis
had discussed these words, and all agreed that both 'image'
and 'similitude' referred to the spiritual nature of man. But
there was disagreement about the difference between image
and similitude. Broadly speaking there were two ways of distinguishing them: either they referred to different faculties, or
to different degrees of intensity of the same faculty. For example, St Bernard followed the first of these alternatives. He referred 'image' to the inalienable gift of free will which mankind
shared with God, and 'similitude' to the habitual virtues which
were formed or deformed by the exercise of free will.[15] But

[15] Bernard, *Sermo in Annunciatione*, I, sect. 7 (*Opera*, edd. J. Leclerq and H. Rochais,
v, 1968, p. 19): 'Ad imaginem nempe et similitudinem Dei factus est homo: in imagine,
arbitrii libertatem; virtutes habens, in similitudine. Et similitudo quidem periit . . .
Imago siquidem in gehenna ipsa uri poterit, non exuri; ardere, sed non deleri.'

Grosseteste, following the example of Augustine, took the view that the two words referred not to different faculties in Man but to different levels of intensity: 'image' meant a complete similarity with God, 'similitude' a likeness capable of being intensified or diminished. Clearly only the one unique God–Man could be a perfect image of God. All others, even in their most perfect state, were an approximation to God so far as the limitations of a created being allowed. This is how Grosseteste sets the scene for his discussion of this problem:

God is all in all, the life of living things, the form of all finely formed things (*formosorum forma*), the species (or perfection) of all species (*speciosorum species*), and Man is in all things God's closest imitative likeness (*similitudo imitatoria*). Therefore Man, as the image of God, is in some sense everything. Therefore a full account of this saying 'Let us make man in our image and after our likeness' requires more even than an explanation of the forms and appearances and substances of all things: it requires also an account of the relationships between God and Man and all other things. Such an explanation is not to be expected from any human being: how much less from one so inexpert as I am. A man could no more explain these things than a point could explain a line, or a grain of sand the sands of the sea-shore, or a drop of rain the water of the ocean, or an atom the system of the whole world. Nevertheless what God will deign to give me, I will stammeringly set forth briefly in such words as I have.[16]

For the background to this passage, we may once more turn to Grosseteste's Index of theological subjects. We have already found him seeking authorities for the proposition 'that all things exist for Man', and failing to make more than a very brief list. Another subject in his Index for which he had an appropriate symbol, and on which he sought illustrations in his authorities, was 'how God is all in all'. On this subject too he found very little, only a single reference in John of Damascus and an uncertain one in Bernard on the *Song of Songs*.[17] But he persevered in his search, and in his *Hexaëmeron* he began his serious discussion of the place of Man in the universe with the words

[16] *Hex.* VIII. i. 2. The many-sided development of Grosseteste's thought on *forma* and *species* may be traced from *Ep.* 1, pp. 4–5, 'Deus est . . . forma formosissima et species speciosissima'; to *Hex.* as above and I. xviii. 2, 'Species in quantum complet materiam, forma est; in quantum inclinat et nititur in actionem, natura est'; to *De Luce*, Bauer p. 56, 'Species et perfectio corporum omnium est lux.' See also above, pp. 32–5, 136–8.

[17] MS Lyons 414, f. 21ᵛ. The symbol is ∧, in contrast to ∨, which signifies 'praising God'. The reference to John of Damascus is to c. 14 of *De Fide Orthodoxa*.

which I have quoted. This avowal of the magnitude of his search is followed by twenty pages of discussion, the most prolonged argument in the whole work. The reader will be lucky if he is not soon lost as Grosseteste picks his way through a subject which he has declared to be beyond the wit of man. He quotes all his favourite authors: chiefly Augustine, Basil, and Gregory of Nyssa, supported by John of Damascus, Chrysostom, and Bernard. He intersperses his quotations with many reflections on memory, imagination, colour, light, the human organs and senses, and the possibility of speaking about God. And then, with a final long quotation from Gregory of Nyssa, he goes on abruptly to the next sentence of *Genesis*, 'And let them have dominion over the fish of the sea'.[18]

Here is Grosseteste in all his remarkable strength and weakness. He takes on a subject larger than any that can be conceived: to speak of 'everything' that God is and that man's nature exhibits, is beyond any human reach. Yet he will say what he can because, having undertaken to explain the words of Genesis, the text requires something to be said. And having said what he can, he will leave it to others to go further if they can. What he says on any subject will often be new, and sometimes (as here) chaotic, but he offers it as his contribution, and then goes on to the next subject. Primarily, he is struggling to explain a difficult text; but he is also struggling to get a view of the whole subject, to know what it is to be a man. As Basil had said 'To know is also to participate', and this is what Grosseteste tried to do. Fragmentary though his thoughts are, they are inspired by a sense of the identification of theology with the study of the created universe and its revelation of the nature of God. This union of the diversity of all things in God is a somewhat nebulous concept, and he was always searching for new ways of expressing it. The more he reached out to comprehend this unity, the more incoherent his thoughts became; then he descended from the summit to the consideration of individual things and he became coherent again. As he wrote later in his *Hexaëmeron* in a revealing, but barely translatable, sentence, 'The individual trees in the paradise of intellectual

---

[18] *Hex.* VIII. i. 1 (p. 236). The discussion of the sentence 'Let us make man in our image, after our likeness', which had started on p. 217, continues to p. 236.

vision are cognitions of individual natures in the light of eternity.'[19] This is what scientific and theological knowledge meant for Grosseteste: the recovery of the lost knowledge of Paradise.

He saw the oneness of all things in God most luminously as shafts of light penetrating the system from top to bottom. The structured unity of scholastic thought, which could be set out diagramatically like a family tree, was not for him. Grosseteste's unity could tolerate large areas of ambiguity. What he saw, he saw clearly, and without the possibility of compromise. What he did not see he left on one side, though sometimes only after he had landed himself in a choking quagmire of words as he tried to explain a text 'brief indeed, but most fertile in most profound and abundant meanings'.

This was the weak side of his preference for insight rather than formal structure. He started with observations on physical objects or fundamental texts and tried to worry his way, now from one side, now from another, into the central mystery of the Being from whom everything flowed. He applied to particulars the imaginative insight, which—as he had learned from Aristotle—was the source of scientific truth, to reach a general understanding of the universe. His theory of the twinkling of stars, which in its main outline he owed to Aristotle and adapted in his own way, may stand as an allegory of his personal stance in the search for knowledge: it is not the stars which twinkle; it is the eye which vibrates as it strains to see them more clearly. Like the soul, the eye is restless till it finds its peace in the knowledge which it seeks. So in this world, the state of man is in a state of permanent agitation as his senses receive impressions, and the mind seeks to understand them, without ever being able fully to understand or see what it seeks.

The conjunction of object, eye, and understanding, in the search for knowledge of physical events and their symbolic meaning, provides an illustration of the unity of all things. The laws which govern the physical universe are an image of the laws of eternity which govern the soul. Yet the physical universe is not just a shadow of eternity, any more than the events of the Old Testament were *only* a shadow of a greater reality to

[19] *Hex.* XI. vii. 1, pp. 313-14: 'In paradiso visionis intellectualis singula ligna sunt singularum naturarum cognitiones in suis eternis rationibus.'

come. The physical universe is both a reality and a symbol of reality; and this conjunction of symbol and reality extended upwards to the celestial spheres and downwards to the most minute atoms. Everything in the universe provides material for studying the nature of God.

III. THE UNITY OF GOD AND NATURE

This was Grosseteste's greatest discovery: nature and the supernatural are one, not only in the old sense that everything in the Old Testament symbolizes God's purpose for man and the whole Creation, but in the broader sense that the physical objects of our sense perceptions, the general laws of nature, the symbolic meanings of every creature, the purposes of the Creator, and (so far as it is knowable) the nature of God, are all parts of a single field of knowledge. 'All created things are mirrors which reflect the Creator'; so Grosseteste wrote in one of his *Dicta*, and he developed the thought in this way:[20]

Consider the smallest and most insignificant object in the universe, a speck of dust. In shape it is the most perfect form known in nature: a sphere, which in symmetry and simplicity is such that a line with one end at its centre will touch the circumference as it moves in any direction. In its beauty of form, it is an image of the whole universe. In duration, it is like the universe itself, showing no tendency to decay or change. Within, it extends an infinite number of lines; without, its circumference offers an infinite number of circles; within and without, it contains every possible geometrical form that can be constructed. It is a complete and inexhaustible treasury of all the primary mathematical constituents from which the whole universe is constructed: points, lines, numbers, proportions. It is a universe in miniature.

Still higher, it is a mirror of the Creator in its unity and trinity: in *unity*, as a simple object; in *trinity*, as combining *potentiality*, representing the power of the Father; *form* (or *essence*), representing the

---

[20] *Dictum*, no. 60, which contains the argument which I summarize here, has been edited in an exemplary fashion by Fr. Servus Gieben, *Franciscan Studies*, xxiv, 1964, pp. 144–59. The word used by Grosseteste to express the smallest indivisible unit of the universe which testifies to the nature and existence of the Trinity is *atomus* and I have followed Fr. Gieben in translating this as 'speck of dust' to avoid connotations which were certainly not in Grosseteste's mind. The difference between Fr. Gieben's exposition and my own may be described by saying that he places the argument in the grand context of a philosophical tradition and I seek to place it in the immediate context of Grosseteste's perceptions.

wisdom of the Son; the *union of the two*, representing the love of Father and Son in the Holy Spirit.

Further. Consider the human mind meditating on the speck of dust. It presents a mirror of the Trinity in the memory, intelligence and uniting love within the human mind: an image of God who remembers everything, understands everything, and loves without beginning, variability, or end.

Wherever we look, therefore, we find vestiges of God, not only as a necessary first cause, but as a Trinity of power, wisdom and love. If we had nothing else to contemplate but a speck of dust, it would display in its essence the nature of God. Similarly, if we had any part of the universe, or the whole of the universe, or just the human mind, the same characteristics of the divine nature could be found. God, nature, and the human mind all lead to the same conclusion.

This is no more than a paraphrase of a small fragment broken off from the large body of Grosseteste's theology. But small though it is, it illustrates several features of his mature theology. It shows that he continued his early scientific habit of considering small things in great detail, and drawing from them the largest conclusions. It shows too that the universe, in his view, was constructed to declare in every detail the nature of God; and these symbolic declarations were never for him (as they tended to be for Alexander Nequam or Gerald of Wales) the inventions of human minds. They were built into the structure of the universe by God. And finally, it shows that when Grosseteste the preacher wanted to appeal to the imagination of his audience, he had recourse to nature. He did not follow the pattern of the popular devotion of his day in concentrating on the human life and sufferings of Christ—these are themes remarkably lacking in his theology—but on the divine wisdom and power and love in the Creation. Here he was at home, and in his full strength.

In his reflections on a speck of dust, Grosseteste took the smallest thing in the visible universe as an indicator of the nature of the whole. More often he appealed to the largest and most pervasive feature of the universe: the phenomenon of light.

I have already mentioned the scientific grounds for his concentration on light—its universality and its strict conformity with the rules of geometry in its behaviour. When he turned to theology, he found equally compelling indications of the fundamental role of light. Commentators on this feature of his

thought often speak of his 'metaphysic of light'. But this is too
remote a concept. He began with something that was immediately present to him in everyday experience, in his scientific work, and in the Bible. The three parts of the Bible on
which his theology were chiefly based—the Creation narrative
in Genesis, the Psalms, and St John's Gospel and Epistles—are
the source of all his theological thinking about light: 'Let there
be Light' (Gen. 1: 3), 'the Lord is my light' (Ps. 27: 1), and a
multitude of phrases in St John—'I have come as light into the
world', 'the true light', 'the true light which lighteth every
man, that cometh into the world' and so on—established light
as a central feature in his biblical theology. There is no need to
look beyond this combination of common experience, science
and biblical doctrine to understand Grosseteste's mature
thought about light.

The theologians of the schools in the twelfth century had
made little of these biblical texts because they raised no clear-
cut issues of the kind that their methods were designed to
resolve. This was not an obstacle for Grosseteste. Quite the
opposite. As a scientist he had found light the most congenial
of subjects. Its properties—especially its travelling in a straight
line, its power of instantaneous self-reproduction, the universality and constancy of its effects, and its fundamental place
in astronomy—combined to make it an ever-recurring subject
of his thought in every branch of knowledge. Finally, as a
theologian, he found it the link between God and the universe:
the natural essence outside the soul which most completely
imitates the divine nature and links the soul with God. Like
God, it has the power of creating by its own operation without
external aid or material. Like God it has the power of pro-
creating itself from within itself as it fills the universe from a
single point. A formula, otherwise only applicable to God,
could also be applied to light: 'Light begetting and splendour
begotten embrace each other and breathe out a mutual
warmth.'[21] Applied to God, this is a mysterious truth about the
divine nature; applied to natural light, it is a fact of experience
on any sunny day. In light the highest truths of divinity and
the commonest physical experience of daily life meet.

More vividly than anything else, light expressed the unity of

---

[21] *Hex.* VIII. iv. 7 (p. 223); and cf. II. x. 1 (pp. 97–8).

all things, and the unity of theology with natural science and common experience. The Bible declared that 'God is light'; and Grosseteste's own observations convinced him that light was the only substance in the physical world of which he could say that it was 'almost pure form'—'the swiftest, most transparent, most luminous form of matter'. 'Light is the first corporeal form'; and 'Every form is a certain kind of light which manifests the matter which it informs.'[22] In these and similar words, Grosseteste goes as close as possible to the limits of orthodoxy in uniting God and the universe.

IV. THE NECESSITY OF GOD'S ENTRY INTO NATURE

This brings us to another—and theologically the most important—part of Grosseteste's message about the unity of God and the created universe.

If we may make a broad distinction between two types of theology—a theology in which Redemption is the central theme, and a theology centred on Creation—Grosseteste is essentially a theologian of Creation. His theology is an examination of the paths by which the operation of God can be traced downwards to the most minute objects in the universe and upwards to the divine nature itself. Each of these paths has two different modes: the first is symbolic; the second, for want of a better word, we may call scientific.

Symbolism is the mode whereby created things convey God's message to intellective beings in a permaent and unchanging way, and they can only convey it in this way, because their natures are themselves unchanging. Symbols can neither change nor be the cause of change; they can only, like signposts, admonish. But there is another dimension to the Creation: the working out of a divine plan in time. For this a different mode of communication is needed, which will not only admonish, but also cause change to take place in human affairs.

To understand the importance of this idea in Grosseteste's thought, it is necessary to turn back to his study of Aristotle. We have seen that he was one of the earliest, and perhaps the first serious, Western student of the *Posterior Analytics*. He was also one of the earliest students of the *Physics*, on which too he

---

[22] *Hex.* ii. x. 4 (p. 100); i. xviii. 2 (p. 78); ii. viii. 2 (p. 96).

wrote a commentary.[23] The first of these works clarified his thought on the process whereby observations of particular events are converted into general laws. The second impressed on him the idea that all development was potentially present in the original constitution of the system in which it takes place.[24] Both of these ideas had a deep influence on Grosseteste's theology. The second in particular helped him to see more clearly that the whole potentiality of Man, including his 'deification' through union with Christ, must have been part of the original constitution of the universe. The highest human potentiality is the capacity for union with God, and this is most fully realized in the union of the human and divine natures in a single person. This union did not take place at the moment of Creation; but it could not have taken place at all unless it had been potentially present from the beginning. It was part—the highest point—of God's design for the universe from the beginning. It was not the sin of the first man which caused the union of God and Man in Christ; the sin of Adam only gave Him a new role as the Saviour as well as the perfecter of humanity.

This was a substantial departure from current theological thought. The questions about the Incarnation to which theologians in the previous hundred years had devoted most attention were, first, why was it necessary and what precisely did it effect? And, second, why was it delayed for so long?[25] On the first of these questions, the explanation of St Anselm had been generally adopted, with some softening at the edges to safeguard the absolute freedom of God. The explanation went thus: God's Incarnation in Christ had its sole cause in Man's sin and redemption. Sin could never be atoned for by Man alone, because even the most perfect obedience to God's will (supposing it to be possible, which it wasn't) would still leave a huge

[23] See above, pp. 133-4.

[24] 'Omne agens aliquo modo habet in se descriptum et formatum opus operandum, unde natura agens habet per modum aliquem descripta et formata in se naturalia fienda.' (These words occur in Grosseteste's introductory remarks on the *Physics*; they are printed with the comments of Duns Scotus, Walter Burley, and Wycliffe by Dales 1963, p. 3).

[25] For the general development, see J. Rivière, *Le Dogme de la Rédemption au début du Moyen Âge*, Bibliothèque Thomiste, 19, 1934. And for a fuller account of Grosseteste's view, see D. J. Ungar, 'Robert Grosseteste on the Reasons for the Incarnation', *Franciscan Studies*, xvi, 1956, 1–3.

unpaid debt for which God's justice demanded satisfaction. No man, however perfect, can pay more than he owes, because everything that can be paid is owed. God alone, therefore, could 'pay the debt' which sinful Man owed to God. But justice demanded that the debt be paid by a human being on behalf of other human beings. In this dilemma, the only solution was that God himself should become Man, and thus enable human nature to pay the debt which was beyond the resources of all mankind.

What Grosseteste found unsatisfactory in this account was that it made the fulfilment of the greatest potentiality of human nature, its union with God, a contingent event in history—contingent, too, not on the realisation of the highest qualities of human nature, but on its corruption. Anselm seems not to have felt this difficulty. Why should Grosseteste have been troubled by it? Because he took seriously the scientific principle which he had learnt from Aristotle that a cause must be greater than its effects. But the Fall of man, however overwhelming in its consequences, could not be greater than the Incarnation. Indeed, it was the whole point of the Incarnation that it made possible an atonement greater than all human sin. It was greater than anything that had ever happened in history, greater even than the Creation. Therefore, its cause could not lie within history. It must have preceded Creation, if not in realization, yet as part of the original design.

Having once got hold of this idea, Grosseteste found that it unlocked many doors. God, he argued, must at the Creation have intended to give his creatures all the goodness, blessedness and glory that their natures were capable of receiving. Otherwise, God would not be the supremely good, loving and all-giving Being whom Christians acknowledge. It follows from this that, since human nature is *capable* of union with the divine nature in Christ, this union must have been part of the original plan, irrespective of sin and the consequent need for atonement for sin.

Moreover—and here is the purely scientific argument—the universe must have a single unifying principle, comparable to the unifying principle in the human body. The unifying principle in the body is the activity of the heart which holds it together so long as it is alive. What is the unifying principle of the universe? Not God, because as Creator, God cannot be within nature as its unifying principle. Not Man, because the unifying principle must be one, and mankind is many. Besides, the unifying principle of the whole must be greater than all its parts, and all mankind is not greater than the whole universe. Despite this, Man must in some way provide the unifying principle because Man alone participates in every part of the created universe: he has in him the four elements which make up the whole material universe; he has the vegetative soul which he shares with plants, the sensitive soul which he shares with the beasts, and the rational soul which he shares with God and the angels. Only Man, therefore, participating in every part of the universe, could meet the requirements of its unifying principle; but neither all men collectively, nor any single man, could be this principle. Conversely, God, alone giving life and form to all its parts, could be the unifying principle; but He, being outside the system, cannot be this principle. It follows from this that the unifying principle must be a God-Man, within the system, yet transcending all its parts. Only so could the human race achieve its fullness of being; only so could the Creation be complete and Nature beatified.[26] Grosseteste expressed the fullness of this beatitude in a phrase that occurs in a work which will concern us presently: 'Beautiful though Nature was when separated from God, it became a hundred times more beautiful when its Creator took a natural form.'[27]

The Incarnation, therefore, was the necessary conclusion to the work of Creation. This was Grosseteste's most original theological idea. He speaks of it with the mixture of pride and humility of one who had made a great discovery, which still needed to be tested by its reception:

[26] It will be noticed that the shape of the argument (God alone *can*; but Man *must*) is identical with that of Anselm in his *Cur Deus Homo*, but it goes behind Anselm's starting-point in sin to Grosseteste's starting-point in Creation and the place of Man in the cosmos: in effect, it transforms Anselm's Redemption theology into a Creation theology. Moreover, although Grosseteste had read the *Cur Deus Homo* very carefully (the abundance of his symbols in the copy of the text in St John's College, Cambridge, MS 17 testifies to this), and though he was influenced by its argument, he did not accept its conclusions and, in his Commentary on Galatians (Magdalen College, Oxford, MS 57, f. 32), he continued to uphold the role of the Devil, which Anselm thought he had disproved. For the biblical foundation of his new argument about the role of the Incarnation in Creation, see 1 Peter 1: 20.

[27] *Le Château d'Amour de Robert Grosseteste*, ed. J. Murray, 1918, lines 866–72. The title is certainly not original, but the authorship seems beyond question. See below, pp. 227–8.

By these and other arguments it seems possible to conclude that God would have become Man even if man had never sinned. I confess I do not know if I am right, and I am afflicted by my ignorance on this matter. As I have said above, I do not remember that any authority has come to this conclusion, and I do not wish or dare to pronounce conclusively on so hard a question without express authority, knowing how easily a plausible argument may mislead my poor skill and learning. But if it is true that God would have become Man even if mankind had never sinned, this entails the subjection of all creatures to that Man–God who is head of the Church of men and angels alike.[28]

On this view, the incarnate Christ was necessary to hold together all parts of the Creation. But, if so, why did He wait so long—4,000 years at a rough computation—to appear? This was a problem also for those who believed that the Incarnation was contingent upon the Fall, for it was agreed that the Fall happened almost at once after the Creation. So everyone who believed in the Incarnation had to explain why it had been so long delayed. But those for whom the Incarnation was contingent on human sin had a fairly simple answer: the delay was caused by the need to prepare the fallen human race to recognize and receive the incarnate Son of God, and this required a long preparation of law and prophets as described in the Old Testament. This explanation might still, even on Grosseteste's view, be partly true. But if the whole Creation stood in need of the Incarnation for its completion from the beginning, why did it not happen at once before Man sinned?

Grosseteste's answer to this question is complicated, but broadly he argues that Man was not created with his potentiality fully developed. Sin apart, a period of probation was necessary, which could have been brief if the initial test had been successfully passed. A similar requirement had been imposed on the angels: at their creation, they had everything their nature allowed, *except* confirmation in their blessedness. To obtain this, they had to make a deliberate choice of obedience to God. Those who made it were confirmed for ever; those who followed their own ambition were for ever deprived, for they had rebelled against the fundamental law of their nature.

Adam and Eve had their initial test under different con-

[28] *De Cess. Leg.* III. ii. 1.

ditions. Unlike the angels, they were subjected to two kinds of law, not only to the law of their nature, but to a positive and less fundamental command to abstain from the fruit of the forbidden tree. This distinction, well known in political theory, was mankind's salvation: Adam and Eve disobeyed the positive command; but they did not, as the disobedient angels, reject the law of their nature. Therefore the way to restoration was not closed; but a long period of preparation was needed before human potentiality had reached a state of preparedness for the Incarnation. Grosseteste envisaged this preparation as the emergence of an inner recognition of total dependence on God. He put it this way:

Let us imagine a man fallen into a deep pit. And let us imagine that there is one alone who can get him out without any other aid. And let us assume that the whole happiness of the man in the pit lies in recognizing the full extent of his debt and loving his rescuer accordingly. This requires time: if he were rescued at once he would think that, given time, or a lamp, or a rope, or a ladder he could have got out by his own efforts. In order to disabuse him, he is given each one of these in turn—time, the light of natural law, the rope of the Commandments, the ladder of the ceremonial law. All to no avail. Now at last he knows that, even with every possible aid, he can do nothing by his own efforts. If his rescuer now appears and pulls him out without any extraneous aid, the rescued man will recognize that he owes everything to his Saviour, and his devotion to him will be immeasurably increased by this knowledge. Will not his happiness in devotion to his Saviour be correspondingly greater?[29]

In passages like this, Grosseteste the searcher for truth becomes the advocate of love: the theologian becomes a preacher. The transition was an essential part of his theological programme. The aim of his theology was the increase of devotion: not mere knowledge, but knowledge with love, a pastoral aim. Nevertheless, his Latin sermons do not give the impression that he found it easy to descend to a popular level. Nearly all of them contain intricate and elaborate arguments which might defy the efforts of the most conscientious listener to understand. At best, they could have been intelligible only to the clergy, and often not even to them. But he wrote one outline of theology for the laity. It was the nearest he came to a *Summa Theologiae*.

[29] *De Cess. Leg.* I. viii. 7-13.

It is also the fullest expression of his pastoral theology for a popular audience.

V. *THE CHÂTEAU D'AMOUR*: A PASTORAL THEOLOGY

Grosseteste's so-called *Château d'amour* is a poem of about 1,800 lines, written in French, probably intended to be sung or declaimed, perhaps with some kind of instrumental backing, to a lay audience, whom the author addresses as *Seigneurs!* Its general style suggests an audience of knightly retainers and officials in a great household. The metre is the popular narrative octosyllabic couplet which had become popular in the twelfth century and was still used by Scott in the *Lay of the Last Minstrel*. It is unlikely that it could have been performed at a single sitting, and it is broken up into several sections, with new beginnings recalling the point reached in the argument and charting the course that lies ahead.[30] The literary genre to which it belongs is so far removed from contemporary forms of scholastic or doctrinal theology that its importance as a witness to Grosseteste's theological thought has escaped attention. It was clearly designed to provide an audience without theological training with an outline of Christian theology. But, though popular in intention, it contains curious technicalities which might have puzzled any audience. To understand its mixture of popular design and technical background we must begin by distinguishing its two Parts and the main sections of each:

Part I

1 (ll. 1–200). An account of the Creation, Fall, and Old Testament Law.

2 (ll. 201–482). An allegory of a King (=God) with a Son and four daughters, Mercy, Truth, Justice, and Peace.[31] The

---

[30] In addition to the edition of the *Château d'Amour* cited above, there is an important study of the work, with an edition of the Middle English translations of it, by Kari Sajavaara, *Mémoires de la Société Néophilologique de Helsinki*, xxxii, 1967.

[31] The theme of the four daughters of God who disagree about the proper treatment of sinful Man has been traced back to Hugh of St Victor and St Bernard who elaborated the theme of the four 'sisters' being reconciled at the Incarnation. It became widely popular in the early thirteenth century. See Hope Traver, *The Four Daughters of God*, Bryn Mawr College Monographs, 6, 1907, and Kari Sajavaara, op. cit., pp. 62–90; T. Hunt, 'The Four Daughters of God: A Textual Contribution', *AHDLMA* 48, 1981, 287–316. For the theological background, see J. Rivière, *Le Dogme de la Rédemption*, pp. 309–362.

daughters disagree on the appropriate treatment for sinful man: Justice and Truth favouring severity, and Mercy and Peace mildness. The Son promises to reconcile their difference and to bring about the fulfilment of the prophecy in Psalm 84. 10: 'Mercy and truth are met together; justice and peace have kissed each other.'

3 (ll. 483–518). Prophecies about the coming of Christ are recalled and one of them is selected for fuller treatment. This is Isaiah 9: 6, where the attributes of the Son are listed: 'Wonderful, Counsellor, the mighty God, Father of the Age to come, Prince of Peace.' The rest of the poem consists of a commentary on each of these attributes.

Part II

1 (ll. 519–878). 'Wonderful' is explained with reference to Christ's miraculous birth.

  (a) (ll. 571–748) The Virgin Mary is very elaborately compared to a Castle of up-to-date design.[32]
  (b) (ll. 749–878) The Incarnation is explained in terms which recall Grosseteste's doctrine that it completed the plan of Creation.

2 (ll. 879–1200). 'Counsellor': Christ is represented as a lawyer arguing with the Devil over his right to deliver mankind from prison. The argument is shrewdly strewn with contemporary legal terminology and shows a knowledge of the procdures of the royal courts.[33]

3 (ll. 1201–1352). 'The Mighty God': the phrase is explained with reference to Christ's miracles, seen here (as in the *De Cessatione Legalium*) as irrefutable evidence of his divinity.[34]

---

[32] The comparison of the Virgin Mary with a castle had been developed from an allegorical interpretation of Luke 10: 38, *Ipse [Jesus] intravit in quoddam castellum*. It was a theme first popularized in England by Archbishop Ralph d'Escures of Canterbury (1114–22) in a sermon which was translated into English in the early twelfth century. Thereafter it appears in numerous sermons. What is unusual in Grosseteste's account is the extreme elaboration and modernity of the castle's outworks and fortifications.

[33] For details on natural and positive law, see lines 114–28; for serfdom and inheritance, lines 163–90; for the four judges who are required 'fornir un seul jugement' without which 'jugement ne avra record', lines 407–18; and for the debate on Christ's right 'pur reindre cel prison' i. e. 'gaol delivery', lines 1015–104. (See F. Pollock and F. W. Maitland, *The History of English Law before the time of Edward I*, 2nd edn., Cambridge, 1898, i. 200; ii. 645, for these legal processes.)

[34] *De Cess. Leg.* II. iv. 5.

4 (ll. 1353-1493). 'Father of the Age to come': this is explained as the age of the Church following Christ's Resurrection, Ascension and union with God.

5 (ll. 1493-1768). 'Prince of Peace': this is explained as the final peace under the rule of Christ following the Last Judgement.

I have set out the scheme of the work at some length because it provides the most complete outline of Grosseteste's theology that we have. Its essential characteristics are these:

(i) The greater part of it is a commentary on a single verse of the Bible (Isaiah 9: 6) in which he finds the whole outline of Christian doctrine compressed.

(ii) The central figure is Christ—but a cosmic Christ who glorifies the universe, not the man of sorrow and suffering who was becoming increasingly the object of contemporary devotion.

(iii) The central *human* figure is the Virgin Mary—but not the *mater misericordiae*, the worker of miracles of pity and mercy of contemporary legends, but the Mother, prepared from the beginning, in whom are concentrated every virtue and power, the preserver of the Faith through the ages: she foreshadows the cosmic figure, popular in pictures of the late Middle Ages and seventeenth century, standing on the moon, crowned with stars, with clouds beneath and angels above.

(iv) And, finally, though writing for a popular audience, Grosseteste does not hesitate to express the unity of God and nature, both in the Creation and Incarnation, in surprisingly technical terms:

Nature was much embellished when God, 'natura naturans', was joined to Nature, 'natura naturata'. Then was Nature purified a hundred times more than it was before Adam paid the forfeit of sin. [35]

For a popular poem, this is a remarkably complicated thought with its distinction between Nature (*Natura naturans*), which is

[35] Lines 866-72: 'Mult est nature enbelie / Kant nature naturante / A nature est ioygnante, / Ke nature est naturee. / Lores est nature puree / Cent tant plus ke einz ne esteit / Avant que Adam forfet aveit.' At several points in this passage I have amended Murray's text with readings from MSS B (Bodley 399), O (Bodley 652), and M (Lambeth Palace 522), but a satisfactory text will only be possible when the relationship of the MSS has been worked out. A new edition is badly needed.

God the source of all nature, and Nature (*Natura naturata*) the created universe. Then, as if this were not enough, the listener is required to envisage the integration of these two Natures in the Incarnate Christ and the embellishment of the whole universe by that event. It is not surprising that the fourteenth-century translator of the poem into English omitted this whole passage, rightly judging it beyond the comprehension of a popular audience.[36]

There is a further oddity in this passage: the idea it expresses is not only complicated, but new and highly controversial. The description of God as 'natura naturans' seems to have made its way into Latin through Aristotle's *Physics* which drew a distinction between Nature as First Cause and Nature as that which was caused; and the phrase *natura naturata* may have come from the Latin translation of Averroes's commentary.[37] That Grosseteste should have used it in a work intended for an unlearned audience shows how difficult he found it to separate the various parts of his mind. Those not very attractive phrases, 'natura naturans' (God), and 'natura naturata' (the created universe), must have stirred echoes of Denys's Hierarchies and of the divine nature flowing through the Creation and drawing all things back to their source. It was in association with this chain of being that he saw the Incarnation as the central event in the glorification of nature and the deification of Man.

He could not keep these thoughts out of his theology even on the most popular level. Advanced scientific learning and theological concepts on the fringe of eccentricity flowed irresistibly into his poetry of popular instruction. The theological implications must have been unintelligible to most hearers, but the whole poem was alive with vivid contemporary imagery and stirring appeals for the audience's attention:

---

[36] See Sajavaara, op. cit., pp. 222, 388.

[37] For the origin of the phrases *natura naturans* and *natura naturata*, see H. Siebeck, 'Über die Enstehung der Termin "natura naturans" und "natura naturata" ', *Archiv für Geschichte der Philosophie*, iii, 1889, 370–8, and H. A. Lucks, 'Natura naturans—Natura naturata', *New Scholasticism*, ix, 1933, 1–24. The passages in Averroes which may have given rise to their use are in his commentary on Aristotle's *Physics*, 193^b 13, and *De Celo*, 268^a 16. The phrases 'natura naturans' and 'natura naturata' are used by Bonaventure, *c.* 1250–54, in his *Commentary on the Sentences*, iii, dist. 8, *resp. ad dubium* 2 (ed. 1877, vol. iii, p. 197) and Vincent of Beauvais, 1247–59, in his *Speculum Doctrinale*, xvii. 4. They are fairly common in the second half of the century, but no example has yet been found earlier than this passage of Grosseteste.

Hue e Huche, e hue e crie!
Duce Dame, aie! aie!
Reine Dame, ovrez! ovrez![38]

No doubt such words as these were accompanied by a good deal of clamour, and the whole performance has a brightness and variety that evidently appealed to the audience. It was the only one of Grosseteste's works for which there is evidence of a lively and uninterrupted circulation from his own lifetime to the end of the Middle Ages.

Grosseteste undoubtedly looked on it as a work of popular instruction, although, as we have seen, it contained passages of considerable intellectual difficulty. In order to hold the attention of the audience, it must in some degree have been entertaining, and Grosseteste seems also to have made some allowance for this. But how far could this go? Certainly not as far as the new kinds of miracle play which were beginning to make their appearance in open-air performances. They had a great future ahead of them; but not a future that Grosseteste approved. When he became a bishop, he ordered his archdeacons 'utterly to exterminate them'.[39] He gave no reasons for his violent hostility, but it is likely that they were the same as those of all later critics from the fourteenth century onwards. To paraphrase one of the earliest, the objection ran as follows: 'The miracles of Christ and his saints were effectual for our salvation, and to use them as an occasion for play and jest is to turn from Christ and to scorn God. Such playing and jesting with the holy works of God destroys the dread of offending God and undermines our faith and salvation'.[40] Levity in sacred things has been abhorred by puritanical minds at all times, Grosseteste among them. Later Lollard critics of miracle plays held Grosseteste in the highest esteem on grounds which he would not always have approved. But it is likely that on this

---

[38] Lines 793–5. For references to the singer and his audience, see lines 20–1 ('Ke la buche de chanteur / Ne seit close de Deu loer'), 26–8 ('En romanz . . . Pur ceus ki ne sevent mie / Ne lettreure ne clergie'), 43 ('Oez seigneurs communement'), 201–2 ('Ici reposera mun dit, / si vus dirrai un respit'), 483 ('Ore oiez de si grant ducur'), 519 ('Ores entendez a mei tus'), etc.

[39] *Ep.* 107, p. 318; also Powicke and Cheney, i. 480.

[40] 'A Sermon against Miracle-Plays', *Reliquiae Antiquae: Scraps from Ancient Manuscripts illustrating chiefly early English Literature*, ed. T. Wright and J. O. Halliwell, ii, 1843, pp. 42–57.

point he would have agreed with them. The buffoonery of the market place was abhorrent to him when it touched sacred things. But lively and learned speech and declamation in the halls of the great were a different matter. Where was the line to be drawn? This was just the fringe of a problem which was to haunt the rest of Grosseteste's life, and to pursue his memory long after his death. These conflicts will concern us when we turn to his work as a bishop. But, first, we may briefly review the unifying force in his theology.

VI. A THEOLOGY OF RECONCILIATION

If, in the end, we ask what Grosseteste's theological vision amounts to, 'fitful' and 'unifying' are the words that best describe it. There were some things which he saw clearly and held to tenaciously: the unity of all things in God; the necessity for the Incarnation in holding everything together and imparting the fullness of being to the created universe; the need for conformity to the divine purpose at every level of activity; the need to draw all men and women into this unity of purpose. These are the threads that ran through everything he wrote. Round these points of clarity there were great areas of uncertainty where a plethora of superlatives, which Grosseteste was adept at inventing, stood for the great truths which eluded precise statement.

Essentially he was a solitary thinker. He belonged to and created no school. This was both his strength and his weakness. It was his weakness because, when his vision failed, he had no well-defined structure of thought to fall back on. It was his strength because his loneliness allowed full scope for his exceptionally powerful and independent mind. His thought was the product of his own genius shaped by the provincial tradition in which he had grown up, shaped too by the independence which came from the obscurity of his birth at a time when nobility of birth was generally considered an essential requirement for nobility of thought and aim. He had had to make his own way in the world through long years of obscurity, without the support of a great religious order or a ready-made patron, remote from the traditions and assured methods of the great schools, but strong in his sense of the presence of physical nature and the scientific tradition which was perhaps more easily assimilated in England than anywhere else in Europe. The other great liberating influence which had come to him through the circumstances of his time was that of the Greeks, whose books and language and tradition of theology became known to him through returned administrators like John of Basingstoke. So he gradually built up a coherent world with a structure and view of the past distinctly different from that which had transformed western Europe in the twelfth century.

Grosseteste's theological studies came at a good moment for appreciating the Greeks. The channels of communication with the Greek world of Constantinople were more open than they had been for several centuries. The squalid circumstances of the Latin conquest had faded from memory, and the hope of a doctrinal accommodation between the two Churches had not yet been blighted by new disagreements. Grosseteste shared the hopes of reconciliation. The Greeks provided a source of support for thoughts which came naturally to him, and he acknowledged his debt by giving them a large place among his quotations from the Fathers. His balancing of Greeks with Latins, which becomes increasingly conspicuous in his theological quotations after 1230, is reminiscent of Dante's balancing of pagan with Christian in his illustrations of great virtues in the *Divine Comedy*: it was a balance which expressed an appreciation for the virtues of those on the other side of a great divide.

It was while translating John of Damascus that Grosseteste was moved to make his most memorable statement about unity in discord. The work he was translating was an exposition of the liturgical chant 'Holy, Holy, Holy'. It consisted largely of extracts from the Greek Fathers, Athanasius, Basil, Chrysostom, Cyril, Gregory of Nyssa, and Gregory of Nazianzus, on the Holy Trinity; at the end it had a statement of the Greek doctrine of the procession of the Holy Spirit, *from* the Father but *of* or *through* the Son. This of course differed from the Western doctrine, which had recently received its final and authoritative statement at the Lateran Council of 1215, that the Procession is *from* both Father and Son. Undeterred, or possibly ignorant of this recent decree, Grosseteste wrote that two honest men, one Greek and the other Latin, who sought the truth rather than victory, might find that their discordant words had the same meaning. For who, he added, could suppose that the Greek Fathers just mentioned were heretics, any more than Jerome, Augustine, and Hilary? Besides, he reflected, there are many ways in which such words as *by* or *from* or *of* can be understood, and the difference of words may conceal an identity of doctrine.[41]

In these words in his most relaxed manner, Grosseteste set himself against the current of scholastic discussion of the last hundred years, which had aimed at precise and authoritative definitions of words and doctrines. And two generations after his death his words earned him the reproof of Duns Scotus; 'Be that as it may; the Catholic Church [and he quoted the Council of 1215] has now declared that the Holy Spirit proceeds *from* both Father and Son, and this must now be firmly believed.'

Clearly, the idea of concord which Grosseteste had formed for himself was a good deal less rigorous than that of most of his scholastic contemporaries and successors. It was in music that he found the best expression, and perhaps the inspiration for his idea, of the place of discord in a general harmony.[42] Reconciliation of all the parts of the universe in a unity of temper rather than of logical structure was the chief note of his theology: the reconciliation of God and the world, of God and man, of Greeks and Latins. The universe was incomplete without the incarnate presence of God in it; all created things were incomplete without the bestowal on them of all the excellences that they were capable of receiving; Christ was necessary for the perfection of mankind; mankind was necessary for the perfection of the universe in association with God; light flowing from God through all its parts was necessary for the perfection of the created universe; the Greeks were necessary to complete the theology of the Latins.

How could such doctrines, so distinct from those which were shaping Western Christendom, be effective in the practical world? It is to this problem that we must now turn.

[41] For the text of John of Damascus, see PG 95. 21–61. Grosseteste's words are at the end of his translation in Magdalen College, Oxford, MS 192, f. 215ʳ; and in Exeter College MS 21, f. 137. They are also quoted in full by Duns Scotus, *Opera Omnia*, v, 1959, pp. 2–4 (*Ordinatio* 1, dist. 11, q. 1), and xvii, 1966, p. 128 (*Lectura in Sent.* 1, d. 11, q. 1).

[42] For his love of music, see below, p. 318. For the musical image which expressed his recognition of the place of discord in harmony, see *De Cess. Leg.* iv. iii. 2.

III

GROSSETESTE'S THOUGHT IN ACTION

NOTE ON THE DIOCESE OF LINCOLN

To give some idea of the complexity and size of the organization for which Grosseteste became responsible as bishop of Lincoln, it must suffice to say that the diocese included the whole area of the counties of Lincoln, Huntingdon, Northampton, Leicester, Oxford, Buckingham, Bedford and Rutland, together with the greater part of Hertfordshire, with the exception of the Liberty of St Albans, geographically within the diocese but practically exempt from the bishop's authority. This whole area of the Midlands from the Humber to the Thames was divided into eight archdeaconries, roughly coextensive with the counties from which they took their names. Each archdeaconry was divided for purposes of ecclesiastical administration and discipline into deaneries, which contained on average about twenty parishes each. The archdeacons were appointed by the bishop and stood in a relationship to him roughly comparable to that of the sheriffs to the king. The deans, seventy-seven in all, were also appointed by the bishop and provided a normal channel of communication between him and the parishes, approximately sixteen hundred in number.

In detail, these divisions may be summarized thus:

Archdeaconries

Lincoln (Lincolnshire except for the West Riding of Lindsey): 23 deaneries; about 500 parishes.

Huntingdon (Huntingdonshire and part of Hertfordshire): 5 deaneries in Hunts. with about 100 parishes; 4 deaneries in Herts. with 68 parishes.

Northampton (Northamptonshire): 10 deaneries with about 250 parishes.

Leicester (Leicestershire with Rutland): 7 deaneries in Leics. with 203 parishes; 1 deanery in Rutland with 44 parishes.

Oxford (Oxfordshire): 9 deaneries with 265 parishes.

Buckingham (Buckinghamshire): 8 deaneries with 186 parishes.

Bedford (Bedfordshire): 6 deaneries with 222 parishes.

Stow: (West Riding of Lindsey): 4 deaneries with about 100 parishes.

Episcopal administration

Apart from his official and archdeacons, whom Grosseteste chose from among his closest advisers, the bishop had a substantial household of clerks whose names and careers, so far as they are known, are listed by Dr Kathleen Major in Callus, 1955, pp. 216–241. As a rough indication of the size of his household, it may be noted that canon law allowed a bishop on his visitations to demand payment for the expenses of a retinue of thirty mounted men, and a great deal of Grosseteste's time must have been spent on horseback. His main places of residence are listed in *Rotuli Roberti Grosseteste*, pp. x–xii. By far the most important of these was at Buckden in Huntingdonshire, where most of the regular diocesan business appears to have been conducted. Grosseteste also often resided at his manor at Liddington in Rutland, a smaller house which he may have used for study and retirement. Other manors at which he stayed occasionally were scattered throughout the diocese from Dorchester in Oxfordshire and Fingest in Buckinghamshire to Sleaford and Nettleham in Lincolnshire. He also had a London house in Holborn at the Old Temple which he used for national and provincial meetings with bishops, barons and king.

The episcopal visitations which were a main commitment of Grosseteste's administration are discussed below. Their frequency and extent cannot be determined exactly; but it would appear from the list of heads of religious houses deposed in 1235 that his first visitation may have included the archdeaconries of Lincoln, Leicester, Oxford, and Buckingham. A further visitation reported by the Dunstable annalist in 1238 was clearly a major operation, and this may have included the archdeaconries omitted in 1235. After this date it is impossible to form any picture of Grosseteste's routine visitations.

He was absent from England at the papal court for the greater part of two years, 1245 and 1250, during his eighteen years as bishop.

Sources

The geographical divisions of the dioceses can be gathered (with numerous omissions and ambiguities) from the *Taxatio* of Pope Nicholas IV compiled c. 1291 and published by the Record Commission in 1802. The details from this and other sources are collected with some critical discussion in the articles on Ecclesiastical History in the relevant volumes of the *Victoria County History*. The details of archdeaconries and their holders will all be found in D. E. Greenway, *Fasti Ecclesiae Anglicanae*, iii, *Lincoln*, 1977. The evidence for the bishop's London house (as Dr Greenway pointed out to me) is in *The Rolls and Register of Bishop Oliver Sutton*, Lincoln Record Society, vol. 48, ed. Rosalind Hill, iii, 1954, p. xxv and n.; the Introduction to this volume contains an excellent account of the daily life of a bishop of Lincoln half a century after Grosseteste.

10

Grosseteste in his Diocese

I. THE PROGRAMME OF ECCLESIASTICAL DISCIPLINE

As bishop of Lincoln, from 1235 to 1253, Grosseteste was—far more effectively than the king could ever be—the ruler of about one-fifth of the whole population of England, as well as being a landlord of baronial rank and wealth. Suddenly, he became a man of power and notoriety. Suddenly, too, the records which have been so scanty for so long become almost embarrassingly abundant. They would allow us to follow his administration in great detail; but we are not concerned with his daily routine. We are concerned only to ask how far and in what ways the special features which we have noticed in his scientific and theological thought, and in his social and intellectual background, affected his work as a bishop. Effectively this means asking whether his methods of scientific and theological enquiry and his strongly marked emphasis on the Bible made any difference to his ideals or activity as a man of power and influence in the Church.

The question has a special importance for Grosseteste because (as we have found) he does not seem to have studied at any of the great schools of Europe, and the methods and principles of their thought were not his. Yet it was these schools and these principles which created the theory and practice of ecclesiastical government as it existed in the thirteenth century. It was above all in Paris and Bologna that the principles of a unified society under papal sovereignty were given the means of becoming a reality. In Bologna especially, the rules of canon law and the hierarchy of ecclesiastical courts, which gave effect to this law, were chiefly elaborated; in Paris, the doctrinal formulas, which were the obligatory statements of belief for all full members of Western society, were given their sharpest edge.

In both, the detailed rules of confession, penance, marriage and morals were worked out. None of these essential ingredients of ordinary religious life would have been the same if they had not passed through the mill of the *questiones, disputationes*, and magisterial definitions in the great schools. The schools were the parliaments of the twelfth century, defining the principles and laying down the rules of conduct of society, and in large part training the executives who would enforce them. Within his diocese, the bishop presided over the whole programme.

Looking at the social consequences of these developments more closely, we can distinguish two periods in the contribution of the great schools to European life. In the first period, during the century from about 1070 to 1170, the essential doctrines, especially those of the Eucharist, the Trinity, confession and penance, and the essential structure of courts and procedures were defined. Before 1170, this process mainly affected the top layers of society. It was in the second period, after 1170, that the task of taking these doctrines and institutions into the lives of ordinary people began in earnest. The main instruments for this programme were of two kinds: textbooks on preaching, confession and penance, and on other matters of faith and practice, gave the whole body of society a single set of rules; and legislative acts of universal and provincial councils gave legal effect to this body of teaching at a parochial and individual level. The visible signs of all this work were to be seen in ordinary parish churches in the confessionals, the carrying of candles, the bowing and kneeling at the moments of consecration in the Mass, and other outward expressions of orthodoxy which now became stereotyped and obligatory. These things have become so much a part of what everyone understands by Catholicism that it is hard to realize how new most of these adjuncts to religious life were to the greater part of the population in the thirteenth century. In their definitive form they depended on the disputes and definitions of the schools. And in their legislative form they depended on the decrees of councils and synods, which were largely composed of former masters of the schools. They were the outward and visible signs that the schools, which had begun by creating a universal system of doctrine and institutions, had now turned to the task of bringing the results of their work to the people.

When Grosseteste became a bishop, this work had already reached a fairly advanced state. Englishmen, going to Paris and Bologna for their training from a country with one of the most effective systems of government in Europe, had taken a large share in this work. Among them, none were more deeply committed to the task of enforcing religious discipline than Robert Curzon, the papal legate in several parts of France from 1213 to 1218, and Stephen Langton, archbishop of Canterbury from 1206 to 1228. These were not gentle, mild, liberal men; nor were they humdrum, conscientious administrators: they were the active agents and advocates—and, when necessary, the violent enforcers—of a new religious ordering of Western society. Both of them had spent many years in the schools of Paris. Langton was the first archbishop of Canterbury with a thorough grounding in Parisian theology. Both were made cardinals by Innocent III, and both belonged to that select team of preachers and prelates appointed by the pope to make the new disciplines and requirements of the Church known far and wide among the laity.[1] Grosseteste had seen both Curzon and Langton in action on one of their preaching tours in France inveighing against usurers. Indeed, his recollection of this incident is the only event in his past which, so far as I know, he ever mentioned; and, since he did so on his death-bed, looking back to a time forty years earlier, it is clear that the experience made a deep impression on him.[2]

There are many grounds for believing that the ideals of this group of papally inspired bishops were shared by Grosseteste. This is not surprising. In the decade after 1220, when Grosseteste was beginning belatedly to rise in the world as a theologian

[1] Teams of preachers, commissioned or encouraged by Innocent III, are found on several occasions between 1198 and 1216 preaching the Crusade against Muslims or Albigensians, denouncing usury, or the holding of markets on holy ground, or the desecration of Sunday. For various aspects of these missions, see J. L. Cate, 'The English mission of Eustace of Flay, 1200-1', *Études d'histoire à la mémoire de H. Pirenne*, 1937, 67–89, and 'The Church and market reform in England during the reign of Henry III', *Essays in honour of J. W. Thompson*, 1938, 27–65; M. R. Gutch, 'A Twelfth-century Preacher, Fulk of Neuilly', *Essays presented to D. C. Munro*, 1928, 183–206. Also the Conciliar decrees of Avignon, 1209, c. 1; Paris, 1212, c. 8; Rouen, 1214, c. 9; Lateran, 1215, c. 10 (J. Mansi, *Sacrorum Conciliorum nova et amplissima collectio*, xxii, pp. 735, 786, 821, 901); see also the chronicles of Roger of Howden and Roger of Wendover, which preserve important notices of these missions. P. Fink, *Jakob von Vitré, Leben und Werke*, 1909, gives details of papal directions for preaching against the Albigensians.

[2] For the details, see above, p. 66 n.

and administrator, Langton was the dominant personality and
legislator in the English Church. Grosseteste's own legislation
as bishop was clearly inspired by Langton's; and to understand
Grosseteste's episcopal activity we must begin with Langton
and the ways in which he tried to give effect to the contemporary authoritative ideal of a Christian society.

For our present purpose, there are two documents which tell
us most of what we need to know about this activity. The first
is a sermon; the second a small body of legislation. The sermon,
delivered by Langton in August 1213 to a large gathering of
Londoners in St Paul's cathedral, contains his first public words
after he set foot in England at the end of his long exile.[3] Grosseteste may well have heard it.[4] It expressed to perfection the
mood and policy which were to guide the English Church in its
dealings with the great body of the laity—not the aristocracy—
during Grosseteste's lifetime.

The occasion was full of drama. The six years' general strike
of the whole ecclesiastical hierarchy—for the formidable Interdict was nothing more nor less than a strike called as a means
of forcing the king to accept Langton as archbishop—was coming to an end. The king had given in; the archbishop had come
to England; all that remained was to fix the terms of the king's
capitulation. While these negotiations went on, the strike continued: Church services and the normal administration of the
sacraments were still suspended.

Many people thought that this continued suspension was an
unreasonable hardship for the large mass of people, who had
had no part in the quarrel but were the main sufferers from its
consequences. These people hoped for some words of con-
ciliation and encouragement from the archbishop whom they
now saw for the first time. But the archbishop was in no mood
to give them what they wanted. The Londoners, he said, had
listened too long to popular preachers—presumably clergy who
had continued to preach in defiance of the Interdict. These had
fed them with comfortable words. After this rich diet, he would
offer them words that would seem dry and tasteless. He would

[3] For the text and occasion of the sermon, see G. Lacombe, 'An Unpublished
Document on the Great Interdict', *Catholic Historical Review*, 1930, NS ix, 408–20; and
for a contemporary report, see Waverley Annals 1213 (*Ann. Mon.* ii. 277; repr. in
Powicke and Cheney, i. 20).

[4] There is a striking similarity between Langton's words on foundation stones and
those of Grosseteste; see above, p. 174.

speak about the innumerable sins with which the English people were burdened, and especially about their drunkenness and gluttony, accopanied by cries of 'wassail!', for which they were well known throughout the world. Also about their meanness in alms-giving, the foundation of eternal life:

Foundations need large stones, not small ones: look round on the buildings in London, and you can see this for yourselves. So it is with the foundations of eternal life: big stones are needed. It is not enough for a man with £100 to give a penny.

Further, there was the question of continence. They must learn this:

I tell you plainly, intercourse out of marriage is mortal sin and leads to Hell. When I was in Paris, I often preached on the text 'Let your moderation be known unto all men': this is especially important for the English who are known everywhere only for their incontinence, gluttony and drunkenness.

Some of you will say to me and to the other bishops, 'We trusted in you and you haven't helped us. Why are the churches still shut now that you have returned to England? You do nothing but speak ill of us.' I tell you this: you are laymen, and you should trust your prelates to act discreetly and wisely; and you ought to obey the pope who is lord of Christendom.

Here is an example which will show you your folly: if your mother had a fever, would you give her beef and fatted goose to eat, and take her out for a drink? Clearly not. Well the Church is your Mother. For six years she has had a fever brought on by the power of wicked men. She is just beginning to recover. But this is no time for rejoicing. There are still many evils to be remedied. The Church has been despoiled of her goods. Till these are given back, she is not safe from her enemies. She has begun to recover, because the king has begun to listen to good advice. But the work of restoration is only just beginning. When it is finished, then it will be time to sing. If I were offered the whole world to relax the Interdict now, I would refuse till everything has been restored. There will be no relaxation till then. It is only through repentance and confession that a full recovery can come.

We are dried up and putrid with sin; but if we repent and confess our sins we can blossom again. Once, in Paris, I was passing a public house when a drunken sot called out to me 'This is a naughty world.' That was the confession of a rascal, who spoke what he did not think.

A good confession is not like this, it calls for a full account of our sins one by one—they must be driven out of the inward parts of our minds. Only so can we come to the joys of Paradise.

These are only small fragments of all that Langton said, but I have attempted to preserve the spirit and drive of his whole discourse, for it marks the start of the new period of ecclesiastical discipline in which Grosseteste operated. He called for the obedience of the laity to their ecclesiastical superiors; for the careful and regular practice of confession; for the rooting out of notorious vices; for the strict observance of the Church's rules of life; and, as a preliminary, for the restoration in full of the properties of the Church, and for the silencing of popular and unauthorized preachers. All this was said in the harshest terms, without compromise, without any balm of kindness, and in the plainest language.

As a contribution to reconciliation between the Church and the people who had been kept at arm's length for the past six years, it was certainly an unpromising beginning. Langton treated his hearers as if they were rather worse than the king who was the cause of all the trouble. The king at least had begun to listen to good advice, while the people had been listening to unauthorized preachers. At one point, his hostility to the people caused a disturbance. A protester began to shout out. He was silenced with blows and removed. The archbishop went on denouncing the sins of the people with unabated vigour. Intransigence was the hallmark of his whole message. And yet, though the attitude and message were uncompromising and unpopular, the words had a common touch in anecdotes, popular imagery, and an appeal to ordinary experience. This was all part of the new technique for conveying the teaching of the schools to the people. One cannot help remarking on the one hand the number of times he refers to his days as a master in Paris, and on the other the way in which scenes of common life form part of these recollections.

Here then we have a first outline of the programme which began with Langton and continued in a steady flow of episcopal legislation diocese by diocese for the rest of the century. Langton's own two councils, at Canterbury in 1213/14 and at Oxford in 1222 were the models for this legislation. They aimed for the first time at the detailed direction and discipline of the whole population in the spirit of Langton's sermon of 1213.[5]

The second of these councils was the scene of the first judicial execution in English history for apostasy—a deacon handed over to the sheriff for burning because he had been circumcised. Also an old woman and young man were walled up to die— the one for thinking she was the Virgin Mary, the other for thinking he was Christ. Here was a warning that the new message was not for preaching only. Yet—like Langton's ser- mon—harsh and menacing though the programme was, it had a certain moderation and sense of the possible. It did not seek extraordinary methods of probing into hidden sins. It searched the pockets of offenders in exacting petty fines; but it left their souls to the privacy of the confessional. This vigour combined with moderation is one of the marks of the scholastic thought of which it was the practical expression. The debates of the schools, with their careful balancing of objections and their attempts to arrive at solutions which would take account of all objections, brought an element of compromise into all schol- astic solutions. Compromise in both theory and practice was the greatest strength of the whole system. It was also, from a different point of view, its greatest weakness.

With this background in mind, we may turn to Grosseteste and ask how far his words and actions as bishop fitted into this programme. Did he accept its severities? Did he accept its compromises and limitations?

It might be expected that, with his humble social back- ground, his limited sympathy with the methods of scholastic thought and his intense interest in nature, he might be more sympathetic to ordinary people and natural instincts, and bet- ter disposed towards secular rights and claims, than his more rigorously trained scholastic contemporaries. But whatever pe- culiarities may appear in his practical ideals, there are several reasons for thinking that they will not have a liberal or secular tendency.

The first reason is that many observers who criticized scho- lastic methods in law and theology did not disapprove of the doctrine and regimen which had been arrived at by these me- thods. It was possible to approve of a unified Christian order

[5] For the texts, see Powicke and Cheney, i. 23–36, 100–25.

under papal sovereignty, the dominance of clerical rule, the whole system of canon law and ecclesiastical courts, the sharpened disciplines of confession and penance and doctrinal instruction, without sympathizing with the intellectual procedures which had produced these results. Indeed, someone who looked at the system without a scholastic training was more likely to blame its compromises than its severities. These compromises were of many kinds—compromises with secular power, easy penances for common sins, a general lack of rigour in dealing with sins not easily discoverable. Theoretical justifications could be found for these laxities; but they could seem mere casuistry to an impatient outsider.

The second reason, which has special relevance to Grosseteste, is that the natural order in which he was interested was intimately associated with the divine and supernatural direction of the world. Everything in the natural world pointed upwards to the eternal mind of which it was the mirror. Nature, therefore, did not point towards a greater freedom for natural instincts, but towards a greater subordination of these instincts to an overriding authority. The idea of hierarchy gave Grosseteste's thinking its strong unitary drive: it stamped his science, his theology, and finally his practical administration with zeal for the subordination of the visible event to the invisible source of its being. There was no room for dualism in Grosseteste's mind; consequently no room for compromise, and little room for debate.

These two features of his administration, his impatience with the normal compromises of his day, and his persistent tendency to view every detail in its relationship to an ideal whole, can be traced in all his activities both as archdeacon and bishop. In the light of these habits of thought, we can now view his major problems as they arose.

II. GROSSETESTE AS ARCHDEACON

The Jews of Leicester

As we know, Grosseteste was archdeacon of Leicester from 1229 till his resignation in 1232. A few of his letters have survived from these years, which contain several interesting sidelights on his personality and friendships. But only one deals with a problem of substantial importance: his letter to the Countess of Winchester about the Jews recently expelled from his archidiaconal town of Leicester. It does not show Grosseteste in an attractive light, and it is necessary first to restrain the sense of disgust which is inseparable from a consideration of the brutalities perpetrated, condoned, and glorified by some of the most responsible characters in Europe, and to concentrate on the facts as they saw them. First, they saw that the Jews presented a threat to the faith of Christendom. No doubt, this threat was exaggerated in imagination, but it was substantiated by some startling examples of bishops and clergy being converted to Judaism: the deacon condemned in Oxford in 1222 was a local example of a wider threat. And secondly, they saw that the Jews lived by practising the trade of usury condemned in the Bible as inadmissible among brethren, and only marginally permissible to degraded outsiders under severe restrictions—to slaves, so to speak, so long as they were kept in chains. The condemnation of usury was soon to get even stronger expression, as utterly contrary to nature, in Aristotle's *Politics* when it became known in the West. So, here too, science did not bring greater mildness, but greater severity. Before the problem was given this new twist, there seemed to be good theoretical grounds for outlawing usury, while permitting Jews to practise it under restraint; afterwards, usury became utterly unacceptable and the Jews were deprived of their livelihood. In the upshot they were expelled, and the way was clear for the Christian financiers of the fourteenth century.

In the early thirteenth century, the practical position was more complicated. The trade of usury could not be dispensed with at a time when people of every rank in society were chronically short of ready cash. So the Jews were necessary. But the Jewish monopoly as suppliers of ready cash was being broken by a variety of devices and subterfuges, which allowed Christians more or less respectably to exact interest for money on loan without incurring the guilt of usury. To the extent that this came about, the necessity for tolerating Jewish communities, which had flourished in every important centre of population in northern Europe since the eleventh century, became progressively weaker.

Matters had reached this state when Grosseteste became involved in the problem—or, more truly, threw himself into the problem without provocation. In 1231, while he was arch-deacon of Leicester, an important change took place in the lordship of the town. After a long period of uncertainty, in August 1231, the young Simon de Montfort was granted the lands of the earldom of Leicester, thus obtaining lordship over the greater part of the town.[6] This marked the renewal of a long friendship between the archdeacon and the earl. Despite their differences of age and background, they had much in common: they were both independent, outspoken, original characters, with a strong tendency towards extremes. One of Montfort's first actions was to expel from Leicester the colony of Jews. Where were they to go? Apparently, they went to Winchester, which had one of the biggest Jewish colonies in England with a royal office to regulate their affairs. They were welcomed on her land by the Countess of Winchester. But Grosseteste, not content with having got rid of the Jews from his own archdeaconry, sent the Countess a letter of bitter re-proof and condemnation of her hospitality.[7] The terms in which it is written, and the fact that he should have intervened at all in the fate of people who had passed beyond his jurisdiction, suggest that he may himself have been the instigator of their expulsion from Leicester by Earl Simon. Certainly he was bent on pursuing them to the full extent of his power, by words if no other weapon was within reach.

The Countess should remember, he wrote, that the Jews were guilty of murdering the Saviour of the world. As a penalty for this sin, which had been inspired by the fear of losing their land and nationhood, God had condemned them to lose the very thing which they had sought to preserve. He had made them wanderers and the slaves of all nations, and this state of affairs would last until the end of history when their redemption would come. Meanwhile, the rulers of the world had a duty to keep them captive—not killing them, but allowing them to live by

[6] For the circumstances of Simon de Montfort's claims to the earldom of Leicester, see Powicke, *Henry III and the Lord Edward*, i. 51-2, 202-3, and the literature cited there. His association with Grosseteste at this time is of particular interest, for it is a further illustration of Grosseteste's familiar relationship with members of the baronage which we have already noticed above, p. 82.

[7] *Ep.* no. 5.

the sweat of their brow. They were like the descendants of Cain, cursed by God, given over to slavery, but not to be killed: they were to live as unconscious witnesses to the truth of Christianity, not cherished by Christian rulers, nor allowed lives of ease on the profits of usury. Rulers who indulged them became themselves guilty of their sin: as St Paul said 'Not only those who do these things, but those who consent to them are worthy of death.' This means that anyone who allows what he can prevent is guilty of the sin to which he consents. Rulers who receive any benefit from the usuries of Jews are drinking the blood of victims whom they ought to protect: their hands and garments are steeped in blood and they themselves become fuel for the eternal fire.

In this summary, I have softened rather than exaggerated the violence of Grosseteste's words, which extend to four pages of print. The letter is of a date too early to have been influenced by Aristotle's philosophical arguments against usury; but Grosseteste has already drawn the extreme conclusion—going beyond the strict limits of the biblical text in this—that usury was against nature and wholly inadmissible, whether practised by Jews or anyone else. All but one of the texts which he quoted were from the Bible, and they were used to produce the maximum effect of blood and horror. The only non-biblical text was a sentence from Augustine justifying the policy of not killing the Jews 'because they are the bearers of the books which prophesy the coming of Christ'.[8]

Here we see Grosseteste in an unfavourable light, but it is a light which we shall do well to get accustomed to, because it will illuminate a great deal of his later career. It is unfavourable to him, because it shows that in an area of conduct where brutality was the rule, he was prepared to go to even greater lengths of brutality, because he took the principles on which it was based more seriously than most men. He thought with more energy, with more fierce commitment, and with a more urgent desire to give practical expression to his thoughts than most men in high positions, who had worked their way to the

---

[8] Quoting Augustine on Ps. 58: 12, 'slay them not lest my people forget.' The subject of usurers has a place in Grosseteste's Index, designated by the suggestive symbol , but the list of references is missing (Lyon MS 414, f. 18).

top by many compromises. Grosseteste had risen almost by a single bound. He had had no lessons in keeping silent. He was a man of the people, and he spoke with a peasant's violence and passion to those above him as well as to those beneath. Langton, with all his harshness of tone, was a man of discretion and compromise, who reserved his violent words for those beneath him, and spoke with discretion to his equals and superiors. He was, after all, the son of a country gentleman.

We happen to be able to observe the difference in temper between Grosseteste's approach to this problem and one inspired by a complete scholastic training. About forty years later, around 1270, the duchess of Brabant sent Thomas Aquinas some questions about the way in which she should treat the Jews in her duchy. After expressing some doubts about his having the necessary experience for answering these questions, and 'without prejudice to a better opinion', he replied with his usual efficiency.[9]

Her first question was whether she was allowed to tax the Jews, and in this way profit from their illicit trade. In reply to this, Aquinas adopted the same premiss as Grosseteste that the guilt of the Jews had caused them to be condemned to perpetual slavery. From this he concluded that all their goods belonged to the lord of the place where they lived. But the practical consequences of this were moderate: they might indeed be taxed, but only in moderation and only in a customary way; they were not to be harassed by novelties.

On the further question whether the proceeds of their usury could be taxed or confiscated, Aquinas replied that, since the profits of usury were unlawful, they should be restored to the victims where possible; but when this was impossible, they might be used for other purposes, such as charity or the common good.

Next: could they be fined? Yes—and more than other men; but always with the proviso that they must be allowed the means of livelihood, and that the ruler must not make a personal profit from their usury except to the extent that he or she had been a victim of usury.

Could gifts be received from Jews? Yes, provided that any

---

[9] *De Regimine Judaeorum ad Ducissam Brabantiae*, in P. Mandonnet, *Thomae Aquinatis Opuscula Omnia*, i, 1927, 488–94.

proceeds of usury were restored to the victims or applied to the common good.

Finally, the same rules were to apply to Christian usurers, such as the money lenders of Cahors, whose expulsion from all places, wherever they were found, was the policy urged by Langton and approved by Grosseteste.[10]

It will be seen that Aquinas's basic assumptions are the same as Grosseteste's: the perpetual slavery of the Jews; the depravity of usury; the inadmissibility of profit for Christian rulers from usury. But the habits of thought, the atmosphere of moderation, and the practical consequences are different. In the first place, Aquinas replied, and then only reluctantly, to specific questions; he hedged his answers with provisos which safeguarded customary limitations; he condemned violent changes; he left much scope for the conscience and judgement of the secular rulers in providing for the common good. Cool reason and moderation prevail. With Grosseteste, it is quite different. Full of fire and zeal, he charged unbidden into the problem, shooting off biblical quotations in all directions, and coming to the quite impracticable conclusion that the Jews should be settled on the land to work with the sweat of their brow for the benefit of princes in return for receiving a pittance for the support of their wretched lives (*suae infelicis vitae qualemcunque sustentationem*).

III. THE PROBLEMS OF A BISHOP

We turn from this scene of violence to the quieter complexities of ecclesiastical life. Grosseteste was elected bishop of Lincoln in March and consecrated in June 1235. He set to work with extraordinary promptitude like a man fully armed for the conflicts that lay ahead of him. He was equipped with a programme for enforcing discipline among clergy and laity alike. Among the laity, he sought to put an end to notorious drunkenness, incontinence and gluttony, to enforce regular confession and penance, and to explain their duties in sermons with a popular appeal. Among the clergy—in addition to all this—he insisted on their competence to perform their pastoral duties. Looked on as a distant ideal, the programme can scarcely be called revolutionary. These were the aims of every well-

[10] See *Chron. Maj.* v. 404.

instructed bishop of the century, and they all used the same aids of diocesan synods and instructions to archdeacons. But a common plan can become revolutionary when it is acted on with an urgent expectation of success. Grosseteste threw himself into the task with a strong desire for immediate results, reinforced by his conviction of personal responsibility for the soul of every individual in his diocese. In addition he had a wonderful power of organization and rapidity of execution, allied to an unbending tenacity in applying general principles to the smallest details of behaviour.

But before he could perform his episcopal functions, Grosseteste needed to be consecrated by the archbishop of Canterbury, and this did not take place without eliciting from him a characteristic display of detailed argument and large generalization. The question was, where should it happen? A minor question, but one which gave forewarning of the awkwardness of having in a high position a man accustomed to look closely into details and to draw from them the largest conclusions without regard to common convenience.

1. Consecration

The question of the place where bishops should be consecrated was one which, like most questions of formal procedure, had a long history of dissension between the parties whose interests were in even the remotest ways affected. Kings, archbishops, bishops, the monks of Canterbury, had all had their say on various occasions. Inevitably the monks were the advocates of their traditional and (as they claimed) legal right to have all consecrations performed in the cathedral church. The king, the archbishop and other bishops were chiefly concerned with practical convenience. The struggle between these two principles had been going on for well over a century, and practical convenience was gradually winning the day. The archbishops had got into the habit of consecrating bishops at some mutually convenient place, generally in London. But, more recently still, the monks of Canterbury had bestirred themselves to upset this lax arrangement, and had discovered or invented grounds for insisting that consecrations should take place in their church.[11] At some date between the king's consent to his election in April and his consecration in June 1235, Grosseteste paid a visit to Canterbury with some members of his household, probably to arrange the details of his consecration. He was then told about (but not shown) an alleged charter of Archbishop Thomas Becket, confirmed by Pope Gregory IX, forbidding episcopal consecrations elsewhere than in Canterbury without the consent of the whole body of monks. Some of Grosseteste's officials seem to have been sceptical about the claim, but he himself accepted it with all the enthusiasm of a man glad to be inconvenienced in a good cause. He at once wrote a letter to the archbishop, which showed that no detail was too unimportant for his personal attention or for the full force of scriptural authority being brought to bear on it.[12]

He wrote to say that he had heard of the monks' objection to his consecration taking place elsewhere than in Canterbury, and he begged as a personal favour—expensive and inconvenient for him though it would be—that it should take place there. He was not at all concerned about the legal rights, privileges, charters, or institutional precedents which lay so thick on the ground, but simply with this: 'If meat scandalizes my brother, I will not eat meat while the world lasts' (1 Corinthians 8: 13). In present circumstances, this meant: 'If my being consecrated elsewhere than in Canterbury scandalizes my brethren, I will not be consecrated elsewhere than in Canterbury while the world lasts.' And very much more to the same effect. He granted that it was a matter of no importance in itself; and yet of the highest possible importance in following the biblical rule of consideration for the weaker brethren: 'Woe to that man by whom offence cometh.'

The archbishop must have been puzzled by this gratuitous

[11] For the monks' claim, see C. R. Cheney, 'Magna Carta beati Thomae: another Canterbury forgery', *Medieval Texts and Studies*, 1973, 78–110, printing a forged charter ascribed to Archbishop Thomas Becket with the clause (no. ix) 'ne episcopi Cantuarensis ecclesie suffraganei alibi consecrentur quam in ecclesia Cantuariensi'. The charter had probably only recently been concocted when Grosseteste was told of it in 1235.

[12] *Ep.* no. 12, where he describes the visit which he and his officials paid to Canterbury; he accepted the monks' claim without demur, but he had (rather unconvincingly) to deny the allegation that his officials had spoken harsh words about it.

self-sacrifice by the new bishop in a matter which chiefly concerned himself and the monks, and for which there was a whole
mass of legal precedents and documents. In addition, he may
have had more than an inkling that the monks' charter, which
had so greatly impressed Grosseteste, was almost certainly a
recent forgery.[13] At all events, he took no notice of Grosseteste's
offer, and the consecration took place at the mutually convenient town of Reading.

This was often to be the fate of Grosseteste's interventions in
the next eighteen years. He took his stand on the highest possible grounds of the Gospel, the law of mutual love, and the
salvation of souls, only to find that the world had worked out
other rules whereby things worked more smoothly. This was
further demonstrated by the first large problem which he en-
countered after his consecration.

2. The bastardy problem

Within a few weeks of his consecration, a problem arose which
brought the contrast between the universal laws of nature and
the Gospel and the practice of the accredited agents of secular
and ecclesiastical government even more forcibly to his attention. On the surface, the problem was only a marginal dispute
in the complicated story of conflicting secular and ecclesiastical
jurisdictions, but it raised issues of a much deeper kind for
Grosseteste. The main issue was simple: did children who had
been born out of wedlock and then legitimized in Canon Law
by the later marriage of their parents have the right to succeed
to secular estates? A simple question, but one which cut deeply
into the organization of a society based primarily on the hereditary tenure of land. For such a society, certainty and stability
in hereditary succession was of the first importance. In 1235,
the rule in England was that legal succession belonged only to
those who had been born in wedlock. How this rule had become
established it is hard to say, for at an earlier period legitimacy
of birth had played a much smaller part in succession, and even
the greatest estates had passed to bastards. But, for whatever
reason, all this had changed in England by the late twelfth

[13] The forgery was very easily and quickly detected as soon as it was challenged (see
Cheney, op. cit. , pp. 99–100).

century and only those who were *born* 'legitimate' could succeed. Those whose interests were most closely affected wanted no change, for any change might disturb existing rights and create unforeseen uncertainties.

Despite the weight of baronial opinion against change, the question had become a controversial one in 1234, probably as the result of the issue of a new code of canon law by Pope Gregory IX. This code contained for the first time a letter from Pope Alexander III to the bishop of Exeter written in about 1175. Although it was sixty years old, it seems to have passed without earlier remark, perhaps because its practical consequences were not clear, perhaps too because, so far as they were clear, they were unwelcome. The letter laid down as a matter of theological principle that those who were born out of wedlock became legitimate by the subsequent marriage of their parents, unless they had been born as a result of adultery. It was the clear intention of the letter, though not clearly expressed, that in the absence of this bar, the children subsequently legitimized would succeed to their parents' estates.[14]

In October 1234, before Grosseteste became a bishop, the king had held a meeting of bishops and barons to discuss the question whether the existing law was consistent with Alexander III's letter. The archbishop of Canterbury and the other eight bishops who were present thought that it was, provided that the question of the *legitimacy* of the children was not called in question, but only their right of succession. It was agreed that if an heir suspected of having been born before his parents' marriage claimed succession to secular estates in the royal court, the question should be referred to the ecclesiastical courts, which alone were competent to decide questions relating to marriage. The ecclesiastical courts would not be asked, 'Is this person a bastard or not?', but 'Was this person born before the marriage of his parents or after?'[15] The royal courts would then decide the question of succession in the light of the answer and in conformity with current practice. In this way it was hoped to avoid any challenge to the papal pronouncement

---

[14] *Decret. Greg.*, IV. xvii, c. 6 (*Corpus Iuris Canonici*, ed. E. Friedberg, 1881, ii. 712).

[15] The writ which was drawn up as a result of this meeting and the relevant documents concerning it are printed in Powicke and Cheney, i. 198–201, with an excellent summary of the course of events from 1234 to 1236.

about legitimacy, and still maintain the existing rule of succession.[16]

This was the position of the bishops and barons who discussed
the matter in 1234. But the question still remained whether the
ecclesiastical courts would consent to answer the question in
the form in which it was put to them. Very soon it became
clear that there was one dissentient diocese—that of Lincoln.
Grosseteste, of course, had not been present at the meeting in
October 1234. But as soon as he took over the affairs of his
diocese in April 1235, he was faced with letters from the royal
courts demanding an answer along the lines agreed by the
archbishop and bishops in the previous year. He reacted with
an energetic refusal to co-operate. Already by October 1235
his continuing refusals had reached a stage where they could
not be ignored and he was summoned to the royal court to
answer for them. Meanwhile he was in correspondence with
the royal justice William Raleigh, with whom (as appears from
the letters they exchanged) he had long-standing ties of friendship. Grosseteste set about the task of persuading Raleigh to
adopt his point of view with remarkable pertinacity and depth
of research. He wrote two letters to him, of which the first is a
major treatise of four or five thousand words dealing with every
aspect of the question.[17] It is astonishing that he had time to
write so much and to let his mind range in such detail over
every aspect of the problem, for (as we shall see) he had plenty
of other problems to deal with at the same time.

As always, he went straight to the foundations. He argued
that the existing law on succession was contrary to divine law,

[16] The theoretical doctrine which underlay this procedure is admirably summarized
by Henry Bracton, who had become a clerk of the royal judge William Raleigh shortly
before 1234: 'To the pope and the priesthood belong all things spiritual; to the king
and kingdom those that are temporal . . . Hence it does not belong to the pope to
order or dispose of temporal things, any more than it belongs to the king to order
spiritual things. Let neither put his sickle with the other's harvest. Just as the pope can
dispose of spiritual ranks and dignities, so can the king dispose of temporal inheritances
according to the custom of the kingdom; for each kingdom has its own customs, and
there may be one rule of succession in England and another in France' (*De legibus et
consuetudinibus Angliae*, ed. G. E. Woodbine, revised by S. E. Thorne, 1977, iv. 298; see
also Thorne's remarks on the subject, vol. iii, pp. xv–xvii).

[17] *Ep.* no. 17, pp. 76–94. The terms in which he addressed Raleigh provide evidence
of a long-standing connection and friendship: 'copularis insuper mihi arctius ceteris in
curia degentibus, filiatione spirituali, dilectione diuturna et speciali, et multiplicis be-
neficii collatione liberali' (pp. 76–7).

contrary to nature and natural law, contrary to reason, as well
as being contrary to canon law, to old English custom, and
to the theory of the relations between secular and spiritual
authority. In direct opposition to all the practical wisdom of
the English episcopate and baronage, he asserted that they
were flying in the face of God, nature, reason, law, custom, and
properly constituted authority. He called on the whole universe
to testify against the iniquity of excluding legitimized bastards
from succession to English estates. He did not deal with the
question primarily as a jurisdictional matter, nor even as a
matter of canon law or theology in any narrow sense. It was a
question of fidelity to the law of nature, the fundamental law
of the universe.

In interpreting this law, he challenged one of the commonest
assumptions about past events. We normally assume that nothing can alter the past. We may pardon a crime, but we
cannot obliterate it; stolen goods do not become unstolen by
subsequent payment, though the consequences of the theft may
be changed; and so on. But Grosseteste set out to prove that
the nature of past events can be changed by what happens
later. To support this view, he first called in the Bible. For
example, the crossing of the Red Sea was an historical event;
but its nature was only disclosed when the event which it
foretold—the process of Redemption—was complete. In this
incident and hundreds of others in the Old Testament, future
events gave an entirely new meaning to the past. As we have
seen, the retrospective role of the Incarnation was peculiarly
highly developed in Grosseteste's theology: it changed the status of everything that had happened in the past, even of the
Creation itself. It was on this principle that he argued for the
power of marriage to cast its shadows backwards and alter
the natural (not merely legal) status of children born before
marriage.

He pursued this theme through four pages of biblical
examples, and then turned to the world of nature. Here too
he discovered the same principle at work in natural bodies:
changes in the constitution of a body cause changes not only in
future offshoots of the body, but in those which already existed.
For instance, a change in the humours of a body in old age
causes not only the hairs which grow *after* the change to be

grey, but also those which had already grown.[18] Similarly with
the plumage of birds: a change of climate or season causes
changes which affect not only new feathers but old ones also.
Grosseteste gave several examples of similar organic changes
which have a retrospective effect on the products of natural
bodies. He attached great importance to them, because they
showed that the same principle, which worked in theology,
worked right through the whole system of nature. Consequently
those who denied the possibility of retrospective changes were
the enemies of nature as well as of God.

Then he turned to reason 'which prevails over all law and
custom'. The most telling point he makes here is in the form of
a conundrum. He refers to the question asked in the royal writ,
'Was so-and-so born before or after the marriage of his parents?'
and he asks: suppose the child was conceived before, but born
after marriage, on what basis do you reckon him (as you undoubtedly will under the terms of the writ) the legitimate in-
heritor of his father's estate? Surely only on the basis that the
marriage altered the status of the illegitimate child in the womb
and made him capable of legitimate succession. So even the
upholders of the existing law admitted in practice that later
events could change the nature of earlier acts.

I shorten the arguments and curtail the subtleties of the
presentation, which are protracted beyond endurance. Enough
has been said to indicate the scope of the arguments which he
deployed. By contrast with the length of these arguments, he is
brief on the purely legal arguments, and equally brief in insisting on the duty of Christian rulers to obey the rules of canon
law. He is rather fuller in asserting the principle that all the
powers of secular rulers come from the Church, which they
are therefore unconditionally bound to obey.[19] But the real
substance and individuality of his thought lies in the biblical,
scientific and rational analogies by which he sought to give a
universal setting to the legal issue. It is here that he displayed
the energy of his richly original and independent mind, brushing aside the legal distinctions with which his episcopal col-

[18] Grosseteste would have been familiar with Aristotle's discussion about the causes
of greyness in his *Historia Animalium*, but the use to which he put his scientific information was quite his own.

[19] The main source of Grosseteste's doctrine at this point appears to be St Bernard's
De Consideratione, IV. iii. 7.

leagues had sought to adjust the competing claims of secular and ecclesiastical courts.

Grosseteste's letter struck Raleigh as a curious irrelevance. He wrote back in jocular mood thanking Grosseteste for his *long* brief. He quoted the authority of the great justiciar Richard de Lucy against Grosseteste's account of the ancient English custom of legitimizing bastards, made a few other observations, and excused himself from replying more fully.[20] Grosseteste was clearly hurt by the levity of one whom, as his 'dearest son', he had a special obligation to instruct. The correspondence was dropped without rancour, but with disillusionment on both sides. It must by now have been clear that neither could hope for any help from the other. The bishops now changed their minds and supported Grosseteste. As for the barons, they persisted in their refusal to change the law, and the royal officials were left to devise new expedients for preserving the status quo, which they did without too much difficulty.[21]

The incident illustrates the strengths and weaknesses of Grosseteste as a practical statesman. His strength lay in his detailed yet universal view of the question, and in the unexpected range of learning which he could muster. These qualities sufficed to make the bishops withdraw from the position that their representatives had adopted in 1234. But in the end even they found his arguments practically irrelevant.

3. His visitations

Grosseteste's controversial stand on the question of legitimization, which caused a temporary split between the baronage and the bishops, might have seemed a sufficient occupation for the first few months of a new bishop. But, while this controversy was going on, Grosseteste had already embarked on his first general visitation of his diocese.

[20] The text of Raleigh's reply has not survived, but the gist of it can be gathered from Grosseteste's detailed reply to it, *Ep*. no. 24. The letter which follows (*Ep*. no. 25) from Grosseteste to Hugh Pattishall, the royal treasurer, is not concerned with the question of bastardy, but it provides further evidence of Grosseteste's close personal relations with leading figures in the royal administration and his concern for their pastoral welfare.

[21] For the later practice of the royal courts in such cases, see G. O. Sayles, *Select Cases in the Court of King's Bench*, Selden Soc. 86, 1957, 74–5; Holdsworth, *History of English Law*, i (7th edn.), 622; ix. 151.

Episcopal visitations were not a novelty in 1235, but Grosseteste brought to his task an idea which was substantially new,
and we can describe it in his own words. In speaking to the
pope in the course of his visit to the papal curia in 1250, he
recalled the novelty which he had introduced into his diocese—
within weeks, so it would seem, of his consecration:

The bishops of Lincoln in the past were accustomed to visit the religious houses of the diocese which were subject to them, and to receive
from these houses the expenses necessary for their visitation. It is not
my intention now to speak about these charges, which had become
approved and tolerable through custom, but (if you will be kind
enough to listen) I shall say a few words about some novelties.

When I became a bishop I believed it to be necessary to be a
shepherd of the souls committed to me, whose blood would be required
of me at the Last Judgement unless I used all diligence in visiting
them as Scripture requires. So I began to perambulate my bishopric,
archdeaconry by archdeaconry, and rural deanery by rural deanery,
requiring the clergy of each deanery to bring their people with their
children together at a fixed place and time in order to have their
children confirmed, to hear the Word of God, and to make their
confessions. When the clergy and people were assembled, I myself
frequently preached to the clergy, a Friar Preacher or Minor preached
to the people, and four friars heard confessions and imposed penances.
Then, having confirmed the children on two days, I and my clerks
gave our attention to enquiring into things which needed correction
or reform so far as they lay within our power.[22]

Grosseteste went on to say that, during his first circuit, various
people came to him complaining that what he was doing was
new and unaccustomed: 'to which I replied that any novelty
that builds up the new man and destroys the old is blessed and
acceptable to Him who came to renew mankind.'

We shall have later to consider the circumstances in which
he gave this remarkably detailed account of his innovation at
the beginning of his episcopate. For the moment it will suffice to
notice the immense and apparently unprecedented task which
Grosseteste had set himself. His diocese covered eight counties,
including some of the most thickly populated parts of England.
As his chief local officers he had eight archdeacons, and under
them seventy-seven rural deans with oversight over nearly two
thousand parishes. To make a circuit of all these deaneries on

---

[22] Gieben, 1971, pp. 375-6. See also Powicke and Cheney, i. 261-5.

the scale he described could scarcely have taken less than a year. Probably, in practice, it took several years. We do not know how fully the plan was implemented, but there are records of visitations in several of Grosseteste's years as bishop, and there is no reason to doubt the substantial accuracy of what he told the pope. Least of all can we doubt the intention that lay behind his plan: he intended to introduce the careful supervision of a disciplined Christian life into every one of the parishes in his diocese.

It was a plan which represented a huge extension of the bishop's pastoral function. I have remarked earlier that it was the task of the thirteenth-century Church to extend the organizational and doctrinal developments of the twelfth century into the lives of all members of the community. But what Grosseteste attempted went far beyond the aim of any contemporary, or even future, bishop. His visitation, as he describes it, and as the surviving documents fitfully reveal, was a mixture of royal eyre, sheriff's tourn, and itinerant preaching mission.[23] He would have liked to use the royal procedure of sworn inquest to uncover irregularities and took it ill that it was denied him. In his general plan, the group of friars in his household were his missioners, and his archdeacons were his chief local agents comparable to royal sheriffs. To this office he appointed men who were his closest collaborators in his learned enterprises and administration—such men as John of Basingstoke, Thomas Wallensis, William Lupus, William of Arundel, Richard of Gravesend, and Robert Marsh.[24] If he had had his way, episcopal government would have become the strongest ruling force in England.

In the course of his first visitation in 1235-6, his enquiries 'into things which needed correction' brought many practices to light which Grosseteste viewed as highly inimical to the disciplined life of the Church. They provoked a stream of directions to his archdeacons.[25] They also provoked a stream of protests and complaints and appeals to the papal court against

---

[23] For these parallels, see Pollock and Maitland, op. cit. i. 151-2 (with some interesting remarks on Grosseteste), 530, 556-60; ii. 519-20.

[24] For these men and their archdeaconries, see Greenway, 1977, 25-6, 28, 34, 37.

[25] Powicke and Cheney, i. 201-5 (a much better edition than *Ep.* nos. 21 and 22, where the same texts are printed).

his decisions, to which Grosseteste responded with counter-appeals. One of the more sensational of these was Grosseteste's successful counter-appeal against the restoration of the prior of St Frideswide's in Oxford, whom he had deposed for fornication and whom the papal court had reinstated. This incident, casually recorded, was only the tip of an iceberg. Grosseteste had in fact deposed no less than eleven heads of religious communities in his first year as bishop. Ten of them were heads of abbeys or priories of Augustinian canons—more than a quarter of all communities of this Order in his diocese. Here, as everywhere else, Grosseteste's standards were clearly more exacting than those of his contemporaries and more brusquely and energetically enforced.[26]

4. General directives and papal collaboration

In the documents of these early months we learn almost everything we need to know about the special objects of his disapproval and concern; also about the arguments with which he supported his claims, and about his methods for making them effective. In principle, it is hard to see much difference between his programme and that of Langton.[27] But in all his

---

[26] The papal letters arising out of the business of his visitation are summarized in *Calendar of Entries in Papal Registers relating to Great Britain and Ireland*, ed. W. H. Bliss, i, 1893, p. 155 (15 July 1236: against clerks in the diocese of Lincoln holding offices of justice or sheriff); ibid. (26 June 1236: against markets in sacred places in the diocese of Lincoln); p. 163 (22 June 1236: annulling the restoration by papal judges delegate of the prior of St Frideswide's, Oxford, whom Grosseteste had removed). The Dunstable Annals, the best chronicle source for Grosseteste's administration, list the heads of religious communities deposed in 1236. Arranged according to archdeaconries (in brackets) they were: (Lincoln) the abbots of Thornton and Bourne; (Leicester) the abbots of Leicester and Ouston and prior of Launde; (Oxford) the abbot of Dorchester, and the priors of St Frideswide's, Oxford, and Cold Norton; (Buckingham) the abbots of Notley and Missenden, and the prior of Bradwell. All of them were Augustinian canons except the last, which was a small Benedictine priory. Their geographical distribution suggests that the visitation of 1235 embraced the four archdeaconries of Lincoln, Leicester, Oxford, and Buckingham. The same source also records a visitation in 1238 of *monasteria et archidiaconatus et decanatus*. This tallies with Grosseteste's own account of his system of visitations, and suggests that he visited monasteries as they occurred in his itinerary. It may also indicate that in 1238 Grosseteste visited the archdeaconries omitted in 1235. (See *Ann. Mon.* iii. 143, 147–8.)

[27] The fullest expression of what may be called his 'programme' is to be found in the statutes for the diocese of Lincoln printed in Powicke and Cheney, i. 265–78, of uncertain date but in their main lines clearly operative during his early years as bishop. For his directives to his archdeacons, see i. 201–5, 479–80. On the prohibition of

aims, arguments, and methods, he goes beyond the conventions and common processes of law in the assertion of his episcopal responsibility.

Like Langton, he was no lover of country pleasures, and he began his episcopal career with an attack of even greater particularity than Langton's and much greater violence. His earliest directives to his archdeacons included prohibitions of all drunken parties. With comprehensive medical precision, he explained how they deformed the image of God in man by taking away the use of reason, by inhibiting physical activity, inducing morbid passions, shortening life, and leading to apostasy and other evils. He forbade popular jousting (rumbustious imitations of the real thing) which led to brawls and homicide, and were specially inappropriate on Holy Days when even useful and legitimate work was forbidden. Then, following the same line of argument, he forbade all games in churches and cemeteries, which were places set apart for holy uses and not for secular occupations, least of all for mere amusements. By parity of reasoning, all miracle plays and May Day and Yuletide festivities, all indecencies and disorders at wakes and on the vigils of saints' days, were forbidden. And so the list continued. The archdeacons were to see to these and many other matters.

Several of these prohibitions appear also in the directives of other bishops of the time. One cannot help suspecting that many bishops were glad to legislate freely and comprehensively on matters which could arouse no opposition from important people. But Grosseteste directed his bolts with impartial energy in all directions. His attack on popular behaviour was chiefly remarkable for his knowledge of popular goings-on, and his readiness to bring up very big generalities and statements of principle in denouncing minor disorders. Whether his archdeacons had any zeal for stemming the flow of human passions is another matter; Grosseteste did what he could to prod them into action.

A slightly more contentious object of his hostility in his early legislation was the use of churches and churchyards for weekly markets. The attack on these markets was not new. It goes back

miracle plays and other theatrical spectacles, see E. K. Chambers, *English Literature at the Close of the Middle Ages*, 1945, 12–16, 83.

at least as far as the popular preaching mission of Eustace of
Flay in the first years of the century, and there had already
been some local legislation against particular markets.[28] But
Grosseteste's legislation struck a new note in its com-
prehensiveness. Besides taking the opportunity of the king's
presence in Northampton to get his help in excluding mer-
chants from the church and cemetery of All Saints in that town,
he went on to lay down the general rule of exclusion and
required his much harassed archdeacons to see that it was
observed. Here, as so often, Grosseteste was going a little further
than any existing ecclesiastical laws on the subject. That was
why he turned for support to the king.[29] Then he sent messengers to the papal court. Their main business was to oppose
objections against the actions he had taken during his diocesan
visitation, but they also sought papal support for banning markets from churches and consecrated ground throughout the
diocese. They duly obtained papal letters ordering Grosseteste
to follow the policy he had adopted.[30]

This was the kind of collaboration with the pope that he
desired: the bishop initiated measures necessary in his diocese;
the pope supporting the local bishop with his universal authority. Grosseteste's general view of the relationship seems to
have been largely influenced by St Bernard's *De Consideratione*,
a work for which he had a high regard. An important theme
in this rich and varied work was the place of the pope among
his co-bishops: a position, no doubt, of authority and superi-
ority, but based on the same privileges and duties that belonged
to all bishops. Eugenius (Bernard had written) was to remember that the Roman Church was the mother not the lord
of other churches, and that the pope was not the lord over the
bishops but one of them, a brother of those who loved God and

[28] In the early years of Henry III, several local markets had been moved from
Sunday to a weekday and from churchyards to secular sites, but there does not seem
to have been any general legislation against them before Grosseteste. See J. L. Cate,
'The Church and Market reform in England during the reign of Henry III', in *Essays
in honour of J. W. Thompson*, Chicago, 1938, 27–65. Powicke and Cheney, i. 202–3 quote
the relevant documents: the earliest known general enactment is in 1285.

[29] He had found the king an apt pupil: Grosseteste told his archdeacons that the
king had not only assented to his brief exhortation but had himself quoted the example
of Christ in the Temple. (Powicke and Cheney, p. 202).

[30] *CPR*, p. 155 (26 July 1236).

a partner of those who feared him.[31] This was a thought that Grosseteste approved, as also was Bernard's condemnation of the business managers of the papal court, who claimed precedence over the pope's fellow-priests on the ground of their closeness to his person.[32]

In Grosseteste's view, a bishop was *unconditionally* subordinate to the pope in only one respect: in his geographical limitation. Once appointed, within the area assigned to him, his authority and responsibility, like that of the pope himself, came from God. The pope had a general pastoral responsibility for the whole Church; a bishop had an equally God-given pastoral responsibility for his diocese. Within his diocese it was the bishop's duty to make decisions with regard to his whole flock in the light of the fundamental laws of the Gospel to which both he and the pope were subject.[33] If, in following these Gospel laws, the bishop stepped beyond the limits of the positive law of the Church—as in the case of markets on consecrated ground—then it was proper for him to seek the pope's support: proper also for the pope to give this support, for they were both subject to the Gospel law. Unless we understand this common subordination of both pope and bishop to the Gospel, we cannot understand how Grosseteste reconciled his very exalted view of the position of the pope as the universal representative of Christ on earth with his equally firmly held view that within his own diocese it was the bishop's duty to uphold the Gospel even against the positive commands of the pope, when these commands were contrary to the Gospel, even if strictly within the rights which papal government claimed as its own.

[31] *De Consideratione*, IV. vii. 23 (*Opp. S. Bernardi*, ed. J. Leclercq and H. M. Rochais, 1963, iii. 466).

[32] Ibid. IV. v. 16 (p. 461).

[33] In his conception of papal power, as on many other subjects, Grosseteste was willing to go beyond the limits laid down by law. On the one hand he allowed the pope powers beyond the law in *Ep*. 49 (p. 145): 'Scio et veraciter scio domini papae et sanctae Romanae ecclesiae hanc esse potestatem, ut de omnibus beneficiis ecclesiasticis libere possit ordinare.' Canon law, however, did not give the pope as wide a power as this until after Grosseteste's death. (See *Corpus Iuris Canonici, Sext*. III. iv, c. 2 (ed. Friedberg, ii. 1021).) But, on the other hand, he allowed the pope less than law here: 'Admittere enim personam aliquam ad ecclesiasticum beneficium et regimen animarum vel recusare personam aliquam ad illud, solius episcopi, unde episcopus est, officium et opus est' (*Ep*. no. 72, p. 228). Notice the phrase 'episcopi *unde* episcopus': *unde* is here used to mean *qua*, 'the bishop *qua* bishop'—a new usage which appears at this time.

Grosseteste's practice and theory of episcopal government, exercised with royal and papal support, worked without a hitch in the matter of markets and popular sports. Although there was no general legislation on which he could base his Gospel-inspired action, what he proposed clashed with no important interest. But his messengers, who obtained papal letters on this subject in June 1236, were also charged with another piece of business more contentious and far-reaching: the refusal of important corporations within the diocese to submit to the bishop's jurisdiction. Chief among these was the bishop's own community of canons at Lincoln, who refused to recognize his right of visitation.

5. The canons of Lincoln

The canons presented a peculiarly difficult problem. On the one hand the bishop could scarcely hope to succeed elsewhere if he could not enforce his authority at home. But, equally, the canons saw that, if the bishop were to have a finger in all their affairs, they could never breathe again in freedom. Grosseteste's dispute with his chapter dragged on and on, with endless appeals and counter-appeals to the papal court.[34] Superficially the pope generally gave him what he wanted, but always in terms that left an opening for further objections and delays on the part of the chapter. In the course of the dispute Grosseteste wrote a long letter to the dean and chapter stating his case with the fullest amplitude. The letter occupies seventy-five pages of the printed edition of his letters, and though it is impossible to read it all with patience, it contains the most important statement of his view of the episcopal office.[35]

With a moderation which is not always conspicuous in his writings, but with the overwhelming accumulation of biblical

[34] The dispute already existed in 1239 when Matthew Paris described the appeals and counter-appeals on both sides (*Chron. Maj.* iii. 528-9). Grosseteste's first visit to the *curia* in 1245 was the occasion for a definitive papal decision which gave the bishop the right of visitation but exempted the canons from taking an oath of obedience (*CPR*, p. 219, 25 August 1245; for the text, see *Chron. Maj.* iv. 497-501).

[35] *Ep.* no. 127, pp. 357-431. Grosseteste had his own ideas on the proper length of a letter, derived from the practice of St Augustine and St Jerome: when William Raleigh made merry about the length of his letter on the legitimization of bastards, Grosseteste told him that he would not have thought it long if he had read the letters of the Fathers (*Ep.* no. 24, p. 95).

texts which he used whenever he was deeply moved, he set out his view of his responsibilities. Within his own diocese, the bishop was as Moses to the Israelites, as David keeping his father's sheep, as Samuel judging Israel, as the sun in heaven, as a husband with his wife, as a craftsman with his material, as a watchman in the vineyard, as a parent with his child. He proposed model after model, held it up for examination, and applied it to illustrate his rights and duties towards the chapter. The letter is a remarkable example of the range of symbols, drawn from sacred history and from the natural world, which stamped Grosseteste's whole view of the universe. Considering that the whole affair was at bottom a legal and jurisdictional one, nothing is more remarkable than the almost complete absence from it of any reference to canon law, which, from a practical point of view, provided the only texts that mattered. The Bible and Nature, looked at from every angle and illustrating every activity, dominate the whole statement. At first, the accumulation seems simply repetitive; but if it is looked at in detail, every example adds some new dimension to the bishop's position, answering objections, removing limitations, enlarging its spiritual character or placing its functions in a new light. As a treatise, it has the lack of system, the variety of illustrations, the breadth of original thinking, and the persistent return to fundamentals which are characteristic of his thought. It is like a great work of nature, chaotic, colourful, without logical order, yet deeply impressive in its unity of tone and temper and unshakeable conviction. On its recipients it seems to have had no effect whatsoever.

6. Pastoral care and secular involvement

The last point on which Grosseteste's envoys at the papal court in June 1236 sought the pope's support proved to be more difficult than those we have so far noticed. Small in itself, it led to issues of fundamental importance for the whole conduct of government. It arose in this way.

There was one class of person in his diocese which aroused Grosseteste's deepest animosity: clerks who held parochial benefices while engaged in secular government. His detestation of such men rose to a special height of violence if they were engaged in the administration of the royal forests—and the royal forests covered a main part of three of the nine counties in his diocese and substantial parts of three others; his two main residences were in royal forests—they were part of his daily life. He spoke of the clerks who administered them with biblical violence. If frolickings and chafferings on consecrated ground on feast days were a desecration of the sanctity of holy things, the diversion of tithes, which a score of biblical texts declared to be sanctified to the Lord, to the uses of such persons was wholly repulsive. It throws an interesting light on the rigidity of the compartments of thirteenth-century thought that even so independent a thinker as Grosseteste, who recognized the inhumanity of forest law, did not demand that it should be more humane. He demanded only that it should not be administered by beneficed clergymen. Since all clerks engaged in government hoped to be rewarded with benefices, and since clerks were as necessary in forest administration as in every other branch of royal government, Grosseteste's demand could not fail to lead to trouble. The trouble started straightaway.

In his campaign to get these men out, and keep them out, of the parishes in his diocese, canon law gave him only uncertain support. The Lateran Council of 1179 had forbidden clerks to act as advocates in secular courts or to hold stewardships of towns or secular jurisdictions under secular rulers; and the Council of 1215 had forbidden clerks to pronounce, record, execute, or be present at judgements involving the shedding of blood.[36] So much was fairly clear. But between these points of clarity there were huge areas of obscurity which could only have been clarified by a large body of case law—and of case law relevant to this issue, there was, in England at least, no trace. Doubtless because nobody wanted it, except Grosseteste.

His messengers at the papal court in 1236, amidst all their other business, sought papal help against such men. The pope

---

[36] Lateran III (1179), c. 12, and IV (1215), c. 18. The current legislation of Church councils and papal letters on the subject was assembled in the compilation issued by Gregory IX in 1234 in Bk. III, tit. 50. But even in this compendious form it left many loopholes and uncertainties, and in the texts available before this date the position was even more obscure. (It may be noted, as indications of the fluidity in these matters, that in the text of Lateran III preserved in the Chronicle of Gervase of Canterbury (i. 257) the main part of c. 12 was omitted; and the Council's prohibition of advocacy in secular courts was omitted in Gregory IX's definitive compilation.

was ready to go some way to meet Grosseteste's wishes. On 15 July a papal mandate was issued requiring him to proceed against clerks in his diocese, holding many benefices and trying to get more, who acted as sheriffs or sat as judges in criminal cases, even if they withdrew before judgement of death or mutilation was passed.[37] This was a complicated mandate, which (as was wont to happen) gave Grosseteste something, but not enough. He was required 'to proceed': but precisely on what grounds, and with what penalties, and against whom? Against those with *many* benefices—but how many? Was not *one* too many? Was the culprit to lose all his benefices, or only the one in dispute?[38] There were no answers to most of these questions, and ten years later Grosseteste was still trying to get greater clarity. In February 1246, the pope once more ordered him to 'exercise his office *without fear*' against rectors of churches who undertake the offices of judge, sheriff, bailiff or notary in secular courts.[39] Here the ground had shifted from stopping secular officials accumulating benefices to stopping beneficed clergy taking secular offices. But it clarified nothing, least of all the kind of support from the pope that Grosseteste could expect if he ejected men who had long held secular offices. The shifting ground illustrates the difficulty of an effective practical action of the kind that Grosseteste desired. No one who mattered wanted him to win. Indeed, if he had won all along the line, government would have come to a standstill.

A special object of Grosseteste's animosity at this time was Robert Passelewe, one of the large army of middle-range officials on whom the royal government depended. What made him specially obnoxious to Grosseteste was that, while holding ecclesiastical offices and seeking an additional cure of souls in the diocese of Lincoln, he was a specialist in *forest* administration.[40] Grosseteste was outraged. But there were few who

[37] *CPR* (15 July 1236), p. 135.

[38] On 23 January 1239, Gregory IX clarified some points about plurality of benefices in answer to Grosseteste (ibid., p. 178).

[39] Ibid., p. 230.

[40] See *Ep.* nos. 124-6. The stages in Passelewe's career in the royal service from 1232 to his death in 1252 are documented in *Close Rolls of the Reign of Henry III*, vols. ii-vi. Powicke, *Henry III and the Lord Edward*, has some admirable pages on the man and his work (see esp. i. 103-5). Grosseteste's aversion to him may go back to the period when Passelewe was a baronial agent in 1223-4 and possibly the compiler of Fawkes de Breauté's *apologia* after his expulsion at the instigation of Archbishop Langton and his associates (see Powicke, i. 65).

shared his sense of outrage. Passelewe seems to have been a conscientious performer of his duties, either in person or by proxy, whether he was acting as archdeacon of Lewes, or as a royal judge, or keeper of the royal forests, or rector of a parish. It could reasonably be urged that the Christian community required the performance of all these duties, and Passelewe could perform them, or see that they were performed, better than most. The king pressed Grosseteste to accept him as rector of a parish. The archbishop made the same request. They were not unreasonable men. Grosseteste could only repeat that it would be contrary to divine and canonical laws for him to accept for spiritual office someone who inquired into thefts of venison, imprisoned accused persons, and passed judgement on them. To receive such a man would be to commit the sin of idolatry, and he asked the archbishop to restrain his official from pestering his suffragans with men like this.[41]

On this issue Grosseteste was able to get his way. It would have been impossible for the king to force him to accept Passelewe, and persistence in the attempt could have led to a complete breach between the bishop and the king, such as was later to come about between the bishop and Innocent IV. Henry III had no wish to press his case to this extreme. He believed in the co-operation of *sacerdotium* and *regnum* in the tasks of government.[42] He saw the relationship in a different light from Grosseteste, but this difference did not prevent a large measure of collaboration and friendship.

There was no lack of warmth in the relations between the two men. In the letter in which he rejected the king's request to institute Passelewe to a benefice, he replied to Henry's enquiry about the effect of unction on the royal position—not at great length, but sufficiently to assure the king that he took a benevolent view of his sacramental gifts. The royal anointing (he told the king) had bestowed on him the seven gifts of the Holy Spirit which gave him power and authority not possessed by unanointed princes. It entitled him to order the affairs of his kingdom according to the eternal law of the whole universe, in association with the hierarchy of angels, as decreed by God's

[41] *Ep.* no. 126, p. 356.
[42] We owe this piece of Henry III's thought to Grosseteste's reply to his letter (*Ep.* 124, p. 348).

eternal wisdom. But let not him be misled into thinking that it gave him an office on the same level as the priesthood. On this point, Grosseteste was able to quote one of the most venerable documents—if only it had been genuine—in human history: nothing less than the Testament of the Patriarch Judah in which he acknowledged his subordination to his brother Levi, the bearer of the *sacerdotium*.[43] No one before Grosseteste could have expounded the royal office in quite this way. His whole account is influenced by the thought of Denys the Areopagite, which he was one of the first in the West to assimilate; and the decisive quotation in favour of the *sacerdotium* came from a document which he himself had rescued and translated. So, here as elsewhere, we find a highly conservative view expressed with a characteristic breadth of vision, and with a novelty that came from his own discoveries.

The king could receive these instructions without resentment because they came from a very learned man, who was also his friend. Besides, he had no difficulty in making suitable provision elsewhere for his loyal servant Robert Passelewe. There were few dioceses in which a man of his ability and connections would not have been welcome. So Passelewe did not suffer from Grosseteste's hostility. In addition to his benefices and the benefits which he enjoyed from his temporary guardianship of various vacant bishoprics and abbeys, he ended his life as archdeacon of Lewes and with all his secular offices intact.

The right to reject men presented by patrons for benefices, for which Grosseteste judged them to be unsuitable on account of their involvement in secular government or insufficiency of learning for pastoral work, was one of the most persistent and contentious of his claims. But what was most important was that, in pursuing this aim, he discovered that the pope, like every other ruler, also needed benefices for his officials and for members of his household. The pope could not be forever weighing up the spiritual qualities of those to whom, for necessary purposes, he had promised benefices. All he could do was to ensure, so far as law could ensure anything, that they would

---

[43] *Ep.* no. 124, pp. 350-1. For Grosseteste's part in recovering and translating the Testaments of the Twelve Patriarchs, see Matthew Paris, *Chron. Maj.* iv. 232-3: the entry is in the year 1242, but introduced with the formula 'ipsis quoque temporibus', which indicates that the date is only approximate.

appoint suitable deputies to perform their spiritual functions while they took most of the revenue.

Up to a point—but never far enough—the pope and canon law could support Grosseteste in his drive against secular officials in spiritual offices, so long as these officials were the king's. But when these officials were the pope's, neither pope nor canon law would help him. Gradually, therefore, the emphasis of Grosseteste's campaign for spiritual purity in his diocese, having shifted from graveyards and markets and joustings on feast days to royal forest officials having the care of souls, shifted again from these to papal appointees, and from them to the papal curia and the pope himself.

Before following Grosseteste from his local environment to encounter the problems of the over-all government of the Church, we may pause to review his first ten years of diocesan administration. What qualities had he shown? What habits of thought had he developed in dealing with practical affairs? With what success had he operated in this limited field of action?

Clearly he had shown a remarkable abundance of energy, especially when it is remembered that, while dealing with all the problems I have sketched, he had also directed a uniquely comprehensive scholarly enterprise, which entailed the collection, translation, and commenting on the works of Ps.-Denys and John of Damascus, as well as the *De Caelo* and *Ethics* of Aristotle, and the so-called Testaments of the Twelve Patriarchs—work which alone would have made him a name among the innovative scholars of the century.

With regard to his habits of thought in practical affairs, he had shown the same qualities as those which he had developed in his scientific and theological work: the same persistent urge to return to fundamental questions and to solve them with the help of fundamental sources; the same depreciation of intermediate solutions and intermediate authorities such as legal texts and customary practices. He had also shown the same intense interest in details, and the same power of placing them in their universal setting. And not only had he shown a power of drawing conclusions, but also of acting on them with intrepid zeal and fearlessness of consequences.

But in all this we may detect a practical weakness. Whereas

in theoretical subjects, no detail can safely be neglected; in practical affairs, the art of government lies in knowing what to neglect. The ruler who wakens all sleeping dogs, will generally waken them only to be bitten. Grosseteste was a compulsive wakener of sleeping dogs, because he saw them all as symptoms of a state of affairs which needed to be corrected. He had much practical wisdom, but no political prudence. He did not understand the need for moderation in dealing with deeply ingrained habits and institutions. But it should be added that it was his political imprudence, his 'extremism', which aroused enthusiasm in the shires of his diocese a century and a half after his death. We shall deal with this later. Immediately we must consider his dealings with the papacy on matters arising from the government of his diocese.

11

Grosseteste's Prophetic Vision

I. THE PROBLEM OF THE PAPACY

GROSSETESTE's first letter to Pope Gregory IX, written soon after he became bishop, expressed his devotion in terms which can only be called fulsome. The superlatives, which he always had at his disposal, flowed out in superabundance to describe the measureless obedience, reverence, awe and fear with which he approached the pope. He wished to have some task imposed upon him to prove the intensity of his obedience: 'I offer myself as one wholly prepared to carry out, to the full extent of my modest power, whatever task you may wish to impose upon me.'[1] He seems to be soliciting a post of special danger or difficulty. Perhaps he saw himself as an emissary to Constantinople or to a mission field even more remote: he would have been wonderfully well equipped for such a mission. But nothing happened. It is hard to know what impression his letter can have made on the pope and curia. They may have sensed that a man so ready for the greatest trials might be less reliable in carrying out the more humdrum, but more immediately necessary, task of providing suitable benefices for the nominees of the pope and cardinals. He had already, as archdeacon, provided a benefice for one of the cardinals, and, already as bishop, another for a nephew of the pope. He was soon to have further requests.[2] This, it seemed, was the chief task which the pope and cardinals wished to impose upon him, and he very soon began to be uneasy about nominees who had so little intention of settling in England to carry out their duties. But, apart from this anxiety, the problem of the papacy did not arise in any serious way during the first ten years of his episcopate. When he wanted papal support, he generally got it. It

[1] *Ep.* no. 35.
[2] For these early demands and the problems they raised, see *Ep.* nos. 36, 46, 49.

is true that this support proved to be very fragile in practice. This could be put down to the wills of wicked men who could always find ways of spinning out the web of objections and exceptions to any papal mandate. But when it came to the employment of unsuitable men in spiritual offices in order to provide them with incomes for performing non-spiritual duties in legal and administrative business, he found that the papacy was as much involved in this practice as any secular ruler.

The whole problem ultimately went back to the lack of funds sufficient to support the growth of government, whether ecclesiastical or secular. The revenue derived from the universal payment of tithes was the only general and regular source of public income which was not ear-marked for military purposes. Strictly speaking, of course, it was not public income. It was paid, chiefly by the laity, for the support of their local church, divisible into three parts for the priest, the maintenance of the fabric, and the relief of the poor. In an ideal world, these three purposes would have absorbed the whole of this income to produce an educated clergy, magnificent churches, and contented poor. But in practice—and, short of a total revolution in society and education, there was no remedy—little of this income was spent in the parish and a large surplus was available for other purposes. Among these other purposes, the needs of government made the most urgent claim.

It is clear that Grosseteste had no objection in principle to draining off parochial revenues for non-parochial purposes. He himself appointed parish rectors who were going to spend their time in learned work and diocesan administration. But he insisted on two conditions: first, that the governmental needs which were supported by the tithes of churches should be strictly ecclesiastical; and secondly, that those who received this income, even if they were chiefly employed elsewhere, should be *capable* of performing the pastoral duties of preaching and administering the sacraments, for which the tithes were primarily intended.

This limited diversion of parochial revenues for the general purposes of the Church might seem reasonable. But it had two defects. First, the peace and safety of the Church depended on secular administration no less than on ecclesiastical administration. The king was a consecrated servant of Christ no less (though with different functions) than the bishop. The modern separation between Church and State simply did not exist in the thirteenth century, though some notable historians have thought that it did.[3] Secondly, many ecclesiastical officials, who were unexceptionable holders of benefices, performed functions indistinguishable from those of secular officials in collecting revenues, bringing defaulters to justice, and preparing for wars which were not obviously more holy than those of secular rulers. This was especially true of the papal collectors and other officials whom the pope sought to provide with rectories in the diocese of Lincoln and everywhere else when vacancies occurred.

This was Grosseteste's first dilemma. The second was equally serious. He had no hesitation in giving the care of parishes to men who were engaged in ecclesiastical administration or learned work useful to the Church. But he insisted that they should be priests (not deacons like most administrators), and have the knowledge and eloquence necessary for performing their pastoral duties, even if in practice they were otherwise employed. The lack of these qualifications had helped to fuel the ferocity of his objection to Robert Passelewe. And yet, a reasonable man might well ask: if a man was going to perform his parochial duties by proxy, did it really matter whether he was a priest rather than a deacon, or an eloquent preacher rather than a tongue-tied mumbler, or capable of explaining the doctrine of the Trinity or of hearing the confessions of a village population? Is it not pointless to ask whether a man is suitable for duties which he will not perform, so long as he is conscientious in seeing that he has a deputy who will do all that is required? To these questions Grosseteste could only have reiterated his fundamental objection to spiritual appointments being held by men incapable of carrying out spiritual duties.

It was this objection which finally drove Grosseteste into an embittered clash with the papal *curia* and ultimately with Pope Innocent IV himself. The question at once arises: why did he allow himself to be driven into this position? It is easy to answer that he was temperamentally incapable of compromise, and it

[3] Maitland's brilliant, and on most points wholly convincing, account of the thirteenth-century Church in *Roman Canon Law in the Church of England*, 1898, is seriously flawed by his conception of a straightforward conflict between Church and State.

is quite likely that he was. But, if so, this psychological state was closely connected with his strongly held views on episcopal responsibility. As bishop, he was immediately responsible for every individual soul committed to his care. Since he must have helpers, he would only have those who were equipped to do the work: he would not put unqualified men into a position which gave them the responsibility for finding a competent substitute, for how could they recognize qualities which they did not possess? It would be like asking a saddle-maker to judge the quality of a horse, or a crew-member to appoint the captain. This was an image, Aristotelian in origin, which he was to use in his final and most ferocious confrontation with Innocent IV. His soul abhorred such a reversal of the order of nature. That was why he resisted even papal claims, firmly established in canon law though they were, to nominate for pastoral office in his diocese men whom he judged incompetent.

But the more important, more general, cause of his intransigence lay in the whole character of his thought. I have earlier drawn attention to its strongly unitary structure in binding together everything from God to the smallest created object. This unity was not just a unity of causes and effects; it was a unity of similarities, of congruities, of illumination by the same single source of light. Revealed truth and scientific truth had the same source, which flowed along the same channels of vision or—to speak more truly—revelation. There is no room for compromise in knowledge coming from God revealing himself in a double flow of created symbols and revealed truths.

His commitment to these divine sources of knowledge set Grosseteste apart from most of his contemporaries, and especially those contemporaries who had most fully absorbed the principles of scholastic thought. The main body of scholastic thought, at least until the last decades of the thirteenth century, required a careful distinction between nature and the supernatural, between revelation and reason, between the rights of organized society and the privileges of many divergent groups and individuals. The need for keeping a balance among all these interlocking rights must have been always present to the wise and intensely political Innocent IV, and may have led him to give this fatherly advice to Grosseteste: 'You have unburdened your soul against your enemies. Let that suffice.

What is it to you if I give them relief? Is your eye evil because
I am good?'[4] But Grosseteste was not made of such malleable
stuff: his character and his habit of thought drove him to take
global views of every problem, and to press on to their solution.

II. GROSSETESTE AT THE PAPAL COURT

Until 1245, Grosseteste conducted his business at the papal
court through letters and messengers. After this, he twice
judged it necessary to go himself. His first visit, which kept him
out of England for nearly a year in 1245, was mainly prompted
by his desire to settle his dispute with the canons of Lincoln
once and for all.[5] The second visit, which occupied most of
1250, was chiefly concerned with his continuing attempt to
stem the flow of papal privileges granting exemption from episcopal control to privileged communities; but he also went prepared to make his general views on papal government known—
and, if possible, to get them accepted.[6] The first visit seems to
have raised no important issue which we have not already
discussed; and, so far as business went, the same might have
been said about the second; but Grosseteste was determined to
go further, and to make known his general views and the causes
of their development in the previous fifteen years. In brief, his
experience during these years had turned a ruler of souls of
boundless energy and dedication into a prophet. The moment
when the prophet emerged from the shadows can be determined with great accuracy.

On Friday 13 May 1250, after many weeks of miscellaneous
business to little purpose, Grosseteste, accompanied by his archdeacon of Oxford, Richard of Gravesend, appeared before the
pope and cardinals to make a statement. He had prepared the
ground carefully in advance. Copies were distributed to the
pope and to three of the cardinals, one of whom read the text

[4] Matthew Paris, *Chron. Maj.* v. 98.

[5] He left England in mid-November 1244 ('in octavis sancti Martini', Matthew
Paris, *Chron. Maj.* iv. 390). There is no record of his playing any part in the Council of
the following year, but the legal definition of his case against the canons of Lincoln,
along with many other cases, was settled as part of the aftermath of the Council. He
did not return to England until October 1245 (see *Ep.* no. 114).

[6] He left England in late January 1250 (*Chron. Maj.* v. 96), and returned about the
end of September ('circa festum S. Michaelis', ibid., 186).

to the assembly.[7] It would have taken about an hour. Its purpose was to communicate the conclusions to which he had been driven by his experience of the obstacles put in his way in carrying out his pastoral duties. It may be looked on as a final extension of his scientific method of observing individual phenomena, and detecting in them the general laws by which they are governed. In accordance with this procedure, Grosseteste reviewed his episcopal experiences, applied to them the doctrines of the Bible, considered them in the light of history, and reached a general view of the historical development of Christendom.

The observed phenomena were these:

exemptions from his pastoral visitations based on real or pretended papal privileges;

limitations imposed, mainly by secular authority, but with papal connivance, on his power to investigate the sins of his flock;

opportunities for avoiding episcopal judgements by appeals from one court to another;

subtleties of legal procedure which prolonged every kind of opposition to episcopal action;

and, above all, the entrusting of pastoral care to men who were unable and unwilling to carry out their duties.

Here we have many and varied phenomena, but they all have a single effect: the frustration of pastoral care directed towards the salvation of souls, which is the central function of the Church. But a single effect must have a single cause and this single cause must be greater than the whole effect.[8] In nature, it was the drying up of the sap—symbolically the word of God—which caused the leaves of trees to fall. In the Church,

---

[7] The documents relating to this occasion were first fully and satisfactorily edited by Fr. Servus Gieben in *Collectanea Franciscana*, xli, 1971, 340–93. The manuscript tradition suggests that the dossier remained among Grosseteste's papers in the Franciscan library in Oxford unnoticed or unstudied till the mid-fourteenth century, except for one summary of his main speech which Fr. Gieben found in a miscellaneous volume in the Bibliothèque Nationale in Paris (MS lat. 10358). The address to the *curia* on 13 May 1250 will be referred to below as the *Memorandum*.

[8] *Memorandum* 7 (p. 353): 'unius enim una est causa, et oppositorum causae oppositae.' Cf. Grosseteste's discussion of Aristotle's question in the *Posterior Analytics*, ii. 16, 98^b 25, 'can a single effect have more than one cause?' Rossi, 391–8.

it was the drying up of the word of God in pastoral care which caused its purpose to fail. The instrument of this desiccation was the papal curia which choked the system with privileges, exemptions, the creation of legal tangles, the tolerance of evils and active support for evil-doers, in order to forward the family interests and political ambitions of the pope and cardinals.[9] This single cause was therefore the source of all the evils which he had experienced in his own diocese: they flowed through the channels listed above and frustrated the work of the Church.

Then he went further. Taking a more general view of the contemporary Church, he found the same cause at work everywhere over an extended period of time with similar effects. The Church had once grown with miraculous speed from a few persecuted individuals to embrace the whole known world. Now it was confined to a small corner of the world, and it was surrounded by triumphant enemies—Mongols, Muslims, unbelievers of every kind. Even the small part of the world which was still Christian was split by schism and torn by heresies; and the heresies, which were strongest in the most populous parts of Western Europe, showed no sign of abating. Worse still, even those parts of Christendom which were formally neither heretical nor schismatic were in large part separated from the body of Christ by notorious and unreproved deadly sins.[10]

Once more, he asked what was the cause of all this? Why

[9] The essence of the argument on this point is in *Memorandum*, paragraphs 10 and 17 (pp. 355 and 358), in which these are the essential words: '10. Sed quae est huius tanti mali prior et originalis causa, fons et origo? . . . Causa, fons et origo est haec curia, non solum eo quod haec mala non dissipat . . . sed et eo amplius quod ipsamet per suas provisiones, dispensationes et collationes curae pastoralis tales quales praetacti sunt pastores, immo mundi perditores, in oculis solis huius [*in full daylight*] constituit. . . . 17. Facta huius curiae sunt liber et doctrina mundi, unde . . . docet et provocat omnes habentes ius patronatus in ecclesiis parochialibus, vel ob affectionem cognationis et carnis, vel propter obsequii remunerationem, vel ut complaceant potentibus, vel propter aliquid huiusmodi, tales . . . ad curam pastoralem provehere et sic oves Christi perdere.' The *curia*, therefore, is the source of the greatest evil in Christendom and deserves the greatest condemnation on the ground that 'causa mali magis [est] malo [mala: *edit.*] suo causato'.

[10] *Memorandum*, 6, p. 353, sketches this state of affairs with dramatic intensity. The emphasis on the smallness of Christendom—a theme which only began to penetrate the consciousness of the West with the appearance of the Mongols in the 1230s—is especially striking: 'Plurimam namque partem occupavit infidelitas . . . De parte vero dicta Christiana magnam partem separavit a Christo schisma. De parte autem residua, quae respectu duarum praenominatorum, admodum ut puto et parva et pauca, non modicam portionem separavit a Christo heretica pravitas. Quasi autem totalitatem residui concorporaverunt diabolo et a Christo separaverunt septem criminalia peccata.'

had the early expansion of the Church given way to this dismal tale of retreat and division? The answer was always the same: the decay of the pastoral office. In the early days, the abundance of true pastors, and the liberty they enjoyed to exercise their pastoral office, had led to the growth of the Church. In recent times, the abundance of evil pastors, and the stifling of pastoral power, had led to the contraction and division of the Church. Whether he looked at his own diocese or extended his view to the whole world, he saw the same cause everywhere at work producing the same effect. This homogeneity of all the parts was just what his scientific principles had taught him to expect: the same cause always produces the same effect, and the cause is always *within* the system of which the effects form part.[11]

I do not think that any earlier observer of the state of Christendom had ascribed its manifold corruptions to a single general cause. They had often satirized the venality of the papal *curia*, but only to work off a grievance or to impute moral blame to its members. They had often been eloquent about the bestialities of the Muslims, the perfidy of the Greeks, the vileness of heretics, and they had sometimes seen one or more of these as a danger to Christendom. And, more generally, they had very often seen the disorders of the present as a symptom of the impending end of the world. But Grosseteste alone looked for a single cause of general corruption at the heart of the whole system: 'What (he asked) is the prior and original cause, the *fons et origo*, of so great an evil?' This was his greatest application of scientific method to practical affairs. Here is his answer:

I speak with the most vehement fear and trembling, but I cannot keep silent. To get to the cause of so great an evil we must go to the source. It lies in this *curia*, not only in what it has *failed* to do in not having purged the world of abominations, as it is in duty bound to do, but even more in what it *has* done. In the full light of day, it has been responsible for handing over to eternal death many thousands of souls for whose salvation Christ endured a shameful death.[12]

He tells the *curia* that they are worse than those who crucified

---

[11] Cf. Grosseteste on Aristotle's *Physics* (ed. R. C. Dales, 1963, p. 3): 'Omne agens aliquo modo habet in se descriptum et formatum opus operandum'—words which were much commented on in the fourteenth century.

[12] *Memorandum*, 10, p. 355.

Christ. *They* had not known what they were doing, and would not have done it if they had known. But the *curia* knows what it is doing, and it has set itself up as a model for the whole world. It is, he says, the textbook for the world, provoking in others the destruction of souls, a contempt for eternity, and the glorification of transitory things. All events require causes greater than themselves, and the greatest events require the greatest causes. What greater event could there be than this general corruption of Christendom? What cause could be found for so great an evil as this? Only the greatest thing in Christendom—the papacy.

It was here that he found the greatest possible cause for the greatest possible corruption. In the throes of this discovery the words tumble out:

Above all, the most prodigious fact in the world is the perversion of Christ's representative on earth acting contrary to Christ in his principal operations. The papal see, the throne of God, the sun of the whole world . . . which should, like the sun, give light, life, nutrition, growth, preservation and beauty to the earth, has lost its proper functions, its *rationes causales*, the reason for its existence. It has been perverted and it has become a source of perdition and destruction. He who bears the *persona* of Christ has divested himself of this *persona* and taken that of his earthly relatives and of his own flesh and blood. Such a one is no longer the true possessor of Christ's throne, and if he receives universal obedience then indeed the last days of darkness are at hand, when the Son of Perdition will be revealed.[13]

Grosseteste drew back from this conclusion: 'Absit; absit', he says, 'Let it not be that this most sacred see and its occupant, whose commands receive universal obedience, should order anything contrary to the will of Christ.'[14] But then he takes up his theme again and presses resolutely on in a passage which ties together secular and sacred science, Aristotle's *Ethics* and the Bible:

Just as a ship must be commanded by a man who understands the art of navigation and not by the cabin boy, and an army by a general who understands the art of war and not by a saddle-maker, so the most divine and absolutely overriding art of saving souls must be given to those who understand the Gospel of Christ as set forth in the

[13] Ibid., 22, 25, 26 (pp. 359–63).
[14] Ibid., 27, p. 363.

Old and New Testaments, without the interference of those who understand only the subordinate arts of secular administration.[15]

Here we have the whole man packed into a few pages of passionate prose: his science, his biblicism, his merging of physical and spiritual reality, his freedom from laws and conventions, his impatience with established routines of government, his profound sense of pastoral responsibility. He ranges over everything from the smallest detail to the cosmic scene and at the end he returns to the source of all these reflections—the obstacles put in the way of bishops and priests in doing their pastoral duty, by privileges, exemptions, restrictions and legal processes of which the papal system of government is the source. It was as if the sun itself, with its life-giving function in the world, had erected an impenetrable barrier between its influence and the world which it was designed to serve. Until this barrier had been cleared away there was no hope for the world. The present state of affairs, unless corrected forthwith, foreshadowed the imminent appearance of Antichrist and the end of the world.[16]

III. THE POPE AND ANTICHRIST

There are two points which require a brief note before we leave this astonishing scene. The first concerns Grosseteste's essential orthodoxy. Comentators have often—indeed generally in recent years—attempted to normalize the thoughts expressed in his speech by pointing out the very wide liberty of criticism of the pope and curia which was compatible with obedience to the papacy. This is no doubt an important consideration which deserves attention. But Grosseteste was not simply attacking the political and family policies of Innocent IV, though these were very prominent in his thought. He was attacking a long historical development going back far into the past—a development which was responsible for the growing strength of Islam, for the schism between the Greek and Roman Churches, for the heresies which had been proliferating in the West for at least a hundred years; a development which had brought about

[15] Ibid., 33–4, pp. 365–6.
[16] Ibid., 25–6, pp. 361–2.

the use of parochial patronage and parochial revenues for military and other secular ends by rulers from the pope downwards. It was in the light of all this, and not simply of Innocent IV's policies, that he concluded that the virtue had gone out of the 'most sacred seat, the throne of God . . . the *principalissima sedes inter mortales*'.

There are ambiguities in Grosseteste's great speech which it would be wrong to exploit in one direction or another. Sometimes he speaks of a long-standing historical development; sometimes of the curia rather than the pope; sometimes of a situation which is not finally hopeless; sometimes of a situation in which obedience to a pope, who has assumed the mantle of his own flesh and blood or of the world, would be separation from Christ and the Church. General obedience to such a pope would announce the day of Antichrist. With such an array of possibilities, it is not easy to know where we stand. But the clear implication is that the true Church is on the very brink of having to make a decision of general disobedience to Innocent IV, and that the grounds for this decision have been building up for some long time under his predecessors also. Indeed, the inner logic of the argument would seem to point to some source of corruption in the remote past, such as Dante imagined the Donation of Constantine to have been, and which later Reformers attributed to the Hildebrandine papacy. When all allowances have been made for the frequent violence of Grosseteste's expression, it is hard to fit the substance of his speech into any normal pattern of orthodoxy. But then it is often hard to fit Grosseteste into any normal pattern. That is why later dissidents were able to claim him as one of themselves, while their opponents saw him as a pillar of orthodoxy.

The second point that needs to be noticed is that in his talk of the coming of Antichrist and the end of the world, Grosseteste was clearly influenced by apocalyptic expectations which were circulating very widely in Europe in the middle years of the century. In one way or another most of these expectations were derived from the prophecies of Joachim of Fiore which had been known in England since the begining of the thirteenth century. Grosseteste certainly knew about them, and some of the men who were closest to him, like Adam Marsh, were

deeply impressed by them.[17] Indeed, it is unlikely that anyone
was totally immune from belief or half-belief in the imminent
appearance of Antichrist. But, however far Grosseteste may
have gone along this road, there is one important difference
between his thinking and Joachim's. The foundations of Joachim's visions of catastrophe lay in the mysterious symbols of the
Book of Daniel and the Apocalypse. They were given chronological shape by calculations based on Daniel's 'four great
beasts', 'a time, two times, and half a time' and 'seventy weeks
of years', and the number 666 of the Apocalypse, and so on.[18]
From these indications, a scheme of persecutions of the Church
which would culminate in the appearance of Antichrist in or
around the yea 1260 became common property during the first
half of the thirteenth century.

There is not the slightest indication, even in his most heated
moments, that Grosseteste thought along these lines. It is,
indeed, surprising, given his intense biblicism and his interest
in mathematical and chronological problems, that he does not
seem to have indulged in speculations about the end of the
world based on the biblical prophecies which inspired Joachim.
His argument in 1250, though it pointed to the possibility of
an imminent end of the world, had quite different foundations.
It was based on his experience in his diocese, and on reflections
about the course of history with its evidence of the contamination of spiritual things by secular ambitions, not only in
his own small corner but throughout the Christian world. At

[17] At an unknown date, Adam Marsh sent him 'paucas particulas de variis expositionibus abbatis Joachim' which had been brought by a friar from the Continent.
From these, Adam wrote, the bishop would be able to judge whether the Last Days
were approaching; and he asked Grosseteste to have the book read to him in the
presence of secretaries and to return it after it had been copied (*Epistolae Adae de
Marisco*, pp. 146–7, in *Monumenta Franciscana*, ed. J. S. Brewer, RS, 1858). Further,
Hugh of Digne, the earliest Franciscan follower of Joachim, whom Grosseteste probably
met on his first visit to the papal *curia* at Lyons in 1245, told the chronicler Salimbene
in 1248 that among the four friends whom he loved most, he counted Robert Grosseteste 'one of the greatest clerks in the world, who translated John of Damascus, the
Testaments of the Twelve Patriarchs, and many other books' (*Chronica fratris Salimbene
de Adam*, ed. O. Holder-Egger, MGH, *Scriptores*, xxxii, 1905, p. 233). But, suggestive
though these passages are for the company Grosseteste kept, they tell us nothing about
his own response to Joachim's prophecies.

[18] Dan. 7: 3–7, 9: 24, 12: 7; Rev. 12: 14, 13: 18. For the whole subject of Joachim
and his influence in the thirteenth century and later, see M. E. Reeves, *The Influence of
Prophecy in the Later Middle Ages* (1969); see also Reeves and B. M. Hirsch-Reich, *The
Figurae of Joachim of Fiore* (1972).

first, he had thought that the contamination could be removed by visitations, rigid discipline and the strict exercise of episcopal oversight. But then he discovered that the law itself, and the source of the law, and the universal pastor of souls, were equally contaminated. So he came to see that the source of corruption was at the centre of the Christian Church, and that only reform there could bring reform elsewhere. From this it followed that, without this reform, an accelerating decay would soon bring about a total collapse and the rule of Antichrist.

By a different process, therefore, Grosseteste reached a conclusion which coincided with that of Joachim of Fiore. But, just as they differed in method, so their conclusions differed in quality. Joachim's conclusion was already foreseeen in the prophecy of Daniel: it marched from stage to stage with the inevitability of a divine plan. Grosseteste's conclusion, like the process which brought it about, was man-made. That was why he attached so much importance to his exposition at the papal court: he was explaining the nature of their actions and their inevitable consequences to the men who were responsible for their actions and might change. The apocalyptic conclusion was inevitable only so long as the cause remained unchanged. If the cause was removed—if, that is, the pope and cardinals listened to his warnings and reverted to their true pastoral role in the world—then the process of deterioration would be arrested, the steady advance of the Church's enemies would be reversed, and with the purification of the Church the expansion of the early centuries would come again.

Grosseteste's system was, therefore, like Joachim's, a world view; but it was founded, not on biblical prophecies, but on the scientific principles of experience, observation, and reflection. These principles had become clear to him in his scientific work and in studying the *Posterior Analytics*. From these sources he had learned to examine the phenomena which present themselves to the senses; to penetrate beneath the surface of events to the structure in which they had their origin; and then to look still deeper to the elemental particles which underlie the structure. This was the procedure he had followed in studying the Church: his experiences of frustration as a bishop had led him to penetrate the surface of events to the structure of secular interests, embracing pope and curia along with other magnates and officials, which kept pastoral care in chains; and, looking still deeper to the elemental particles of this structure, he found family and territorial interests in all their vast ramifications at the root of the matter. The analysis was clear; the remedy was not in doubt. The only question was whether the remedy would be adopted.

IV. GROSSETESTE'S DESCENT INTO DESPAIR

It is an awe-inspiring thought to contemplate Grosseteste at the moment when the reading of this tirade was completed. He had packed into it everything that his experience, his science, and his knowledge of the Bible could contribute towards resolving the greatest of all problems. He had prepared everything with the utmost care—the distribution of copies to the assembled cardinals, the long and solemn reading, his own presence as an old man of eighty. With every mark of respect and reluctant criticism, he had concluded with a devastating criticism of the curia as the source of all the evil of a radically corrupted Christendom. He must have waited with some anxiety to discover whether he had moved his hearers by his arguments, either to repent, or to take vengeance on their traducer.

We know nothing of what was said, if indeed anything was said. Popes and curia had listened to many attacks on them at one time or another, and they were aware of many other attacks made by absent moralists and satirists. It is unlikely that they had ever listened to an attack so comprehensive in its range or so original in its method. Thy must have noticed that this was no ordinary prophetic utterance claiming that the fatal year of the Beast was now at hand and that the moment had come when Antichrist would sit in the papal chair. What they had heard was either wild nonsense or a damning condemnation of themselves. It was not a message of inevitable doom, but a physician's diagnosis of a disease and a prediction of what would follow if steps were not taken to cure it. Grosseteste had written of the diseased heart of Christendom in the hope of repentance and reform. He left knowing that he had failed.

Whatever effect he might have had would in any event have been blunted by the need to get on with practical business.

Grosseteste had come to the papal court not only on his own affairs, but also as the leader of a deputation of English bishops protesting about the large payments demanded by the archbishop of Canterbury and others as they went round the countryside on papal business.[19] Grosseteste had mentioned this subject at the end of his great speech, and one cannot help thinking that it would have been more in keeping with the gravity of the occasion if he had omitted this small pin-prick. But, of course, his whole point was that the disease of Christendom showed itself in countless small iniquities, and he was always ready to step from the smallest incident to the largest conclusion and back again. A few days later, he had to appear again before the pope and cardinals to make a formal complaint on behalf of the English clergy about the exactions of their archbishop and perhaps to defend himself from a similar charge.[20] The descent from the lofty heights of his previous harangue to pettifogging complaints about archiepiscopal procurations was steep; and it may well have occasioned the pope's explosion reported by Matthew Paris: 'Oh you wretched Englishmen, always biting and robbing one another. How hard you work to satisfy your own cupidity, preventing your own men of religion from carrying out their duties of prayer and hospitality, to enrich others—and foreigners too as likely as not!'[21] This would have been a very stupid comment on Grosse-

[19] The only record of this protest which has survived is Grosseteste's dossier of documents relating to his visit to the *curia* in 1250. It is printed by Gieben, loc. cit., pp. 373-5 under the title *Conquestio cleri anglici*. Grosseteste refers to the grievance in *Memorandum*, paragraph 40, p. 368.

[20] Ibid., p. 373: 'post primo proposita paucis elapsis diebus'. It was on this occasion that Grosseteste gave his account of his own visitations (ibid. pp. 375-7). His point was that, though *he* had been careful not to impose any financial burden on the parishes he visited, he feared his successors, like the archbishop of Canterbury, would not be so forebearing unless the Holy See provided a remedy against the exactions of archbishops and bishops alike.

[21] Matthew Paris, *Chron. Maj.* v. 98. Matthew Paris's knowledge of the whole incident was remarkably sketchy. He knew nothing about Grosseteste's main speech nor about the complaint against the archbishop of Canterbury. He thought that the reason for Grosseteste's visit was to answer appeals against him (ibid., 97); and that, on being rebuffed, he stayed on simply to avoid giving the impression that he had achieved nothing. This ignorance seems to indicate that Grosseteste had kept, and continued to keep, his main purpose a secret. The two remarks of Innocent IV reported by Matthew Paris are meaningless in the context which he gives them; but in the context as we know it, they are pertinent and may have been remembered and reported by those who heard them.

teste's earlier speech, and it is always rejected as apocryphal. But as a comment on Grosseteste's intervention on behalf of the English bishops, it would be both witty and ironical.

To Grosseteste, however, the subject of his second speech was quite as important as the first, and he developed it with equal learning and independence, and at almost equal length: it presented the other side of the decline of Christendom.[22] His first speech had dealt with the obstacles to pastoral care, and he had conducted the argument in the spirit of a scientific enquiry into the root cause and fatal consequences of a widespread phenomenon. In it we are constantly reminded of his scientific work and the method of scientific generalization, which Aristotle's *Posterior Analytics* and *Physics* had helped him to define. His second speech was in a different mode. It was a philosophical enquiry into the principles of just government and the way in which the burden of its expense should be properly distributed. In this enquiry he was investigating one of the greatest problems of the later Middle Ages: how the growing cost of the ever increasing activities of government was to be fairly distributed, taking account of the good of the community and the needs of the ruler. On this subject—in addition, as always, to the Bible—Grosseteste's main inspiration came from Aristotle's *Ethics*. Translating this work, collecting its ancient commentaries, and supplementing them with his own annotations, had been his greatest learned enterprise in recent years. Probably it had been completed shortly before 1250.[23] Certainly Grosseteste's mind was full of it at Lyons in his thinking about the principles of government, the common good, and the rational use of law.

Superficially, all these matters were very far from the simple problems with which his second speech was concerned. His immediate concern was the excessive demands for expenses made by the archbishop of Canterbury, and probably in the view of his critics by Grosseteste himself, in the course of his visitations. There was a growing body of canon law on this subject, and to most of his hearers it must have seemed that it

[22] Gieben, 1971, 373-87.
[23] The most recent survey of Grosseteste's work on Aristotle's *Nicomachean Ethics* is in Mercken, 1973, 33*-66*. Quotations from the *Ethics* in his second speech are in Gieben, 1971, pp. 378, 386.

was a question best left to lawyers.[24] But, as always, Grosseteste
wanted to go behind the law and establish principles which
would reconcile the resources and rights of the governed with
the needs of government. His broad argument was that, instead
of relying on laws which could never take account of individual
circumstances—the relative wealth, for instance, of individual
sees—a new spirit was needed in determining these matters: a
spirit of equity and moderation rather than a too rigorous
insistence on legal rights. At this point, the *curia* must have
been astonished to be instructed on the difference between
ἐπιείκεια and ἀκριβοδίκαιος, between a spirit of equity and
concern for the general good, and a too precise standing on
one's rights in all circumstances. The lesson would not have
been made more palatable by Grosseteste's clear conviction
that the curia was addicted to the latter.[25]

It must be confessed that Grosseteste is imprecise on the ways
in which the virtue of moderation could be promoted. He could
only suggest that charges for visitations should not be increased
beyond what was customary; and he went to some pains to
describe the great increase of activity which he had been able
to initiate without increasing the charge to his flock. But he
feared for the future, and (as in his earlier speech) he thought
that the curia should set an example and reduce the possibility
of extortionate demands in future.

Practical measures could scarcely be expected from such a
harangue. As in his earlier speech, what Grosseteste pleaded
for was a change of heart at the centre of Christendom which
would spread down through all the parts of the Church. The
papal heart proved obdurate. But the speech displays a new
facet of his mind. In most of his actions and arguments as
bishop we have observed a tendency to excessive rigour in the
face of human frailties. In this last speech, though he is as
rigorous as ever in condemning the greed and worldliness which
were destroying the Church, he strikes a milder note in his plea
for moderation in the exercise of power. Aristotle's *Ethics* seems
to have given him a vocabulary for expressing the more urbane
side of his nature, which even the critics of his harshness re-

---

[24] *Corpus iuris Canonici*, ed. E. Friedberg, 1881, ii. 625–33, collects the contemporary
legal texts (*Decretalium Coll. Gregorii IX*, iii. xxxix, cc. 14–27).
[25] Gieben, p. 386; and cf. p. 380.

cognized in his social behaviour. The word and the nature of ἐπιείκεια made a strong appeal o him. One of his last notes on the section of the *Ethics* in which it appears runs as follows:

It is a word with many meanings. Inwardly, it expresses a quality which shows itself in thoughtfulness, grace, modesty and love of self-knowledge. Outwardly, it expresses moderation in applying the rules of positive law, and in softening the rigours of the law according to circumstances in unusual cases.[26]

These were the qualities which he urged the chief source of power in Christendom to exhibit. Infuriating though it must have been to listen to such instructions, the two speeches contain a panoramic view of the visionary and practical powers of his mind still in their full vigour.

On his return to England, Grosseteste knew he had failed in his greatest endeavour. All the scientific and philosophical learning, the experience and biblical pondering which had gone into his appeals had been brushed aside. But he did not give up. In order to save something from the wreckage—'hoping', as he wrote, 'that so great an effort should not be thought entirely wasted'—he sent a memorandum to his friends among the cardinals, setting out once more his general view of the papal office, and emphasizing the impossibility of his accepting for benefices men whom he thought unsuitable.[27] To Simon de Montfort, who was himself under attack for his oppressive rule in Gascony, he sent that part of his second speech which dealt with the difference between just rule and tyanny;[28] and he suggested that the two of them should combine in some great enterprise for the salvation of souls. We do not know the details, but they included an arduous journey, so he was perhaps think-

---

[26] The text of this note was printed by M. Grabmann, *Forschungen über die lateinischen Aristoteles Übersetzungen des xii. Jhts*, *BGPMA*, xvii, 1916, p. 252. For the manuscripts in which it occurs, see Mercken, loc. cit. and S. H. Thomson, 'The *Notule* of Grosseteste on the *Nicomachean Ethics*', *Proc. of the British Academy*, xix, 1934.

[27] This memorandum also is preserved only in Grosseteste's dossier of documents and printed by Gieben, loc. cit., pp. 387–93. The account given in the dossier of the circumstances in which the supplementary memorandum was written is confused, but the most likely interpretation seems to be that Grosseteste wrote it, and perhaps read it to the pope before he left, and sent it to the cardinals on his return 'ne tantus suae peregrinationis labor neglectus putaretur aut ab aliquibus incuriae traderetur' (p. 393).

[28] *Mon. Franciscana*, p. 110. I accept the identification made by Thomson, 1940, p. 145. The date is probably early 1251.

ing of some kind of Crusade and preaching mission.[29] In addition, he sent a copy of his new translation of Aristotle's *Ethics*, which had so greatly influenced his second speech on justice at the *curia*, to his Franciscan friend Hugh of Digne, whom he had perhaps met at Lyons.[30] In every possible way, therefore, he completed the work he had set out to do at the papal court and awaited the result.

Here matters rested for another two years. No one in England outside his immediate circle seems to have known anything about his speeches or their reception. For another hundred years, so far as we know, his words attracted no attention.[31] Evidently, therefore, neither Grosseteste nor any of his intimate friends spoke about the incident on their return to England. His appeal had fallen on deaf ears.

Then came the final crushing affront to all that he had believed in and worked for as bishop. Innocent IV sent letters addressed not to Grosseteste himself, whom he clearly now regarded as unmanageable, but to the papal agent in England and to the archdeacon of Canterbury, instructing them to put the pope's nephew in possession of a canonry and benefice in Lincoln, and declaring null and void in advance any attempt to grant his benefice to anyone else.[32] This was a direct chal-

[29] Ibid. p. 111: Adam Marsh writes to Grosseteste: 'Locutus est mihi comes Leycestriae super saluberrimo triumphalis magnificentiae proposito liberandis animis cordi vestro coelitus immisso . . . et amplectitur, ut video, ardenti promptitudine grandium conceptuum . . . (sed) non videt qualiter tanta difficultatum discrimina personaliter aggredi valeatis.' The language recalls Grosseteste's earlier proposal to the pope (*Ep.* no. 35: see above, p. 272; also *Ep.* no. 49, where he speaks of his desire to offer his life 'in ultimas Saracenorum regiones pro fide Christi et caritate inserendis et promovendis').

[30] *Mon. Franciscana*, p. 114. For the identification of Hugh de Berions with Hugh of Digne, see F. M. Powicke, 'Robert Grosseteste and the Nicomachean Ethics', *Proceedings of the British Academy*, xvi, 1930, 85–104.

[31] A collector of Grosseteste's sermons, rummaging as we may suppose among his literary remains after his death, included the *Memorandum* among the sermons (MS BL Royal 7 D. xv, ff. 28ᵛ–34), and another collector in the first half of the fourteenth century (MS Exeter College, Oxford, 21, ff. 117–33) included the greater part of the dossier in his collection. One copy of the *Memorandum* with some notes, made perhaps by one of his audience in 1250, survives in an independent tradition in a Paris MS BN lat. 10358. But Ranulf Higden, revising his Chronicle *c.*1340, was the first to mention the *Memorandum* in a confused form; then Wycliffe gave it full publicity.

[32] We owe the text of the letter to Matthew Paris, *Chron. Maj.* (*Additamenta*), vi. 229–31, where it appears with the note 'literae quae episcopum Lincolniensem Robertum ad iram provocaverunt'. Its date is 26 January 1253. The fact that it is addressed to the pope's agent and the archdeacon of Canterbury supports Matthew Paris's earlier statement that Grosseteste had been suspended from his episcopal functions by Inno-

lenge to Grosseteste in his own diocese, and he wrote a letter of protest to the pope's agent. In language similar to that which he had used in 1250, he declared: 'There is not and cannot be any sin so contrary to evangelical and apostolic doctrine, so hateful and detestable to Christ, or so deadly to the human race as the slaying of souls by defrauding them of pastoral care.'[33] Once more he listed the signs of the papal alliance with Lucifer and Antichrist. By being the cause of so great a sin and by killing the image of God in man, the pope had moved his seat still closer to the throne of the Prince of Darkness. Consequently, to obey the pope now would be to cut himself off from the body of Christ and to join the Prince of Darkness. What he had envisaged as a possibility in his speech of 1250 was now a proximate reality.

V. GROSSETESTE'S LAST WORDS

Grosseteste's life was now drawing to an end and we come to his last great scene: his death-bed. It is the main set-piece in Matthew Paris's account of Grosseteste. It has been received with considerable scepticism by modern historians, and it must be treated with caution. At the same time, before we ascribe its highly coloured details to Matthew Paris's journalistic exaggerations, we may reasonably ask once again whether his critics are not themselves moved by a normalizing interpretation of Grosseteste which may be misleading. The questions which can properly be asked are these. First, is there evidence that Matthew Paris systematically misrepresented Grosseteste's words and actions? Second, did Matthew Paris have a trustworthy source? And third, are the words which he reports in this scene consistent with other words known to have been written or spoken by Grosseteste?

cent IV in Lent 1251 for his refusal to institute an earlier Italian nominee of the pope on the grounds of his ignorance of English (*Chron. Maj.* v. 227). Other sources, notably the Lanercost chronicle, say that he was excommunicated. But in view of Matthew Paris's emphatic denial, this is unlikely. Suspension was a disciplinary measure which had been taken even against Stephen Langton, who had hastened to make his peace with the pope. But we know nothing about the scope or duration of Grosseteste's suspension.

[33] *Ep.* no. 128. The letter got into the main chronicles of the day: *Chron. Maj.* v. 389–92, with the note 'optima epistola episcopi Lincolniensis R.'; also in Burton Annals (*Ann. Mon.* i. 311–13); and hence into many others.

As for the first of these questions, I have already given some reasons for thinking that Matthew Paris's account of Grosseteste was a good deal more balanced and thoughtful than has often been supposed. On the second question, the source was as good as could be imagined: Matthew Paris got his information from Grosseteste's physician and friend of twenty years' standing, the Dominican friar John of St Giles who attended him in his last illness. The third question is the most important and can only be answered by considering what Grosseteste is reported to have said, and comparing it with his other utterances.

In his reported words, Grosseteste began by asserting that it was *heresy* for the friars not to denounce the sins of the rich. He then asked John of St Giles to give him a definition of heresy. When he hesitated, Grosseteste himself provided one: 'Heresy', he said, 'in its Greek etymology means "choice": it is a choice made for human ends, contrary to Holy Scripture, openly declared, and stubbornly maintained.' He then went on to apply his definition to the papal *curia* and to the pope himself: 'To give the care of souls to anyone chosen for human ends, whether of family or politics, is contrary to Holy Scripture; to announce this choice openly in a formal document, and to defend this choice by suspension, excommunication or war against those who resist, is to fulfil all the conditions of heresy.' Every faithful believer, he continued, is obliged to oppose such a heretic so far as he can; and whoever does not do so must be judged an accomplice, as St Gregory declares. According to Matthew Paris, Grosseteste applied his definition of heresy first to the friars who were silent about the sins of the rich; but it was equally, and more immediately, applicable to the pope and justified his own recent action in rejecting the papal nomination of his nephew to a benefice.[34]

Of course, this was not the common view of the nature of heresy. The great contemporary canonist, Henry of Susa, the cardinal bishop of Ostia, whom lawyers knew as Hostiensis, gave a very different account in his encyclopaedia of canon law. His long article on the subject, replete with quotations from all the best authorities, led to the conclusion that the central meaning of heresy was deviation from the articles of

[34] *Chron. Maj.* v. 401-2.

faith of the Catholic Church.[35] This undoubtedly reflected the main trend of scholastic thought, with its strong emphasis on doctrinal conformity as the essential test of orthodoxy. If Matthew Paris is right, Grosseteste's emphasis diverged from that of his scholastic contemporaries. He was certainly not lax in his enforcement of the doctrinal tenets of the Church; but he saw secular motives and secular ambition as the real threat to the Church, and the cause of the doctrinal heresies by which the Church was torn apart. He had failed to persuade the papal curia of this and his suspension, as a prelude to foisting a nephew of the pope into a cure of souls within his own diocese was the measure of his failure. He concluded that the pope, unless he desisted, was worthy of eternal death, for [he added] 'as the Apostle says, "Not only those who do such things, but those who consent to their being done, are worthy of death." ' 'Indeed,' he concluded, with a rare reference to canon law, 'canon law itself allows that heresy is a crime for which a pope can be put on trial.'[36]

It can never be completely established that these words were substantially those that Grosseteste used, but they are all fore-shadowed in his speech of 1250 and his letter of 1253. Certainly, the precise identification of the misuse of papal power with heresy is new; but in 1250 he had said that evil pastors are heretics, and he had identified the *curia* as the source of this evil.[37] Since 1250, the pope had shown himself, despite Grosse-teste's solemn and deferential warnings, to be the worst of the lot in nullifying the power of the bishop in order to thrust an unworthy nephew into a canonry in Grosseteste's own cath-edral. So it was not only the papal curia which was the root cause of all the evils in Christendom which were leading to the

[35] Hostiensis, *Aurea Summa*, ed. Venice, 1609, Bk. 5, cols. 1528–42, *De hereticis*: *largo sumpto* the word has a wide range of meanings, but *stricto modo* a heretic is one 'qui aliter sentit de articulis fidei quam Romana ecclesia'.

[36] *Chron. Maj.* v. 402.

[37] *Memorandum*, paragraph 9, pp. 354–5: 'Cumque pastorum conversatio gregis sit liber, doctrina, et instructio, ipsi sunt evidenter magistri malorum omnium. Et quo-modo non tunc heretici, maxime cum verbum operis efficacius suadeat verbo oris?' Cf. also 20, p. 358: 'opus curae pastoralis consistit . . . in veraci doctrina veritatis vitae.' The equation *conversatio pastorum* = *doctrina gregis* is the foundation of Grosseteste's pastoral theology, as also of his diagnosis of the Church's ills. It is also closely linked with his doctrine, derived from Augustine, that to know is to love: 'nullus novit bonum nisi amaverit'. (Marginal note in BL MS Royal 5 D x, f. 50[v] with Grosseteste's symbols and notes on Augustine's *De LXXXIII Quaestionibus*).

final catastrophe of Antichrist and the end of the world; it was the pope himself. The case against him seemed to be complete.

Most of the remainder of the conversation of these last days follows the same line of thought. In 1250, he had said that evil pastors who assumed the *persona* of Christ without preaching the Gospel of Christ—even if they did not add other evils to their score—were antichrists; he had added that the curia was the *causa, fons et origo* of this evil; that obedience to it was separation from Christ; and that, in these circumstances, the revelation of the Son of Perdition was at hand.[38] In 1253, he went a step further and asked whether the pope who persisted in the destruction of souls whom Christ had come to save could not properly be called Antichrist himself.[39] Once more he went over all the details of the obstacles he had met in carrying out his episcopal duties: the pope's support for Christian usurers, worse even than Jews; the pope's sale of indulgences for the Crusade; his conferring of benefices on the unworthy; his collusion with the king in the appointment of worldly bishops. Filled with indignation at these betrayals, he broke into tears, sighs and lamentations, and died uttering his final prophetic words: 'The Church will not be freed from servitude except by the edge of a bloody sword. What we have already suffered is little in comparison with what is still to come—and that shortly, within the next three years.'[40]

This final prediction is puzzling. In 1250 Grosseteste had seen that the day of Antichrist was at hand and could only be averted by the reform of the curia. Since then, the scene had darkened. The pope had shown that he was personally responsible for the depravities that Grosseteste had described. The pope seemed more than ever to have identified himself with Antichrist. So we might have expected that his prediction of the end of the world would have sharpened. And yet, his last prediction, if we can trust Matthew Paris's report, was *relatively* mild. It was not a prediction of the end of the world, but of imminent violence, bloodshed and tribulation which would free

---

[38] *Memorandum*, paragraphs 7, 10, 26, pp. 353–4, 355, 362–3.

[39] *Chron. Maj.* v. 402: 'suspirans ait, "Christus venit in mundo ut animas lucraretur"; ergo si quis animas perdere non formidet, nonne Antichristus merito est dicendus?'

[40] 'Nec liberabitur ecclesia ab Aegyptiae servitute nisi in ore gladii cruentandi; sed haec profecto levia; sed in brevi, scilicet hoc triennio, ventura sunt graviora.' *Chron. Maj.* v. 407.

the Church from servitude. Grosseteste seems to have shrunk
from a full-scale apocalyptic statement. Perhaps, despite his
violence of language and imagery, and despite his cosmic anx-
ieties, he was held back from predicting the final catastrophe
by some practical sense of the limits of his knowledge. What he
certainly knew was that he had failed to achieve the reform for
which he had fought during his years as bishop and for which
he had argued so dramatically at Lyons in 1250. It had been his
fate in all things to seek a living unity, and to find everywhere
irremediable decay and destruction.

12

Grosseteste's Place in History

At his death, Grosseteste had indeed failed, and he had failed more comprehensively than he knew. As a man of action, he had set himself against the system of legal compromises on which papal government was based, and the system had been too strong for him. As a scientific observer of causes and predictor of consequences, he had come to believe that the end of the world, or at least a decisive eruption of violence that would change the world, was at hand, and the world continued unchanged. As a theologian he had resisted contemporary tendencies to equate orthodoxy with doctrinal definitions and to dilute the unique authority of the Bible with the authority of the *Sentences*. Yet doctrinal definitions of orthodoxy became increasingly minute, and even before his death the Oxford friars of all people had succumbed to the allurements of scholastic procedures. His name was revered, but his influence on the main stream of even Franciscan theology was small.[1]

The meagreness of his influence even in Oxford becomes very conspicuous when we get to Duns Scotus. Scotus had access to all Grosseteste's literary remains, and it is clear that he had looked at them with care but without admiration. He quoted from Grosseteste's commentary on the *Posterior Analytics*, which was the most widely quoted of all his works; also from his *Hexaëmeron* and *Dicta* and from his notes on the *Ethics* and his translations of Ps.-Denys, and from other notes, sermons and memoranda preserved in the Franciscan library. These quotations are widely distributed in his works, but they are seldom important. They formed no part of the structure of Scotus's thought. Grosseteste pointed towards an integration of science and theology, and of Greek and Latin thought, on generous lines; Scotus initiated a new stage of scholastic refinement.

---

[1] On this subject, see the forthcoming study of Fr. Peter Raedts SJ, *Richard Rufus of Cornwall and the Tradition of Oxford Theology*.

It was implicit in Grosseteste's scientific method that he began with individual cases and worked outwards to general rules. He found it difficult to know when to stop, whether in mere length of exposition or in the ramifications of his arguments. We have noticed a remarkable example of this habit in his eighty-page letter to the canons of Lincoln expounding scriptural passages and scientific analogies bearing on his right of visitation. Much of what he wrote has a similar tendency, though seldom given such unbridled scope. He brushed aside all petty or intermediate considerations to reach fundamental conclusions. But fundamental conclusions were apt to elude definition and to end inconclusively. Consequently, Grosseteste's writings contain a treasury of arguments and insights which could be used for purposes that he would not have approved. He was an opener-up of new prospects, rather than a definer of the state of the question; and he often reopened questions which had seemed to be solved, and ended without solving them. Scotus shut down the lid rather sharply on one of the prospects to which Grosseteste had devoted much of his later energies—the reintegration of Greek and Latin theology.[2] In this area a new rigidity had set in, and when Greek again began to absorb the energy of men of Grosseteste's stature, the inspiration was widely different from his—more literary, more 'humane', less ecclesiastical, less theological.

We may gather from this that Grosseteste's place in history is not to be found in continuity of influence. Even his scientific work does not seem to have been a major stimulus to the Oxford scientists of the fourteenth century. He was never forgotten, and his commentary on the *Posterior Analytics* was a commonly quoted book in the faculty of Arts; but he does not appear to have been recognized as a conspicuous or coherent influence in the major developments of the period before 1350.

What mainly kept an interest in his thoughts alive was the bequest of his books and notes to the Franciscan library in Oxford. This bequest was the most successsful practical decision he ever took. Instead of mouldering in a forgotten corner of Lincoln cathedral library, the records of his thought were lodged at the centre of English intellectual activity, looked at with curiosity, and with occasional moments of deeper interest,

[2] See above, pp. 231-2.

by a long succession of Oxford scholars. But it was not until
Wycliffe saw his works in the 1360s that they came to the notice
of a thoroughly receptive mind.

I. WYCLIFFE'S DISCOVERY OF GROSSETESTE

Wycliffe found Grosseteste's thought stimulating, perhaps even
inflammatory, as no one had done since Roger Bacon. But for
different reasons. Bacon had found inspiration in Grosseteste's
scientific observations and method, in his translations from
Greek, and in his programme of study which he identified with
his own. Like Bacon, Wycliffe also saw his own reflection in
Grosseteste's works, but the image was quite different. He saw
successively a philosopher, theologian, reformer and persecuted
Christian in a hostile world, with whom at every stage he
could identify himself: a much more complicated image than
Bacon's—in some ways truer, in others more distorted; an image based on a much closer study of Grosseteste's writings, but
in circumstances widely different from those in which they were
written.

Wycliffe's earliest study of Grosseteste's works belongs to the
time when he was lecturing on logic from about 1361 to 1370.
Like most lecturers on logic, he knew Grosseteste's commentary
on the *Posterior Analytics*, and went on from this to study his
incomplete commentary on Aristotle's *Physics*. He evidently
liked what he found in these works because he always quoted
them in support of views which he favoured—the reality of
universals, the apprehension of a continuum as a series of points
without magnitude, the incorruptibility of heavenly bodies, the
possibility of geometry without sense data, and the existence of
a primary material essence of the universe 'which *Lincolniensis*
calls light'.[3] All these references show that Wycliffe felt a close
affinity to Grosseteste before he became a theologian. Already
he placed him in the roll of great names of the past: 'those more
subtle thinkers like Pythagoras, Democritus, Plato, Epicurus,
and, among the moderns, *Lincolniensis* and others'.[4] Naturally,

---

[3] *De Logica*, ii. 32–3; iii. 2–3, 35, 109, 119.
[4] *De Logica*, iii. 19. The third part of the *Logica* has sometimes been dated late in
Wycliffe's career because of a remark (iii. 183) which might indicate 1383 as the date
of its composition; but against this is the evidence (iii. 217) that he was not yet a
theologian, and the suggestion of a late date has now been generally abandoned.

Wycliffe counted himself among the 'others'; so the line of descent ran from Pythagoras to Wycliffe, with Grosseteste as the only modern link in a line coming down from a legendary antiquity.

Even more important than his points of agreement with Grosseteste was the similarity of temperament which he discovered. Like Grosseteste, Wycliffe was not interested in going over again in greater detail the points which had already been covered by his near contemporaries. He struck out in a new direction: 'I have been moved', he wrote, 'by friends of God's law to write a treatise setting forth the logic of Holy Scripture.'[5] He was still a Master of Arts when he wrote these words, and he left the deeper questions of the biblical text to theologians;[6] but he was stretching out beyond the ordinary limits of the arts course, a lonely voice, supported by choice spirits of the past. He needed their support—and he would need it increasingly in the course of time. He asked his readers not to deride what he wrote, though he knew that it differed from earlier authorities and undermined many opinions and imaginings of the moderns: 'Reason must guide me, for it was reason which led Aristotle, Plato, Parmenides and Democritus to the truths which they discovered.'[7] This sentence was written when Aristotle was still a name to be mentioned with favour, and perhaps before he had discovered his close affinity with Grosseteste. But he was beginning to single out *Lincolniensis* and to find in him a kindred spirit before he had finished his *Logic*.

Wycliffe did not become a fully fledged Doctor of Theology until 1372/3 when he was about forty years old. But for several years before this date, his writings were becoming increasingly theological in content, and as his interests widened the range of his quotations from Grosseteste became more extended. He began to quote Grosseteste's treatises on Truth and Free Will, his *Dicta*, his *Hexaëmeron*, and the spurious (as I think) *De Generatione Stellarum*. In all these works he found his own views expressed: he agreed that the existence of Truth implied the existence of God, and that the Incarnation would have happened if Man had never sinned. He approved Grosseteste's

[5] *De Logica, Proemium*, p. 1.
[6] Ibid., iii. 217.
[7] Ibid., iii. 132.

sympathy for the Greeks and his tolerance of differing formulations of the same theological truth :

> Would that modern writers would pay more attention to the writings
> and opinions of this good man, whose intention was to reconcile
> the ancient doctors of the Church, gathering together their Catholic
> opinions and expounding them in a favourable sense, rather than
> attacking dead men by forcing them into equivocal positions, so that
> their writings may be trampled on and those of their critics glorified,
> as is the odious fashion of too many nowadays.[8]

On every issue, and generally in contrast to most recent writers,
Grosseteste belonged to the right tradition: to the tradition of
Augustine and Anselm in thinking that Truth was inseparable
from God; to the tradition of Augustine, Anselm and Richard
of St Victor, in thinking that the doctrine of the Trinity could
be proved from the analogies of Nature.[9]

This community of thought, which grew in scope as he read
more widely in Grosseteste's works, was well established by the
time Wycliffe started lecturing in theology, and it continued as
he extended his quotations to Grosseteste's *De Cessatione Legalium* and *De Decem Mandatis*, to the whole body of his surviving
letters and sermons, and to his comments on the Psalms and
Epistle to the Galatians. Most important of all, by the mid-
1370s, he began to quote the accounts of Grosseteste's life in
the chronicles of Ranulf Higden and Matthew Paris, and he
studied the documents relating to his visit to the papal court in
1250. They had an explosive effect on his image of Grosseteste.

It has often been remarked that Wycliffe's treatise *On Civil
Government*, which is now generally dated 1376, marked a
turning-point in his life. The vigorous, original, self-confident,
but still wholly orthodox theologian of earlier years began to
emerge as an increasingly violent critic of the papacy, the religious orders, the ecclesiastical hierarchy, the negligent clergy,
and finally of the Eucharistic doctrine as defined in 1215. What
has not, I think, been remarked is that this change was accompanied by the earliest quotations from Matthew Paris and

---

[8] *Tractatus de Trinitate*, ed. A. du Pont Breck (1962), pp. 144–5.

[9] Ibid. p. 2. In addition to the passages quoted above, the most important references
to Grosseteste in Wycliffe's early works are *De Actibus Animae* in *Misc. Philosophica*, i.
96, 171, 180; *De Ente*, 7–8, 104, 313; *Tract. de Trinitate*, 15, 41, 45, 61–2, 174; *De
Benedicta Incarnatione*, 88, 96, 128, 177 (and cf. 79).

from Grosseteste's speech to the curia in 1250. Now, for the first time, Wycliffe saw Grosseteste, not only as a congenial philosopher and theologian, but as an uncanonized and unjustly excommunicated saint, the critic of the papacy, the advocate of the pastoral office of the clergy, the denouncer of unworthy priests and presentations. On all the subjects which became the leading themes of his later years, he was able to find something in Grosseteste which confirmed, or at least encouraged, him in his views: on heresy, on the primacy of Scripture, on errant monks, on the true functions of the pope, cardinals and bishops, and on the papacy as the cause of the decline of Christendom.[10] From 1376 till his death in 1384 Wycliffe claimed Grosseteste's support at every step: he was the 'archidoctor', the saint, the catholic theologian, and in his *Trialogus* even more emphatically than in his *Logic*, he gave Grosseteste his place as the modern representative of the great tradition going back to the remote past:

Democritus, Plato, Augustine and *Lincolniensis* were far more distinguished philosophers, and more sublime in the metaphysical sciences, than Aristotle.[11]

But, after all, we may ask, how important was Grosseteste in Wycliffe's development? And was Wycliffe justified in the use he made of him?

On the first question, Grosseteste was clearly not an influence with anything like the same importance as Augustine or even Anselm in shaping his theological system. And we can never know whether the discovery of Grosseteste's final attacks on papal policy helped to propel Wycliffe along a similar course,

[10] For the references to Grosseteste on these subjects in *De Civili Dominio*, see i. 308-9, 374, 457, on unjust excommunication; i. 318, 341; ii. 112, on tithes, unworthy priests, and presentations; i. 384-94, 457, on the limits to obedience to the pope; ii. 17, 395, on the true functions of pope, cardinals and bishops; i. 396-7 on Holy Scripture; ii. 19-20 on errant monks; i. 31, 341; ii. 24-5, 124, 210, 263; iv. 395, 397, on the responsibility of the laity for correcting abuses; ii. 58, on heresy; ii. 61, on the cause of the decline of Christendom. On heresy, it would seem that, in addition to the death-bed talk reported by Matthew Paris, Wycliffe had seen a treatise of Grosseteste which has not survived: 'Docet Lincolniensis in quodam libello speciali istius materie quod heresis est dogma falsum Scripture Sacre contrarium pertinaciter defensatum . . . et istum sensum dicit Lincolniensis se extraxisse a Grecorum sententiis, et concordant Latini catholici.' *De Civili Dominio*, ii. 58-9.

[11] *Trialogus*, 83. The epithet 'Archidoctor' is used in connection with Grosseteste's refusal of obedience to the pope (*De Officio Regis*, 64).

or simply lent support to a line he was already beginning to take. But we can be sure that this support was very important. Like all rebels Wycliffe felt his isolation and needed the past to compensate for the hostility of the present. Grosseteste was his nearest support in time, in place, and in circumstances—in Oxford, an Englishman, and persecuted by the pope. Wycliffe had earlier discovered an unfolding congruity of view in philosophy and theology. Now he discovered that they thought alike on the state of Christendom and the source of its corruptions in the papacy. These similarities help to explain the value he attached to Grosseteste's support, and his disappointment when he failed to find it. Wycliffe was not quite uncritical of his heroic predecessor. He blamed the fulsome terms of Grosseteste's initial letter to Gregory IX, and thought that his later tribulations were perhaps a divine punishment for his frailty.[12] And, though he believed that Grosseteste's own philosophical principles required him to take the same view of the Eucharist as he did, he had to admit that he had been ambiguous.[13] Wycliffe's recognition of these blemishes shows that his critical sense did not desert him in reading Grosseteste but it may also suggest that he was dishonest in claiming Grosseteste's support for statements which went far beyond anything that Grosseteste intended. As we shall see, Wycliffe's enemies were quick to make this allegation. Is it justified?

Whatever the right answer may be, it cannot be simple. Wycliffe's quotations were often partial, and he sometimes quoted from an uncertain memory of what he had read. I do not think he was exceptional in this regard: and he had the additional difficulty of working with a huge, unsorted mass of material. Besides, by the mid 1370s he was bristling with contentious opinions, anxious to see them anticipated in Grosseteste's words, and liable to see substantial agreement in vague uncertainties. In nearly every case, Wycliffe pressed

[12] *De Potestate Papae*, 248–56, 261: this mild criticism occurs in the context of a long account of Grosseteste's view of papal power drawn from several different sources, mainly Grosseteste's letters.

[13] For Wycliffe's account of Grosseteste's view of the Eucharist, see *De Apostasia*, 62–4, 181, 192–3, 216, 227, 245; *Trialogus*, 265. It is in the last of these passages that Wycliffe attempts to explain Grosseteste's phrase with regard to the Eucharist, 'accidens forte est sine subiecto'. The explanation is tortuous, but he was surely right in thinking that Grosseteste's expression was ambiguous in speaking of a clearly defined doctrine.

Grosseteste further and in a different direction than Grosseteste intended. But this also would be true of very many *bona fide* quotations in scholastic debates. In every scholastic exercise, ancient sources were quoted in contexts unforeseen by their authors to support conclusions which were certainly not intended. In these circumstances, the most we can do is to draw a distinction between 'legitimate' extensions of Grosseteste's arguments, in the sense that they could reasonably be held to be implicit in Grosseteste's words, and 'illegitimate' extensions, which are clear distortions.

We can find an example of the first of these tendencies in the way in which Wycliffe developed the argument of Grosseteste's great speech of 1250. Grosseteste had argued that the weaknesses of western Christendom and the strength of its enemies were caused by the political ambitions of the papacy, which had brought about the neglect of pastoral care at all levels in the Church. This was a significant enlargement of the common criticism of the papal curia, and Wycliffe accepted it gladly. But there was a gap in the argument: it is not evident why the worldliness of the papacy, or the neglect of pastoral care arising from it, should be a *cause* of European weakness. Indeed, the very opposite is what we might have expected. No doubt the great political popes of the thirteenth century looked on their military and political manoeuvres as undesirable in themselves, but as a necessary protection against disorders which would have weakened the collective strength of Christendom. Grosseteste never faced this possibility: he simply observed that Christendom had never grown so fast as when it was weakest from a worldly point of view, and most dedicated to pastoral work. The mechanics of politics did not interest him. He simply trusted in the efficacy of the Spirit in frustrating the designs of the flesh.

Wycliffe filled this argumentative gap, not systematically but effectively, by observing that the worldly power of the papacy had weakened the Church by causing internal dissensions. For instance, the papal claims to supremacy over Alexandria, Antioch, Jerusalem, and Constantinople had turned the Christians of these regions against the western Church. Moreover, the secularization of a power which should have been spiritual had given Christianity the same legalistic characteristics as Islam, without giving it the conviction or simplicity of Islam. The multiplication of laws, which had their origin in the desire to dominate, made Christianity less intelligible to ordinary Christian people than Islam to ordinary Muslims. The pride of popes and prelates caused ordinary Christians to fall away from the Church in disgust, whereas the poverty and suffering of Christ and the Apostles had drawn people to it in sympathy. These remarks, scattered throughout Wycliffe's works, show an acute political intelligence at work. Wycliffe shared the view which Grosseteste had put forward in 1250, and instinctively he filled the gaps that Grosseteste had left in the argument.[14] Wycliffe saw that Christendom had become weak by trying to be strong in the way that Islam was strong; and it could never beat Islam at that game, because worldly strength, which lay at the heart of Islam, was a perversion of Christianity. With a new emphasis, and with fuller support from intermediate causes, he was able to write, 'I make bold to say that infidelity will grow until the clergy returns to the poverty of Jesus Christ: as Aristotle says in his fourth book of his *Meteors*, "Opposites are resolved by their opposites,"[15] that is to say, the weaknesses caused by wealth and pride will be cured by poverty and humility.'[16] This was a wholly Grossetestean argument both in spirit and expression, and it correctly interpreted and enlarged the point he had made, with the addition of a political insight that Grosseteste lacked.

But alongside these legitimate elaborations of Grosseteste's argument, there are also passages in Wycliffe's *Civil Lordship* where he quoted Grosseteste with approval, and then claimed or implied his support for a further step which Grosseteste did not take. Examples of this 'illegitimate' in-filling became more numerous as Wycliffe branched out in new directions. It may be said in defence of Wycliffe that Grosseteste's open-ended methods of argument—his invitations to readers to make their

---

[14] The various ways in which the avarice, self-seeking, legal chicanery, over-elaboration of ceremonies and laws, and temporal ambitions of the papacy and clergy had caused the weaknesses and divisions in Christendom are clarified by Wycliffe in his *De Ecclesia*, p. 517; *De Blasphemia*, pp. 48, 74, 84, 275; *De Potestate Papae*, 110, 232–3; *Opus Evangelicum*, i. 19, 177; *De Officio Regis*, 63, 129, 278; *Dialogus* (*Speculum ecclesiae militantis*), 91; *De Christo et suo Adversario Antichristo* (*Polemical works*, ii. 672); *Ad Argumenta emuli veritatis* (*Opera minora*, p. 290).

[15] *Meteorologica*, iv. 6 (383[b] 15).

[16] *De Veritate Sacrae Scripturae*, pp. 366–7.

own additions, his disclaiming completeness, and his tentative conclusions—often make it uncertain how far, or in which direction, he would himself have gone. Besides, Wycliffe did not have the possibilities of easy reference and comparison, which would have given him an overall view of Grosseteste's position and have warned him how widely Grosseteste would have differed from his final position. But it is also likely that he did not want to know: he saw Grosseteste as the solitary upholder of his own views in recent time, and he had to hold onto him.

Wycliffe has left many examples of his going beyond anything that Grosseteste could have intended while invoking his name. For instance, he gladly accepted Grosseteste's statement that Christ is the whole subject-matter of theology, giving theology its unity and making it a genuine science. He elaborated the various kinds of unity which Christ supplied: unity with the Father, unity of God and Man, unity with all believers, unity of physical and spiritual. All these positions could reasonably be drawn from Grosseteste; but when he concludes that 'it follows that every creature in its intelligible being is God', he has left Grosseteste far behind. It would be wrong to think that there is any malign misrepresentaton here: it is only the free and discursive development of an idea found in a favourite author.[17]

Perhaps the development was not always innocent. On the sacredness of tithes, he followed Grosseteste in deriving their sanctity both from the Bible and from the mathematical perfection of the number ten, which embraces all the constituent elements of the universe. Like Grosseteste and other numerical symbolists, Wycliffe believed that the all-embracing perfection of the number ten reflected its fundamental role in the created universe. So far, so good. But then Wycliffe took the further step. He argued that, just because the institution of tithes in human affairs had the same fundamental role as the number ten in the universe, their regulation was not a matter for ecclesiastical jurisdiction alone. Consequently, their misuse by

---

[17] There are two passages in *De Dominio Divino*, pp. 42-3, 198, in which Wycliffe elaborated this theme, quoting Grosseteste's *Hexaëmeron* (i. 1-3, pp. 49-50). Wycliffe gives a wrong reference to c. 7; and what he calls a *contention* of Grosseteste is in reality a report of a view which Grosseteste does not explicitly accept, though his later remarks are favourable. There are many differences in detail, but no more than we might expect in a passage which Wycliffe is clearly quoting from memory.

delinquent clerks justified their seizure by the royal power responsible for the good order of the world. The logical consistency of this argument deserves to be recognized. But it depends on the view that secular government, which chronologically is prior to ecclesiastical government, is also prior in nature and divine purpose. Grosseteste's letters are full of his denial of this principle, and Wycliffe could scarcely have failed to recognize this. He implicated Grosseteste in this position by association rather than direct assertion, but his followers did not notice the subtle difference.[18]

We enter here the slippery ground where genuine agreement and legitimate development melt away into support by association or implication. Once this process has begun there is no end to the possibilities of misrepresentation. Grosseteste did not support Wycliffe's views on the right of the laity to take over and administer ecclesiastical revenues; or on the lack of necessity for confession to a priest; or on the priesthood of all believers; or on the Eucharist. But he provided arguments or suggested doubts which allowed Wycliffe to use his name on all these issues.[19]

Yet when all deductions have been made, there is still a substantial area in which Wycliffe could legitimately claim Grosseteste's support: on the sufficiency of the Bible; on the primacy of pastoral care; on the essential place of preaching in the work of the church; on the connection between the vices of the papacy and the decline of pastoral care, the rise of Islam, the divisions within the Church; on the necessity for the Incarnation to complete the work of Creation; on the merits of the Greeks; on the need for new translations from Greek. As he turned from one of these subjects to another, he found that Grosseteste had been there before him.

Wycliffe could not have known—what is so evident to us— how different he was from Grosseteste in personality, in aims, and in circumstances. The differences leap at once to the historical eye, and they show themselves in many ways. For instance, we have noticed some of the lists of great names of

[18] *De Civili Dominio*, pp. 317–58: the important citations of Grosseteste's *De Luce* and Comments on Ps. 4: 16–17 are on pp. 318 and 341.

[19] On confession and the priesthood of all believers, see Wycliffe's discussion of Grosseteste's views in *De Blasphemia*, 145–8, quoting *Dictum* 108; and *Opera Minora*, 177–8, quoting *Dictum* 3. On the Eucharist, see above, n. 13

the past with which Wycliffe fortified his position, and the high place which Grosseteste occupied in these lists. But, far from proving their similarity, these lists of names are an indication of an important difference, which may be summed up by saying that Wycliffe, with all his violence, which is not un-characteristic of Grosseteste, was a much more scholastic writer than Grosseteste. He was more dependent on authorities, more concerned with organization, more optimistic about the possi-bility of practical solutions. Where Grosseteste was a visionary who could see the end more clearly than the steps towards it, Wycliffe was fertile in expedients. Both were men of remarkable force and originality; both were willing to reopen questions which others regarded as settled; both were dangerous to es-tablished institutions. But they were all of these thing in dif-ferent ways. Grosseteste wanted a change of heart; Wycliffe a change of management. Grosseteste expected the end of the world to follow if the papacy persisted in its corruptions; Wycliffe thought that these corruptions were an invitation to the secular ruler to enlarge his power. Wycliffe was more reck-less than Grosseteste; but recklessness too is a symptom of an optimism which had no place in Grosseteste's character.

Wycliffe was much shriller than Grosseteste. This has not endeared him to modern scholars who find shrillness more disturbing than their predecessors did. By contrast Grosseteste was never shrill: the fierceness of his indignation, and the ex-tremism of his conclusions, came from a more capacious soul than Wycliffe's. Wycliffe in recent days has had the misfortune of appealing neither to lovers of ancient order, nor to advocates of social revolution: so he is no one's hero in the modern world. Grosseteste is everyone's, partly because his ambiguities suggest a richer variety of possibilities, partly because he is just more likeable. Nevertheless, Wycliffe was the first man after Roger Bacon to read Grosseteste with passionate interest and with a broad understanding of his point of view.

II. GROSSETESTE AND THE LOLLARDS

Besides giving him his personal admiration, Wycliffe performed another service for Grosseteste in giving his works a central place in English theological and ecclesiastical controversy for the next two generations. Something like three-quarters of the surviving manuscripts of Grosseteste's works belong to the period after 1370, and a substantial number can be directly associated with Wycliffite controversies. For modern students of Grosseteste the greatest service which these controversies performed was that they led to the proliferation of manuscripts of his works. But, in his own time, Wycliffe's greatest service was that he made *Lincolniensis* a name which stirred the hearts of the unlearned. The 'great subtle clerk *Lincoln*' became a talisman for Lollard preachers and pamphleteers: the invocation of his name made them invulnerable to the charge that they had no learning. No matter how little they knew of his works, they knew that he was on their side:

The great clerk *Lincoln* proveth that true preaching of the Gospel passeth other good works that man doeth on earth.

If any priest say he cannot preach, one remedy is, resign up his benefice; another remedy is that he take the Sunday Gospel and tell it to his people, that is if he understand Latin. . . . But if he understand no Latin, let him go to one of his neighbours that understand it to expound it to him, and thus let him edify his flock. Thus saith *Lyncoln*.

Since the life of prelates is book and example to their subjects, as Lincoln saith, those prelates be heretics and masters of heresy that teach wickedness to the commons by their own wicked life that is a book to their subjects.

Robert Grosted clepeth exemption of religious houses, bought dearly from the pope for to be exempt from visitations of bishops and their just correction, the devil's nets.[20]

The men who listened to sentiments like these found a special consolation in the fact that Grosseteste, despite his great works and miracles, had *not* been canonized, but (as they believed) excommunicated. These were facts that emphasized the partiality of papal judgements and the unreliability of canonization as a test of sanctity. They made Grosseteste more than ever one of themselves:

---

[20] For these and other Lollard references to Grosseteste, see Anne Hudson, *Selections from English Wycliffite Writings* (1978), and 'The Dissemination of Wycliffite Thought', *JTS*, NS xxiii (1972), 65–81; C. F. Bühler, 'A Lollard Tract on Translating the Bible into English', *Medium Aevum*, vii (1938), 167–83 (esp. 174); T. Arnold, *Select English Works of John Wycliffe*, 3 vols. (Oxford, 1869–71); F. D. Matthew, *English Works of Wyclif hitherto unprinted*, EETS, 74, 1880 (2nd edn. 1902), pp. 61, 92, 112, 224.

If any true man will impugn the worldly life [of popes], and announce their cursedness to the people, they will not canonize him, be he never so fervent in charity, as befell Robert Grosseteste. How glorious a cause he had, and what glorious books he wrote, more than any other great saint of this land to the common profit of Christendom![21]

So, in his neglect, as well as in his doctrine, he was on the side of the common people. One may smile at the frequency with which the learned *Lincoln* is brought on the stage to give countenance to doctrines which he would certainly have condemned. Popular preachers with very little literature seem to have had a small core of quotations attributed to Grosseteste which they could call on to give a sense of solidity to what they said. Yet, by however devious a route, these ignorant eulogists understood Grosseteste's insistence on taking the Gospel to ordinary people. They understood the essential point of his final words about heresy—words which had their antecedents in several of his sermons—that 'heresy of false life is worse than heresy only in heart or words'.[22]

These words express the essence of the Lollard understanding of Grosseteste. To penetrate thus far into the heart of his teaching was no small achievement. It was not the whole of Grosseteste's message, but it summed up a large part of his experience as a bishop. He wanted to bring religion more directly to the hearts of the people than most contemporary bishops. This work of evangelization appeared to him the ultimate and only effective safeguard of Christendom against its external and internal enemies; and his views on benefices made him the enemy, if not of the papacy, yet of any conceivable medieval pope.

III. THE ANTI-WYCLIFFITE DISCOVERY OF GROSSETESTE

While Wycliffe and the Lollards were raising Grosseteste's fame to the highest pitch of popular acclaim, their enemies discovered—largely as a result of having to answer the acclamations of the new heretics—that Grosseteste's works provided as much ammunition for them as for their enemies.

[21] Arnold, op. cit., iii. 230–2.
[22] Matthew, op. cit., 61.

John Tissington

So far as we know, the first scholar to make this discovery was
the Oxford Franciscan John Tissington, who held the position
of *lector* to the Franciscans which Grosseteste had held 150 years
earlier. In 1380 in Oxford, Wycliffe had made his declaration
about the Eucharist in which, while maintaining the Real Presence, he contested the corporeal identity between the Eucharistic bread and the Body of Christ. Tissington produced an
immediate reply to this in a rather carelessly, and no doubt
rapidly, written onslaught on Wycliffe's position.[23] He gave a
new turn to the controversy by his use of the *Hierarchies* of
Denys the Areopagite and Grosseteste's commentaries on them.
Wycliffe had already used them fairly extensively in his later
writings—perhaps he was the first Oxford scholar to do so.[24]
As we have seen, he had had some difficulty in reconciling what
he found there with his own views. Tissington exploited his
difficulty, and he showed how Grosseteste's work on Denys
could be used as a main witness against Wycliffe. For both of
them, the importance of Denys was that he represented antiquity: he had learnt his doctrine from St Paul. The importance
of Grosseteste was that he represented modernity: Tissington
made the extravagant claim for him that he was among modern
writers like the sun in comparison with the moon in its eclipse.[25]
Together, they linked the primitive and modern Church.

For Tissington, therefore, as for Wycliffe, Grosseteste had
an importance greater than his doctrinal contribution to the
debate. And Tissington probably owed Grosseteste another
debt in introducing him to a new witness to the Eucharistic
doctrine of the primitive Church: the letter of Ignatius of

---

[23] Wycliffe's declaration of 1380 and Tissington's reply are printed in *Fasciculi
Zizaniorum Magistri Johannis Wyclif cum Tritico, ascribed to Thomas Netter of Walden*, ed.
W. W. Shirley, RS (1858), pp. 115–180. The descriptions of Denys and Grosseteste
quoted above are on pp. 135 and 137. For Tissington's career, see *BRUO*, iii. 1879–80.

[24] For Wycliffe's quotations from Grosseteste's translations and commentaries, see
De Dominio Divino, 195; *De Veritate Sacrae Scripturae*, i. 41, 43, 115; *De Potestate Papae*, 54
(?); *De Apostasia* 62–4, 227, 345; *Trialogus*, 265; *Sermones*, iii. 496. For the long delay in
the use of Grosseteste's work on Ps.-Denys, even in Oxford, see B. Smalley, 'John
Russel O.F.M.', *RTAM*, xxiii, 1956, pp. 310–11 (reprinted in *Studies in Medieval Thought
and Learning*, 1981, 238–9); Callus, 1955, 60–1; H. F. Dondaine, *Le Corpus dionysien de
l'Université de Paris au 13ᵉ siècle*, Rome, 1953, 20–1.

[25] For Tissington on antiquity, see *Fasciculi*, p. 137, and on Grosseteste, ibid. 135;
for Wycliffe on Denys as 'testis precipuus post auctores Scripturae', see *De Potestate
Papae*, 54.

Antioch, 'a disciple of St John the Apostle', to the church of
Smyrna.[26] So far as we know, Grosseteste had been the only
writer before Tissington to use the letters of Ignatius in a Latin
translation, and it is highly likely that Grosseteste was himself
the translator.[27] Grosseteste had quoted Ignatius in his commentary on Denys; and Wycliffe, with his usual sharp eye,
noticed this and used it in his *De Apostasia* to support his view
of the Eucharist. But Tissington went further. He found the
translation itself, perhaps among Grosseteste's manuscripts in
the library of the Oxford Franciscans, and he used the letters
as an independent witness to the doctrine of the primitive
Church. So Grosseteste—besides being the greatest of the moderns as Tissington believed—also gave him access to the doctrines of the early Church in the works of Ignatius. As we know,
one of the main inspirations of the translations of Grosseteste's
later years was his desire to make primitive documents available to the western Church. If Wycliffe was the first con-
troversialist to grasp the importance of this intention,
Tissington—following in Wycliffe's footsteps with a hostile intention—was the second.

Tissington's reply evidently made a powerful impression. It
was ordered to be preserved in the university archives and three
copies of it survive.[28] But, important though it was in sketching
the outline of an orthodox reply to Wycliffe, it was no more
than an occasional pamphlet rapidly composed to meet an
immediate crisis. The line of thought which it introduced
needed to be greatly enlarged to be effective. This was the task
undertaken by the Oxford Carmelite, Thomas Netter.

Thomas Netter[29]

Netter was a man of the next generation. Whereas Tissington
had been a regent doctor of theology in 1380, Netter first
studied in Oxford as a young Carmelite priest from London

[26] *Fasciculi*, p. 136; and cf. pp. 151, 152.
[27] That Grosseteste was the translator of the letters of St Ignatius was first suggested
by Archbishop Ussher (*Polycarpi et Ignatii Epistolae*, Oxford 1644, p. xv). The suggestion
was supported by J. B. Lightfoot (*The Apostolic Fathers*, Part II: *S. Ignatius; S. Polycarp*,
1885, 589-90), but rejected on inadequate grounds by Thomson 1940, pp. 59-61, who
accepted however that Grosseteste was the translator of the spurious letters of Ignatius,
which seem to have turned up during the Council of Lyons in 1245, at which Grosseteste was present. The evidence that he also translated the genuine letters is circumstantial, but (as Ussher and Lightfoot recognized) very strong.
[28] *Fasciculi*, p. lxxx; *BRUO*, iii. 1879.
[29] For Netter's career, see *BRUO*, ii. 1343-4. His *Doctrinale* was printed in three
volumes at Venice in 1571 and reprinted 1757-9. My references are to the first edition.

about 1396. His vast anti-Wycliffite *Doctrinale Fidei Catholicae* occupied the greater part of his life from the early years of the fifteenth century till his death in 1430. It covered in a systematic way every possible subject of theological debate between Wycliffe and his adversaries. The number of quotations from the Fathers is beyond calculation, and those from Ps.-Denys, Rabanus, Isidore, Anselm and Bernard are quite numerous. Those from Grosseteste become increasingly numerous as the work proceeds. Netter's work is a characteristic piece of late scholastic argument, more personal, more heavily weighted with long quotations, less dialectical, than the scholastic writings of earlier days. The important place occupied by Denys and Grosseteste is symptomatic of the new intellectual atmosphere of fifteenth-century Oxford.

We can observe the formation of this new intellectual outlook in the course of Netter's work. In his first volume, when he dealt with the Church, the papacy and Antichrist, he did not mention Grosseteste. Even when he cited Denys the Areopagite he was careful to mention that he used the translation of John Scotus Erigena and the commentary of Thomas of Vercelli[30]— not those of Grosseteste. But when he came to Wycliffe's attack on the mendicant orders, Netter was able to expose a crude distortion of Grosseteste's views. Wycliffe had quoted—and the quotation became a favourite text among his followers— Grosseteste's description of members of religious orders who left their cloister to wander in the world as 'corpses leaving their tombs wrapped in their burial sheets'. Netter looked up the text and found that though Grosseteste had undoubtedly used the phrase as quoted, he had distinguished between those who were engaged in the business of the community and those who wandered at their own sweet will: it was only the latter who were the objects of Grosseteste's satire. Netter made great play with Wycliffe's dishonesty in not having menioned this fact, and concluded that 'there was nothing in common between Wycliffe the heretic and that just man, the holy *Lincolniensis*.'[31] Clearly, he had scored a point. Equally clearly, he too failed to mention that he had earlier found *Lincolniensis* less than sound on the papacy.

---

[30] Op. cit., i. 179, 299, 316ᵛ, 318ᵛ.
[31] Ibid., i. 523. Netter quotes the sermon from *Dicta* no. 135.

After this uncomfortable start, Netter's use of Grosseteste became increasingly common. On the Eucharist, baptism, priests, deacons and the ceremonies of the liturgy, he quoted Grosseteste's translation and commentaries on Denys extensively and with good effect. The numerous passages he selected for quotation and his own comments on them form perhaps the finest medieval memorial to Grosseteste's last years as translator, commentator and theologian working on a congenial and stimulating text.[32] This was an important moment in the medieval rehabilitation of Grosseteste.

In the course of his quotations and appreciations of Grosseteste's comments, Netter was moved to make a remark which went to the heart of the contrast between Grosseteste and Wycliffe: 'the feet of the first stand in a spacious place, while Wycliffe looks for truth in narrow corners where it cannot be found.'[33] The judgement is that of a partisan; but the image is just. It comes from a man who had spent several years with both writers, and had felt Grosseteste's power of filling the formulas of theological debate with warmth and largeness of vision.

Thomas Gascoigne[34]

What we have so far observed in the anti-Wycliffite students of Grosseteste is their almost exclusive reliance on his work on Denys the Areopagite. No doubt, for the practical purposes of debate, this emphasis was well justified. But the time was ripe for a closer study of his other works. The scholar who, hot on the heels of Netter, undertook this task was another Oxford doctor, Thomas Gascoigne. A greater contrast to Wycliffe can scarcely be imagined. Wycliffe is all vinegar, Gascoigne all unction; a solemn but somewhat laughable figure in his pedantic self-importance. He was a man of substance from Yorkshire, proud of his family, learned in a widely ranging, discursive way, combining a deep veneration for the past with

---

[32] The most important quotations from Grosseteste's commentary are ii. 140^v, 142, 151^v, 158; iii. 59^v-60, 65^v, 66^v, 67, 68^v-69^v, 77, 78, 84^v-86, 88^v-89, 91-2, 95, 97^v-99^v, 105^v-106, 113^v, 119, 120, 146-147^v, 151^v, 180, 208^v. On ii. 131, Netter also quotes from 'a certain book *de studio magni Lincolniensis inter Minores Oxon*', which appears to be an annotated copy of Grosseteste's *Hexaëmeron* different from any that has survived.   [33] Netter, op. cit., ii. 142.

[34] For Gascoigne's career, see *BRUO*, ii. 745-8; also W. A. Pronger, 'Thomas Gascoigne', *EHR* liii (1938), 606-26; liv (1939), 20-37.

a love of local gossip. Yet he too had something of the spirit of Grosseteste in undertaking a large programme of independent reading, in going back to the original sources, and in neglecting the current controversies of the schools. He spent the last twenty-four years of his life, from 1434 when he incepted in theology till his death in 1458, compiling a huge theological encyclopaedia consisting of extracts from the choicest writers of the past, enlivened by anecdotes of the present.[35] Apart from the Bible, he went only to the Fathers and those among their successors whom he judged worthy of their company. Among the Fathers, Jerome comes easily first with 2,200 quotations. Grosseteste, with 550 quotations, is first among post-Patristic writers, standing strangely on the same level as Augustine. Of other medieval writers, the great biblical commentator Hugh of Vienne comes closest to Grosseteste with 500 quotations. The rest lag far behind: Duns Scotus, 110; Aquinas, 35; the *Glossa Ordinaria*, 15; Bonaventure, 7. William of Auvergne, Stephen Langton, Bede, Rabanus, Clement of Lanthony make rare appearances.[36] Besides quoting Grosseteste frequently—indeed, as a first step to quoting him at all—Gascoigne, probably like Wycliffe, Tissington, and Netter before him, undertook what we might call original research into the materials which Grosseteste had bequeathed to the Franciscans in Oxford. But, whereas Wycliffe had read hastily, picking out and shaping what he found for his own purposes, Gascoigne read doggedly, and extracted copiously, giving minute attention not only to the texts which he transcribed but also to the books in which he found them. He was by far the most persistent and leisurely reader which these materials ever had, and he was the last to have a chance to read them as a whole before they were dispersed. In 1434, when he was just beginning his work, he wrote after one of his quotations:

I, Thomas Gascoigne, born in the diocese of York in England, saw in Oxford these words of the lord bishop of Lincoln, Robert Grosseteste, written with his own hand in his comment on the fifth chapter of the

---

[35] The work survives in Lincoln College, Oxford MSS 117 and 118, from which a selection was printed by J. E. Thorold Rogers, *Loci e Libro Veritatum* (1881). There are some further extracts from Grosseteste made by Gascoigne in Bodleian MS Lat. th. e. 33.

[36] I take the figures from Prosser, *EHR* liv. 34.

epistle of the Apostle to the Romans, when I was beginning my alphabetically arranged book of Truths gathered from Holy Scripture and from the writings of the holy doctors.[37]

Passages like this appear again and again in Gascoigne's great work, combining the curious quirk of a man who never tired of writing his own name with the pride of the researcher who is confident that he has gone to the very fountain-head of knowledge. One of his first acts as a young master in theology was to begin his thorough search of the materials which Grosseteste had left to the Franciscans, and he pursued his researches there for the rest of his life, making new discoveries which he labelled in a similarly ponderous fashion, often noting the year, and the fact that it was written in Grosseteste's own hand, and that it came from a book catalogued as 'Ep. Pauli A' or 'Lincoln E', or from the comments of Grosseteste on the Psalms which did not go beyond Psalm 100, or from a sermon, or from his *Dicta*. Towards the end, in 1455, he remarked in connection with one quotation, 'I believe that the works of Robert Grosseteste, which I have seen and which were written with his own hand, are equal in length to the works of Nicholas of Lyre (the greatest of all medieval commentators) on Holy Scriptures.'[38] It was in this company—in the succession of the greatest expounders of Scripture from Jerome to his own day—that Gascoigne wished to place Grosseteste. Of all Grosseteste's new admirers, Gascoigne was the most industrious and the most thoroughly convinced of his orthodoxy. The company he placed him in was very different from Wycliffe's list of the mighty dead; but he too put him in the highest class—close to Augustine and far above Aquinas. In this blaze of glory, the history of Grosseteste as an influence in a continuing tradition of thought comes to an end.

GROSSETESTE'S POSITION IN MEDIEVAL THOUGHT AND ACTION

For the first and last time in their history, the works of Grosseteste were studied sympathetically and as a whole by a succession of scholars in the century between 1360 and 1460. They

---

[37] Lincoln Coll. MS 118, p. 14.
[38] Lincoln Coll. MS 117, p. 629 (see also p. 251).

read them, not as historical documents, but as links in an unbroken tradition of thought to which they too belonged. They came to widely differing conclusions about them, more sharply polarized and no less diverse than the conclusions of later historical scholars. They all agreed about his importance; but whether his contribution to the tradition was one of consolidation or disintegration remained obstinately inconclusive. Wycliffe and Netter could face each other with some unanswerable quotations; and Gascoigne could pour oil on the troubled waters in limitless quantities without comment; but where Grosseteste really stood remained unclear. What is clear is that he could not have appealed to both Wycliffe and Gascoigne unless he had possessed qualities which they both admired and themselves possessed. Wycliffe was right to see in him a neo-Platonic thinker for whom all things were united in God; and he was right to see a restless searcher for a perfect Christian order in the world. Equally Gascoigne was right to see a fellow-searcher who shared his urge to read the sources of Christian doctrine for himself, and not to receive at second-hand the numerous snippets round which scholastic debates clustered: a scholar like himself, therefore, firmly embedded in the broad tradition of Christian thought.

It is no longer necessary to choose between the two: both are true, and any preference for one or the other must largely reflect a personal reaction which cannot be tested by any impartial measure. For myself, I think that Gascoigne's learned passivity is much further removed from Grosseteste than Wycliffe's forceful and abrasive search for truth. Wycliffe comes closest to Grosseteste in philosophical and theological outlook, and in the way in which he viewed the natural world. He shared his indignation at the state of Christendom, though he gave indignation the final push into institutional rebellion, which Grosseteste would certainly have abhorred. Discontent leading to the reshaping of institutions was not his line at all: reshaping implies manipulation; manipulation calls for compromise; and, for Grosseteste, one compromise was as bad as another. Wycliffe, in his pastoral emphasis, his insistence on preaching, his willingness to use new translations of the Bible, his appeal to Scripture, his overwhelming sense of the corruption of Western Christendom, and his tracing of these corruptions, as well as the rise of Islam and the Greek schism, to the worldly ambitions of the papal curia, could reasonably claim Grosseteste's support; but on all points of institutional reorganization or doctrinal revision, Grosseteste would have been his enemy.

The same judgement can be made about all later movements of anti-papal reform. On the pastoral side, they could claim Grosseteste's support; but not in their proposals for reform by institutional change. He was an extremist; but not a revolutionary. And the reason for this was that, however great his hostility to the pope and papal curia, his hostility came not from the pope's claiming too much, but from his being too little what he claimed to be. As the *persona Christi* there was no limit to what he could claim; but when by his actions he renounced this *persona*, he became nothing. No one else could take his place except Antichrist. The pope must be one or the other; there could be no half-way house. Many later Puritans also thought this; and they drew the conclusion that the church must be built on something other than the papacy. Grosseteste drew the conclusion that the end of the world was at hand. He could not have envisaged the possibility of replacing the pope by an assembly of presbyters, still less by a consecrated king. There was no remedy save the end: 'Even now there are many Antichrists, whereby we know that it is the last hour.'[39] Grosseteste, therefore, distances himself both from the moderation and methods of scholastic thought and from the alternatives offered by later reformers of institutions.

In some of his latest words, he comes close to joining the apocalyptic visionaries who grew in numbers and variety from the early thirteenth century onwards. But his habits of thought are widely different from theirs also. *They* began with the apocalyptic visions of the Bible, and worked out the details with the aid of chronological data provided by the Bible; and they did this with much bitterness of spirit in the midst of persecutions and threats to their existence. Grosseteste began with a different set of data—with the abuses he had failed to remedy in his own diocese, with his observation of the principles on which the papal curia acted, and with his further observation of the ever-lengthening chain of effects springing from

---

[39] 1 John 2: 18. The argument of Grosseteste's speech to the *curia* in 1250 may be looked on as an elaboration of this theme.

this single cause of corruption sub-dividing in all directions. He approached the disease in the spirit of a physician observing the spreading decay of the human organism, which could be arrested if the patient would stop taking alcohol or whatever. But since the patient would not stop—since the popes would not renounce their secular and dynastic ambitions—there was nothing to be done about it but wait for the end.

This was not the spirit of apocalyptic prophecy with its white-hot emotions and fundamental sense of insecurity. Grosseteste seems to have felt no personal insecurity and certainly no sense of personal grievance until at the end Innocent IV brushed aside his episcopal authority. Until this moment the general impression he gave, despite all his grievances, was one of cheerfulness. Long after his death, it was remembered that his greatest delight was in the music of the harp, and that he kept a domestic harpist in the room next to his study so that he could enjoy the sound of the harp by day or night. It was also remembered that he gave a characteristic explanation of his delight in this music: it sharpened his wits; it drove off Satan; it reminded him of the joys of heaven; it recalled the last Psalm of David.[40] These words sound like those of a cheerful man. And perhaps this cheerfulness was possible because the future did not lie in his hands. It was in his power to follow the Gospel teaching, and there was nothing more he could do. All observers agreed that he was no morose planner of a future Utopia. He was a practical man prepared to give everyone advice on their immediate problems. He kept his own household in perfect order. He was lavish in expenditure, hospitable, generous, the patron of scholars, the educator of noble youths, a genial and courteous host; practical, moreover, in all ordinary affairs. He was ready to tell the countess of Lincoln how to conduct her affairs down to the minutest detail:

You ought to know that any ploughland which does not give you 100 measures of corn is giving you a poor return. Then you should know the number of your ploughlands. With this knowledge, you can calculate the gross yield of corn you can expect. This will tell you how

[40] See the passage in Robert de Brunne's early fourteenth-century poem 'Handlying Synne', ll. 4739-74 in F. J. Furnivall's edition of this work, EETS (1901), pp. 158-9. I owe this reference to Professor J. C. Holt.

much you can use, how much you need to keep for seed, and how much you can distribute every day to the poor.[41]

Close attention to details, and to the general rules into which the details could be fitted, had inspired his early scientific studies: detail was the foundation, and the rules were the result of reflection on the details. Even the great question of the end of the world could be approached in a similar spirit, proceding from the diversity of details to the recognition of the operation of a general law.

This scientific spirit of observation and reflection separated him not only from apocalyptic visionaries, but also from those with prophetic gifts receiving inspiration directly from God, and from those who cultivated the miraculous in their study of sanctity. I do not think that Grosseteste ever mentions the miracles of the Virgin Mary though she had a central place in his cosmic theology.[42] In all things, he liked to proceed from small occurrences to general conclusions; in practical life, from the careful calculation of corn yields to the surpluses which would make large charitable gifts possible; in the religious life, from the manual work of the Rhineland beguines to a way of holiness which he judged superior to that of the begging Franciscans; in the organization of the Church, from the pastoral care of parishes to the purification of the whole Church and its release from heresies, schisms, and external enemies; in theology, from Genesis 1: 3, 'Fiat lux', to the primordial role of light in the universe; in science, from geometry to the con-

---

[41] 'Les reules qe le bon Eveske de Nichole seynt Robert Groseteste fist a la Contesse de Nichole de garder e governer terres e ostel', printed in *Walter of Henley's Husbandry*, ed. E. Lamond (1890), pp. 123-45 (see esp. pp. 143 and 127-9). These rules, which form a comprehensive guide to the management of a great estate, were probably written for Hawice de Quincy, who was Countess of Lincoln in her own right from 1232 to 1243.

[42] In the later Middle Ages Grosseteste was generally reckoned to have been an early supporter of the doctrine of the Immaculate Conception of the Virgin Mary. This does not, however, seem to be supported by the texts. He held that the Virgin Mary had been sanctified after conception but before birth, *either* at the moment of infusion of the rational soul (which, as he believed, took place some time after conception) *or* at some later moment before birth. Nevertheless, both in the sermon in which he explains his position and elsewhere (notably in his *Château d'Amour*) the role of the Virgin in the cosmic plan is heavily emphasized. On the whole subject, see especially Fr. Servus of S. Anthonis (Gieben), 'Robert Grosseteste and the Immaculate Conception with the text of the Sermon *Tota pulchra es*', *Collectanea Franciscana*, xxviii (1958), 211-27.

stitution of the universe. All these processes of thought are as
far removed from apocalyptic visions or prophesyings as they
are from the procedures of scholastic thought.

Both in the detailed observations with which his arguments
begin, and in the large visions with which they end, Grosseteste
broke away from the central body of scholastic thought and
from the organized compromises which were the gift of scholasticism to practical affairs. No doubt, all serious people broke
away from this central ground in some degree, but Grosseteste's
breakaway was peculiarly his own. It came from his personality, his upbringing, his opportunities, his interests. Equally,
all serious people were conscious of the threat of a breakdown
in the ordering of the Christian society of the West. Some saw
the main threat in the turbulence of townspeople, or in agrarian
discontent, or in external or internal enemies of one kind or
another. They sought refuge from these threats in various
ways—in the hardening of doctrinal statements and insistence
on their acceptance, in sharpening the weapons against heresy,
in organizing Crusades, and above all in a practical alliance
between secular and ecclesiastical authorities for the protection
of the status quo. Grosseteste's adherence to these measures
varied. He had no quarrel with established doctrines, and he
had no tenderness for heretics or for sin in any shape or form.
But he had no use for the secular-ecclesiastical alliance which
was the practical basis of later medieval order. He wanted the
spiritual power to be supreme, but he wanted it first to be
spiritual. There was a contradiction here which could never be
resolved. The spiritual could never continue to be spiritual and
yet rule the world, for it could not rule without resorting to the
compromises which make it possible to rule. Grosseteste wanted
it to rule without compromise, and this was impossible.

Then too, at a deeper level, with all his conservatism and
veneration for the ideal of papal authority, his manner of
thought threatened the stability of Christendom in a number
of subtle ways. He had no quarrel with established doctrines,
but he would go back independently to fundamental sources;
he would look at details, whether in biblical texts or in the
physical world, with his own eyes; he would make his own
selection of authorities, neglecting some and introducing others
on his own initiative; he would look again at issues which had

long been settled, and leave them more unsettled than before; and then, as his attitude to the Greeks shows, he would introduce a broader concept of orthodoxy than that formulated in the scholastic debates in the twelfth century and accepted by the fourth Lateran Council.

In all these ways he introduced an element of indeterminism which had only to become widespread to become dangerous to the established order. The stability of Western Christendom was increasingly based on a mixture of doctrinal rigidity and practical compromise. These were two sides of the same coin: the secular aristocracy supported doctrinal orthodoxy in return for the moral and political compromises which left their position in society intact; and the ecclesiastical hierarchy found these compromises acceptable because they preserved the framework of doctrinal orthodoxy and clerical authority. Practical compromises in matters of rights, jurisdictions, and revenues, ensured the stability of the ecclesiastical hierarchy. The guarantee of orthodoxy made the compromises acceptable to the highest of high churchmen; and the maintenance of their practical interests and way of life made doctrinal intransigence acceptable to the secular aristocracy. If one or other of these essential supports were removed, the whole system would be threatened with the collapse which took place in varying degrees in the sixteenth century.

It was Grosseteste's peculiar threat to this balance that he was against both sides of it for different reasons, and in different degrees. He was in favour of a strongly authoritarian Christian society in which the discipline of the spiritual authority was rigorously enforced; but he was against the exploitation of the Church by the secular interests, whether of the ecclesiastical or lay hierarchy, which had to be satisfied to procure the enforcement of doctrinal orthodoxy. But then, he was also against making a formal doctrinal unity the acceptable basis of peaceful coexistence. This was not because he was against formal orthodoxy but because he wanted more than this: nothing less than an out-and-out attack on sin in all its forms by all possible means. He wanted, not a society of moderate external uniformity, but a society of God's people. Genial and courteous though he was, he was ready to be a tyrant to achieve this end. One of his grievances against royal government was that the king would not allow him to use the process of sworn inquest to uncover sins, as the royal justices uncovered crimes. He could not see that, if compulsory Christianity, of which he approved, was to be the basis of organized society, it could only be tolerable by being formal; and that, if spiritual Christianity were to be the aim, it could not be compulsory.

As a result of this inner contradiction, he was an enigma to his contemporaries; and those in succeeding generations, who thought they understood him, did so by leaving out some essential ingredient in his composition. His support could be claimed both by the advocates of radical changes in the organization and doctrines of the Church, and by the conservative defenders of papal authority and established practices. He would have agreed with neither side, nor with any other appropriator of his words. And I am quite doubtful whether he would have agreed with all that I have written of him here. He was a man difficult to please and difficult to follow. In his science and theology, in his combination of the two, and his application of them to the government of the Church, he had a personal vision which embraced the orthodoxy of his day and yet pointed to its dissolution. His words set up reverberations in the minds of others, ambiguous and disturbing in their implications, foreshadowing many of the dilemmas of the later Middle Ages—an English voice, provincial in interests and universal in application, eliciting unrest and demanding obedience, a mirror of the future.

Bibliography

WITH ABBREVIATED TITLES

There are full bibliographies of Grosseteste in McEvoy, 1982, and Gieben, 1969. The following list contains only the main books, articles, and editions which are mentioned above, with the abbreviated titles by which they are referred to in the notes.

1. Original Sources

1. *Works by or attributed to* ROBERT GROSSETESTE

BAUR, Ludwig, 1912.*Die philosophischen Werke des Robert Grosseteste*, BGPM, ix, 1912.

BROWN, E., 1690. *Fasciculus rerum expetendarum ac fugiendarum*, London, vol. ii, pp. 244–307. [Selections from Grosseteste's Sermons and *Dicta*.]

Château d'amour, ed. J. Murray, *Le Château d'Amour de Robert Grosseteste, évêque de Lincoln*, Paris, 1918.

DALES, R. C., 1963, ed. *Roberti Grosseteste Commentarius in VIII Libros Physicorum Aristotelis*, Boulder, Colorado.

—— 1966, ed. 'The Text of Robert Grosseteste's *Questio de fluxu et refluxu maris*, with an English Translation', *Isis*, lvii. 455–74.

De Cess. Leg.: *De Cessatione Legalium*, ed. R. C. Dales and E. B. King, Auctores Britannici Medii Aevi, British Academy, London, 1986.

De Decem Mand.: *De Decem Mandatis*, ed. R. C. Dales and E. B. King, Auctores Britannici Medii Aevi, British Academy, London (forthcoming).

Ep.: *Roberti Grosseteste Episcopi quondam Lincolniensis Epistolae*, ed. H. R. Luard, RS, 1861.

GIEBEN, Servus, 1958. 'Robert Grosseteste and the Immaculate Conception, with the text of the sermon *Tota pulchra es*', *Coll. Franc.*, xxvii. 211–27.

—— 1964. 'Traces of God in Nature according to Robert Grosseteste, with the text of the *Dictum, Omnis creatura speculum est*', *Franc. Stud.* xxiv. 144–58.

—— 1967. 'Robert Grosseteste on Preaching, with an edition of the sermon *Ex rerum initiatarum* on Redemption', *Coll. Franc.* xxxvii. 100–41.

—— 1971. 'Robert Grosseteste at the papal curia, Lyons 1250: edition of the documents', *Coll. Franc.* xli. 340–93.

Hex.: *Hexaëmeron*, ed. Richard C. Dales and Servus Gieben OFM Cap., Auctores Britannici Medii Aevi, vi, British Academy, London, 1982.

McEvoy, James, 1974. 'The sun as *res* and *signum*: Grosseteste's commentary on Ecclesiasticus, 43, 1–5', *RTAM*, xli. 38–91.

—— 1980. 'Robert Grosseteste: Theory of Human Nature, with the text of his conference, *Ecclesia sancta celebrat*', *RTAM*, xlvii. 131–87.

Mercken, H. P. F., 1973. *The Greek Commentaries on the* Nicomachean Ethics *of Aristotle in the Latin translation of Robert Grosseteste*, i [vols. ii–iii to follow], Leiden.

Rossi, Pietro, 1981, ed. Robertus Grosseteste, *Commentarius in Posteriorum Analyticorum Libros*, Unione Accademica Nazionale Corpus Philosophorum Medii Aevi, Testi e Studi, ii.

Rotuli Roberti Grosseteste, episcopi Lincolniensis, 1235–853, ed. F. N. Davis, Canterbury and York/Lincoln Record Society, 1913.

Steele, Robert, 1926, ed. *Opera hactenus inedita Rogeri Baconi*, fasc. 6: *Compotus Fr. Rogeri*. [The volume contains also the *Computus Correctorius* of Grosseteste.]

Thomson, S. H., 1933. 'The text of Grosseteste's *De Cometis*', *Isis*, xix. 19–25.

—— 1957. 'Grosseteste's *Quaestio de Calore, De Cometis*, and *De Operationibus Solis*', *Med. Hum.* xix. 34–43.

Wenzel, S., 1970. 'Robert Grosseteste's Treatise on Confession, *Deus Est*', *Franc. St.* xxx. 218–93.

2. *Chronicles and other Sources*

Ann. Mon.: *Annales Monastici*, ed. H. R. Luard, RS, 5 vols., 1864–9.

Bacon, *Op. Maius*: *The 'Opus Maius' of Roger Bacon*, ed. J. H. Bridges, 3 vols., Oxford, 1897–1900.

Baeumker, C., 1923, ed. *Liber magistri Alvredi de Sareshel ad magistrum magnum Alexandrum Nequam de motu cordis, BGPM, xxiii.*

Brewer, J. S., 1859, ed. Fr. Rogeri Bacon, *Opera hactenus inedita*, RS.

Chron. Maj.: *Matthaei Parisiensis, monachi S. Albani, Chronica Majora*, ed. H. R. Luard, RS, 7 vols., 1872–83.

Close Rolls: *Calendar of Close Rolls of the Reign of Henry III*, Public Record Office Calendars, London, 1902–38.

CPR: *Calendar of Entries in the Papal Registers relating to Great Britain and Ireland*, i. *1198–1304*, ed. W. H. Bliss, London, 1894.

Eccleston: A. G. Little, ed. *Fratris Thomae vulgo dicti de Eccleston Tractatus de adventu fratrum minorum in Angliam*, Manchester, 1951.

Fasciculi: *Fasciculi zizaniorum magistri Johannis Wyclif cum tritico*, ascribed to Thomas Netter of Walden, ed. W. W. Shirley, RS, 1858.

GIRALDUS CAMBRENSIS, *Opera*, ed. J. S. Brewer, J. F. Dimock, and G.
F. Warner, 8 vols., RS, 1861-91.
HIGDEN: *Polychronicon Ranulphi Higden*, ed. J. R. Lumby, RS, 9 vols.,
1865-86.
Hist. Angl.: *Matthaei Parisiensis monachi S. Albani Historia Anglorum*, ed.
F. Madden, RS, 3 vols., 1866-9.
HUNT, R. W., 1970. 'Verses on the life of Grosseteste', *Med. Hum.* NS
i. 241-51.
Lanercost Chronicle, 1201-1346, ed. J. Stevenson, Bannatyne Club, 1839.
POWICKE, F. M., and CHENEY, C. R., *Councils and Synods and other
Documents relating to the English Church, 1205-1313*, 2 vols., Oxford,
1964.
ROGER OF WENDOVER, *Chronica sive Flores Historiarum Rogeri de Wend-
over*, ed. H. O. Coxe, 5 vols., English Historical Society, London,
1841-4.
WYCLIFFE, JOHN, *Latin Works*. [All quotations are from the editions
published by the Wyclif Society 1883-1921 with the exception of
those mentioned below or indicated in the footnotes.]
—— *Tractatus de Trinitate*, ed. A. du Pont Breck, Boulder, Colorado,
1962.
—— *Trialogus*, ed. G. V. Lechler, Oxford, 1869.

2. Books and Articles

ALLAN, D. J., 1950. 'Medieval versions of Aristotle *De Caelo* and of
the commentary of Simplicius', *MARS*, ii. 82-120.
BENSON, R. L., and CONSTABLE, G., 1982, ed. *Renaissance and Renewal
in the Twelfth Century*, Cambridge, Mass.
BRUO: A. B. Emden, *A Biographical Register of the University of Oxford*,
3 vols., Oxford, 1957-9.
CALLUS, D. A., 1943. 'Introduction of Aristotelian learning to
Oxford', *Proceedings of the British Academy*, xxix. 229-81.
—— 1955, ed. *Robert Grosseteste, Scholar and Bishop*, Oxford.
CROMBIE, A. C., 1953. *Robert Grosseteste and Scientific Method*, Oxford
(second edn. 1962).
DALES, R. C., 1961. 'Robert Grosseteste's scientific works', *Isis*, lii.
381-402.
—— 1962. 'The authorship of the *Questio de fluxu et refluxu maris* attributed to Robert Grosseteste', *Speculum*, xxvii. 582-8.
—— 1977. 'Adam Marsh, Robert Grosseteste and the treatise on the
tides', *Speculum*, lii. 900-1.
—— and GIEBEN, Servus, 1968. 'The Prooemium to Robert Grosseteste's *Hexaemeron*', *Speculum*, 451-61.
FRANCESCHINI, E., 1933. *Roberto Grossotesta, vescovo di Lincoln, e le sue*

traduzioni latine, Venice.

GIEBEN, Servus, 1969. 'Bibliographia universa Roberti Grosseteste, 1473–1969', *Coll. Franc.* xxxix. 362–418.

GREENWAY, D. E., 1977, ed. *Fasti Ecclesiae Anglicanae, 1066–1300*, ii-i.*Lincoln*. London, Institute of Historical Research.

HASKINS, C. H., 1924. *Studies in the History of Mediaeval Science*, Harvard (2nd edn. 1927).

HUNT, R. W., 1953. 'Manuscripts containing the indexing symbols of Robert Grosseteste', *Bodleian Library Record*, iv. 241–55.

—— 1955. 'The Library of Robert Grosseteste', Callus 1955, pp. 121–45.

HUO: History of the University of Oxford, i. *The Early Oxford Schools*, ed. J. I. Catto, Oxford, 1984.

McEVOY, James, 1982. *The Philosophy of Robert Grosseteste*, Oxford.

—— 1983. 'The Chronology of Robert Grosseteste's writings on Nature and Natural Philosophy', *Speculum*, lviii. 614–55.

RUSSELL, J. C., 1932. 'Hereford and Arabic Science in England *c.* 1175–1200', *Isis*, xviii. 14–25.

—— 1944. 'Richard of Bardney's Account of Robert Grosseteste's early and middle life', *Med. Hum.* ii. 45–54.

THOMSON, S. H., 1940. S. H. Thomson, *The Writings of Robert Grosseteste, Bishop of Lincoln*, Cambridge.

THOMSON, Williell R., 1983, *The Latin Writings of John Wyclyf: an annotated catalog*, Toronto.

UNDER, D. J., 1956. 'Robert Grosseteste on the reasons for the Incarnation', *Franc. Stud.* xvi. 1–36.

VAUGHAN, Richard, 1958. *Matthew Paris*, Cambridge.

Index